The Austrian Codification of Administrative Procedure

THE COMMON CORE OF EUROPEAN

ADMINISTRATIVE LAWS

General Editors:
Giacinto della Cananea, Professor of Administrative Law at Bocconi University; and Mauro Bussani, Professor of Comparative Law at the University of Trieste and Adjunct Professor of Comparative Law at the University of Macau

OTHER TITLES IN THE SERIES:

Tort Liability of Public Authorities in European Laws
Edited by Giacinto della Cananea and Roberto Caranta

Administrative Justice **Fin de siècle**
Early Judicial Standards of Administrative Conduct in Europe (1890–1910)
Edited by Giacinto della Cananea and Stefano Mannoni

Judicial Review of Administration in Europe
Procedural Fairness and Propriety
Edited by Giacinto della Cananea and Mads Andenas

Procedural Requirements for Administrative Limits to Property Rights
Edited by Martina Conticelli and Thomas Perroud

European Research Council
Established by the European Commission

The Common Core of European Administrative Law (CoCEAL) project has received funding from the European Research Council (ERC) under the Horizon 2020 Research and Innovation Programme 'Advanced Grant' Excellent Science (Grant Agreement No 694697).

The Austrian Codification of Administrative Procedure

Diffusion and Oblivion (1920–1970)

Edited by

GIACINTO DELLA CANANEA

ANGELA FERRARI ZUMBINI

OTTO PFERSMANN

OXFORD

UNIVERSITY PRESS

OXFORD
UNIVERSITY PRESS

Great Clarendon Street, Oxford, OX2 6DP,
United Kingdom

Oxford University Press is a department of the University of Oxford.
It furthers the University's objective of excellence in research, scholarship,
and education by publishing worldwide. Oxford is a registered trade mark of
Oxford University Press in the UK and in certain other countries

First Edition published in 2023

Published in the United States of America by Oxford University Press
198 Madison Avenue, New York, NY 10016, United States of America

British Library Cataloguing in Publication Data

Data available

Library of Congress Control Number: 2022951996

ISBN 978–0–19–886762–3

DOI: 10.1093/oso/9780198867623.001.0001

Printed and bound by CPI Group (UK) Ltd,
Croydon, CR0 4YY

General Editors' Preface

This is the fifth book of the series, The Common Core of European Administrative Laws (CoCEAL), based on comparative research for which the European Research Council has awarded us an Advanced Grant. From the outset it was decided that this research would have two major themes. The first concerns the methodology of comparative analysis. Our intent is to compare a plurality of legal systems, going beyond the mainstream scrutiny of the most influential ones, and seeking to understand the role of various legal formants therein. Second, and more importantly, this comparison has a particular end in view. Our intent is to launch a large-scale debate not only on commonalities and diversities within the European legal space but also, and more importantly, on how commonality and diversity have stretched out and interact with one another, within and across legal systems, both diachronically and synchronically, in the past and today.

From the first point of view, the methodology adopted in our research owes a great deal to the pioneering seminars held at Cornell Law School during the 1960s and to the 'Common Core of European Private Law' project launched in 1993. This methodology is based on a 'factual analysis' in the sense that it is based on hypothetical cases that are first subject to scrutiny during workshops with the experts of the legal systems selected for comparison, in order to ascertain whether those cases are plausible and meaningful. Only at a later stage are these cases sent to the experts, who elaborate their answers on the basis of all relevant legal formants. A further step consists in comparing these answers, with a view to understanding the relevance and significance of both the commonality and diversity.

From the second point of view, this new research is strongly focused on administrative procedure and thus considers various types of administrative action, including adjudication and rulemaking, without overlooking the importance of traditional sets of issues, such as those relating to judicial review and government liability in tort. These are precisely the ones with which we have chosen to open this new series, because they are, at the same time, both 'classic' and important. They allow us to take into due consideration the works of those who have gone before, using legal comparison for various purposes. They permit us to call for heightened attention to what is new and original in the European legal space, where national legal systems interact one with one another and with the two regional organisations, the European Union and the Council of Europe.

The project website, www.coceal.it, provides useful information on past initiatives and next steps.

We wish to express our gratitude to those who contributed, in various ways, to the elaboration of the research project; that is, Mads Andenas, Jean-Bernard Auby, Roberto Caranta, Martina Conticelli, and Marta Infantino. We are also grateful to other colleagues who, in a number of conferences, seminars, and workshops held in various corners of Europe, gave advice and feedback, not without critical remarks on some aspects, thus helping us to adjust and broaden our initial views, including Stanislaw Biernat, Marcello Clarich, Victor Comelles, Delphine Costa, Luca De Lucia, Bruno De Witte, Luis Maria Diez-Picazo, Mariolina Eliantonio, Leonardo Ferrara, Claudio Franchini, Michel Fromont, Diana-Urania Galetta, Michele Graziadei, Jeffrey Jowell, Marco Mazzamuto, Oriol Mir Puigpelat, Mauro Renna, Aldo Sandulli, Alec Stone Sweet, Stefan Storr, Robert Thomas, Simone Torricelli, Aldo Travi, Takis Tridimas, András Varga, Ellen Vos, and Jacques Ziller. The support of the universities of Rome 'Tor Vergata', Bocconi, and Trieste is gratefully acknowledged, as well as that of the Centro Studi di Diritto Comparato of Trieste and of the Fondazione Manes of Rome.

Giacinto della Cananea and Mauro Bussani
Rome and Trieste, 29 March 2022

Editors' Preface

A distinctive feature of the new comparative research concerning European administrative laws is the idea that an adequate comparison must be not only synchronic, but also 'diachronic', in order to give a sense of how legal ideas, institutions, and norms have changed over time. The underlying idea is that both history and comparison give a sense of the relativity of such ideas, institutions, and norms and help explain their change. The first diachronic comparison in this series (*Administrative Justice* Fin de siècle: *Early Judicial Standards of Administrative Conduct in Europe (1890–1910)*) has shown that, in all the legal systems selected for our comparison, between the last decade of the nineteenth century and the first decade of the twentieth the courts defined and refined general principles in order to prevent misuses and abuse of power by public authorities. The principle of legality expressed these related ideas. It was supplemented by various requirements aiming at achieving procedural fairness and propriety.

This new book, too, focuses on administrative procedure, but in a different way. To begin with, it looks at it from the viewpoint of its codification. Moreover, it is an inquiry into the nature, causes, and consequences of the administrative procedure legislation which was adopted in Austria in 1925. According to some observers, such legislation was the most influential within the civil law tradition for a long period of time. Our comparative enquiry has two main purposes, which are related but distinct. First, in connection with the research's focus on both commonality and diversity, we seek to understand whether it is accurate to suggest that Austria and some of its neighbours—including Czechoslovakia, Poland, and Yugoslavia—adopted similar principles and institutions, if not the same, and in this case whether it makes sense to group them together in this way, even though they later embraced state Socialism. We are equally interested in understanding whether the Austrian legislation was not relevant for other legal systems, such as those of France, Germany, and Italy. Second, while there is much talk about the influence of 'foreign' ideas and institutions, a more precise conceptual approach is necessary. In this respect, the concept of 'diffusion' can be used as a working hypothesis, in order to see whether and how a legal tradition can be shared by various legal systems, each with its own set of institutions, procedures, and rules. This is crucially important for a better understanding of how the 'common core' of European administrative laws has evolved.

One or two things should be said about the elaboration of this book. When the research questions had been elaborated and the group had been formed, a first workshop should have taken place, but it was postponed, due to the pandemics.

One webinar was thus organised, in October 2020, followed by a workshop, which was held in Rome (June 2021), with the participation of public lawyers, historians of law, and members of judicial institutions, whose comments were taken into account and, in most cases, published here. Readers will also find both the transcript of the original text of the Austrian general law on administrative procedure (which was so far available only in Gothic script) and its English translation—by Ian Silver—in parallel text. Our hope is that this may contribute to the advancement of knowledge in this field. There are various influential traditions of administrative law in Europe, such as those of England, France, and Germany. This book is about another legal tradition, the Austrian one, which has been often overlooked, but which is interesting in itself and from a comparative perspective.

We owe considerable debts of gratitude to many people. Mauro Bussani and Stefano Mannoni provided valuable advice on the formulation of the questionnaire. Sabino Cassese took part in the webinar, with very helpful comments. The CoCEAL research team (including Martina Conticelli, Leonardo Parona, Laura Muzi, and Paola Monaco) and two university officers (Paola Calogero and Paolo Paolini) assisted us in a number of ways, and in particular organised the various meetings. Adrian Bedford and Paola Monaco reviewed all the chapters from a linguistic point of view and on the basis of the OUP guidelines, respectively. To all, our thanks.

Giacinto della Cananea
Angela Ferrari Zumbini
Otto Pfersmann
Rome, 31 January 2022

Contents

Detailed Contents

Table of Legislation

AUSTRIA

CZECHOSLOVAKIA

FRANCE

GERMANY

HUNGARY

ITALY

LIECHTENSTEIN

POLAND

SPAIN

YUGOSLAVIA

List of Abbreviations

AB	*Ausschussbericht* (Committee report) (Austria)
Adm Sci	Administrative Sciences
Admin L Rev	Administrative Law Review
Áe	Act I of 1981 on Amendments to General Rules of Administrative Procedure (Hungary)
AJCL	American Journal of Comparative Law
Ákr	Act CL of 2016 on general administrative regulations (Hungary)
Am Pol Sc Rev	American Political Science Review
Ann Am Acad Pol Soc Sci	Annals of American Academy of Political Science
APA	Administrative Procedure Act
Art/Arts	article/s
AVG	*Allgemeines Verwaltungsverfahrensgesetz*
B C Int'l & Comp L Rev	Boston College International and Comparative Law Review
BGBl	*Bundesgesetzblatt* (federal law gazette) (Austria)
CLJ	Cambridge Law Journal
Colum L Rev	Columbia Law Review
DVBl	*Deutsches Verwaltungsblatt*
ECHR	European Convention of Human Rights
ed(s)	editor(s)
edn	edition
EGVG	*Einführungsgesetz zu den Verwaltungsverfahrensgesetzen* (Introductory Act to the Administrative Procedure acts) (Austria)
eHLFL	*Historisches Lexikon des Fürstentums Liechtenstein online* (Liechtenstein)
ELG	*Entscheidungen der liechtensteinischen Gerichtshöfe* (Liechtenstein)
ERPL	European Review of Public Law
Et	Act IV of 1957 on General Rules of Administrative Procedure (Hungary)
EU	European Union
Eur LJ	European Law Journal
Eur Pub L	European Public Law
ff	following
Foreign Aff	Foreign Affairs
Foro it	*Foro italiano*
GAiPP	*Gazeta Administracji i Policji Państwowej* (Poland)
Geo Mason L Rev	George Mason Law Review

Harv L Rev	Harvard Law Review
ibid	ibidem
ICLQ	International and Comparative Law Quarterly
Iowa L Rev	Iowa Law Review
IRAS	International Review of Administrative Sciences
It J Pub Law	Italian Journal of Public Law
J Comp Leg	Journal of Comparative Legislation and International Law
J of Law & Soc	Journal of Law and Society
J L Econ & Org	Journal of Law, Economics and Organization
JCL	Journal of Comparative Law
Ket	Act CXL of 2004 on General Rules of Administrative Procedure and Services (Hungary)
Kp	Act I of 2017 on Administrative Court Procedure (Hungary)
L & Soc Rev	Law & Society Review
LGBl	*Liechtensteinisches Landesgesetzblatt*
LHR	Law and History Review
LI	*Liechtenstein-Institut*
LI LA	*Liechtensteinisches Landesarchiv*
LJZ	*Liechtensteinische Juristen-Zeitung*
Louisiana LR	Louisiana Law Review
LPS	*Liechtenstein—Politische Schriften*
LR	*Register zur systematischen Sammlung der liechtensteinischen Rechtsvorschriften* (Liechtenstein)
Maastricht J Eur & Comp L	Maastricht Journal of European and Comparative Law
Mich L Rev	Michigan Law Review
MLR	Modern Law Review
Monist	The Monist
para(s)	paragraph(s)
PL	Public Law (Journal)
Pol Sci Q	Political Science Quarterly
PrGS	*Preußische Gesetzessammlung*
R Adm	La Revue administrative
Rev Fr Dr Const	Revue Française de Droit Constitutionnel
Rev hist droit fr étrang	Revue historique de droit français et étranger
RGBl	*Reichsgesetzblatt* (law gazette of the Autro-Hungarian Empire) (Austria)
RIDC	Revue internationale de droit comparé
Riv trim dir pub	Rivista trimestrale di diritto pubblico
RV	*Regierungsvorlage* (government bill) (Austria)
Stan L Rev	Stanford Law Review
StF	*Stammfassung* (original version) (Austria)
StGH	Staatsgerichtshof (Liechtenstein)
TLQ	The Lawyer Quarterly
transl	translation
Tul L Rev	Tulane Law Review

Un Chicago Legal Forum	University of Chicago Legal Forum
Un Pa L Rev	University of Pennsylvania Law Review
VBI	*Verwaltungsbeschwerdeinstanz* (Liechtenstein)
VGH	*Verwaltungsgerichtshof* (Liechtenstein)
VHVFL	*Verlag des Historischen Vereins für das Fürstentum Liechtenstein* (Liechtenstein)
Virginia L Rev	Virginia Law Review
VLAG	*Verlag der Liechtensteinischen Akademischen Gesellschaft* (Liechtenstein)
VwGH	*Verwaltungsgerichtshof*
Wash L Rev & St B J	Washington Law Review and State Bar Journal
Yale LJ	Yale Law Journal
ZNR	*Zeitschrift für Neuere Rechtsgeschichte* (Liechtenstein)
ZöR	Zeitschrift für öffentliches Recht

List of Contributors

Jean-Bernard Auby Emeritus Public Law Professor of Sciences Po Paris (France)

Ino Augsberg Professor of Legal Philosophy and Public Law, Kiel University (Germany)

Javier Barnes Professor of Administrative Law, University Pompeu Fabra (UPF), Barcelona (Spain)

Mario P. Chiti Emeritus Professor of Administrative Law, University of Florence (Italy)

Giacinto della Cananea Professor of Administrative Law, Bocconi University (Italy), Principal Investigator of the CoCEAL project

Angela Ferrari Zumbini Professor of Administrative Law, University of Naples Federico II (Italy)

Clemens Jabloner Hans Kelsen Professor, Department of Legal Philosophy at the University of Vienna (Austria)

Filip Křepelka Doc. JUDr., PhD, Faculty of Law, Masaryk University, Brno (Czech Republic)

Stevan Lilić PhD, Professor of Administrative Law and Administrative Procedure Law, University of Belgrade Faculty of Law, retired (Serbia); Professor of Administrative Law, University of Donja Gorica Faculty of Legal Sciences (Montenegro)

Stefano Mannoni Professor of History of Medieval and Modern Law, University of Florence (Italy)

Marko Milenković PhD, Research fellow, Institute of Social Sciences Belgrade (Serbia); Affiliated research fellow, Center for Constitutional Studies and Democratic Development, JHU SAIS Bologna (Italy)

Thomas Olechowski Professor of Austrian and European Legal History, University of Vienna (Austria)

Otto Pfersmann Professor of Law, École des hautes études en sciences sociales (France)

Wojciech Piątek Professor of Administrative and Comparative Law, Faculty of Law and Administration of the Adam Mickiewicz University in Poznan (Poland)

Lukáš Potěšil JUDr., PhD Faculty of Law, Masaryk University, Brno (Czech Republic)

Emanuel Schädler Dr. iur., LL.M., Senior Research Fellow in the Department of Law, Liechtenstein Institute, Gamprin-Bendern (Principality of Liechtenstein)

Dian Schefold Emeritus Professor of Public Law, University of Bremen (Germany)

Stefan Storr Professor of Public Law and Public Economic Law, University of Graz (Austria)

András Zs. Varga Professor of Administrative Law, Pázmány Péter Catholic University, Faculty of Law and Politics (Hungary)

Original German Text of the 1925 Law with English Parallel Translation

I. Teil Allgemeine Bestimmungen.

1. Abschnitt: Behörden.

Zuständigkeit

§ 1. Die sachliche und örtliche Zuständigkeit der Behörden richtet sich nach den Vorschriften über ihren Wirkungsbereich und nach den Verwaltungsvorschriften.

§ 2. Enthalten die im § 1 erwähnten Vorschriften über die sachliche Zuständigkeit keine Bestimmungen, so sind in den Angelegenheiten der Bundesverwaltung in erster Instanz die politischen Bezirksbehörden (Bundespolizeibehörden), in zweiter Instanz der Landeshauptmann und in dritter Instanz das Bundeskanzleramt sachlich zuständig.

§ 3. Soweit die im § 1 erwähnten Vorschriften über die örtliche Zuständigkeit nichts bestimmen, richtet sich diese

a) in Sachen, die sich auf ein unbewegliches Gut beziehen; nach der Lage des Gutes;

Part I. General Provisions.

Section 1: Authorities.

Jurisdiction

§1 The subject matter and territorial jurisdiction of the authorities shall be governed by the provisions on their scope of activities and by the administrative regulations.

§2 If the provisions on subject-matter jurisdiction mentioned in §1 do not contain any provisions, the political district authorities (federal police authorities) shall have subject-matter jurisdiction in matters of federal administration in the first instance, the governor of the state[1] in the second instance and the Federal Chancellery in the third instance.

§3 Insofar as the provisions mentioned in §1 do not determine territorial jurisdiction, this shall be governed by the provisions of §3

a) in matters relating to immovable property; according to the location of the property.

[1] General comments regarding the text:

- To keep as close as possible to the original text as requested, the 'antiquated' phrasing from 1925 has been retained in the translation.
- The original German text almost exclusively uses the definite article when referring to authorities (*die Behörde* = the authority). In English the indefinite would often fit better (*eine Behörde* = an authority) because a section/paragraph is establishing a general rule applicable to any authority undertaking some action. This also happens frequently with reference to cases. We have again remained true to the original German and used 'the' in the translation.
- For one or two German terms where there is no single English equivalent, we have used a word or words that most closely reflect the German word and left a footnote regarding this (eg for the German word '*Land*' in §2).
- §29 contains a reference to the 'majority of people'. It is unclear in the German what exactly this refers to. We have adhered as closely as possible to the original German and the meaning here remains rather unclear in English also.

Translator's note: state = federated or federal state (from the German *Land*).

b) in Sachen, die sich auf den Betrieb einer Unternehmung oder sonstigen dauernden Tätigkeit beziehen; nach dem Ort, an dem das Unternehmen betrieben oder die Tätigkeit ausgeübt wird oder werden soll;

c) in sonstigen Sachen: zunächst nach dem Wohnsitz (Sitz) des Beteiligten, und zwar im Zweifelfalle des belangten oder verpflichteten Teiles, dann nach seinem Aufenthalt, hierauf nach seiner Heimatgemeinde, schließlich nach seinem letzten Wohnsitz (Sitz) im Inlande, wenn aber keiner dieser Zuständigkeitsgründe in Betracht kommen kann oder Gefahr im Verzuge ist, nach dem Anlaß zum Einschreiten; kann jedoch auch danach die Zuständigkeit nicht bestimmt werden, so ist die sachlich in Betracht kommende oberste Behörde zuständig.

b) in matters relating to the operation of a business or other permanent activity; according to the place where the business is operated or the activity is or is to be carried out.

c) in other matters: first according to the domicile (seat) of the participant, namely in the case of doubt of the party sued or obligated, then according to his residence, thereafter according to his home municipality, finally according to his last domicile (seat) in Austria, however, if none of these grounds for jurisdiction can be considered or if there is a case of imminent danger, according to the cause for intervention; if however, jurisdiction still cannot be determined after this, the highest authority coming into consideration shall be competent.

§ 4. (1) Ist gemäß den in §1 erwähnten Vorschriften die örtliche Zuständigkeit mehrerer Behörden gegeben und für diesen Fall nicht anderes bestimmt oder begründen die im § 3 unter a und b angeführten Umstände die örtliche Zuständigkeit mehrerer Behörden, so haben diese Behörden einvernehmlich vorzugehen.

(2) Gelangen sie in der Sache zu keinem Einvernehmen, so geht die Zuständigkeit auf die sachlich in Betracht kommende Oberbehörde und, wenn danach verschiedene Behörde berufen sind und auch diese sich nicht zu einigen vermögen, auf die sachlich in Betracht kommende gemeinsame Oberbehörde über.

(3) Bei Gefahr im Verzuge hat jede der im Absatz 1 bezeichneten Behörden in ihrem Amtsbereiche die notwendigen Amtshandlungen unter gleichzeitiger Verständigung der anderen Behörde vorzunehmen.

§4 (1) If, according to the provisions mentioned in §1, the local jurisdiction of several authorities exists and no other provision is made for this case, or if the circumstances mentioned in §3 a and b establish the territorial jurisdiction of several authorities, these authorities shall proceed by mutual agreement.

(2) If they fail to reach agreement on the matter, jurisdiction shall pass to the relevant superior authority and, if thereafter different authorities are competent and these are also unable to reach agreement, to the common superior authority competent for the matter.

(3) In the case of imminent danger, each of the authorities referred to in paragraph 1 shall perform the necessary official acts within its area of jurisdiction while simultaneously notifying the other authorities.

§ 5. (1) Über Zuständigkeitsstreite zwischen Behörden entscheidet die sachlich in Betracht kommende gemeinsame Oberbehörde.

(2) Die Bestimmung des § 4, Absatz 3, gilt auch in diesem Falle.

§5 (1) Disputes over jurisdiction between authorities shall be decided by the joint superior authority competent for the matter.

(2) The provision of §4, paragraph 3, shall also apply in this situation.

§ 6. (1) Die Behörde hat ihre sachliche und örtliche Zuständigkeit von Amts wegen wahrzunehmen; langen bei ihr Anbringen ein, zu deren Behandlung sie nicht zuständig ist, so hat sie diese ohne unnötigen Aufschub auf Gefahr des Einschreiters an die zuständige Stelle weiterzuleiten oder den Einschreiter an diese zu weisen.

(2) Durch Vereinbarung der Parteien kann die Zuständigkeit der Behörde weder begründet noch geändert werden.

Befangenheit von Verwaltungsorganen.

§ 7 (1) Verwaltungsorgane haben sich der Ausübung ihres Amtes zu enthalten und ihre Vertretung zu veranlassen;

1. in Sachen, an denen sie selbst, der andere Eheteil, ein Verwandter oder Verschwägerter in auf oder absteigender Linie, ein Geschwisterkind oder eine Person, die noch näher verwandt oder im gleichen Stande verschwägert ist, beteiligt sind;
2. in Sachen ihrer Wahl oder Pflegeeltern, Wahl oder Pflegekindern, ihres Mündels oder Pflegebefohlenen;
3. in Sachen, in denen sie als Bevollmächtigte einer Partei bestellt waren oder noch bestellt sind;
4. wenn sonstige wichtige Gründe vorliegen, die geeignet sind, ihr volle Unbefangenheit in Zweifel zu setzen;
5. im Berufungsverfahren, wenn sie an der Erlassung des angefochtenen Bescheides in unterer Instanz mitgewirkt haben.

(2) Bei Gefahr im Verzuge hat, wenn die Vertretung durch ein anderes Verwaltungsorgan nicht sogleich bewirkt werden kann, auch das befangene Organ die unaufschiebbare Amtshandlung selbst vorzunehmen.

2. Abschnitt: Beteiligte und deren Vertreter.

Beteiligte; Parteien.

§ 8. Personen, die eine Tätigkeit der Behörden in Anspruch nehmen oder auf die sich die Tätigkeit der Behörde bezieht, sind Beteiligte und insoweit sie an der Sache vermöge eines Rechtsanspruches oder eines rechtlichen Interesses beteiligt sind, Parteien.

§6 (1) The authority shall *ex officio* exercise its subject-matter jurisdiction and territorial jurisdiction; if it receives applications which it has no jurisdiction to deal with, it shall forward them to the competent authority without unnecessary delay, at the risk of the applicant, or direct the applicant to that authority.

(2) The jurisdiction of the authority may not be established or modified by agreement of the parties.

The bias of administrative bodies.

§7 (1) Administrative bodies shall refrain from exercising their office and arrange for their substitution;

1. in matters involving themselves, their spouse, a relative or relative by marriage in the ascending or descending line, a sibling or a person still more closely related or related by marriage in the same degree;
2. in matters of their parents of choice or foster parents, or children of choice or foster children, their ward or charge;
3. in matters in which they have been or are still appointed as agents of a party;
4. if there are other important reasons which are likely to cast doubt on their full impartiality;
5. in the appeal proceedings if they participated in the issuing of the contested decision in the lower instance.

(2) In a case of imminent danger, if substitution by another administrative body cannot be effected immediately, the body that is prejudiced shall perform the official act that cannot be postponed.

Section 2: Participants and their representatives.

Participants; parties.

§8 Persons who make use of the activity of the authorities or to whom the activity of the authority relates are participants and, insofar as they are involved in the matter by virtue of a legal claim or a legal interest, parties.

Rechts und Handlungsfähigkeit.

§ 9. Insoweit die persönliche Rechts und Handlungsfähigkeit von Beteiligten in Frage kommt, ist sie von der Behörde, wenn in den Verwaltungsvorschriften nicht anderes bestimmt ist, nach den Vorschriften des bürgerlichen Rechts zu beurteilen.

Vertreter

§ 10. (1) Die Beteiligten und ihre gesetzlichen Vertreter können sich, sofern nicht ihr persönliches Erscheinen ausdrücklich gefordert wird, durch eigenberechtigte Personen vertreten lassen, die sich durch eine schriftliche Vollmacht auszuweisen haben. Vor der Behörde kann eine Vollmacht auch mündlich erteilt werden; zu ihrer Beurkundung genügt ein Aktenvermerk.

(2) Inhalt und Umfang der Vertretungsbefugnis richten sich nach den Bestimmungen der Vollmacht; hierüber auftauchende Zweifel sind nach den Vorschriften des bürgerlichen Rechtes zu beurteilen. Die Behörde hat die Behebung etwaiger Mängel unter sinngemäßer Anwendung der Bestimmungen des § 13, Absatz 3, von Amts wegen zu veranlassen.

(3) Als Bevollmächtigte sind solche Personen nicht zuzulassen, die unbefugt die Vertretung anderer zu Erwerbszwecken betreiben.

(4) Die Behörde kann von einer ausdrücklichen Vollmacht absehen, wenn es sich um die Vertretung durch amtsbekannte Familienmitglieder, Haushaltungsangehörige, Angestellte oder durch amtsbekannte Funktionäre von beruflichen oder anderen Organisationen handelt und Zweifel an über Bestand und Umfang der Vertretungsbefugnis nicht obwalten.

(5) Die Beteiligten können sich eines Rechtsbeistandes bedienen und auch in seiner Begleitung vor Amt erscheinen.

(6) Die Bestellung eines Bevollmächtigten schließt nicht aus, daß der Vollmachtgeber im eigenen Namen Erklärungen abgibt.

Legal capacity and capacity to act.

§9 Insofar as the personal legal capacity and capacity to act of participants are in question, it shall be assessed by the authority in accordance with the provisions of civil law unless otherwise provided for in the administrative regulations.

Representatives

§10 (1) The participants and their legal representatives may, unless their personal appearance is expressly required, be represented by persons of full age and legal capacity and who must identify themselves by a written power of attorney. A power of attorney may also be granted orally before the authority; a note in the file shall suffice for its authentication.

(2) The content and scope of the power of representation shall be governed by the provisions of the power of attorney; any doubts arising in this respect shall be assessed in accordance with the provisions of civil law. The authority shall *ex officio* arrange for the rectification of any deficiencies, applying the provisions of §13, paragraph 3, *mutatis mutandis*.

(3) Persons shall not be allowed as authorised representatives if they represent others without authority for gainful purposes.

(4) The authority may dispense with an express power of attorney in the case of representation by family members, members of the household, employees, when they are known to the authorities, or by functionaries of professional or other organisations known to the authorities and if there are no doubts as to the existence and scope of their power of representation.

(5) The participants may avail themselves of the services of a legal counsel and may also appear before the authority in his company.

(6) The appointment of a representative shall not preclude the person who has granted a power of attorney from making declarations in his own name.

§ 11. (1) Soll von Amts wegen oder auf Antrag gegen einen handlungsunfähigen Beteilgiten, der eines gesetzlichen Vertreters entbehrt, oder gegen eine Person, deren Aufenthalt unbekannt ist, eine Amtshandlung vorgenommen werden, so kann die Behörde, wenn die Wichtigkeit der Sache es erfordert, auf Kosten des Beteiligten durch ein in ihrem Amtsbereiche gelegenes Bezirksgericht einen Kurator (Beistand) bestellen lassen.

(2) Der gesetzliche Kurator (Beistand) hat die Stellung eines gesetzlichen Vertreters.

§11 (1) If an official act is to be performed *ex officio* or on application against a participant who lacks the capacity to act and is devoid of a legal representative, or against a person whose whereabouts are unknown, the authority may, if the importance of the matter so requires, have a guardian (counsel) appointed by a district court in which the authority is located, at the expense of the participant concerned.

(2) The legal guardian (counsel) shall have the position of a legal representative.

§ 12. Die Vorschriften dieses Gesetzes über die Beteiligten sind auch auf deren gesetzliche Vertreter und Bevollmächtigten zu beziehen.

§12 The provisions of this Act relating to the participants shall also apply to their legal representatives and authorised representatives.

3. Abschnitt: Verkehr zwischen Behörden und Beteiligten.

Anbringen

§ 13. (1) Anträge, Gesuche, Anzeigen, Beschwerden und sonstige Mitteilungen können, sofern in den Verwaltungsvorschriften nicht anderes bestimmt ist, bei der Behörde schriftlich oder telegraphisch und, soweit es der Natur der Sache nach tunlich erscheint, auch mündlich angebracht werden. Rechtsmittel und Eingaben, die an eine Frist gebunden sind oder durch die der Lauf einer Frist bestimmt wird, sind schriftlich oder telegraphisch einzubringen.

(2) Zur Entgegennahme mündlicher Anbringen ist die Behörde, außer bei Gefahr im Verzuge, nur während der für den Parteienverkehr bestimmten Zeit, zur Entgegennahme schriftlicher Eingaben nur während der Amtsstunden verpflichtet. Die Amtsstunden und die für den Parteienverkehr bestimmte Zeit sind bei der Behörde durch Anschlag kundzmachen.

Section 3: Interactions between authorities and participants.

Submissions

§13 (1) Unless otherwise provided for in administrative regulations, applications, petitions, notifications, complaints and other communications may be submitted to the authority in writing or by telegraph or, if the nature of the matter so requires, also orally. Appeals and submissions that are subject to a time limit, or by which the duration of a time period is determined, shall be submitted in writing or by telegraph.

(2) Except in the case of imminent danger, the authority is only obliged to accept oral submissions during the hours designated for communication by parties and written submissions only during official hours. The official hours and the hours designated for the communication of parties shall be announced by a notification at the authority.

(3) Formgebrechen schriftlicher Eingaben wie auch das Fehlen einer Unterschrift berechtigen an sich die Behörde noch nicht zur Zurückweisung, sie hat deren Behebung von Amts wegen zu veranlassen und dann den Einschreiter die Behebung der Formgebrechen oder die schriftliche Bestätigung telegraphischer oder mündlicher Anbringen mit der Wirkung auftragen, daß das Anbringen nach fruchtlosem Ablaufe einer gleichzeitig zu bestimmenden Frist nicht mehr berücksichtigt wird. Wird das Formgebrechen rechtzeitig behoben, so gilt die Eingabe als ursprüglich richtig eingebracht.

(4) Die Behörde ist nicht verpflichtet, Anbringen, die sich auf keine bestimmte Angelegenheit beziehen, in Verhandlung zu nehmen.

(3) Irregularities in the form of written submissions, as well as the absence of a signature, shall not in and of themselves entitle the authority to reject the submission, it shall occasion their rectification *ex officio* and then order the applicant to rectify the irregularities or to provide written confirmation by telegraphic or oral submission with the effect that the submission shall no longer be taken into account after the fruitless expiry of a period to be determined at the same time. If the irregularity is remedied in due time, the submission shall be deemed to have been originally submitted correctly.

(4) The authority shall not be obliged to hear submissions that do not deal with a specific matter.

Niederschriften

§ 14. (1) Mündliche Anbringen von Beteiligten sind erforderlichenfalls ihrem wesentlichen Inhalt nach in einer Niederschrift festzuhalten. Niederschriften über Verhandlungen (Verhandlungsschriften) sind derart abzufassen, daß bei Weglassung alles nicht zur Sache Gehörigen der Verlauf und Inhalt der Behandlung richtig und verständlich wiedergegeben wird.

(2) Jede von der Behörde aufgenommene Niederschrift hat außerdem zu enthalten:

a) Ort, Zeit und Gegenstand der Verhandlung und, wenn schon frühere darauf bezügliche Verhandlungen vorliegen, erforderlichenfalls eine kurze Darstellung des dermaligen Standes der Sache;
b) die Benennung der Behörde und die Namen des Leiters der Amtshandlung und der sonst mitwirkenden amtlichen Organe, der anwesenden Beteiligten und ihrer Vertreter sowie der etwa vernommenen Zeugen und Sachverständigen;
c) die eigenhändige Unterschrift des die Amtshandlung leitenden Organes.

Transcripts

§14 (1) Oral submissions by participants shall, if necessary, be recorded in transcripts so as to convey their essential content. Transcripts of hearings (protocols of hearings) shall be drawn up in such a way that the course and content of the proceedings are correctly and comprehensibly reproduced, omitting everything that is not relevant to the matter.

(2) Every transcript recorded by the authority shall also contain:

(a) The place, time and subject-matter of the hearing and, if there have been previous hearings relating thereto, a brief statement of the previous state of the case if necessary.
(b) The designation of the authority and the names of the head of the official act and the official bodies otherwise involved, of the parties present and their representatives as well as of any witnesses and experts heard.
(c) The signature of the authority overseeing the official act, by his own hand.

(3) Jede Niederschrift ist den vernommenen oder sonst beigezogenen Personen, wenn sie nicht darauf verzichten, vorzulesen und von ihnen durch Beisetzung ihrer eigenhändigen Unterschrift zu bestätigen. Kann eine Person nicht oder nur mittels Handzeichens fertigen, hat sie die Fertigung verweigert oder sich vor Abschluß der Niederschrift oder des ihre Aussage enthaltenden Teiles der Niederschrift entfernt, so ist unter Angabe des Grundes, aus dem die Fertigung nicht erfolgte, die Nichtigkeit der schriftlichen Wiedergabe von dem die Amtshandlung leitenden Organe ausdrücklich zu bestätigen.

(4) In dem einmal Niedergeschriebenen darf nichts Erhebliches ausgelöscht, zugesetzt oder verändert werden. Durchstrichene Stellen sollen noch lesbar bleiben. Erhebliche Zusätze oder Einwendungen des Vernommenen wegen behaupteter Unvollständigkeit oder Unrichtigkeit der Niederschrift sind in einen Nachtrag aufzunehmen und abgesondert zu bestätigen.

(5) Die Niederschrift kann, wenn kein Einwand erhoben wird, auch in Kurzschrift abgefaßt werden; sie ist nachträglich in Vollschrift zu übertragen.

(3) Unless they waive this requirement, every transcript shall be read out to the persons heard or otherwise consulted and confirmed by them by affixing their handwritten signature. If a person is unable to sign the transcript or can only sign it by initial, if the person has refused to sign it or if the person has left before the transcript or the part of the transcript containing his testimony has been completed, the invalidity of the written record shall be expressly confirmed by the authority conducting the official act, stating the reason why the transcript was not completed.

(4) Nothing significant may be erased, added or changed in what has been written down. Passages that have been crossed out shall remain legible. Significant additions or objections by the person heard on account of the alleged incompleteness or incorrectness of the transcript shall be recorded in an addendum and confirmed separately.

(5) The transcript may, if no objection is raised, also be written in shorthand; they shall subsequently be transcribed in full.

§ 15. Soweit nicht Einwendungen erhoben wurden, liefert eine gemäß den Bestimmungen des § 14 aufgenommene Niederschrift über den Verlauf und den Gegenstand der betreffenden Amtshandlung vollen Beweis. Der Gegenbeweis der Unrichtigkeit des bezeugten Vorganges bleibt zulässig.

§15 Unless objections have been raised, a transcript of the proceedings and the subject matter of the official act in question, taken in accordance with the provisions of §14, shall provide full evidence. The counter-evidence of the incorrectness of the witnessed procedure shall remain admissible.

Aktenvermerke.

§ 16. (1) Amtliche Wahrnehmungen und Mitteilungen, die der Behörde telephonisch zugehen, ferner mündliche Belehrung, Aufforderungen und Anordnungen, über die keine schriftliche Ausfertigung erlassen wird, schließlich Umstände, die nur für den inneren Dienst der Behörde in Betracht kommen, sind, wenn nicht anders bestimmt und kein Anlaß zur Aufnahme einer Niederschrift gegeben ist, erforderlichenfalls in einem Aktenvermerk kurs festzuhalten.

(2) Der Inhalt des Aktenvermerkes ist vom Amtsorgan durch Beisetzung von Datum und Unterschrift zu bestätigen.

File notes.

§16 (1) Official perceptions of and telephone communications received by the authority, as well as oral admonition, requests and orders for which no written copy is issued, and finally circumstances which are only relevant for the internal workings of the authority, shall be, if necessary, recorded in a file note, unless otherwise stipulated and no reason for a transcript is given.

(2) The content of the file note shall be confirmed by the authority by affixing the date and his signature.

Akteneinsicht.

§ 17. (1) Die Behörde hat, sofern die Verwaltungsvorschriften nicht anderes bestimmen, den Parteien die Einsicht und Abschriftnahme der Akten oder Aktenteile zu gestatten, deren Kenntnis zur Geltendmachung oder Verteidigung ihrer rechtlichen Interessen erforderlich ist.

(2) Von der Akteneinsicht ausgenommen sind Beratungsprotokolle, Amtsvorträge, Erledigungsentwürfe und sonstige Schriftstücke (Mitteilungen anderer Behörden, Meldungen, Berichte u. dgl.), deren Einsichtnahme durch die Parteien eine Schädigung berechtigter Interessen einer Partei oder dritter Personen oder eine Gefährdung der Aufgaben der Behörde herbeiführen oder den Zweck des Verfahrens beeinträchtigen würde.

(3) Allen an einem Verfahren beteiligten Parteien muß auf Verlangen die Akteneinsicht in gleichem Umfang gewährt werden.

(4) Gegen die Verweigerung der Akteneinsicht ist kein Rechtsmittel zulässig.

Erledigungen.

§ 18. (1) Die Behörde hat Anbringen soviel als möglich, insbesondere im Falle von Belehrungen und vorläufigen informativen Verhandlungen mündlich oder telephonisch zu erledigen und den wesentlichen Inhalt der Amtshandlung, wenn nötig, in einer Niederschrift oder einem Aktenvermerk festzuhalten.

(2) Die Behörde und ihre Organe sind verpflichtet, zur möglichsten Förderung des mündlichen Verkehres auch die gelegentliche Anwesenheit der Beteiligten am Amtssitze zu benützen und bei Dienstreisen keine Gelegenheit außer acht zu lassen, um die geeignete Erhebung oder Vorkehrungen auf die einfachste und mindest kostspielige Weise zu veranlassen.

(3) Eine schriftliche Ausfertigung ist jedenfalls auszufolgen oder zuzustellen, wenn dies in den Verwaltungsvorschriften ausdrücklich angeordnet ist oder von der Partei verlangt wird. Die Ausfertigung kann auch telegraphisch erfolgen, wenn die Kosten von der Partei gedeckt werden.

Inspection of files.

§17 (1) The authority shall, unless the administrative regulations provide otherwise, allow the parties to inspect and make copies of files or parts of files when knowledge of which is necessary for the assertion or defence of their legal interests.

(2) Files exempted from inspection are transcripts of consultations, official presentations, drafts of final decisions and other documents (communications from other authorities, notifications, reports, etc.), the inspection of which by parties would cause damage to the legitimate interests of another party or third persons, jeopardise the tasks of the authority or impair the purpose of the proceedings.

(3) All parties to a proceeding must be granted, upon request, the same extent of access to files.

(4) No appeal shall be admissible against the refusal to grant access to a file.

Conclusions.

§18 (1) The authority shall deal with applications as much as possible, in particular in the case of briefings and preliminary informative hearings, orally or by telephone and, if necessary, record the essential content of these official acts in a transcript or a file note.

(2) The authority and its bodies shall be obliged, in order to promote oral communication as far as possible, also to make use of the occasional presence of the participants at the official seat and, in the case of business trips, not to disregard any opportunity to arrange for the appropriate inquiry or arrangements in the simplest and least costly manner.

(3) A written apograph shall be delivered or served in any case if this is expressly ordered in the administrative rules or requested by a party. The apograph may also be issued by telegraph if the costs are covered by the party.

(4) Alle schriftlichen Ausfertigungen müssen die Bezeichnung der Behörde enthalten sowie mit Datum und mit der Unterschrift dessen versehen sein, der die Erledigung genehmigt hat. An die Stelle der Unterschrift des Genehmigenden kann die Beglaubigung der Kanzlei treten, daß die Ausfertigung mit der Erledigung des betreffenden Geschäftsstückes übereinstimmt und das Geschäftsstück die eigenhändig beigesetzte Genehmigung ausweist. Das Nähere wird durch Verordnung geregelt.

(4) All written apographs must contain the name of the authority and be dated and signed by the person who approved the conclusion. The signature of the approver may be replaced by the certification of the registry that the apograph corresponds to the conclusion of the relevant document and that the document shows the approval affixed by hand. Further details shall be regulated by decree.

(5) Für Bescheide gelten die Vorschriften des III. Teiles, für Ladungsbescheide überdies die Bestimmungen des § 19.

(5) The provisions of Part III shall apply to decrees, and to summonses the provisions of §19 shall apply additionally.

Ladungen.

§ 19. (1) Die Behörde ist berechtigt, Personen, die in ihrem Amtsbereiche ihren Aufenthalt (Sitz) haben und deren Erscheinen nötig ist, vorzuladen.

(2) In der Ladung ist außer Ort und Zeit der Amtshandlung auch anzugeben, was den Gegenstand der Amtshandlung bildet, in welcher Eigenschaft der Geladene vor der Behörde erscheinen soll (als Beteiligter, Zeuge u.s.w.) und welche Behelfe und Beweismittel mitzubringen sind. In der Ladung ist ferner bekanntzugeben, ob der Geladene persönlich zu erscheinen hat oder ob die Entsendung eines Vertreters genügt und welche Folgen an ein Ausbleiben geknüpft sind.

(3) Wer nicht durch Krankheit, Gebrechlichkeit oder sonstige begründete Hindernisse vom Erscheinen abgehalten ist, hat die Verpflichtung, der Ladung Folge zu leisten und kann zur Erfüllung dieser Pflicht durch Zwangsstrafen verhalten oder vorgeführt werden. Die Anwendung dieser Zwangsmittel ist nur zulässig, wenn sie in der Ladung angedroht waren und die Ladung zu eigenen Handen zugestellt war; sie obliegt den Vollstreckungsbehörden.

(4) Gegen die Ladung oder die Vorführung ist kein Rechtsmittel zulässig.

Summons.

§19 (1) The authority shall be entitled to summon persons who have their residence (seat) in its area of jurisdiction and whose appearance is necessary.

(2) The summons shall state, in addition to the place and time of the official act, the subject matter of the official act, the capacity in which the summoned person is to appear before the authority (as a participant, witness, etc.) and which supporting documents and evidence are to be brought along. The summons shall also state whether the summoned person is to appear in person or whether the sending of a representative is sufficient and what consequences are attached to non-appearance.

(3) Anyone who is not prevented from appearing through illness, infirmity or other justified obstacles shall be obliged to comply with the summons and may be forced to comply with this obligation by means of coercive penalties or forcibly brought before the bench. The application of these means of coercion is only permissible if they were threatened with them in the summons and the summons was placed in the person's own hands; this is the responsibility of the enforcement authorities.

(4) No appeal shall be allowed against a summons or enforced appearance before the bench.

§ 20. (1) Steht die zu ladende Person in einem öffentlichen Amte oder Dienste oder im Dienste eines dem öffentlichen Verkehr dienenden Unternehmens und muß voraussichtlich zur Wahrung der Sicherheit oder anderer öffentlicher Interessen eine Stellvertretung während der Verhinderung dieser Person eintreten, so ist gleichzeitig deren vorgesetzte Stelle von der Ladung zu benachrichtigen.

(2) die Vorführung eines Heeresangehörigen oder eines Beamten der Heeresverwaltung hat durch das vorgesetzte militärische Kommando (Dienststelle) zu erfolgen.

§20 (1) If the person to be summoned is in public office or service or is in the service of an enterprise providing public transport services and if it is likely that a deputy will have to act in order to ensure safety or other public interests while that person is not available, the person's superior authority shall be notified of the summons at the same time.

(2) The summons to an army member or an official in army administration shall be made by the superior military command (office).

4. Abschnitt: Zustellungen.

Section 4: Servicing.

Art der Zustellung.

§ 21. Die schriftlichen Ausfertigungen werden durch die Post, durch Organe der Behörde oder durch die Gemeinde zugestellt.

Mode of servicing.

§21 Written apographs shall be served by post, by bodies of the authority or by the municipality.

Ort der Zustellung.

§ 22. (1) Die Zustellung hat in der Wohnung, in der gewerblichen Betriebsstätte, im Geschäftsraume oder am Arbeitsplatze der Person, der zugestellt werden soll (Empfänger), und bei Anwälten und Notaren in deren Kanzlei zu erfolgen; eine außerhalb dieser Räume vorgenommene Zustellung ist nur gültig, wenn die Annahme des Schriftstückes nicht verweigert wurde.

(2) In Ermangelung einer Wohnung (gewerbliche Betriebsstätte, Geschäftsraum, Arbeitsplatz) können Zustellungen vorgenommen werden, wo der Empfänger angetroffen wird.

Place of delivery.

§22 (1) Service shall be effected at the home, business premises, place of business or place of work of the person being served (addressee) and, in the case of lawyers and notaries, at their offices; service effected outside these premises shall only be valid if acceptance of the document has not been refused.

(2) In the absence of a home (commercial premises, business premises, workplace), service may be effected where the addressee is found.

Ersatzzustellung.

§ 23. (1) Wird der Empfänger in der Wohnung (Kanzlei, gewerblichen Betriebsstätte, Geschäftsraum, Arbeitsplatz) nicht angetroffen, so kann an jeden daselbst befindlichen, dem Zusteller bekannten erwachsenen Angestellten oder zur Familie gehörigen Hausgenossen des Empfängers zugestellt werden.

Substituted service.

§23 (1) If the addressee is not found at his home (office, business premises, place of work), service may be made on any adult employee or member of the addressee's family who is known to the servicing agent.

(2) Werden auch solche Personen nicht angetroffen, so kann das zuzustellende Schriftstück dem in demselben Hause wohnenden Vermieter oder einer von diesem bestellten, ebenda wohnenden Aufsichtsperson eingehändigt wedrden, wenn diese Personen zur Annahme bereit sind.

(3) Die Behörde kann die Personen bezeichnen, an die eine Ersatzzustellung wegen ihres Interesses an der Sache nicht erfolgen darf.

(4) Ist die Zustellung auf diesem Wege nicht möglich, so ist das zuzustellende Schriftstück, wenn die Zustellung durch die Post zu vollziehen war, bei dem zuständigen Postamt, in allen anderen Fällen aber beim Gemeindeamt des Zustellungsortes zu hinterlegen. Diese Hinterlegung ist durch eine an der Tür der Wohnung (Kanzlei) oder an der Eingangstür der gewerblichen Betriebsstätte (Geschäftsraum) zu befestigen schriftliche Anzeige und nach Tunlichkeit auch durch mündliche Mitteilung an die Nachbarn bekanntzumachen.

(5) An der Eingangstür eines verschlossenen Geschäftes darf die Anzeige nur an einem Werktage befestigt werden.

(6) Die vorschriftsmäßige Hinterlegung des zuzustellenden Schriftstückes hat die Wirkung der Zustellung. Die Beschädigung oder das Abreißen der Anzeige hat auf die Gültigkeit der Zustellung keinen Einfluß.

(7) Wenn der Empfänger seinen gewöhnlichen Aufenthaltsort nur vorübergehend verlassen hat und ihm das zuzustellende Schriftstück nicht rechtzeitig nachgesendet werden kann, so ist es der Behörde zurückzustellen.

Zustellung zu eigenen Handen.

§ 24. (1) Wenn es von der Behörde aus besonders wichtigen Gründen angeordnet wird, sind die schriftlichen Ausfertigungen zu eigenen Handen zuzstellen.

(2) If such persons cannot be found the document to be served may either be handed over to the landlord living in the same house or to a person in charge appointed by him and living there if these persons are prepared to accept it.

(3) The authority may designate persons to whom substituted service may not be made because of their interest in the matter.

(4) If service is not possible in this way, the document to be served shall be deposited at the competent post office if service was to be effected by post but in all other cases at the town hall of the place of service. This deposit shall be announced by means of a written notice affixed to the door of the dwelling (offices) or to the entrance door of the commercial establishment (business premises) and, if possible, also by verbal notice to neighbours.

(5) The notice may only be affixed to the entrance door of a locked business on a working day.

(6) The deposit of the document to be served in accordance with the regulations shall have the effect of service. Damage to or tearing off of the notice shall not affect the validity of the service.

(7) If the addressee has left his habitual residence only temporarily and the document to be served cannot be forwarded to him in time, it shall be returned to the authority.

Servicing to one's own hand.

§24 (1) If ordered by the authority for particularly important reasons, written apographs shall be serviced to the addressee's own hand.

(2) Kann eine solche Zustellung nicht bewirkt werden, so ist der Empfänger durch eine in seiner Wohnung (Kanzlei, gewerbliche Betriebsstätte, Geschäftsraum) zurückzulassende oder, falls diese Räume verschlossen sind, an deren Eingangstür zu befestigende schriftliche Anzeige anzufordern, zur Annahme des Schriftstückes an einem genau zu bestimmenden Zeitpunkte in dem betreffenden Raume anwesend zu sein. Wird dieser Aufforderung nicht entsprochen, so ist nach § 23, Absatz 4 bis 6, vorzugehen.

(3) Die Vorschrift des § 23, Absatz 7, findet Anwendung.

(2) If such service cannot be effected, the addressee shall be requested by a written notice to be left in his home (office, commercial premises, business premises) or, if these premises are locked, to be affixed to their entrance door, to be present in the relevant room at a time to be precisely determined in order to accept the document. If this request is not complied with, it is to be proceeded with in accordance with §23, paragraphs 4 to 6.

(3) The provision of §23, paragraph 7, shall apply.

Zustellnachweis.

§ 25. (1) Der Vollzug der Zustellung ist von dem Zusteller zu beurkunden (Zustellschein). Der Zustellschein ist an die Behörde zurückzuleiten.

(2) Von der Beigabe eines Zustellscheines kann bei Schriftstücken, die nicht zu eigenen Handen zuzustellen sind, abgesehen werden, wenn die Behörde den Nachweis der Zustellung für entbehrlich hält.

Proof of delivery.

§25 (1) The execution of the service shall be certified by the servicing agent (service receipt). The service receipt shall be returned to the authority.

(2) The enclosure of a service receipt may be dispensed with in cases where documents are not to be served in one's own hand if the authority considers the proof of service to be dispensable.

Bestimmungen für besondere Fälle.

§ 26. (1) Ist eine im Inlande wohnende Person zum Empfange der für einen Beteiligten bestimmten Schriftstücke ermächtigt, so erfolgen die Zustellungen an diese.

(2) Haben mehrere Beteiligte aus eigenem Antrieb oder infolge behördlicher Aufforderung einen gemeinsamen Vertreter oder Bevollmächtigten, so wird mit der Zustellung einer einzigen Ausfertigung des Schriftstückes an diesen die Zustellung an alle Beteiligten vollzogen. Wird ein Gesuch oder ein sonstiges schriftliches Anbringen von mehreren Beteiligten gemeinsam eingebracht, so gilt im Zweifel derjenige, dessen Unterschrift an erster Stelle steht, als gemeinsamer Zustellungsbevollmächtigter namhaft zu machen.

Provisions for special cases.

§26 (1) If a person residing in the national territory is authorised to receive documents intended for a participant, service shall be effected to that person.

(2) If several participants have a joint legal representative or authorised representative of their own accord or as a result of an official request, the service of a single apograph of the document on that representative shall constitute service on all participants. In cases of doubt, when a request or any other written application is submitted jointly by several participants, the person whose signature appears first shall be deemed to be the joint representative for service.

§ 27. Wird die Annahme eines Schriftstückes von einer Person, der gültig zugestellt werden kann, verweigert, so ist das Schriftstück am Zustellungsorte zurückzulassen oder, falls dies nicht möglich ist, bei dem zuständigen Postamt oder Gemeindeamte zu hinterlegen. Die Zurücklassung oder Hinterlegung hat die Wirkung der Zustellung.

§27 If a person who can be validly served refuses to accept a document, the document shall be left at the place of service or, if this is not possible, deposited at the competent post office or town hall. Leaving or depositing the document has the same effect as service.

§ 28. (1) Eine Partei, die während eines Verfahrens ihre Wohnung ändert, hat dies der Behörde mitzuteilen.

(2) Die Unterlassung dieser Mitteilung hat zur Folge, daß alle weiteren, die Verwaltungssache betreffenden Zustellungen am bisherigen Wohnort nach den Vorschriften des § 23, Absatz 4, jedoch ohne die dort vorgesehene schriftliche Anzeige vorgenommen werden können, falls die neue Wohnung nicht ohne Schwierigkeit festgestellt werden kann.

§28 (1) A party who changes his residence during proceedings shall notify the authority thereof.

(2) Failure to give such notice shall have the effect that all further notifications concerning the administrative matter may be effected at the previous place of residence in accordance with the provisions of §23, paragraph 4, but without the written notice provided for therein, if the new place of residence cannot be established without difficulty.

§ 29. (1) Zustellung an Personen, deren Wohnung unbekannt ist, oder eine Mehrheit von Personen, die der Behörde nicht bekannt sind, können, wenn kein Vertreter bestellt ist, durch öffentliche Bekanntmachung erfolgen und gelten, sofern in den Verwaltungsvorschriften nicht anderes bestimmt ist, als vollzogen, wenn seit dem Stichtage an der Amtstafel der Behörde zwei Wochen verstrichen sind.

(2) Der Behörde bleibt es anheimgestellt, die öffentliche Bekanntmachung in ortsüblicher oder anderer Weise zu ergänzen.

§29 (1) Service on persons whose residence is unknown or the majority of persons, who are unknown to the authority, may, if no representative has been appointed, be effected by public notice and, unless otherwise provided in the administrative regulations, shall be deemed to have been effected if two weeks have elapsed since the reference date on the official notice board of the authority.

(2) It shall be left to the discretion of the authority to supplement the public notice in a locally customary manner or by other means.

§ 30. Alle einer Person zuzustellende Schriftstücke sind dieser unmittelbar bei der Behörde gegen schriftliche Empfangsbestätigung auszufolgen, wenn sie sich zur Empfangnahme des Schriftstückes einfindet, bevor das Schriftstück der Post übergeben oder die sonst zum Vollzuge der Zustellung nötige Einleitung getroffen ist.

§30 All documents to be served on a person shall be delivered directly to that person at the authority upon written acknowledgement of receipt if that person arrives to receive the document before the document has been handed over to a post office or before any other steps necessary for the completion of the service have been taken.

Mängel der Zustellung.

§ 31. Unterlaufen bei der Zustellung Mängel, so gilt sie als im Zeitpunkte vollzogen, in dem das Schriftstück der Person, für die es bestimmt ist (Empfänger), tatsächlich zugekommen ist.

Deficiencies in servicing.

§31 If there are deficiencies in servicing, the service shall be deemed to have been effected at the time when the document actually reached the person for whom it was intended (addressee).

5. Abschnitt: Fristen.

§ 32. (1) Bei der Berechnung von Fristen, die nach Tagen bestimmt sind, wird der Tag nicht mitgerechnet, in den der Zeitpunkt oder die Ereignung fällt, wonach sich der Anfang der Frist richten soll.

Section 5: Time limits.

§32 (1) When calculating time limits that are determined by days, the day shall not be counted in which the point in time or event falls as the basis of which the beginning of the time limit is to be determined.

(2) Nach Wochen, Monaten oder Jahren bestimmte Fristen enden mit dem Ablaufe desjenigen Tages der letzten Woche oder des letzten Monates, der durch seine Benennung oder Zahl dem Tage entspricht, an dem die Frist begonnen hat. Fehlt dieser Tag in dem letzten Monate, so endet die Frist mit Ablauf des letzten Tages dieses Monates.

(2) Time limits determined by weeks, months or years shall end with the expiry of that day of the last week or of the last month which, by its designation or number, corresponds to the day on which the time limit began. If this day is missing in the last month, the period shall end with the expiry of the last day of that month.

§ 33. (1) Der Beginn und Lauf einer Frist wird durch Sonn oder Feiertage nicht behindert.

(2) Fällt das Ende einer Frist auf einen Sonn oder Feiertag, so ist der nächste Werktag als letzter Tag der Frist anzusehen.

(3) Die Tage des Postenlaufes werden in die Frist nicht eingerechnet.

(4) Durch Gesetz oder Verordnung festgesetzte Fristen können, wenn nicht ausdrücklich anderes bestimmt ist, nicht geändert werden.

§33 (1) The commencement and running of a time limit shall not be hindered by Sundays or public holidays.

(2) If the end of a period falls on a Sunday or public holiday, the next working day shall be deemed to be the last day of the period.

(3) The days of the postal run shall not be included in the time limit.

(4) Time limits set by law or regulation may not be altered unless expressly otherwise provided for.

6. Abschnitt: Ordnungs und Mutwillensstrafen.

Ordnungsstrafen.

§ 34. (1) Das Verwaltungsorgan, das eine Verhandlung, Vernehmung, einen Augenschein oder eine Beweisaufnahme leitet, hat für die Aufrechterhaltung der Ordnung und für die Wahrung des Anstandes zu sorgen.

(2) Personen, die Amtshandlung stören oder durch ungeziemendes Benehmen den Anstand verletzen, sind zu ermahnen; bleibt die Ermahnung erfolglos, so kann ihnen nach vorausgegangener Androhung das Wort entzogen, ihr Entfernung verfügt und ihnen die Bestellung eines Bevollmächtigten aufgetragen werden oder gegen sie eine Ordnungsstrafe bis 100 S und, falls diese nicht einbringlich ist, Haft bis zu drei Tagen verhängt werden. Bei erschwerenden Umständen ist die selbständige oder gleichzeitige Verhängung einer Haftstrafe bis zur abgegebenen Dauer zulässig.

(3) Die gleichen Ordnungsstrafen können von der Behörde gegen Personen verhängt werden, die sich in schriftlichen Eingaben einer beleidigenden Schreibweise bedienen.

Section 6: Administrative penalties and penalties for wanton acts.

Administrative penalties.

§34 (1) The administrative body conducting a hearing, examination, inspection or the taking of evidence shall ensure the maintenance of order and the preservation of decency.

(2) Persons who disturb official proceedings or offend decency by unseemly behaviour shall be admonished; if the admonition is unsuccessful, they may, after prior warning, be deprived of their right to speak, ordered to be removed and instructed to appoint an authorised representative, or ordered to pay an administrative fine of up to 100 Schillings and, if this is not recoverable, imprisonment of up to three days. In the case of aggravating circumstances, the independent or simultaneous imposition of a custodial sentence up to the given duration is permissible.

(3) The same administrative penalties may be imposed by the authority on persons who use offensive language in written submissions.

(4) Gegen öffentliche Organe, die in Ausübung ihres Amtes als Vertreter einschreiten und einem Disziplinarrecht nicht unterstehen, verhängte Ordnungsstrafen dürfen nicht in Haft umgewandelt werden. Gegen öffentliche Organe und gegen Bevollmächtigte, die zur berufsmäßigen Parteienvertretung befugt sind, wenn sie einem Disziplinarrecht unterstehen, keine Ordnungsstrafe zu verhängen, sondern lediglich die Anzeige an die Disziplinarbehörde zu erstatten.

(5) Die Verhängung einer Ordnungsstrafe schließt die strafgerichtliche Verfolgung wegen derselben Handlung nicht aus.

Mutwillensstrafen.

§ 35. Gegen Personen, die offenbar mutwillig die Tätigkeit der Behörde in Anspruch nehmen oder in der Absicht einer Verschleppung der Angelegenheit unrichtige Angaben machen, kann die Behörde eine Mutwillensstrafe bis 300 S und im Falle der Uneinbringlichkeit Haft bis zu drei Tagen verhängen.

Widmung und Vollzug der Ordnugns und Mutwillensstrafen; Rechtsmittel.

§ 36. (1) Die Ordnungs und Mutwillensstrafen fließen der Gebietskörperschaft zu, die den Aufwand der Behörde zu tragen hat. Die §§ 12, 54 und 67 des Verwaltungsstrafgesetzes finden auf Ordnungs und Mutwillensstrafen Anwendung.

(2) Gegen den Bescheid, mit dem eine Ordnungs oder Mutwillensstrafe verhängt wird, ist Berufung ohne aufschiebende Wirkung an die vorgesetzte Behörde zulässig, die endgültige entscheidet.

II. Teil. Ermittlungsverfahren.

1. Abschnitt: Zweck und Gang des Ermittlungsverfahrens.

Allgemeine Grundsätze.

§ 37. Zweck des Ermittlungsverfahrens ist, den für die Erledigung einer Verwaltungssache maßgebenden Sachverhalt festzustellen und den Parteien Gelegenheit zur Geltendmachung ihrer Rechte und rechtlichen Interessen zu geben.

(4) Administrative penalties imposed on public bodies that intervene in the exercise of their office as representatives and are not subject to disciplinary law may not be converted into imprisonment. No administrative penalty shall be imposed on public bodies and on authorised representatives which represent parties professionally if they are subject to a disciplinary law, instead, only a report shall be made to the disciplinary authority.

(5) The imposition of an administrative penalty shall not preclude criminal prosecution for the same act.

Penalties for wanton acts.

§35 Against persons who apparently wilfully make use of the authority's services or provide false information with the intention of delaying the matter, the authority may impose a penalty for wanton acts of up to 300 Schillings and, in the event of uncollectibility, up to three days' imprisonment.

Dedication and execution of administrative penalties and penalties for wanton acts; appeals.

§36 (1) Administrative penalties and penalties for wanton acts shall accrue to the regional body which shall bear the expenses of the authority. §§12, 54 and 67 of the Administrative Penal Code shall apply to administrative and wanton penalties.

(2) Against a decision imposing administrative penalties and penalties for wanton acts, an appeal to the superior authority without suspensive effect shall be admissible, which shall make the final decision.

Part II. Investigation procedure.

Section 1: Purpose and course of the investigation procedure.

General principles.

§37 The purpose of the investigation procedure is to establish the facts relevant for the conclusion of an administrative matter and to give the parties the opportunity to assert their rights and legal interests.

§ 38. Sofern die Gesetze nicht anderes bestimmen, ist die Behörde berechtigt, im Ermittlungsverfahren auftauchende Vorfragen, die als Hauptfragen von anderen Verwaltungsbehörden oder von den Gerichten zu entscheiden wären, nach der über die maßgebenden Verhältnisse gewonnenen eigenen Anschauung zu beurteilen und diese Beurteilung ihrem Bescheide zugrunde zu legen. Sie kann aber auch das Verfahren bis zur rechtskräftigen Entscheidung der Vorfrage aussetzen, wenn die Vorfrage schon den Gegenstand eines anhängigen Verfahrens bei der zuständigen Behörde bildet oder ein solches Verfahren gleichzeitig anhängig gemacht wird.

§38 Unless otherwise provided by law, the authority shall be entitled to assess the preliminary questions arising in the investigation procedure, which would have to be decided as main questions by other administrative authorities or by the courts, according to its own view of the relevant circumstances and to base its decision on this assessment. However, it may also suspend the procedure until the preliminary question has been legally decided if the preliminary question is already the subject of pending proceedings before a competent authority or if such proceedings are pending at the same time.

§ 39. (1) Für die Durchführung des Ermittlungsverfahrens sind die Verwaltungsvorschriften maßgebend.

(2) Soweit die Verwaltungsvorschriften hierüber seine Anordnung enthalten, hat die Behörde von Amts wegen vorzugehen und unter Beobachtung der in diesem Teile des Gesetzes enthalten Vorschriften den Gang des Ermittlungsverfahrens zu bestimmen; sie kann insbesondere auch eine mündliche Verhandlung nach den Bestimmungen der §§ 40 bis 44 von Amts wegen oder auf Antrag durchführen. Gegen die Ablehnung eines solchen Antrages ist kein Rechtsmittel zulässig. Die Behörde hat sich bei allen diesen Verfügungen von Rücksichten auf mögliche Zweckmäßigkeit, Raschheit, Einfachheit und Kostenersparnis leiten zu lassen.

§39 (1) Administrative regulations shall govern the conduct of the investigation procedure.

(2) Insofar as administrative regulations contain an order to this effect, the authority shall proceed *ex officio* and, observing the provisions contained in this part of the Act, determine the course of the investigation procedure; in particular, it may also hold an oral hearing in accordance with the provisions of §§40 to 44 *ex officio* or upon application. No appeal is admissible against the rejection of such a request. In all such orders, the authority shall be guided by considerations of possible expediency, speed, simplicity, and cost-saving.

Mündliche Behandlung.

§ 40. (1) Mündliche Verhandlungen sind unter Zuziehung aller bekannten Beteiligten sowie der erforderlichen Zeugen und Sachverständigen vorzunehmen und, sofern sie mit einem Augenschein verbunden sind, womöglich an Ort und Stelle, sonst am Sitze der Behörde oder an dem Ort abzuhalten, der nach der Sachlage an zweckmäßigsten erscheint.

(2) Die hat Behörde hat darüber zu wachen, daß die Vornahme eines Augenscheins nicht zur Verletzung eines Kunst, Betriebs oder Geschäftsgeheimnisses mißbraucht werde.

Oral hearings.

§40 (1) Oral hearings shall be held with the participation of all known participants as well as the necessary witnesses and experts and, if connected with a visual inspection, they if possible shall be held on the spot, otherwise at the seat of the authority or at the place which appears to be the most expedient according to the facts of the case.

(2) The authority shall ensure that a visual inspection is not misused for the purpose of violating an art, trade or business secret.

§ 41. (1) Die Anberaumung einer mündlichen Verhandlung hat durch persönliche Verständigung der bekannten Beteiligten zu erfolgen und wird nach Bedarf überdies noch durch Anschlag in der Gemeinde oder durch Verlautbarung in der für amtliche Kundmachungen im Lande bestimmte Zeitung bekanntgemacht.

(2) Die Verhandlung ist so anzuberaumen, daß die Teilnehmer rechtzeitig und vorbereitet erscheinen können. Die Verständigung (Kundmachung) über die Anberaumung der Verhandlung hat die für Ladungen vorgeschriebenen Angaben einschließlich des Hinweises auf die gemäß § 42 eintretenden Folgen zu enthalten. Falls für Zwecke der Verhandlung Pläne oder sonstige Behelfe zur Einsicht der Beteiligten aufzulegen sind, ist dies bei Anberaumung der Verhandlung unter Angabe von Zeit und Ort der Einsichtnahme bekanntzugeben.

§41 (1) The convening of an oral hearing shall be effected by personal notification of the known participants and shall, if necessary, also be proclaimed by notice in the municipality or by publication in the newspaper designated for official announcements in the country.

(2) A hearing shall be scheduled in such a way that the attendees can appear in time and prepared. The notice (announcement) of the convening of the hearing shall contain the information prescribed for summonses, including a reference to the consequences pursuant to §42. If, for the purpose of the hearing, plans or other documents are to be made available for inspection by the participants, this shall be announced when the hearing is convened, stating the time and place of inspection.

§ 42. (1) Wurde eine mündliche Verhandlung durch Anschlag in der Gemeinde oder auch durch Verlautbarung in der für amtliche Kundmachungen im Lande bestimmten Zeitung bekanntgemacht, so hat dies zur Folge, daß Einwendungen, die nicht spätestens am Tage vor Beginn der Verhandlung bei der Behörde oder während der Verhandlung vorgebracht werden, keine Berücksichtigung finden und die Beteiligten dem Parteiantrag, dem Vorhaben oder der Maßnahme, die den Gegenstand der Verhandlung bilden, als zustimmend angesehen werden.

(2) Im Falle einer nur durch Verständigung der Beteiligten anberaumten Verhandlung erstreckt sich die im Absatz 1 bezeichnete Rechtsfolge bloß auf die Beteiligten, die rechtzeitig die Verständigung von der Anberaumung der Verhandlung enthalten haben.

(3) Versäumt derjenige, über dessen Ansuchen das Verfahren eingeleitet wurde, die Verhandlung, so kann sie entweder in seiner Abwesenheit durchgeführt oder auf seine Kosten auf einen anderen Termin verlegt werden.

§42 (1) If an oral hearing has been announced by notice in the municipality or by publication in the newspaper designated for official announcements in the country, this shall have the consequence that objections, which are not raised with the authority at the latest on the day before the beginning of the hearing or during the hearing, shall not be taken into account and the participants shall be deemed to agree to the application, the endeavour or the measure forming the subject-matter of the hearing.

(2) In the case where a hearing is convened only by notification to the participants, the legal consequence referred to in paragraph 1 shall extend only to the participants who have received timely notification of the convening of the hearing.

(3) If the person on whose application the proceedings were instituted fails to attend the hearing, it may either be held in his absence or postponed to another date at his expense.

§ 43. (1) Das mit der Leitung der mündlichen Verhandlung betraute Verwaltungsorgan (Verhandlungsleiter) hat nach Eröffnung der Verhandlung sich von der Persönlichkeit der Erschienen zu überzeugen, ihre Stellung als Parteien oder sonst Beteiligte und die etwaige Vertretungsbefugnis zu prüfen und den Gegenstand der Verhandlung darzulegen.

(2) Der Verhandlungsleiter hat die Verhandlung unter steter Bedachtnahme auf ihren Zweck ohne Zulassung von Abschweifungen oder Weitläufigkeiten so zu führen, daß den Parteien das Recht auf Gehör gewahrt, anderen Beteiligten aber Gelegenheit geboten wird, bei Feststellung des Sachverhaltes mitzuwirken. In der Sache nicht beteiligte Personen dürfen in der Verhandlung nicht das Wort ergreifen.

(3) Jeder Partei muß insbesondere Gelegenheit geboten werden, alle zur Sache gehörenden Gesichtspunkte vorzubringen und unter Beweis zu stellen, sich über die von anderen Beteiligten, den Zeugen und Sachverständigen vorgebrachten oder die als offenkundig behandelten Tatsachen sowie über die von anderen gestellten Anträge und über das Ergebnis amtlicher Erhebungen zu äußern.

(4) Der Verhandlungsleiter bestimmt die Reihenfolge, in der die Beteiligten zu hören, die Beweise aufzunehmen und die Ergebnisse früher aufgenommener Beweise oder Erhebungen vorzutragen und zu erörtern sind. Er entscheidet über die Beweisanträge und hat offenbar unerhebliche Anträge zurückzuweisen.

(5) Dem Verhandlungsleiter steht auch die Befugnis zu, Verhandlungen nach Bedarf zu unterbrechen oder zu vertagen und den Zeitpunkt für die Fortsetzung der Verhandlung mündlich zu bestimmen.

(6) Stehen sich zwei oder mehrere Parteien mit einander widersprechenden Ansprüchen gegenüber, so hat der Verhandlungsleiter nach Tunlichkeit auf das Zustandekommen eines Ausgleiches dieser Ansprüche mit den öffentlichen und den von anderen Beteiligten geltend gemachten Interessen hinzuwirken.

§43 (1) After the opening of a hearing, the administrative body entrusted with the conduct of the oral proceedings (presiding officer of the hearing) shall ascertain the identities of the persons appearing, examine their status as parties or other participants and possible authority to represent them and explain the subject matter of the hearing.

(2) The presiding officer of the hearing shall conduct the hearing with constant regard to its purpose, without permitting digressions or prolixities, in such a way that the right of the parties to be heard is safeguarded and that other parties are given the opportunity to participate in establishing the facts of the case. Persons not involved in the matter may not speak in the hearing.

(3) In particular, each party must be given the opportunity to present and prove all the aspects of the case, to comment on the facts presented by other parties, witnesses and experts or on facts treated as obvious, as well as on applications made by others and on the results of official investigations.

(4) The presiding officer of the hearing shall determine the order in which the parties are to be heard, evidence is to be taken and the results of evidence or investigations determined earlier are to be presented and discussed. He shall decide on the motions for evidence and shall reject motions that are obviously irrelevant.

(5) The presiding officer of the hearing shall also have the power to interrupt or adjourn hearings as necessary and to determine orally the time for the continuation of the hearing.

(6) If two or more parties with conflicting claims oppose each other, the presiding officer of the hearing shall, to the best of his ability, work towards reconciling these claims with the public interests and the interests asserted by other parties.

§ 44. (1) Über jede mündliche Verhandlung ist eine Verhandlungsschrift nach den Bestimmungen der §§ 14 und 15 aufzunehmen.

(2) Schriftliche Äußerungen und Mitteilungen von Beteiligten, Niederschriften über Beweise, die bis zum Schlusse der mündlichen Verhandlung, aber außerhalb dieser aufgenommen wurden, Berichte und schriftliche Sachverständigengutachten sind der Verhandlungsschrift anzuschließen. Dies ist in der Verhandlungsschrift zu vermerken. Teilnehmer an der mündlichen Verhandlung dürfen ihre Erklärungen jedoch nicht schriftlich abgeben.

(3) Sobald die zulässigen Vorbringungen aller Beteiligten aufgenommen und die Beweisaufnahme beendet sind, hat der Verhandlungsleiter die Verhandlungsschrift, insoweit die Beteiligten nicht darauf verzichten, zu verlesen und die Verhandlung, gegebenenfalls nach mündlicher Verkündung des Bescheides (§ 62, Absatz 2), für geschlossen zu erklären.

§44 (1) A transcript of each hearing shall be made in accordance with the provisions of §§14 and 15.

(2) Written statements and communications by participants, transcripts of evidence gathered prior to the conclusion of the oral proceedings but outside of them as well as reports and written expert opinions shall be appended to the transcripts of the hearing. This shall be noted in the transcript of the hearing. However, attendees in the oral proceedings may not submit their statements in writing.

(3) As soon as the admissible submissions of all participants have been transcribed and the gathering of evidence has been concluded, the presiding officer of the hearing shall read out the transcript of the hearing, unless the parties waive this, and declare the hearing closed, after an oral announcement of the administrative decision (§62, paragraph 2) if one is necessary.

2. Abschnitt: Beweise.

Allgemeine Grundsätze über den Beweis.

§ 45. (1) Tatsachen, die bei der Behörde offenkundig sind, und solche, für deren Vorhandensein daß Gesetz eine Vermutung ausstellt, bedürfen keines Zweifels.

(2) Im übrigen hat die Behörde unter sorgfältiger Berücksichtigung der Ergebnisse des Ermittlungsverfahrens nach freier Überzeugung zu beurteilen, ob eine tatsache als erwiesen anzunehmen ist oder nicht.

(3) Den Parteien ist Gelegenheit zu geben, von dem Ergebnis der Beweisaufnahme Kenntnis und dazu Stellung zu nehmen.

§ 46. Als Beweismittel kommt alles in Betracht, was zur Feststellung des maßgebenden Sachverhaltes geeignet und nach Lage des einzelnen Falles zweckdienlich ist.

Section 2: Evidence.

General principles on evidence.

§45 (1) Facts that are obvious to the authority and facts that are presumed to exist by law need not be doubted.

(2) In all other respects, the authority shall, with careful consideration of the results of the investigation procedure, freely assess whether a fact is to be assumed as proven or not.

(3) The parties shall be given the opportunity to take note of and comment on the result of the taking of evidence.

§46 Anything that is suitable for establishing the relevant facts and that is expedient in the individual case shall be considered as evidence.

Urkunden.

§ 47. Die Beweiskraft von öffentlichen und Privaturkunden ist von der Behörde nach den Vorschriften der §§ 292 bis 296, 310 und 311 B.P.D zu beurteilen.

Documents.

§47 The probative force of public and private documents shall be assessed by the authority in accordance with the provisions of §§292 to 296, 310 and 311 ZPO (Civil Procedural Law).

Zeugen.

§ 48. Als Zeugen dürfen nicht vernommen werden:

1. Personen, die zur Mitteilung ihrer Wahrnehmungen unfähig sind oder die zur Zeit, auf die sich ihre Auslage beziehen soll, zur Wahrnehmung der zu beweisenden Tatsache unfähig waren;
2. Geistliche darüber, was ihnen in der Beichte oder sonst unter dem Siegel geistlicher Amtsverschwiegenheit anvertraut wurde;
3. Organe des Bundes, der Länder, Bezirke und Gemeinden, wenn sie durch ihre Aussage das ihnen obliegende Amtsgeheimnis verletzen würde, insofern sie der Pflicht zur Geheimhaltung nicht entbunden sind.

§ 49. (1) Die Aussage darf von einem Zeugen verweigert werden:

a) Über Fragen, deren Beantwortung dem Zeugen, seinem Ehegatten, seinem Verwandten oder Verschwägerten in auf oder absteigender Linie, seinem Geschwisterkind oder einer Person, die mit ihm noch näher verwandt oder im gleichen Grade verschwägert ist, ferner seinen Wahl oder Pflegeeltern, Wahl oder Pflegekindern, seinem Vormund oder Pflegebefohlenen einen unmittelbaren bedeutenden Vermögensnachteil oder die Gefahr einer strafgerichtlichen Verfolgung zuziehen oder zur Schande gereichen würde;

b) Über Fragen, die er nicht, die er nicht beantworten könnte, ohne eine ihm obliegende staatlich anerkannte Pflicht zur Verschwiegenheit, von der er nicht gültig entbunden wurde, zu verletzen oder ein Kunst, Betriebs oder Geschäftsgeheimnis zu offenbaren.

(2) Die zur berufsmäßigen Parteienvertretung befugten Personen können die Zeugenaussage auch darüber verweigern, was ihnen in ihrer Eigenschaft als Vertreter einer artei von dieser anvertraut wurde.

Witnesses.

§48 Witnesses who shall not be examined:

1. Persons incapable of communicating their perceptions or who were incapable of perceiving the fact to be proved at the time to which their testimony should relate;
2. clergy about what was confided to them in confession or otherwise under the seal of spiritual official secrecy;[2]
3. organs of the Federation, the states, districts, and municipalities, if their testimony would violate official secrecy requirements incumbent upon them, insofar as they are not released from the duty of secrecy.

§49 (1) A witness may refuse to give evidence:

a) On questions the answering of which would cause the witness, his spouse, his relative or relative by marriage in the ascending or descending line, his sibling or a person who is even more closely related to him or who is related to him by marriage to the same degree, furthermore his parents of choice or foster parents, children of choice or foster children, his guardian or charge an immediate significant pecuniary loss or the risk of criminal prosecution or would bring him shame;

b) About questions he could not answer without violating an officially recognised duty of secrecy from which he has not been validly released or disclosing an art, trade, or business secret.

(2) Persons authorised to professionally represent parties may also refuse to testify about what has been entrusted to them by a party in their capacity as a representative of that party.

[2] Translator's note: spiritual professional or confessional secrecy (from the German *geistliche Amtsverschwiegenheit*).

(3) Wegen der Gefahr eines Vermögensnachteiles darf die Aussage über Geburten, Verheiratungen und Sterbefälle der im Absatz 1, a, bezeichneten Personen nicht verweigert werden.

(4) Will ein Zeuge die Aussage verweigern, so hat er die Gründe seiner Weigerung glaubhaft zu machen.

(5) Einem Zeugen, der einer Ladung (§§ 19 und 20) ohne genügende Entschuldigung nicht Folge leistet oder die Aussage ohne Rechtfertigung verweigert, kann die Verpflichtung zum Ersatze aller durch seine Säumnis oder Weigerung verursachten Kosten auferlegt werden; gegen einen solchen Anspruch ist die Berufung an die im Instanzenzuge übergeordnete Behörde zulässig.

(3) Because of the danger of pecuniary loss, testimony about births, marriages and deaths of the persons designated in paragraph 1a, may not be refused.

(4) If a witness wishes to refuse to testify, he shall provide prima facie evidence for his refusal.

(5) A witness who fails to obey a summons (§§19 and 20) without sufficient excuse or who refuses to testify without justification may be required to reimburse all costs caused by his failure or refusal; such a claim may be appealed to the higher authority in the proceedings.

§ 50. (1) Jeder Zeuge ist zu Beginn seiner Vernehmung über die für die Vernehmung maßgebenden persönlichen Verhältnisse zu befragen, erforderlichenfalls über die gesetzlichen Weigerungsgründe zu belehren und zu ermahnen, daß er die Wahrheit anzugeben habe und nicht verschweigen bedürfe; er ist auch auf die strafrechtlichen Folgen einer falschen Aussage aufmerksam zu machen und mit Handschlag zur Angabe der Wahrheit zu verpflichten.

(2) Öffentliche Organe, die einen Diensteid oder eine Angelobung geleistet haben, sind als Zeugen über ihre dienstlichen Wahrnehmungen unter Erinnerung an ihren Diensteid oder ihre Angelobung zu vernehmen.

§50 (1) At the beginning of his examination, each witness shall be questioned about the personal circumstances relevant to the examination, instructed, if necessary, about the legal grounds for refusal and admonished that he must state the truth and not withhold it; he shall also be made aware of the criminal law consequences of a false statement and obliged to state the truth, sealed by a handshake.

(2) Public officers who have taken an oath of office or undertaken a swearing-in ceremony shall be heard as witnesses on their official perceptions, recalling their oath of office or swearing-in ceremony.

Wahrnehmung von Beteiligten.

§ 51. Die Bestimmungen der §§ 48 und 49 finden auch auf die Vernehmung von Beteiligten zum Zwecke der Beweisführung Anwendung, doch gilt der Weigerungsgrund des § 49, Absatz 1, a, wegen Gefahr eines Vermögensnachteiles nicht.

Perception of participants.

§51 The provisions of §§48 and 49 shall also apply to the questioning of participants for the purpose of taking evidence, however, if the grounds for refusal pursuant to §49, paragraph 1, a, concerning the risk of a pecuniary loss shall not apply.

Sachverständige.

§ 52. (1) Wird die Aufnahme eines Beweises durch Sachverständige notwendig, so sind die der Behörde beigegebenen oder zur Verfügung stehenden amtlichen Sachverständiger (Amtssachverständige) beizuziehen.

(2) Die Behörde kann aber ausnahmsweise anderer geeigneten Personen als Sachverständige heranziehen und beeiden, wenn Amtssachverständige nicht zur Verfügung stehen oder es mit Rücksicht auf die Besonderheit des Falles geboten erscheint. Der Bestellung zum Sachverständigen hat Folge zu leisten, wer zur Erstattung von Gutachten der erforderten Art öffentlich bestellt ist oder wer die Wissenschaft, die Kunst oder das Gewerbe, deren Kenntnis die Voraussetzung der geforderten Begutachten ist, öffentlich als Erwerb ausübt oder zu deren Ausübung öffentlich angestellt oder ermächtigt ist. Aus solche Sachverständige finden die Vorschriften der §§ 49 und 50 sinngemäß Anwendung.

§ 53. (1) Auf Amtssachverständige sind die Bestimmung des § 7 anzuwenden. Andere Sachverständige sind ausgeschlossen, wenn einer der Gründe des § 7, Absatz 1, Zahl 1 bis 3 und 5, zutrifft; außerdem können sie von einer Partei abgelehnt werden, wenn diese Umstände glaubhaft macht, die Unbefangenheit oder Fachkunde des Sachverständigen in Zweifel stellen. Die Ablehnung kann vor der Vernehmung des Sachverständigen, später aber nur dann erfolgen, wenn die Partei glaubhaft, daß sie den Ablehnungsgrund vorher nicht erfahren oder wegen eines für sie unübersteiglichen Hindernisses nicht rechtzeitig geltend machen konnte.

(2) Über den Ablehnungsantrag entscheidet die Behörde endgültig.

Augenschein.

§ 54. Zur Aufklärung der Sache kann die Behörde auf Antrag oder von Amts wegen auch einen Augenschein, nötigenfalls mit Zuziehung von Sachverständigen, vornehmen.

Experts.

§52 (1) If the taking of evidence by experts becomes necessary, the official experts associated with or available to the authority (official experts) shall be consulted.

(2) The authority may, however, under exceptional circumstances consult and swear in other suitable persons as experts if official experts are not available or if this appears to be necessary in view of the peculiarities of the case. The appointment as an expert shall be obeyed by anyone who has been publicly appointed to provide expert opinions of the required kind or who publicly practices the science, art or trade, the knowledge of which is the prerequisite for the required expert opinions, or who is publicly employed or authorised to practice the same. The provisions of §§49 and 50 shall apply *mutatis mutandis* to such experts.

§53 (1) The provisions of §7 shall apply to official experts. Other experts shall be excluded if one of the grounds of §7, paragraph 1, numbers 1 to 3 and 5 applies; in addition, they may be rejected by a party if the party can produce prima facie evidence that cast doubt on the impartiality or expertise of the expert. The refusal may be made before the expert is heard but later only if the party can produce prima facie evidence that he or she was unable to learn of the reason for refusal beforehand or was unable to assert it in time because of an obstacle that was insurmountable for him.

(2) The authority shall make a final decision on the application for rejection.

Inspection.

§54 In order to clarify the matter, the authority may also, upon application or *ex officio*, conduct an inspection, if necessary, with the assistance of experts.

Mittelbare Beweisaufnahme und Erhebungen.

§ 55. (1) Die Behörde kann Beweisaufnahmen auch durch ersuchte oder beauftragte Verwaltungsbehörden oder einzelne dazu bestimmte amtliche Organe vornehmen lassen oder durch sonstige Erhebungen ersetzen oder ergänzen. Insbesondere können Amtssachverständige außer dem Falle einer mündlichen Verhandlung mit der selbständigen Vornahme eines Augenscheins betraut werden.

(2) Die Gerichte dürfen um die Aufnahme von Beweisen nur in den gesetzlich besonders bestimmten Fällen ersucht werden.

Taking of indirect evidence and investigations.

§55 (1) The authority may also have evidence taken by requested or commissioned administrative authorities or individual official bodies designated for this purpose or replace or supplement the taking of evidence with other investigations. In particular, official experts may be entrusted with the independent performance of an inspection, except in the case of an oral hearing.

(2) The courts may be requested to take evidence only in cases specifically determined by law.

III. Teil. Bescheide.

Erlassung von Bescheiden.

§ 56. Der Erlassung eines Bescheides (Entscheidung oder Verfügung) hat, wenn es sich nicht um eine Ladung (§19) oder einem Bescheid nach § 57 handelt, die Feststellung des maßgebenden Sachverhaltes, soweit er nicht von vornherein klar gegeben ist, nach den Vorschriften der §§ 37 und 39 voranzugehen.

§ 57. (1) Wenn es sich um die Vorschreibung von Geldleistungen nach einem gesetzlich, statutarisch oder tarifmäßig feststehenden Maßstabe oder bei Gefahr im Verzug um unaufschiebbare Maßnahmen handelt, ist die Behörde berechtigt, einen Bescheid auch ohne vorausgegangenes Ermittlungsverfahren zu erlassen.

(2) Gegen einen nach Absatz 1 erlassenen Bescheid kann bei der Behörde, die den Bescheid erlassen hat, binnen zwei Wochen Vorstellung erhoben werden. Die Vorstellung hat nur dann aufschiebende Wirkung, wenn sie gegen die Vorschreibung einer Geldleistung gerichtet ist.

(3) Die Behörde hat binnen zwei Wochen nach Einlangen der Vorstellung das Ermittlungsverfahren einzuleiten, widrigenfalls der angefochtene Bescheid von Gesetzes wegen außer Kraft tritt. Auf Verlangen der Partei ist das Außerkrafttreten des Bescheides schriftlich zu bestätigen.

Part III. Administrative decisions.

Adoption of administrative decisions.

§56 The adoption of an administrative decision (ruling or order) shall, if it is not a summons (§19) or an administrative decision pursuant to §57, be preceded by the determination of the relevant facts, unless they are clear from the outset, in accordance with the provisions of §§37 and 39.

§57 (1) If it is a matter of prescribing monetary payments according to an index established by law, statute, or tariff or, in the case of imminent danger, a matter that cannot be postponed, the authority shall be entitled to issue an administrative decision even without a prior investigation procedure.

(2) An appeal against an administrative decision issued under paragraph 1 may be lodged with the authority that issued the decision within two weeks. The appeal shall only have a suspensive effect if it is directed against the prescribing of a monetary payment.

(3) The authority shall initiate an investigation procedure within two weeks of receipt of the appeal, otherwise, the contested administrative decision shall cease to have effect by operation of law. Upon the request of the party, the expiry of the administrative decision shall be confirmed in writing.

Inhalt und Form der Bescheide.

§ 58. (1) Jeder Bescheid ist ausdrücklich als solcher zu bezeichnen und hat den Spruch und, sofern es sich nicht um den Bescheid eines Bundesministeriums oder einer Landesregierung handelt, die Rechtsmittelbelehrung zu enthalten.

(2) Bescheide sind zu begründen, wenn dem Standpunkte der Partei nicht vollinhaltlich Rechnung getragen oder über Einwendungen oder Anträge von Beteiligten abgesprochen wird.

(3) Im Übrigen gelten auch für Bescheide die Vorschriften des § 18, Absatz 4.

§ 59. (1) Der Spruch hat die in Verhandlung stehende Angelegenheit und alle die allfälligen Kostenfragen in möglichst gedrängter, deutlicher Fassung und unter Anführung der angewendeten Gesetzesbestimmungen, und zwar in der Regel zur Gänze, zu erledigen. Läßt der Gegenstand der Verhandlung eine Trennung nach mehreren Punkten zu, so kann, wenn dies zweckmäßig erscheint, über jeden dieser Punkte, sobald, er spruchreif ist, gesondert abgesprochen werden.

(2) Wird die Verbindlichkeit zu einer Leistung oder zur Herstellung eines bestimmten Zustandes ausgesprochen, so ist in dem Spruche zugleich auch eine angemessene Frist zur Ausführung der Leitung oder Herstellung zu bestimmen.

§ 60. In der Begründung sind die Ergebnisse des Ermittlungsverfahrens, die bei der Beweiswürdigung maßgebenden Erwägungen und die darauf gestützte Beurteilung der Rechtsfrage klar und übersichtlich zusammenzufassen.

§ 61. (1) Die Rechtsmittelbelehrung hat anzugeben, ob der Bescheid noch einem weiteren Rechtszuge unterliegt oder nicht und bejahendenfalls innerhalb welcher Frist und bei welcher Behörde die Berufung einzubringen ist.

(2) Enthält ein Bescheid tatsächlich keine Rechtsmittelbelehrung oder fälschlichen die Erklärung, daß kein Rechtsmittel zulässig sei, oder ist keine oder eine kürzere als die gesetzliche Berufungsfrist angegeben, so gilt die Berufung als rechtzeitig, wenn sie innerhalb der gesetzlichen Frist eingebracht wurde.

Content and form of the administrative decision.

§58 (1) Every administrative decision shall be expressly designated as such and shall contain the ruling and, unless it is a decision of a federal ministry or a state government,[3] the information on the right of appeal.

(2) Reasons shall be given for administrative decisions if the position of the party is not fully taken into account or if objections or applications of the participants are rejected.

(3) In all other respects, the provisions of §18, paragraph 4 shall also apply to administrative decisions.

§59 (1) The ruling shall deal with the matter under consideration and all questions of possible costs, in as concise and clear manner as possible, citing the legal provisions applied, and, as a rule, in their entirety. If the subject matter of the hearing permits division into several points, each of these points may, if this appears expedient, be dealt with separately as soon as a point is ready for a decision.

(2) If the obligation to perform a service or to create a certain condition is decided, the ruling shall at the same time also specify a reasonable period for the performance of the service or creation {of the condition[4]}.

§60 The statement of reasons shall clearly and concisely summarise the results of the investigative procedure, the decisive considerations in the assessment of the evidence and the assessment of the legal question based thereon.

§61 (1) The notice of the right to appeal shall state whether or not the administrative decision is subject to further legal review and, if so, within what period and to which authority the appeal is to be lodged.

(2) If the administrative decision actually contains no notice of the right to appeal or erroneously contains the statement that no appeal is admissible, or if no time limit or a time limit shorter than the statutory time limit for appeal is stated, the appeal shall be deemed to have been filed in time if it was filed within the statutory time limit.

[3] Translator's note: or government of a federated state (from the German *Landesregierung).*

[4] Added by translator for clarity.

(3) Ist in dem Bescheide eine längere als die gesetzliche Frist angegeben, so ist die innerhalb der angegebenen First eingebrachte Berufung rechtzeitig.

(4) Enthält der Beschein keine oder eine unrichtige Angabe über die Behörde, bei welcher die Berufung einzubringen ist, so ist die Berufung auch dann richtig eingebracht, wenn sie bei der Behörde, die den Bescheid ausgefertigt hat, oder bei der angegebenen Behörde eingebracht wurde.

(3) If the time limit specified in the administrative decision is longer than the statutory time limit, an appeal filed within the specified time limit shall be deemed as timely.

(4) If the administrative decision does not contain any information or contains incorrect information about the authority with which the appeal is to be lodged, the appeal shall also be deemed to have been lodged correctly if it was lodged with the authority that issued the administrative decision or with the denoted authority.

§ 62. (1) Wenn in den Verwaltungsvorschriften nicht anderes bestimmt ist, können Bescheide sowohl schriftlich als auch mündlich erlassen werden.

(2) Der Inhalt und die Begründung eines mündlichen Bescheides ist, wenn die Begründung bei einer mündlichen Verhandlung erfolgt, am Schlusse der Verhandlungsschrift, in anderen Fällen in einer besonderen Niederschrift zu beurkunden.

(3) Eine schriftliche Ausfertigung des mündlich verkündeten Bescheides ist den bei der Verkündung nicht anwesend und jenen Parteien zuzustellen, die spätestens drei Tage nach der Verkündung eine Ausfertigung verlangen: über dieses Recht ist die Partei bei Verkündung des mündlichen Bescheides zu belehren.

(4) Die Berichtigung von Schreib und Rechnungs fehlern oder anderen offenbar auf einem Versehen beruhenden Unrichtigkeiten in Bescheiden kann die Behörde jederzeit von Amts wegen vornehmen.

§62 (1) Unless otherwise provided for in administrative regulation, administrative decisions may be issued both in writing and orally.

(2) The content of and reasons for an oral administrative decision shall be recorded at the end of the transcript of the hearing if the reasons are given at an oral hearing, and in a special record in other cases.

(3) A written transcript of an orally pronounced administrative decision shall be served on the parties not present at the pronouncement and on those parties who request a transcript not later than three days after the pronouncement: the party shall be informed of this right when the oral administrative decision is pronounced.

(4) The authority may at any time *ex officio* correct clerical and accounting errors or other unintentional inaccuracies in administrative decisions.

IV. Teil. Rechtsschutz.

1. Abschnitt: Berufung.

§ 63. (1) Der Instanzenzug und das Recht zur Einbringung der Berufung (Rekurs, Beschwerde) und sonstige Rechtsmittel (Vorstellung) richtet sich abgesehen von den in diesem Gesetz besonders geregelten Fällen, nach den Verwaltungsvorschriften.

(2) Gegen nur das Verfahren betreffend Anordnungen ist eine abgesonderte Berufung nicht zulässig. Sie können erst in der Berufung gegen den die Angelegenheit erledigenden Bescheid angefochten werden.

Part IV. Legal remedy.

Section 1: Appeal.

§63 (1) The stages of appeal and the right to appeal (recourse, complaint) and other legal remedies (presentation) shall be governed by administrative regulations, except for the cases specifically regulated by this Act.

(2) A separate appeal shall not be admissible against orders relating only to the proceedings. They may only be challenged in the appeal against the administrative decision settling the matter.

(3) Die Berufung hat den Bescheid zu bezeichnen, gegen den sie sich richtet, und einen begründeten Berufungsantrag zu enthalten.

(4) Eine Berufung ist nicht mehr zulässig, wenn die Partei nach Zustellung oder Verkündung des Bescheides ausdrücklich auf die Berufung verzichtet hat.

(5) Die Berufung ist von der Partei schriftlich oder telegraphisch binnen zwei Wochen bei der Behörde einzubringen, die den Bescheid in erster Instanz erlassen hat. Die Frist beginnt für jede Partei mit der an sie erfolgten Zustellung der schriftlichen Ausfertigung des Bescheides, im Falle bl0ß mündlicher Verkündung mit dieser.

(3) An appeal shall specify the administrative decision against which it is directed and contain a reasoned request for appeal.

(4) An appeal shall no longer be admissible if the party has expressly waived the right to appeal after service or pronouncement of the administrative decision.

(5) An appeal shall be filed by the party in writing or by telegraph within two weeks with the authority that issued the administrative decision in the first instance. The time limit shall commence for each party with the delivery of the written transcript of the administrative decision or, in the case of an oral pronouncement, with the pronouncement.

§ 64. (1) Rechtzeitig eingebrachte Berufungen haben aufschiebende Wirkung.

(2) Die Behörde kann die aufschiebende Wirkung ausschließen, wenn die vorzeitige Vollstreckung im Interesse einer Partei oder des öffentlichen Wohles wegen Gefahr im Verzuge dringend geboten ist. Ein solcher Anspruch ist tunlichst schon in den über die Hauptsache ergehenden Bescheid aufzunehmen.

§64 (1) Appeals filed in due time shall have suspensive effect.

(2) The authority may exclude the suspensive effect if the early enforcement is urgently required in the interest of a party or for public welfare due to an imminent danger. Such a claim shall, if feasible, be included in the administrative decision on the main proceedings.

§ 65. Werden in einer Berufung neue Tatsachen oder Beweise, die der Behörde erheblich scheinen, vorgebracht, so hat sie hievon unverzüglich den etwaigen Berufungsgegnern Mitteilung zu machen und ihnen Gelegenheit zu geben, binnen angemessener, zwei Wochen nicht übersteigender Frist von dem Inhalte der Berufung Kenntnis zu nehmen und sich dazu zu äußern.

§65 If new facts or evidence that appear relevant to the authority are presented in an appeal, the authority shall immediately inform the opponents of the appeal and give them the opportunity to take cognisance of the content of the appeal and to comment on it within a reasonable period of time not exceeding two weeks.

§ 66. (1) Notwendige Ergänzungen des Ermittlungsverfahrens hat die Berufungsbehörde durch die Behörde erster Instanz durchführen zu lassen oder selbst vorzunehmen.

(2) Ist der Berufungsbehörde vorliegende Sachverhalt so mangelhaft, daß die Durchführung oder Wiederholung einer mündlichen Verhandlung unvermeidlich erscheint, so kann die Berufungsbehörde den angefochtenen Bescheid beheben und die Angelegenheit zur neuerlichen Verhandlung und Erlassung eines neuen Bescheides an die Behörde erster Instanz verweisen.

§66 (1) The appellate authority shall have the necessary additions to the investigation procedure carried out by the authority of the first instance or shall carry them out itself.

(2) If the facts of the case before the appellate authority are so deficient that the holding or repetition of an oral hearing appears unavoidable, the appellate authority may set aside the contested administrative decision and refer the matter to the authority of the first instance for a new hearing and the issuing of a new administrative decision.

(3) Die Berufungsbehörde kann jedoch die mündliche Verhandlung und unmittelbare Beweisaufnahme auch selbst durchzuführen, wenn hiermit ein Ersparnis an Zeit und Kosten verbunden ist.

(4) Außer dem im Absatz 2 erwähnten Fall hat die Berufungsbehörde, sofern die Berufung nicht als unzulässig oder verspätet zurückzuweisen ist, immer in der Sache selbst zu entscheiden. Sie ist berechtigt sowohl im Spruch als auch hinsichtlich der Begründung (§ 60) ihre Anschauung an die Stelle jener der Unterbehörde zu setzen und demgemäß den angefochtenen Bescheid nach jeder Richtung abzuändern.

§ 67. Die Vorschriften des III. Teiles des gegenwärtigen Gesetzes gelten auch für die Bescheide der Berufungsbehörde, doch ist der Spruch auch dann zu begründen, wenn dem Berufungsantrag stattgegeben wird.

2. Abschnitt: Sonstige Abänderung von Bescheiden.

Abänderung und Behebung von Amts wegen.

§ 68. (1) Anbringen von Beteiligten, die außer den Fällen der §§ 69 und 71 die Abänderung eines der Berufung nicht oder nicht mehr unterliegenden Bescheides begehren, sind, wenn die Behörde nicht den Anlaß zu einer Verfügung gemäß den Absätzen 2 bis 4 findet, wegen entschiedener Sache zurückzuweisen.

(2) Von Amts wegen können Bescheide, aus denen niemandem ein Recht erwachten ist, sowohl von der Behörde, die den Bescheid erlassen hat, als auch in Ausübung des Aufsichtsrechtes von der sachlich in Betracht kommenden Oberbehörde aufgehoben oder abgeändert werden.

(3) Andere Bescheide kann in Wahrung des öffentlichen Wohles die Behörde, die den Bescheid in letzter Instanz erlassen hat, oder die sachlich in Betracht kommende Oberbehörde insoweit abändern, als dies zur Beseitigung von das Leben oder die Gesundheit von Menschen gefährdenden Mißständen oder zur Abwehr schwerer volkswirtschaftlicher Schädigungen notwendig und unvermeidlich ist. In allen diesen Fällen hat die Behörde mit möglichster Schonung erworbener Rechte vorzugehen.

(3) The appellate authority may, however, conduct oral proceedings and directly take evidence itself if this saves time and costs.

(4) Except for the case mentioned in para 2, the appellate authority shall always decide on the merits of the case, unless the appeal is to be dismissed as inadmissible or rejected as out of time. It shall be entitled to substitute its opinion for that of the lower authority, both in the decision and in the statement of reasons (§60) and accordingly amend the contested administrative decision in any direction.

§67 The provisions of Part III of the present Act shall also apply to the administrative decisions of the appellate authority but reasons shall be given for the ruling even if the appeal is granted.

Section 2: Other Amendments to administrative decisions.

Amendment and rectification *ex officio*.

§68 (1) Applications by parties who, except in the cases of §§ 69 and 71, request the amendment of an administrative decision that is not or no longer subject to appeal, shall, if the authority does not find grounds for an order in accordance with paragraphs (2) to (4), be dismissed on the grounds that the matter has been decided.

(2) *Ex officio*, administrative decisions from which no right has accrued to anyone may be revoked or amended both by the authority that issued the decision and, in the exercise of the right of supervision, by the competent superior authority.

(3) Other administrative decisions may be amended in the interest of public welfare by the authority which issued the decision in the last instance or by the competent superior authority insofar as this is necessary and unavoidable for the elimination of abuses endangering the life or health of persons or for the prevention of serious damage to the national economy. In all these cases the authority shall proceed to offer the greatest possible protection of acquired rights.

(4) Außerdem können Bescheide von Amts wegen in Ausübung des Aufsichtsrechtes von der sachlich in Betracht kommenden Oberbehörde als nichtig erklärt werden, wenn der Bescheid

a) von einer unzuständigen Behörde oder von einer nicht richtig zusammengesetzten Kollegialbehörde erlassen wurde,
b) einen strafgesetzwidrigen Erfolg herbeiführen würde,
c) tatsächlich undurchführbar ist oder
d) an einem durch gesetzliche Vorschrift ausdrücklich mit Nichtigkeit bedrohten Fehler leidet.

(5) Nach Ablauf von drei Jahren nach dem im § 63, Absatz 5, bezeichneten Zeitpunkt ist eine Nichtigkeitserklärung aus den Gründen des Absatzes 4, a, nicht mehr zulässig.

(6) Die der Behörde in den Verwaltungsvorschriften eingeräumten Befugnisse zur Zurücknahme oder Einschränkung einer Berechtigung außerhalb eines Berufungsverfahrens bleiben unberührt.

(7) Auf die Ausübung des der Behörde gemäß den Absätzen 2 bis 4 zustehenden Abänderungs und Behebungsrechtes steht niemand ein Anspruch zu. Mutwillige Aufsichtsbeschwerden und Abänderungsanträge sind nach § 35 ahnden.

(4) In addition, administrative decisions may be declared null and void *ex officio* in the exercise of the supervisory right by the competent superior authority if the administrative decision

a) was issued by an authority lacking competence or by an improperly constituted collegiate authority,
b) would bring about a result contrary to criminal law,
c) is in fact impossible to comply with; or
d) suffers from a defect expressly threatened with nullity by statutory provision.

(5) A declaration of nullity on the grounds of paragraph 4, a, shall no longer be admissible after the expiry of three years from the date referred to in §63, paragraph 5, a.

(6) The powers granted to the authority in the administrative regulations to withdraw or restrict an entitlement outside an appeal proceeding shall remain unaffected.

(7) No person has a claim to the exercise of the right of amendment and rectification to which the authority is entitled under paragraphs 2 to 4. Wanton supervisory complaints and requests for amendments shall be punished in accordance with §35.

Wiederaufnahme des Verfahrens.

§ 69. (1) Dein Antrag einer Partei auf Wiederaufnahme eines durch Bescheid abgeschlossenen Verfahrens ist stattzugeben, wenn ein Rechtsmittel gegen den Bescheid nicht oder nicht mehr zulässig ist und:

(a) Der Bescheid durch Fälschung einer Urkunde, falsches Zeugnis oder eine andere gerichtlich strafbare Handlung herbeigeführt oder sonstwie erschlichen worden ist oder

(b) Neue Tatsachen oder Beweismittel hervorkommen, die im Verfahren ohne Verschulden der Partei nicht geltend gemacht werden konnte und allein oder in Verbindung mit dem sonstigen Ergebnisse des Verfahrens voraussichtlich einen im Hauptinhalte des Spruches anders lautend Bescheid herbeigeführt hätten, oder

Reopening of the proceedings.

§69 (1) A party's application for the reopening of proceedings that have been concluded by an administrative decision shall be granted if an appeal against the administrative decision is not or is no longer admissible and:

(d) the administrative decision has been obtained by the forgery of a document, false testimony, or any other act punishable by law or has otherwise been obtained by fraud; or

(e) new facts or evidence emerge which could not have been asserted in the proceedings through no fault of a party and which, alone or in conjunction with the other results of the proceedings, would probably have led to a different administrative decision in the main substance of the ruling, or

(c) Der Bescheid gemäß § 38 von Vorfragen abhängig war und nachträglich über eine solche Vorfrage von der hierfür zuständigen Behörde (Gericht) in wesentlichen Punkten anders entschieden wurde.

(f) the administrative decision was, pursuant to §38, dependent on preliminary questions and such preliminary questions were subsequently decided differently regarding the essential points by the competent authority (court).

(2) Der Antrag auf Wiederaufnahme ist binnen zwei Wochen von dem Zeitpunkt an, in dem der Antragssteller nachweislich von dem Wiederaufnahmsgrunde Kenntnis erlangt hat, jedoch spätestens binnen drei Jahren nach der Zustellung oder mündlichen Verkündung des Bescheides bei der Behörde einzubringen, die den Bescheid in erster Instanz erlassen hat.

(2) The application for reopening shall be filed with the authority that issued the administrative decision in the first instance within two weeks of the date on which the applicant verifiably became aware of the reason for reopening, but at the latest within three years of the service or oral pronouncement of the administrative decision.

(3) Unter den Voraussetzungen des Absatzes 1 kann die Wiederaufnahme des

Verfahrens auch von Amts wegen verfügt werden. Nach Ablauf von drei Jahren nach Erlassung des Bescheides kann die Wiederaufnahme auch von Amts wegen nur mehr aus den Gründen de Absatz 1, a, stattfinden.

(3) Under the conditions of paragraph 1, the reopening of the proceedings may also be ordered *ex officio*. After the expiry of three years after the administrative decision has been issued, the reopening may also take place *ex officio* only on the grounds of paragraph 1, a.

(4) Die Entscheidung über die Wiederaufnahme steht der Behörde zu, die den Bescheid in letzter Instanz erlassen hat.

(4) The decision on reopening shall be taken by the authority that issued the administrative decision in the last instance.

§ 70. (1) In den die Wiederaufnahme bewilligenden oder verfügenden Bescheide ist, sofern nicht schon auf Grund der vorliegenden Akten ein neuer Bescheid erlassen werden kann, auszusprechen, inwieweit und in welcher Instanz das Verfahren wieder aufzunehmen ist.

(2) Frühere Erhebungen und Beweisaufnahmen, die durch die Wiederaufnahmegründe nicht betroffen werden, sind keinesfalls zu wiederholen.

(3) Gegen die Ablehnung eines Antrages auf Wiederaufnahme steht dem Antragssteller das Recht der Berufung an die im Instanzenzuge übergeordnete Behörde zu. Gegen die Bewilligung oder Verfügung der Wiederaufnahme ist eine abgesonderte Berufung nicht zulässig.

§70 (1) Administrative decisions granting or ordering the reopening shall state to what extent and in which instance the proceedings are to be reopened unless a new administrative decision can already be issued on the basis of the files at hand.

(2) Earlier investigations and hearings of evidence that are not affected by the grounds for reopening shall not be repeated under any circumstances.

(3) The applicant shall have the right to appeal to the authority at the higher level in the stages of appeal against the rejection of an application for reopening. A separate appeal shall not be admissible against the approval of or the order to reopen.

Wiedereinsetzung in den vorigen Stand.

§ 71. (1) Gegen die Versäumung einer Frist oder einer mündlichen Verhandlung ist auf Antrag der Partei, die durch die Versäumung einen Rechtsnachteil erleidet, die Wiedereinsetzung in den vorigen Stand zu bewilligen, wenn:

(a) Die Partei glaubhaft macht, daß sie durch ein unvorhergesehenes oder unabwendbares Ereignis ohne ihr Verschulden verhindert war, die Frist einzuhalten oder zur Verhandlung zu erscheinen, oder

(b) Die Partei die Berufungsfrist versäumt hat, weil der Bescheid fälschlich die Angabe enthält, daß keine Berufung zulässig sei.

(2) Der Antrag auf Wiedereinsetzung muß binnen einer Woche nach Aufhören des

Hindernisses oder nach dem Zeitpunkt, in dem die Partei von der Zulässigkeit der Berufung Kenntnis erlangt hat, gestellt werden.

(3) Im Falle der Versäumung einer Frist hat die Partei die versäumte Handlung gleichzeitig mit dem Wiedereinsetzungsantrag nachzuholen.

(4) Zur Entscheidung über den Antrag auf Wiedereinsetzung ist die Behörde berufen, bei der die versäumte Handlung vorzunehmen war oder die versäumte Verhandlung angeordnet oder die unrichtige Rechtsmittelbelehrung erteilt hat.

(5) Gegen die Versäumung der Frist zur Stellung des Wiedereinsetzungsantrages findet keine Wiedereinsetzung in den vorigen Stand statt.

(6) Die Behörde kann dem Antrag auf Wiedereinsetzung aufschiebende Wirkung beilegen.

(7) Die Wiedereinsetzungsantrag kann nicht auf Umstände gestützt werden, die Behörde schon früher für unzureichend befunden hat, um die Verlängerung der versäumte Frist oder die Verlegung der versäumten Verhandlung zu bewilligen.

Reinstatement to the previous legal position.

§71 (1) In case of the failure to observe a time limit or attend an oral hearing, reinstatement to the previous legal position shall be granted on application by the party who suffers a legal disadvantage as a result of the failure if:

(c) the party provides prima facie evidence that he was prevented by an unforeseen or unavoidable event of no fault of his own from acting within the time limit or from appearing at the hearing, or

(d) the party did not act within the time limit for appeal because the administrative decision incorrectly stated that no appeal was admissible.

(2) The application for reinstatement must be filed within one week of the cessation of the obstacle or after the point in time when the party became aware of the admissibility of the appeal.

(3) If not enacted within the time limit, the party shall perform the missed act simultaneously with the application for the reinstatement to the previous legal position.

(4) The authority before which the omitted act was to be performed or which ordered the missed hearing or issued the incorrect notice of the right to appeal shall be competent to decide on the application for the reinstatement to the previous legal position.

(5) No reinstatement to the previous legal position shall be granted in the case of a failure to observe the time limit for filing the application for the reinstatement.

(6) The authority may attach a suspensive effect to the application for reinstatement.

(7) The application for the reinstatement may not be based on circumstances which the authority has previously found insufficient to grant the extension of the defaulted time limit or the rescheduling of a missed hearing.

§ 72. (1) Durch die Bewilligung der Wiedereinsetzung tritt das Verfahren in die Lage zurück, in der es sich vor dem Eintritte der Versäumung befunden hat.

(2) Durch den Antrag auf Wiedereinsetzung gegen die Versäumung der mündlichen Verhandlung wird die Frist zur Anfechtung des infolge der Versäumung erlassenen Bescheides nicht verlängert.

(3) Hat eine Partei Wiedereinsetzung gegen die Versäumung der mündlichen Verhandlung beantragt und gegen den Bescheid Berufung eingelegt, so ist auf die Erledigung der Berufung erst einzugehen, wenn der Antrag auf Wiedereinsetzung abgewiesen worden ist.

(4) Gegen die Ablehnung eines Antrages auf Wiedereinsetzung steht dem Antragssteller das Recht der Berufung an die im Instanzenzug übergeordnete Behörde zu. Gegen die Bewilligung der Wiedereinsetzung ist kein Rechtsmittel zulässig.

§72 (1) The granting of reinstatement shall restore the proceedings to the position they were in before the default occurred.

(2) The application for reinstatement against the failure to attend the oral proceedings shall not extend the time limit for appealing the administrative decision issued as a result of the failure.

(3) If a party has applied for reinstatement due to the failure to attend the oral proceedings and has appealed against the administrative decision, the appeal shall not be dealt with until the application for reinstatement has been dismissed.

(4) The applicant shall have the right to appeal against the rejection of an application for reinstatement to a higher authority in the stages of appeal. No appeal shall be admissible against the granting of reinstatement.

3. Abschnitt: Entscheidungspflicht.

§ 73. (1) Die Behörden sind verpflichtet, wenn in den Verwaltungsvorschriften nicht anderes bestimmt ist, über Anträge von Parteien (§8) und Berufungen ohne unnötigen Aufschub spätestens aber sechs Monate nach deren Einlangen den Bescheid zu erlassen.

(2) Wird der Partei innerhalb dieser Frist der Bescheid nicht zugestellt, so geht auf ihr schriftliches Verlangen die Zuständigkeit zur Entscheidung an die sachlich in Betracht kommende Oberbehörde über. Ein solches Verlangen ist unmittelbar bei der Oberbehörde einzubringen. Das Verlangen ist abzuweisen, wenn die Verzögerung nicht ausschließlich auf ein Verschulden der Behörde zurückzuführen ist.

(3) Für die Oberbehörde beginnt der Lauf der in Absatz 1 bezeichneten Frist mit dem Tage des Einlangens des Parteiverlangens.

Section 3: Duty to decide.

§73 (1) Unless otherwise provided for in administrative regulations, the authority shall be obliged to issue an administrative decision on applications of the parties (§8) and on appeals without undue delay but no later than six months after the receipt thereof.

(2) If a party is not served with the administrative decision within this time limit, the competence to decide shall be transferred to a competent superior authority upon written request. Such a request shall be submitted directly to the superior authority. The request shall be rejected if the delay is not exclusively due to the fault of the authority.

(3) For the superior authority, the time limit referred to in paragraph 1 shall commence on the date of receipt of the party's request.

V. Teil. Kosten.

Kosten der Beteiligten.

§ 74. (1) Jeder Beteiligte hat die ihm im Verwaltungsverfahren erwachende Kosten selbst zu bereiten.

(2) Inwiefern einem Beteiligten ein Kostenersatzanspruch gegen einen anderen Beteiligten zusteht, bestimmen die Verwaltungsvorschriften. Der Kostenersatzanspruch ist so zeitgerecht zu stellen, daß der Anspruch über die Kosten in den Bescheid aufgenommen werden kann. Die Höhe der zu ersetzenden Kosten wird von der Behörde bestimmt und kann von dieser auch in einem Pauschbetrage festgesetzt werden.

Kosten der Behörden.

§ 75. (1) Sofern sich aus den Bestimmungen der §§ 76 bis 78 nicht anderes ergibt, sind die Kosten für die Tätigkeit der Behörden im Verwaltungsverfahren von Amts wegen zu tragen.

(2) Die Heranziehung der Beteiligten zu anderen als den in den §§ 76 bis 78 vorgesehenen Zeitungen, unter welchem Titel immer, ist unzulässig.

(3) Die gesetzlichen Bestimmungen über die Stempel und Rechtsgebühren des Bundes bleiben unberührt.

§ 76. (1) Erwachsen der Behörde bei einer Amtshandlung Barauslagen so hat dafür, soferne nach den Verwaltungsvorschriften nicht auch diese Amtslagen von Amts wegen zu tragen sind, im allgemeinen die Partei aufzukommen, die um die Amtshandlung angesucht hat.

(2) Wurde jedoch die Amtshandlung durch das Verschulden eines anderen Beteiligten verursacht, so sind die Auslagen von diesem zu tragen. Wurde die Amtshandlung von Amts wegen angeordnet, so belasten die Auslagen den Beteiligten dann, wenn sie durch sein Verschulden herbeigeführt worden sind.

Part V. Costs.

Costs of the participants.

§74 (1) Each participant shall bear his own costs incurred in the administrative proceedings.

(2) The administrative regulations shall determine the extent to which one participant is entitled to claim reimbursement of costs from another participant. The claim for reimbursement of costs shall be filed in a timely manner so that the claim for the costs can be included in the administrative decision. The amount of the costs to be reimbursed shall be determined by the authority and may also be fixed by it as a lump sum.

Costs of the authorities.

§75 (1) Unless otherwise provided for in provisions §§76 to 78, the costs of the tasks of the authorities in the administrative proceedings shall be borne *ex officio*.

(2) The enlisting of participants for acts other than those provided for in §§76 to 78, shall be inadmissible under any title whatsoever.

(3) The statutory provisions on stamps and legal fees of the Federation shall remain unaffected.

§76 (1) If the authority incurs cash expenses in connection with an official act, the party requesting the official act shall, as a general rule, bear such expenses unless the administrative provisions provide that such expenses shall be borne *ex officio*.

(2) However, if the official act was caused by the fault of another participant, the expenses shall be borne by that person. If the official act was ordered *ex officio*, the expenses shall be borne by the participant concerned if they were caused by his fault.

(3) Treffen die Voraussetzung der vorangehenden Absätze auf mehrere Beteiligte zu, so sind die Auslagen auf die einzelnen Beteiligten angemessen zu verteilen.

(4) Ist eine Amtshandlung nicht ohne größere Barauslagen durchführbar, so kann die Partei, die um die Amtshandlung ansucht, zum Erlag eines entsprechenden Vorschusses verhalten werden.

§ 77. (1) Für Amtshandlungen der Behörden außerhalb des Amtes können Kommissionsgebühren eingehoben wurden. Hinsichtlich der Verpflichtung zur Entrichtung dieser Gebühren finden die Bestimmungen des § 76 sinngemäß Anwendung.

(2) Die Kommissionsgebühren sind in Pauschbeträgen (nach Tarifen) oder, soweit keine Pauschbeträge (Tarife) festgesetzt sind, als Barauslagen nach den Vorschriften des § 76 aufzurechnen. Die Pauschbeträge (Tarife) sind nach der für die Amtshandlung aufgewendeten Zeit, nach er Entfernung des Ortes der Amtshandlung von Amte oder nach der Zahl der notwendigen Amtsorgane festzusetzen.

(3) Die Festsetzung der Pauschbeträge (Tarife) erfolgt durch Verordnung der Bundesregierung, für die Behörden der Länder, Bezirke und Gemeinden durch Verordnung der Landesregierung.

(4) Die Kommissionsgebühren sind von der Behörde, die Amtshandlung vorgenommen hat, einzugehen und fließen der Gebietskörperschaft zu, die den Aufwand dieser Behörde zu tragen hat.

(5) Die durch die Entsendung von Amtsorganen anderen am Verfahren beteiligten Verwaltungsbehörden erwachsenen Kosten sind von der die als Barauslagen im Sinne des § 76 zu verhandeln; die von den Beteiligten eingehobenen Beträge sind der anderen Verwaltungsbehörden zu überweisen.

(6) Die Bestimmung des § 76, Absatz 4, gilt auch für die Kommissionsgebühren.

(3) If the prerequisites of the preceding paragraphs apply to several participants, the expenses shall be distributed among the individual participants in an appropriate manner.

(4) If an official act cannot be carried out without considerable cash expenditure, the party requesting the official act may be required to make an appropriate advance payment.

§77 (1) Commission fees may be levied for official acts of the authorities performed away from the office. With regard to the obligation to pay these fees, the provisions of §76 shall apply *mutatis mutandis.*

(2) Any commission fees shall be paid as lump sums (according to tariffs) or, if no lump sums (tariffs) are fixed, as cash expenditure according to the provisions of §76. The lump sums (tariffs) shall be fixed according to the time spent for the official act, according to the distance of the place of the official act from the office or according to the number of the necessary officials.

(3) Lump sums (tariffs) shall be fixed by decree of the Federal Government or, for the authorities of the states, districts, and municipalities, by decree of the state government.

(4) Commission fees shall be received by the authority that performed the official act and shall accrue to the regional body that has to bear the expenses of that authority.

(5) The costs incurred by the secondment of officials from other administrative authorities involved in the proceedings shall in all cases be treated by the authority performing the official act as cash expenditures within the meaning of §76; the amounts collected from the participants shall be remitted to the other administrative authority.

(6) The provision of §76, paragraph 4, shall also apply to commission fees.

§ 78. (1)(Verfassungsbestimmung:) Den Parteien können für die Verleihung von Berechtigungen oder sonstige wesentlich in ihrem Privatinteresse liegende Amtshandlungen der Behörden besondere Verwaltungsabgaben auferlegt werden, sofern die Freiheit von derlei Abgaben nicht ausdrücklich durch Gesetz festgesetzt ist.

(2) (Verfassungsbestimmung:) In den Angelegenheiten der Bundesverwaltung, übertragener Wirkungsbereich der Gemeinden in Bundesangelegenheiten) sind für das Ausmaß der Verwaltungsabgaben, abgesehen von den durch Gesetz besonders geregelten Fällen, durch Verordnung der Bundesregierung zu erlassende Tarife maßgebend, in denen die Abgaben mit festen Ansätzen, die nach objektiven Merkmalen abgestuft sein können, bis zum Höchstbetrag von 100 S im einzelnen Fall festzusetzen sind.

(3) (Verfassungsbestimmung:) Das Ausmaß der Verwaltungsabgaben in den Angelegenheiten der Landes, Bezirks und Gemeindeverwaltung richtet sich nach den auf Grund des FinanzVerfassungsgesetzes und des Abgabenteilungsgesetzes bestehenden landesgesetzlichen Vorschriften.

(4) (Verfassungsbestimmung:) Die Verwaltungsabgaben sind von der in der Sache in erster Instanz zuständigen Behörde einzugehen und fließen der Gebietskörperschaft zu, die den Aufwand dieser Behörde zu tragen hat.

(5) (Verfassungsbestimmung:) Die Art der Einhebung ist für die Bundesbehörde durch Verordnung der Bundesregierung, für die Behörden der Länder, Bezirke und Gemeinden durch Verordnung der Landesregierung zu regeln.

§ 79. Die in den §§ 76 bis 78 vorgesehenen Leistungen sind nur insoweit einzuheben als dadurch der notdürftige Unterhalt des Beteiligten und der Personen, für die er nach dem Gesetze zu sorgen hat, nicht gefährdet wird.

§78 (1)(Constitutional provision:) Special administrative charges may be imposed on the parties for the granting of authorisations or other official acts of the authorities which are essentially in their private interest unless freedom from such charges is expressly established by law.

(2) (Constitutional provision:) In matters of federal administration (direct or indirect federal administration, federal matters delegated to municipalities) the extent of the administrative charges shall, except in cases specifically regulated by law, be determined by tariffs that will be issued by a decree of the Federal Government, in which the charges shall be set at fixed rates, which may be graduated according to objective elements, up to a maximum amount of 100 Schilling per individual case.

(3) (Constitutional provision:) The extent of administrative charges for matters of the state, district and municipal administration shall be governed by the provisions of state law existing on the basis of the Finance Constitution Act and the Levy Sharing Act.

(4) (Constitutional provision:) Any administrative charges shall be collected by the authority competent in the matter in the first instance and shall accrue to the regional body which has to bear the expenses of this authority.

(5) (Constitutional provision:) The method of collection shall be regulated for a federal authority by the decree of the Federal Government, while for the authorities of the federal states, districts and municipalities by a decree of the state government.

§79 The costs for services provided for in §§76 to 78 shall be collected only to the extent that they do not jeopardise the subsistence of the participant and of the persons for whom he is responsible under the law.

VI. Teil. Schlussbestimmungen.

§ 80. (1) Dieses Gesetz tritt gemäß den Bestimmungen des Einführungsgesetzes zu den Verwaltungsverfahrensgesetzen in Kraft.

(2) Die Durchführungsverordnung können bereits von dem der Kundmachung des Gesetzes folgenden Tag an erlassen werden. Sie treten frühestens zugleich mit dem Gesetz in Kraft.

(3) Mit der Vollziehung ist die Bundesregierung betraut.

**Hainisch, Weber, Schneider, Reich, Ahrer
Schürff, Mataja**

Part VI. Final Provisions.

§80 (1) This Act shall come into force in accordance with the provisions of the Introductory Act to the Administrative Procedure Acts.

(2) The implementing ordinances may be issued as early as the day following the promulgation of the Act. They shall enter into force at the same time as the Act at the earliest.

(3) The Federal Government shall be entrusted with enforcement.

**Hainisch, Weber, Schneider, Reich, Ahrer
Schürff, Mataja**

1
Introduction

Giacinto della Cananea

I. The Object and Nature of this Book

This book contains a comparative enquiry into administrative procedure legislation. It has two themes. The first is the Austrian codification of administrative procedure in 1925. The second is the spread of Austrian ideas and institutions to some neighbouring countries. These themes can be briefly outlined as follows.

There is little doubt that the development of administrative procedure legislation has been one of the most significant achievements of the twentieth century as far as administrative law is concerned, although there is a diversity of opinion about its impact. For some, at the beginning of the last third of the twentieth century, administrative procedure legislation had not radically altered the deep structures of administrative law.[1] For others, at the turn of the twenty-first century, adopting general legislation is the 'form *par excellence* of administrative procedure'.[2] In a similar vein, others argue that a sort of '*ius commune*' of administrative procedure has emerged on both sides of the Atlantic.[3]

However, all too often, the comparative study of administrative procedure legislation begins with an examination of texts from around the middle of the twentieth century, such as the US Administrative Procedure Act (APA) of 1946, or even more recent ones, such as the German legislation of 1976. One such example is a recent survey promoted by the International Academy of Comparative Law concerning administrative procedure containing not even one chapter on Austria. This indifference has more than one drawback. Descriptively, ignoring previous forms of legislative regulation—that is, those of Spain (1889) and Austria—prevents an accurate description of relevant legal realities. It also prevents an understanding of the practical importance of other (and potentially better) solutions to similar—if

[1] JP Gilli, 'Review of G. Isaac, La procedure administrative non contentieuse' (1969) 21 RIDC 660.

[2] GA Bermann, 'Foreword' in J-B Auby (ed), *Codification of Administrative Procedure* (Bruylant 2014) v. See also J Barnes, 'Towards a Third Generation of Administrative Procedure' in S Rose-Ackerman and P Lindseth (eds), *Comparative Administrative Law* (Edward Elgar 2010) 337; JM Beerman, 'Common Law and Statute Law in Administrative Law' (2011) 63 Admin L Rev 1 (emphasising the importance of the APA within the context of statutory law).

[3] E Garcia de Enterria, 'Prologo' in A Brewer-Carias, *Principios del procedimiento administrativo. Estudio de derecho administrative comparado* (Civitas 1990) v.

Giacinto della Cananea, *Introduction* In: *The Austrian Codification of Administrative Procedure*. Edited by: Giacinto Della Cananea, Angela Ferrari Zumbini, and Otto Pfersmann, Oxford University Press.
 DOI: 10.1093/oso/9780198867623.003.0001

not identical—problems that concern the business of government.[4] On a more theoretical level, an opportunity is thus lost for comparing Austrian administrative procedure legislation with the later frameworks, which would allow a better understanding of whether they constitute different models and, if so, explain it in terms of values and principles.[5]

There is yet another drawback from a comparative perspective. Austrian administrative procedure legislation was not isolated. Between 1921 and 1930, just a few years after the dissolution of the centuries-old Habsburg Empire, the legislation adopted by other countries was not simply similar to that of Austria but, according to some observers, was clearly influenced by it.[6] This is an important point for consideration as a working hypothesis, and it leads to further questions. We may ask ourselves whether a cluster emerged among those nations and, if so, whether it can be explained either by their shared history and culture or a shared understanding of the new needs of government. There is a further point that looks interesting from a comparative viewpoint. Some of the nations that adopted administrative procedure legislation in the 1920s faced a drastic regime change after 1945 when they fell under Soviet rule. The question that thus arises is whether those principles and rules of administrative procedure survived in one way or another.

Following these remarks, three themes will be interwoven in this introduction. The first concerns the adoption of administrative procedure legislation in Austria almost one century ago. The second theme concerns the spread of Austrian ideas and institutions within other legal systems. The third looks at some issues in methodology.

II. Austrian Administrative Procedure Legislation

To better understand the innovative dimension of Austrian administrative procedure legislation, it is important to be aware of the background. This section will develop the analysis in two related ways. It will be argued from a historical perspective that throughout the nineteenth century—with the notable exception of the Spanish legislation of 1889—administrative law evolved very differently from private law; that is, its general principles and rules were not codified (this term is

[4] See R Parker, 'Book Review: L. Adamovich, Handbuch des österreichischen Verwaltungsrechts. Vol. 1. Allgemeiner und materiellrechtlicher Teil' (1956) 5 AJCL 146, 148 (noting that the Austrian APA regulated problems on which the US one was 'either silent or vague'); R Parker, 'Administrative Procedure in Austria' (1965) 14 AJCL 322, 325 (arguing that the Austrian code 'could furnish some food for thinking to American lawyers').

[5] See G Pastori (ed), *La procedura amministrativa* (Neri Pozza 1964) 72.

[6] See G Langrod, 'La codification de la procédure administrative non contentieuse en Pologne' (1960) 13 R Adm 533, 534 (observing that a group of countries regulated their administrative procedure '*à l'instar du modèle autrichien*') and more recently Z Kmeciack (ed), *Administrative Proceedings in the Habsburg Succession Countries* (Wolters Kluwer Polska 2020).

initially employed comprehensively, encompassing the legislative restatement of existing rules and practice as well as a statement of the new law). Quite the contrary, they were defined and refined by the courts. It will be further argued that attempts made in this direction before the first quarter of the twentieth century come mainly from the Austrian legal experience.

A. Background: Judicial Regulation of Administrative Procedure

Albert Venn Dicey's famous attack on French administrative law[7] consisted of a strong critique of the creation of special courts as these were thought to be grounded in 'ideas *foreign* to the fundamental assumption of our English common law' based on the rule of law. In sum, there was a sharp contrast between common law systems and civil law systems.

However, Dicey's contemporaries, such as American scholars Frank J. Goodnow and their successors, have pointed out that Dicey misconceived the scope and nature of administrative law in England. In the 1950s, according to Martin Loughlin, 'the Diceyan argument that in Britain we had no administrative law had clearly been rejected'.[8] Similarly, not only did he consider just 'one small part of French administrative law and ignored the rest',[9] but he also focused on less recent rules, essentially as they were before 1848.

More specifically, Dicey's sharp divide between common law and civil law systems was untenable for two reasons. First, while the field of private law was characterised in continental Europe by the adoption of systematic codes (France 1804, the Austrian Empire 1811, Italy 1865, Spain 1889, and the German Empire 1896), administrative laws were not codified on both sides of the European civilisation.[10] Second, and consequently, while the structure of judicial systems diverged, depending on whether the disputes concerning the exercise of power by public authorities were under the supervision of ordinary or special administrative courts, their jurisprudence on administrative procedure was not necessarily different. Indeed, as John Bell observed some time ago, 'the French case is not radically different in outcome' from that of the UK.[11] Our previous diachronic comparison concerning six legal systems confirms this similarity, showing that the courts defined and refined general principles to prevent misuse and abuse of power

[7] AV Dicey, *Introduction to the Study of the Law of the Constitution* (first published in 1885, 10th edn, Macmillan 1959, under the supervision of ECS Wade) 328–29.

[8] M Loughlin, *Public Law and Political Theory* (Clarendon 1992) 179.

[9] WI Jennings, 'Administrative Law and Administrative Jurisdiction' (1938) 20 J Comp Leg 99.

[10] J Rivero, *Cours de droit administratif comparé* (Les cours de droit 1956–57) 31. On the ideologies underlying civil codes, see JH Merryman and R Pérez-Perdomo, *The Civil Law Tradition: An Introduction to the Legal Systems of Europe and Latin America* (3rd edn, Stanford UP 2007) 28.

[11] J Bell, 'Discretion and Administrative Procedure in France and England' in L Torchia (ed), *Il procedimento amministrativo: profili comparati* (CEDAM 1993) 15.

by public authorities everywhere.[12] The principle of legality expressed these related ideas. It was supplemented by various requirements aiming to achieve procedural fairness and propriety, including the duty to respect pre-established procedure, the right to be heard, and the duty to give reasons. However, in principle, nothing prevented parliaments from laying down general legislation governing the discharge of administrative functions and powers. Nevertheless, this was not to be.

B. Background: The Nineteenth-Century Debate on the Codification of Administrative Procedure

Ideas and suggestions that administrative procedure should be regulated by legislation date back almost two centuries. In Restoration France, one of the founders of administrative law as an academic discipline,[13] Joseph-Marie de Gérando, was already devoting considerable attention to the study of administrative procedure and suggested its codification.[14] Three decades later, another French public lawyer, Jules Mallein, reconsidered the issue and concluded that the disadvantages of codification vastly exceeded its advantages,[15] a conclusion that would remain unchallenged in France for an extended period. This resulted in a profound difference between administrative and private law, codified in France since 1805. Consequently, despite the influence of French administrative law as far as judicial review is concerned, two other European countries seized the leadership regarding the regulation of administrative procedure, namely Spain and Austria.

In Spain, legislation was approved by Parliament in the same year as the Civil Code (1889). Though the act dealt mainly with the judicial review of the administration, it also laid down a few general provisions concerning administrative procedure, particularly on hearing the interested parties and the notification of administrative acts.[16] Its importance cannot, therefore, be neglected, also because it set an important precedent for the administrative procedure legislation adopted in 1958, as Barnes observes in this volume.[17] However, it must be

[12] G della Cananea and S Mannoni (eds), *Administrative Justice* Fin de Siècle: *Early Judicial Standards of Administrative Conduct in Europe* (1890–1910) (OUP 2021).

[13] J-L Mestre, *Introduction historique au droit administratif français* (PUF 1985).

[14] J-M de Gérando, *De la procédure administrative*, 4 (Thémis 1822) 57, 60. For further remarks, see B Seiller, 'L'administrateur éclairé. La procédure administrative non contentieuse selon Gérando' (2013) Revue d'histoire des facultés de droit et de la culture juridique 425, 428.

[15] J Mallein, *Faut-il codifier les lois administratives: examen de la question?* (Maisonville et fils 1860), who criticised the proposal made by MA Trolley, *Traité de la hierarchie, de l'organisation et de la competence des diverses autorités administratives* (Plon 1854) reviewed by Rodolphe Dareste in the *Revue bibliographique et critique de droit français et étranger* (1854) 72 (noting that it failed to define the administrative act).

[16] Act of 19 October 1889, known as '*Ley Azcarate*'.

[17] See Chapter 3. See also G Langrod, 'La codification de la procédure administrative non contentieuse en Espagne' (1959) 12 R Adm 74 (same remark).

observed that its effectiveness was undermined because each central department developed its own rules of procedure, leading to the emergence of a 'disordered body of rules'.[18]

This explains why the Austrian administrative procedure legislation of 1925 was not the first one.[19] However, with some justification, it is usually regarded as the most important of its time for two reasons. On the one hand, it meant that comprehensive administrative procedure legislation was enacted; on the other, this legislation soon exerted an important influence on other European legal systems. These aspects will be considered in the paragraphs that follow.

Meanwhile, two introductory remarks may be helpful. First, the term 'codification' is used in more than one way. Sometimes, it is taken to mean a statement of existing practice in a piece of legislation. Another option is the definition of general principles with the approval of parliamentary institutions. This may preserve the flexibility of the law, but it is not regarded as a real form of codification, unlike the complete and systematic statement, in the form of a code, of both general principles and detailed rules. There may be various solutions between the last two options, depending on whether the law is stated from sector-specific rules, practice, and judicial decisions, or created.[20]

Second, although Roscoe Pound observed that the 'era of codes' in Europe 'reinforced the idea of law as a body of rules',[21] qualification is necessary, and the Austrian case provides a helpful example. The Austrian Civil Code of 1811 authorised judges to adjudicate cases basing themselves on the 'principles of natural law' if neither an explicit provision nor interpretation by analogy provided an adequate solution. Similarly, at the beginning of the new century, the Swiss Civil Code attributed strong powers to the courts, which were authorised to refer to the 'principles of justice and equity'.[22] These are but a few examples. However, they are interesting because they show the relevance and significance of diversity, even within a shared orientation.

C. The Austrian Turning Point

There is certainly no lack of studies concerning the Austrian administrative procedure legislation of 1925, mainly—though not only—in academic works

[18] L Ortega, 'A Comparison with the Spanish Regulation of Administrative Procedures' (2010) 2 It J Pub L 296, 297.

[19] The opposite view, expressed, among others, by Parker, *Administrative Procedure in Austria* (n 4) 322 is thus inaccurate.

[20] For further analysis, see Merryman and Pérez-Perdomo (n 10) 29.

[21] R Pound, 'Hierarchy of Sources and Forms in Different Systems of Law' (1933) 7 Tul L Rev 475, 480.

[22] For further analysis, see AE von Overbeck, 'Some Observations on the Role of the Judge under the Swiss Civil Code' (1977–78) 37 Louisiana L R 681, 687 (noting the difference compared with Germany).

written in German.[23] It may be helpful to take stock of the existing literature from four points of view. First, Austria benefited from the extensive case law of the Administrative Court (Verwaltungsgerichtshof) created in 1875. For five decades, the Court's rulings obliged public authorities to respect not only traditional rights, such as property and freedom of commerce, but also procedural rights. The Court took important steps in this direction, recognising the right to be heard, legal representation, and the duty to give reasons, thus limiting absolutism.[24] Initially, it judged individual cases without even citing precedent.[25] It thus acted from a sort of micro perspective. A macro perspective was provided by academic works, particularly those of Friedrich Tezner.[26] The macro perspective examined more systemic concerns and sought to address them.

Second, as is often the case with administrative procedure legislation, including that of the United States and Germany,[27] it results from a complex and lengthy political process.[28] As early as 1875, when the Court was created, there was debate as to the principles it had to guarantee, but eventually the very concise formulation approved referred to 'essential procedural infringements'. Subsequently, while some observers argued that the Court's case law did not suffice to ensure adequate protection of individuals' rights, the executive emphasised the need for its action to be 'unhampered by legalistic norms'.[29]

Third, such legislation included five statutes: the first clarified that agencies would be subject to other statutes; the second was the APA; the third act regulated criminal administrative procedure; the fourth concerned the execution of administrative decisions, while the fifth established simplification measures. Regarding the APA, the legislator assumed that the administration was part of the executive branch and exercised discretionary powers but that its action had to be regulated. This assumption had consequences, including the use of terms such as 'parties' and 'interest' and the possibility of legal representation. While the law dealt in detail with administrative adjudication, the procedures for adopting regulations were left outside its remit.

[23] See, in particular, E Mannlicher, *Die Osterreichische Verwaltungsreform des Jahres 1925* (Springer 1926). Among the comments written in other languages, see Parker, *Administrative Procedure in Austria* (n 4); Pastori (n 5); MR Hernritt, 'La nouvelle procédure administrative autrichienne' in *Annuaire de l'institut international de droit public* (PUF 1932) 251; H Schambeck, 'The Development of Austrian Administrative Law' (1962) 28 IRAS 215.

[24] Parker, *Administrative Procedure in Austria* (n 4) 323.

[25] A Ferrari Zumbini, 'Standards of Judicial Review of Administrative Action in the Austro-Hungarian Empire' in della Cananea and Mannoni (n 12) 45 (charting the development of procedural requirements).

[26] F Tezner, *Die rechtsbildende Funktion der österreichischen verwaltungsgerichtlichen Rechtsprechung* (Verlag der Österreich Staatsdruckerei 1925).

[27] See W Gellhorn, 'The Administrative Procedure Act: The Beginnings' (1986) 72 Va L Rev 219(discussing the process that led to adoption of the APA).

[28] Schambeck (n 23) 219 (with a reference to the special commission for administrative reform established in 1911).

[29] Parker, *Administrative Procedure in Austria* (n 4) 324.

Fourth, and consequently, Austrian legislation is commonly regarded as replicating the judicial model.[30] This interpretation has been based on two findings: the imposition of the fundamental requirements of due process law concerning administrative adjudication on the one hand and the lack of norms concerning rule-making procedure on the other. However, there was no lack of awareness that also administrative rules could adversely affect the rights of the individual.[31]

Moreover, one commentator has observed that other requirements of natural justice, for example, that the tribunal be unbiased, were 'not so firmly entrenched in Austrian law'.[32] Nor is it altogether clear what objectives the legislator was pursuing and whether it simply sought to 'codify' the jurisprudence of the Administrative Court. From the former point of view, was legislation passed to make the procedure of federal agencies uniform and to simplify their action? Or was it intended to give a more secure foundation to the emerging administrative State by bringing it closer to the ideals of the *Rechtsstaat*? A related but distinct question concerns the reasons underlying the legislation on Austrian administrative procedure. Was it the product of solely internal forces, or was it somehow promoted or encouraged by external pressure? The other group of questions from a comparative perspective concerns the relationship between the legislator and the courts. Was it a codification of existing law and practice, as some observers have argued,[33] or was it also a statement of new law and standards of procedure? Did it claim to be systematic, like civil codes, or was it a sort of 'residual statute', similar to the US APA?[34] And did its wording prevent further judicial development of the principles of administrative law or, conversely, did the Administrative Court continue to expand procedural requirements? All these questions will be investigated in this book.

[30] L Torchia, 'I modelli di procedimento amministrativo' in Torchia (n 11) 35.

[31] On this line of reasoning, see Parker, *Administrative Procedure in Austria* (n 4) 325 (mentioning Hans Kelsen's intervention in his capacity as member of the Austrian Constitutional Court, to strike down a regulation that directly affected an individual without affording him due process of law and suggesting that the American problem of rate-making procedure was not as important in Europe because most public utilities were owned by the State). See also the decision rendered by the Administrative Court in a sort of 'transnational' case concerning Austria and Hungary in 1911, where the Court denied that some of the interested parties were entitled to an administrative procedure and for further analysis, see E Bousek, 'Decision Rendered by the Imperial Royal Administrative Court of Austria, Involving the Question of Territorial Rights of a River Flowing into a Lower-Lying State' (1913) 7 AJCL 653.

[32] Parker, *Administrative Procedure in Austria* (n 4) 327.

[33] G Langrod, 'Pour une protection efficace du particulier contre les abus de l'administration' (1969) 22 R Adm 631, 635, fn 5.

[34] For this thesis, see M Shapiro, 'Codification of Administrative Law: The US and Europe' (1996) 2 Eur L J 26, 29; Gellhorn (n 27) 232 (for whom the Act was for the most part 'declaratory of . . . standards of good behaviour'). Earlier accounts, however, observed that the APA was in some respects a codification, while in others it was a statement of new law: 'The Federal Administrative Procedure Act: Codification or Reform?' (1947) 56 Yale LJ 670, 673. For further discussion, see I Stewart, 'Australia' in Auby (n 2) 32 (pointing to the various techniques which are used).

III. The Spread of Austrian Ideas and Institutions

The second set of issues that must be examined concerns the spread of administrative procedure legislation in various European countries after 1925. First of all, it may be helpful to put things in perspective by explaining why little attention has been given to the topic so far. Second, it will be argued that adopting general legislation on administrative procedure is an important sign of change, which should not be viewed from the perspective of only one system. Third, and as a development of the preceding argument, it is both interesting and important to understand whether, as some earlier studies suggested, the Austrian codification gave rise to some sort of cluster.

A. Beyond the Conception of Administrative Law as a National Enclave

Before we seek to assess the importance and significance of the Austrian administrative procedure legislation, an important point should be borne in mind about the birth and development of administrative law.

For almost a century, administrative law was dominated by two received ideas. The first was the Diceyan idea that administrative law was not a product of the State, but of some States; that is, only those of continental Europe, while it did not, and could not, exist in England or other common law systems adhering to the postulates of the rule of law. The second was the idea that the French administrative system was much more advanced and, consequently, had been substantially imitated by the rest of continental Europe.[35] It is fair to say at this juncture that although Dicey was the most prominent representative of this line of thought, he was not isolated in this. Suffice it to say that one of the most distinguished comparative lawyers of the past century, Réné David, emphasised the absence of administrative law in England in the distinction between the two Western legal families;[36] around the same time, one of the most influential public lawyers of continental Europe, Massimo Severo Giannini, echoed Dicey's point about the absence of administrative law in common law systems.[37]

With the benefit of hindsight, we are now more aware that these ideas were fraught with difficulties. Administrative law did in fact exist in both the United Kingdom and the Unites States already in the nineteenth century. At the root of the idea that administrative law was a product of the State, of each State, that is to say,

[35] Dicey (n 7) 330.

[36] R David, *Le droit anglais* (PUF 1965) 92 ('la notion d'un droit administratif … est inconnue en Angleterre').

[37] MS Giannini, *Istituzioni di diritto amministrativo* (Giuffè 1981) 8–9.

a sort of national enclave, was a strong belief in the law *tout court*. Namely the conviction, illustrated by Montesquieu in his *Spirit of the Laws*, that law has a strong correlation with its natural and social context.[38] Subsequently, in the works of the nineteenth-century German historical school, this correlation was conceptualised in terms of a biunivocal relationship between the law and the *Volksgeist*, the 'spirit of the people'.[39] The least that can be said is that such a biunivocal correlation was problematic, especially if the main principles were inspired by Roman law.

While this is established in the history of private law, what is less well known is that, even in the field of public law, which Savigny claimed was based on national context,[40] the nineteenth century was marked by borrowings and legal transplants. An enlightening example is that of the French model of judicial control of administrative action, which, due to its prestige, constituted more than a simple source of inspiration for other legal systems in continental Europe, including Italy and, to some degree, the Habsburg Empire and various German States. Interestingly, Dicey was well aware of this. He observed that the corpus of *droit administratif* was worth studying also because 'it had been imitated in most of the countries of continental Europe'.[41] However, this undermined the thrust of the argument that national values and institutions inextricably influenced public law. Subsequently, many academic works have compared the various forms of judicial review, following Laferrière's treatise.[42]

B. National and Transnational Factors of Administrative Procedure Legislation

Late nineteenth-century comparative studies in public law paid no attention to the first attempt to codify administrative procedure, for which Spain was a forerunner (1889). The codification of administrative procedure would be examined by national scholars some decades later, when Austria adopted its general legislation. It was also mentioned by those who illustrated similar reforms in a number

[38] Montesquieu, *L'esprit des lois* (1756; Flammarion, 1987) 304 (bk XI, ch VI). In the secondary literature, see P Stein, *Legal Evolution: The Story of an Idea* (CUP 1980) 15 (according to whom Montesquieu deviated from the natural law tradition because he noted that the 'nature of things' may, and does, differ for different social groups).

[39] FK Savigny, *Vom Beruf unserer Zeit für Gesetzgebung und Rechtswissenschaft* (Mohr und Zimmer1815). See also Merryman and Pérez-Perdomo (n 10) 31.

[40] FK Savigny, *System des heutigen Römischen Rechts von Friedrich Carl von Savigny* (Veit und Comp 1840) I, English translation Willian Halloway, *System of the Modern Roman Law* (Higginbotham 1867) 2 (clarifying that 'private law and not public law is part of our undertaking').

[41] Dicey (n 7) 329. For further discussion of '*nationalisme administratif*, see A Plantey, *Prospective de l'Etat* (CNRS 1975) 198.

[42] E Laferrière, *Traité de la juridiction administrative et des recours contentieux* (Berger-Levrault 1887–88). His treatise was discussed by Frank Goodnow, 'Review of E. Laferrière, *Traité de la juridiction administrative*' (1896) 11 Pol Sci Q 353.

of neighbouring countries. However, with few exceptions, there was a tendency to focus on only one system.

This approach had two weaknesses. First, as Alan Watson has observed, it is always possible to analyse the local factors that either promote or facilitate any legal change, but such an exclusive focus on one legal system inevitably overlooks similar changes in other legal systems, whether or not they have a shared past.[43] However, also for a better understanding of what is regarded as a national peculiarity, for example, the French principles governing the tortuous liability of public administrations, it is helpful to consider other ways of dealing with the same type of problems.

Second, and more importantly for our purposes here, focusing on one legal system does not allow—indeed it actually hinders—a complete understanding of the extent to which legal change within that system is connected with innovations in another legal system. This often leads to an underestimation of the shared and connecting elements between legal systems. A question that arises is why an important legal change—in our case a new way of regulating administrative procedure, ie through general legislative provisions—had not occurred before. Another question is whether there is any evidence of a formal connection, such as 'reception' and the like. In the absence of a formal connection, we may wonder whether, for national policymakers, Austrian legislation had an advantage because it was viewed as being the most advanced form of regulation in light of the evolving needs of government.

The spread of administrative procedure legislation in the territory of the former Habsburg Empire is therefore instructive because it provides fertile ground for discussing the conventional view according to which the law, and a fortiori public law, is inevitably rooted in its social, political, and historical context, so that the legal institutions of other peoples may not be used to guide government on the use of legislative power.

C. The 'Influence' of the Austrian Reform: A Case of the Diffusion?

The point just made concerning the importance of Austrian general legislation on administrative procedure reveals that there are two sides to the same coin. One is empirical, and the other theoretical. The first concerns the nature of the process that led to the adoption of administrative procedure legislation and its duration. The other concerns the theoretical framework best suited to making sense of this process.

[43] A Watson, 'Sources of Law and Legal Culture' (1983) 131 Un Pa L Rev 1121, 1122.

There was no lack of awareness of the relationship between the norms adopted in Austria and some neighbouring nations in the few less recent studies concerning administrative procedure legislation.[44] However, this relationship was referred to, rather than explained, as if, by accepting the Austrian legal infrastructure, each of those nations recognised its technical soundness. The new States would thus abandon developing their own principles and institutions. Arguably, this conventional approach must not be rejected but reconsidered because it pays little attention—or none at all—to the differing paths those nations followed. Nor does it consider whether they interacted. The question that thus arises is not only whether Austria can be viewed as the 'exporter', and the other legal systems as 'importers', but also whether the measures adopted by the latter were of a formal or informal nature, with an added distinction between legislative and executive regulation. Another critical issue is whether adopting these requirements was considered an instrument of administrative reform. In this sense, an American commentator of the US Model APA observed that 'state ... legislators are busy men, working under unfavourable conditions ... with no special training fitting them for the understanding the complications of the administrative law field' and are, therefore, keen to follow the experience of other legislatures.[45]

The durability of administrative procedure legislation is important too because it indicates the degree of stability of general provisions, as opposed to sector-specific ones, which are more likely to alter as a consequence of obsolescence.[46] Moreover, it may be interesting to examine whether those national legislative frameworks changed after 1945, when Poland and Czechoslovakia, among other nations, were subjected to Soviet rule, as well as whether reviewing courts continued to invoke the text of national administrative procedure legislation to check the legality of administrative decisions. Our point is not so much that the new Socialist constitutions were based on an absolute conception of power and thus allowed the executive to act roughly and even arbitrarily. Instead, we are interested in understanding whether administrative procedure legislation was formally maintained, and, if so, whether this somehow mitigated arbitrariness.

The theoretical side requires a slight digression on the concept of 'influence' often employed in this field. Some use it at the macro level, for example, in studies concerning the influence exerted by French administrative or judicial institutions in other legal systems.[47] Others use it at the micro level, for example, concerning

[44] Pastori (n 5); Langrod (n 6); G Isaac, *La procedure administrative non contentieuse* (LGDJ 1968) 109. On the institutional history of the empire, see J Bryce, *The Holy Roman Empire* (3rd edn, Macmillan 1871).

[45] CJ Peck, 'Lobbying for the Administrative Procedure Act' (1963) 15 Admin L Rev 135. On the importance of this 'Model' APA, see also B Schwartz, 'The Model State Administrative Procedure Act' (1958) 33 Wash L Rev & St B J 1.

[46] See WH Allen, 'The Durability of the Administrative Procedure Act' (1986) 72 Va L Rev 235 (observing that the conventional wisdom is that the APA has been 'impervious to change').

[47] See, for example, JM Galabert, 'The Influence of the French Conseil d'Etat outside France' (2000) 49 ICLQ 700.

the influence of the proportionality principle of the European Court of Justice within the legal systems of the Member States of the EU.[48] These examples show that the concept of influence is used in different ways and contexts. Moreover, it does not tell us much about two fundamental features of the spread of ideas and institutions. The first is whether the reception of legal ideas and institutions is voluntary or coerced, as in the case of the imposition of the French codes on Italy in the years after 1805[49] and that of the Japanese Constitution of 1946.[50] The second feature is whether external or 'imported' ideas and legal institutions supplemented domestic law by filling lacunae or gave rise to profound changes in domestic law.[51] Franz Wieacker's analysis of the assimilation of Roman law in the field of private law in Germany confirms this criticism. He observed that 'the simplest concepts, such as "influence" or "impact", are harmless but rather meaningless'[52] and elaborated the contours of 'reception'. Nevertheless, this concept, too, is used in more than one way: generically, with regard to various uses of foreign law in various contexts, and specifically in relation to the dissemination of Roman law in Germany and other parts of Europe at the time of *jus commune*.[53]

That said, criticism of a concept is all well and good, but it must be replaced with something else. In this respect, some strands of thought provide options to use as working hypotheses to explain the legal realities in question.[54] One important strand emphasises the frequency and significance of the processes of borrowing and imitation. The most representative scholar holding this view is Alan Watson, for whom the evolution of law is mainly to be explained by the transplant of legal rules, as is shown, empirically, by the reception of Roman law in medieval Europe and the reception of German and Swiss law in Turkey.[55] This approach has been

[48] See M Cohn, 'Legal Transplant Chronicles: The Evolution of Unreasonableness and Proportionality Review of the Administration in the United Kingdom' (2010) 58 AJCL 583 (proffering an interpretation which highlights exchanges within Commonwealth countries).

[49] See A Kocourek, 'Factors in the Reception of Law' (1935) 10 Tul L Rev 209 (distinguishing accord from conflict and assimilation from imposition).

[50] J Rivero, *Cours de droit administratif comparé* (Les cours de droit 1956–57) 27. For further analysis, see HS Quigley, 'Revising the Japanese Constitution' (1959) 38 Foreign Aff 140 (for a very critical assessment of the 'foreign imposition not wholly suited to a people of very different legal and social tradition', such as that of Japan). But see also J Williams, 'Making the Japanese Constitution: A Further Look' (1965) 59 Am Pol Sc Rev 665 (for whom more recent studies have brought additional information showing that the Japanese side supported innovations).

[51] See W Twining, 'Social Science and the Diffusion of Law' (2005) 32 J Law & Soc 203, 205 (distinguishing the attempts to modernise domestic law as distinct from those to fill gaps).

[52] F Wieacker, 'The Importance of Roman Law for Western Civilization and Western Legal Thought' (1981) 4 B C Intl & Comp L Rev 257, 270; CS Lobingier, 'The Reception of Roman Law in Germany' (1916) 14 Mich L Rev 562.

[53] W Wiegand, 'The Reception of American Law in Europe' (1991) 39 AJCL 229.

[54] Wieacker (n 52) 272.

[55] A Watson, *Legal Transplants: An Approach to Constitutional Law* (2nd edn, U Georgia Press 1993); A Watson, *The Evolution of Law* (Johns Hopkins UP 1986); A Watson, 'The Evolution of Law: Continued' (1987) 5 LHR 537, 550; E Örücü, 'A Synthetic and Hyphenated Legal System: The Turkish Experience' (2006) 1 JCL 261 (2006) (arguing that the Turkish system is 'eclectic', because it benefited from more than one foreign model); W Ewald, 'Comparative Jurisprudence (II): The Logic of Legal Transplants' (1995) 43 AJCL 489.

vigorously challenged by Otto Kahn-Freund and other researchers who have called for greater attention to context[56] and, a fortiori, by those who have affirmed that transplants are simply impossible.[57] There is yet another school of thought that has developed the concept of 'diffusion' (the origin of which is the Roman term '*diffundere*'), conveying the impression of the spread of something across space.[58] While these studies focus essentially on private law, there is recent scholarship concerning borrowing and transplants in constitutional law.[59] There is also another strand underlining the gradual 'convergence' of administrative laws in the European legal area,[60] but it is not particularly apposite here because of its strong focus on the European Union.

The concept of 'diffusion' looks more promising in our case, albeit with a *caveat*. We must be mindful that the metaphor of 'diffusion' is not wholly appropriate, at least in the sense in which it is used in the natural sciences; namely to refer to the spread of molecules from an area of high concentration to one of low concentration, resulting in homogeneity between the two.[61] However, we can accomplish two goals by focusing on 'diffusion'. First, and specifically, we may be able to identify the characteristics that made Austrian administrative procedure legislation significant for other legal systems. Second, and more generally, pinpointing the factors that led to the diffusion of such legislation could help better understand other cases involving similar legislative frameworks, including Spanish administrative procedure legislation in Latin America.

Bearing in mind the said caveat, 'diffusion' may thus be used as a working hypothesis to throw light on both formal and substantive aspects. The former concern the nature of the processes through which various nations adopted administrative procedure legislation. The latter include questions such as the following: was there only a common concern for regulating administrative procedure through legislation, or were there also clear parallels with the Austrian legislation? If such parallels existed, did it make sense to refer to codification? Additionally, what justified them, given that there were no institutional ties among those legal systems after the dissolution of the Habsburg Empire?

Last but not least, arguments about the diffusion of a specific type of legislation often start from the premise that only the normative material of law is both relevant and significant. This is, however, a narrow approach. The level of legislation

56 O Kahn-Freund, 'On Uses and Misuses of Comparative Law' 37 MLR 1 (1974).

57 P Legrand, 'The Impossibility of Legal Transplants' (1997) 4 Maastricht J Eur & Comp L 111.

58 Twining (n 51) 230 (discussing both law and social science literature); W Twining, 'Diffusion of Law: A Global Perspective' (2006) 1 JCL 237; S Farran and C Rautenbach, 'Introduction' in S Farran and others (eds), *The Diffusion of Law: The Movement of Laws and Norms Around the World* (Routledge 2016) 2.

59 See, for example, N Tebbe and RL Tsai, 'Constitutional Borrowing' (2010) 108 Mich L Rev 459.

60 S Cassese, 'Le problème de la convergence des droits administratifs: vers un modèle administratif européen' in *L'État de droit—Mélanges en l'honneur de Guy Braibant* (Dalloz 1996) 47.

61 Z Elkins and B Simmons, 'On Wavers, Clusters, and Diffusion: A Conceptual Framework' [2005] Annals Am Ac Pol & Soc Sci 35.

or executive regulation in cases of formal legal norms or precepts is undoubtedly important, but it is not the only one that matters. There is also the level of judicial doctrines and background theories, including the rule of law.

IV. Methodological Issues

A word or two more is warranted at this juncture about some methodological issues. First, this volume combines history and legal comparison. Second, the criteria for selecting the legal systems included in our analysis must be discussed. Moreover, both positive and negative outcomes are important and must be taken into account.

A. History and Comparison

As observed earlier, although the existence of one kind of administrative procedure legislation or another is increasingly part of the accepted order of events in modern societies, it is a relatively recent phenomenon, encompassing Europe, the Americas, and some parts of Africa and Asia.[62] Therefore, it is both interesting and important to understand the antecedents of our current set of legal principles and institutions. There is something 'faintly absurd about discussing administrative law with only the vaguest idea of how its subject matter has evolved'.[63] A historical perspective enables us to comprehend why and how, in a legal system characterised by the existence of a sophisticated set of general principles defined and refined by a special administrative court, the legal framework of administration—in the practical sense—evolved in an unprecedented way (with the notable exception of the Spanish Act of 1889) and has been a source of inspiration for various nations of Central and Eastern Europe.

In this sense, the approach we have chosen is both historical and comparative. It is historical insofar as it examines how administrative institutions have evolved through time. This can serve to understand which parts of those institutions have lingered into the present and which parts have diverged from the past.[64] In this respect, we have chosen to focus on the five decades between 1920 and 1970 in order to consider not only the processes that led to the adoption of legislation on

[62] Auby (n 2); F Bignami, 'Comparative Administrative Law' in M Bussani and U Mattei (eds), *The Cambridge Companion to Comparative Law* (CUP 2012) 155.

[63] P Craig, *Administrative Law* (5th edn, Sweet & Maxwell 2003) 47; P Craig, *UK, EU and Global Administrative Law* (CUP 2015) (criticising 'temporal parochialism').

[64] See JWF Allison, 'History to Understand, and History to Reform, English Public Law' (2013) 72 CLJ 526 (2013) (criticising the selective and non-transparent uses of history in discourses about public law in England).

administrative procedure legislation but also its durability, in the sense mentioned earlier. Moreover, our approach is comparative in the sense that we examine the solutions that various legal systems have developed for similar problems. An analysis of the choices of a plurality of legal systems in the same time frame can shed light on their shared and distinctive traits. The underlying idea is that both commonality and diversity are important and thus deserve adequate attention.[65]

Two caveats may be helpful. First, the more general conjecture on which this line of research is based is that there are not only numerous and relevant differences between European legal systems but also some common elements, including the principles of legality and procedural fairness—namely a sort of common core. But what matters is not so much that a common core did exist but what kind of common core has emerged and how it has evolved.[66] Second, this research is not without problems, one of which is the choice of the legal systems to be compared.

B. Choice of Legal Systems

The traditional comparative approach is limited to two or three legal systems, assuming that they are the 'major legal systems' of the world or a specific area, in our case Europe. This approach is questionable both in general and in our particular case. It is generally questionable, not only with regard to the intrinsic soundness of the phrase 'major legal systems', but also because history reveals that for specific subject matters, the 'smaller' legal systems must be taken into the utmost consideration for practical and theoretical purposes. The Belgian solution concerning judicial review of administration in the nineteenth century provides an excellent illustration of this point. It was regarded by both German and Italian reformers as a source of inspiration for a 'liberal' approach unlike the French one. In our particular case, limiting the comparison to the major legal systems, such as those of France, Germany, and Italy, would give us only a limited description of legal realities relevant to better understand the spread of Austrian ideas and legal institutions.

To reduce the risk of selectivity,[67] we have compared nine different legal systems: Czechoslovakia, France, Germany, Hungary, Italy, Lichtenstein, Poland,

[65] G della Cananea and M Bussani, 'The Common Core of European Administrative Laws: A Framework for Analysis' (2019) 26 Maastricht J Eur & Comp L 217.

[66] On the concept of common core, see RB Schlesinger, 'Introduction' in RB Schlesinger (ed), *Formation of Contracts: A Study of the Common Core of Legal Systems* (Oceana 1968) 5; RB Schlesinger, 'The Common Core of Legal Systems: An Emerging Subject of Comparative Study' in K Nadelmann, AT von Mehren and JN Hazard (eds), *Twentieth Century Comparative and Conflicts. Law, Legal Essays in Honor of Hessel E. Yntema* (Sijthoff 1961) 65 (observing that it derived plausibility from historical studies, concerning the common roots of legal institutions).

[67] See Allison (n 64) 531; EA Posner and CR Sunstein, 'The Law of Other States' (2006) 59 Stan L Rev 148 (with regard to the issue of citations).

Spain, and Yugoslavia. There are some legal systems—Lichtenstein, Poland, Czechoslovakia, and Yugoslavia—that adopted some kind of administrative procedure legislation in the 1920s. Whether a spatial and temporal cluster thus emerged remains to be seen.[68] Second, other systems—Hungary, in particular—adopted administrative procedure legislation later. The question that thus arises is whether it had anything in common either with the Austrian legislation or with that of another European legal system. If so, the picture would become more complex than the one-way transfer hypothesis suggests. The Spanish case is partially different because general administrative procedure legislation had been in place since 1889, but the new one was adopted in 1958 under an authoritarian regime, albeit of another type.[69] There are, third, legal systems—including France, Germany, and Italy—where no general administrative procedure legislation was produced for at least half a century after 1925. Therefore, it is interesting to discover why their political choices differed from those of Austria and some of its neighbours and whether this reveals different views about the importance of administrative procedure.

However, in excluding a priori both the cultural and normative sides of diffusion, one risks going too far. Beliefs and ideas about what public law is (or should be) must surely form part of any explanatory theory that seeks to consider whether and how legal cultures interact, in our case from the viewpoint of the common core of European administrative law. The general point here is that a study on the diffusion of law requires analysis reaching beyond formal legal sources to include other legal formants.[70]

Our choice has one further implication that deserves autonomous treatment. In some way, it is evident that a conjecture—in our case, that the Austrian administrative procedure legislation constitutes an important chapter in the evolution of the common core of administrative laws in Europe—needs to be tested and that all findings of the investigation are relevant and significant. After all, a scientific enquiry must seek to confirm the initial conjecture through evidence and argument. However, in this research we are not simply affirming that neither result—whether positive or negative—may be ignored when seeking an explanatory theory rooted in practice. We are also arguing that precisely the fact that the Austrian administrative legislation has promoted change elsewhere has yet another ramification; namely, this change has come neither from the continental legal system that traditionally had more prestige in the field of administrative law (ie France)[71] nor from

[68] See Elkins and Simmons (n 61) 35.

[69] See JJ Linz, 'An Authoritarian Regime: The Case of Spain' in E Allard and Y Littunen (eds), *Cleavages, Ideologies, and Party Systems* (Academic Bookstore 1964) 291.

[70] R Sacco, 'Legal Formants: A Dynamic Approach to Comparative Law' (1991) 39 AJCL 1.

[71] F Melleray (ed), *L'argument de droit comparé en droit administrative français* (Bruylant 2007); E Örücü, 'Infusion of the Diffused: Four Circles of Diffusion Infusing the Legal System of Turkey' in Farran and others (n 58) 7 (pointing out the reception of French administrative Law in Turkey after 1868).

the one perhaps most often referred to today (Germany), but from yet another. This may suggest that conventional views about the relationships between administrative laws should be reconsidered.[72]

V. The Structure of the Book

The discussion of Austrian administrative procedure legislation and its diffusion is structured in the following manner. Part I of the book addresses the process by which the Austrian legislation was adopted, the underlying reasons for the policy, and its impact and durability in the long run. Part II follows with a discussion of the various national legal systems. For each of them, one of the main questions is, of course, whether and to what extent legislators and scholars have afforded the Austrian administrative procedure legislation consideration. However, other important questions include whether the legislative provisions set out after 1925 remained in force after the regime changes and whether they still supplied the basic vocabulary for legal discussion about administrative procedure. The answers from the experts of the national legal systems selected for our comparison are, as will be seen, partially similar and partially different. This is why Part III compares these answers to understand the factors that determined their commonality and diversity.

A final word concerns the text of the Austrian administrative procedure legislation which has thus far been seldom studied outside the German-speaking area. We considered that translating the Austrian APA into English could provide a better understanding of its relevance and significance for other scholars.

[72] S Mannoni, 'The Administrative World of Yesterday' in della Cananea and Mannoni (n 12) 311.

PART I

THE AUSTRIAN ADMINISTRATIVE PROCEDURE LEGISLATION OF 1925

2
Administrative Procedure and Judicial Control

Clemens Jabloner

I. Introduction

For a better understanding of the Austrian codification of administrative procedure, it may be helpful to make a few general and introductory remarks on the relationship between administration (and its procedure) and the controlling judiciary, a topic to be considered, first of all, from the perspective of the separation of powers. It ought to be said from the outset that, although most modern constitutions usually establish the separation of powers, it can be, and has been, understood in more than one way. In particular, the English and French political systems are often regarded, with justification, as the leading examples of two opposing ways of conceiving the separation of powers. Thus we have two political models. Second, as there are also various ways of understanding the rule of law, it is crucial to clarify how it evolved in Austrian legal culture. As a final point, it should be observed that the role of the courts that discharge judicial review of administration must be considered dynamically, that is, with an eye on the dimension of change.

II. The Separation of the Judiciary from the Executive

The separation of the judiciary and the administration has a deep historical, and somewhat contradictory, dimension. It is always surprising for students to learn that the principle of separation of judiciary and administration did not initially serve exclusively, nor even primarily, to protect the judiciary but to safeguard the administration. From today's perspective, we see this institutional principle the other way round; that is, the judiciary must be protected against the executive branch because it is the weaker function of the State. This is highly topical in Austria at the moment. However, this reversal of the balance of powers results from a nineteenth-century development.

Clemens Jabloner, *Administrative Procedure and Judicial Control* In: *The Austrian Codification of Administrative Procedure.* Edited by: Giacinto Della Cananea, Angela Ferrari Zumbini, and Otto Pfersmann, Oxford University Press.
 DOI: 10.1093/oso/9780198867623.003.0002

From the French perspective, the original arrangement when judicial control of the administration was introduced is described with wonderful sarcasm by Alexis de Tocqueville in his work *L'Ancien Régime et la Révolution*. He deserves to be quoted in full:

> In no country in Europe were the courts more independent of the government than in France; nor was there any in which more abnormal tribunals existed. The one involved a necessity for the other. Judges whose position was beyond the king's reach, whom he could neither dismiss, displace, or promote, and over whom he had no hold either by ambition or fear, soon proved inconvenient. That led to the denial of their jurisdiction over cases to which the administration was a party, and to the establishment of another class of courts, less independent, which presented to the subject's eye a semblance of justice, without involving, for the monarch, any risk of its reality.
>
> In countries like Germany, where the judges were never as independent of the government as they were in France at this time, no such precaution was ever taken, and no administrative tribunals ever established. The monarch held the common courts in such subjection that he did not need extraordinary ones.[1]

Tocqueville later commented on the English judiciary. He observed that in England alone, four systems of law were in use: common law, statute law, Roman law, and equity. Moreover, he followed Blackstone in his analysis of the courts, noting that England had established an infinite variety of courts with no clear competencies, neither geographically nor on the merits. But he also said that notwithstanding the immense number of courts, there were apparently none close at hand that could hear petty cases promptly and at little expense. Hence, the administration of justice was cumbersome and costly. Despite these defects, in England, everyone, irrespective of rank, and whether their claim was against a private individual or the sovereign, could be more confident of their claim being heard; they also enjoyed better protections regarding their fortune, liberty, or life before the courts. For these reasons, Tocqueville favoured the English system.

In my view, his reflections deserve to be taken into consideration because the situation in England at that time bears some similarity with the European situation nowadays with the various supreme courts in Strasbourg and Luxembourg, and the constitutional courts. Overlapping competencies sometimes lead to tensions or even conflicts between supreme courts. Nevertheless, the individual has a good chance of succeeding in his or her claim.

[1] A de Tocqueville, *L'Ancien Régime et la Révolution* (1856), English translation GG Reisman, *The Old Regime and the Revolution* (Harper 1856), bk II, ch IV, 73.

III. Separation of Powers and the Rule of Law: The Austrian System

As observed earlier, the dimension of change must be taken into account. As far as France was concerned, a huge change, a revolutionary initiative, came from the administration, more precisely from the executive parliamentary committees, which—again quite unlike today—did not confine themselves to general law-making but tried to advance the revolution administratively.

The background to all this was the fact that absolutism, and with it the modern development of public law, was driven, as it were, like a wedge into mediaeval legal thinking. Obviously, the dissolution of all power relations into legal relations and the judiciary itself was highly inefficient in the Middle Ages, but it could still impose certain limits on executive power, which was in the hands of the Crown.

However, the absolutist State, with the expansion of the police, its broad discretionary powers, exceptions to judicial control, and the separation of powers understood in this way, called for resistance in a world that, seen as a whole, was pushing for juridification. The rule of law, at least in Central European terms, meant—as Adolf Julius Merkl pointed out—the juridification of the administration and the forms of administrative jurisdiction, regardless of whether they were based on the French or the German model.[2] From the viewpoint of the sociology of law, these steps can be regarded as a reoccurrence of earlier elements in the modern system of public law.

In any case, the Austrian Administrative Court (Verwaltungsgerichtshof or VwGH), from which my analysis stems, was—and is, in part, still today—clearly marked by this original separation of powers in the subtler sense of a 'balance of powers': according to the Minister of Justice (and eminent scholar) at the time, Josef Unger, the Administrative Court should oversee, not administer. This basic idea was reflected in the elements of fundamental respect for discretionary powers, the petrification of the administrative decision taken (in other words, no innovations were allowed before the Administrative Court), the acceptance in principle of the facts determined by the administration, and above all in the mere cassation of administrative court decisions.

The Austrian Administrative Court was established in 1876. It was understood at the time that the Court had to find standards of review which went beyond pure questions of law and which related to the preceding administrative procedure. After all, the procedure was also to be determined by general regulations whose compliance was to be reviewed. Such internal regulations certainly existed, but they did not reach the status of law.

[2] AJ Merkl, *Allgemeines Verwaltungsrecht* (Springer 1927).

It was therefore clear that the rules for administrative procedure had to be created first. Moreover, indeed, the jurisprudence of the Court developed these rules over the following decades, such as the cardinal principle of the 'right to be heard'—which is the subject of recent research.[3] Austrian administrative procedural law is therefore indeed, at its core, 'judge-made law' in the truest sense. Literarily brought together by Friedrich Tezner,[4] it then formed the basis for the Administrative Procedure Acts, which were codified in 1925—not without a certain economic and political pressure from outside.

With this development, which led to the 'justiciability' of administrative procedure, the young Republic of Austria took on a pioneering role in Europe. Its acceptance was also promoted by the fact that several judges of the old Administrative Court were appointed to corresponding functions in some of the successor States, especially in Czechoslovakia and Poland. In other words, countries having close ties with Austria, which resulted in their having a particular interest in how the administration was regulated there.

IV. Recent Changes, in the Light of European Law

Although the Austrian system of judicial control of the administration had long remained relatively stable, with the advent of the European Convention on Human Rights (ECHR), it found itself in increasing tension with the development of European law. Not only does the European Union (EU) require a much more intensive review of administration, this is also true of the corresponding provision of the ECHR. The tendency is to follow the English model, in which the administration is seen more as a political and less as a legal function, while genuine legal procedure begins in the courts. Tocqueville's thoughts are still enlightening in this respect.

Years of uncertainty as to whether and to what extent the Austrian construction conformed to European law, as well as other motives such as the overloading of the Central Administrative Court, an endeavour to federalise administrative jurisdiction later pushed for a reform of the judicial system, which became effective in 2013. Administrative courts of first instance were now set up in place of the administrative appeal authorities. In addition, these administrative courts were given a much greater leeway to make decisions on the merits.

These changes, in my view, have numerous advantages. First of all, they have reduced the workload of the Administrative Court. Second, they have strengthened

[3] A Ferrari Zumbini, 'Standards of Judicial Review of Administrative Action in the Austro-Hungarian Empire' in G della Cananea and S Mannoni (eds), *Administrative Justice* Fin de siècle: *Early Judicial Standards of Administrative Conduct in Europe (1890–1910)* (OUP 2020) 45.

[4] F Tezner, *Die rechtsbildende Funktion der österreichischen verwaltungsgerichtlichen Rechtsprechung* (Verlag der Österreich Staatsdruckerei 1925).

the federalist element. Third, and more importantly, our system is now more aligned with the European Convention. As the President of the Administrative Court, I supported these changes for all the above reasons. That said, I see a certain disadvantage in the fact that it is difficult to summarise the advantages of different systems in practical terms today. The expansion of administrative jurisdiction has led to a certain reduction in the legal expertise of the administration itself. However, this may be offset by the fact that the procedure for the administrative courts of first instance is quite similar to the procedure for the administrative authorities.

Although the courts of first instance are still searching for their role and judicial self-image to some extent, overall, the reform seems to have proved itself worthy. Ideally, it will bring about a combination of what is good in traditional Austrian administrative procedure and more profound judicial control.

3

The History of the Administrative Procedure in Austria until 1925*

Thomas Olechowski

I. Introduction

> Administrative procedure, in linguistic terms, could be defined as a procedure whereby the State or a self-governing body sets out the activities of the administration in performing its administrative tasks. This would not, however, be an appropriate one. One cannot regulate the creative activity of the administration; if a collective interest is achieved and secured, as long as individual legal spheres do not restrict it, the administration is bound only by the existing laws and is only subject to constitutional controls.[1]

With these words, Viennese lawyer Joseph Ludwig Brunstein introduced a lecture on administrative procedure reform at the Vienna Legal Association on 14 February 1900. His view, namely that the administration could not be regulated by law, at least not to the same extent as the judiciary, was widespread and prevalent at the time. Although the Constitution and the laws had to be observed, Brunstein and his contemporaries saw this instead as a kind of paramount limit for administrative action. Administration and law are alien to one another, and only where the subjective rights of individuals are affected is it possible to establish precise legal rules.

II. 'Old Style' Administrative Justice

The juridification of the administrative procedure in Austria[2] began at the point where the actions of the authorities collided with the well-acquired rights of the subjects. When the administrative and judicial authorities began to diverge in the

* Translation: Mag Dr Miriam Gassner, LLM.

[1] JL Brunstein, *Das Administrativ-Verfahren und seine Reform* (Manz 1900) 3.

[2] The term 'Austria' has three different meanings in this chapter. Before 1867, it denoted the entire Habsburg hereditary kingdoms and lands. From 1867 to 1918, it meant one of the two parts of the Austro-Hungarian monarchy. Thereafter it is used to refer to today's Republic of Austria.

Thomas Olechowski, *The History of the Administrative Procedure in Austria until 1925* In: *The Austrian Codification of Administrative Procedure.* Edited by: Giacinto Della Cananea, Angela Ferrari Zumbini, and Otto Pfersmann, Oxford University Press. © Thomas Olechowski 2023. DOI: 10.1093/oso/9780198867623.003.0003

mid-eighteenth century, the Austrian monarch Maria Theresa determined that a special body, a '*consessus in causis principis et commissorum*', should be created within the new administrative authorities.[3] This body was supposed to decide disputes in the area of public law, and Maria Theresa duly issued her own rules of procedure ('*Consessualordnung*'), which contained relatively precise regulations on bringing complaints and counter-objections, oral hearings, and much more.[4] Even these astonishingly modern-looking regulations were superseded when the adjudication of public law disputes ('*contentiosa publica*') was wholly removed from the administrative authorities and entrusted to the courts designated to civil and criminal law. This happened in two steps, which took place in 1762 and 1782.[5]

However, the term 'court' as it was used at that time must also be examined: judicial independence, essential for the judiciary today, was unknown in the eighteenth-century absolutist States. In practice, judges worked largely independently but had to obtain the monarch's *placet* in the event of death sentences, and monarchs could personally intervene in individual cases at any time. They could instruct and change judges, or decide for themselves, *ex plenitudine potestatis*.[6] This was true regarding tax and construction law, as well as criminal and civil law. It was only under Enlightenment influence that this practice fell into disrepute, and monarchs gradually withdrew from the judiciary. Judicial independence was only constitutionally secured in Austria during the revolution of 1848/49, but such judgements of power seldom occurred after the early nineteenth century. However, a small vestige has survived to the present day in the institute of pardons and the federal president's right of abolition.

This achievement in terms of the rule of law came at a high price: the monarch's withdrawal was limited to civil and criminal justice. They did not want to, and could not, give up other areas of law, ie what we now call administrative law, without shaking the foundations of their rule. For this reason, towards the close of the eighteenth century, a movement began to make access to the courts more difficult or even to declare it inadmissible for administrative matters. Appeals against decisions by administrative authorities could only be brought before superordinate

[3] F Lehne, 'Zur Geschichte der Verwaltungsstreitsache in Österreich' in Verwaltungsgerichtshof (ed), *90 Jahre Verwaltungsgerichtsbarkeit in Österreich* ([self-published] 1966) 26–39, 33; T Olechowski, 'Die Entwicklung allgemeiner Grundsätze des Verwaltungsverfahrens' in M Holoubek and M Lang (eds), *Allgemeine Grundsätze des Verwaltungs- und Abgabenverfahrens* (Linde 2006) 13–40, 16.

[4] These rules of procedure are published by Friedrich Tezner, *Die landesfürstliche Verwaltungsrechtspflege in Österreich vom Ausgang des 15. bis zum Ausgang des 18. Jahrhunderts*, vol II (Hölder 1902) 137–41.

[5] T Olechowski, 'Geschichte der Verwaltungsgerichtsbarkeit in Österreich' in K-P Sommermann and B Schaffarzik (eds), *Handbuch der Geschichte der Verwaltungsgerichtsbarkeit in Deutschland und Europa*, vol II (Springer 2019) 1099–1130, 1101.

[6] H Erwin, 'Machtspruch' in A Cordes and others (eds), *Handwörterbuch zur Deutschen Rechtsgeschichte*, vol 3 (2nd edn, Erich Schmidt 2016) 1119–22.

administrative authorities.[7] This development in Austria corresponded to a general trend on the continent. Among many others, the French law of 16 August 1790, prohibiting court interference in administrative matters, is deserving of mention.[8] In the light of this legislation, France began to develop its own way of legal protection in administrative matters, headed by the Conseil d'Etat. In Austria, however, similar efforts floundered at the planning phase. It would be an exaggeration to say that there were no procedural rules on administrative matters in Austria at the beginning of the nineteenth century. Those that existed were decidedly imperfect; for the most part, they were directly concerned with substantive administrative law and only clarified individual questions, such as under which conditions an appeal could take place.[9]

An example to illustrate the situation at the time is an ordinance issued by the Minister of the Interior in 1859, which consisted of three points. Whereas the first two regulate specific administrative matters (citizenship, etc.), the third generally stipulates that appeals against decisions by the political authorities must be submitted to the authority whose decision is being contested within 60 days.[10]

At that time, comprehensive regulations were the exception to the rule. Particularly noteworthy are the provisions of the Criminal Code on Serious Police Violations of 1803, which would be referred to as administrative criminal law today.[11] They were divided into two sections, the first containing substantive penal provisions and the second procedural norms. The latter were inspired mainly by criminal procedural law and thus exhibited a remarkable level of rule of law. The Financial Criminal Code of 1835[12] also contained both a substantive and a procedural part.

In 1854 an imperial ordinance was issued to regulate general enforcement procedures.[13] Some parts appear remarkably modern. For example, a categorisation of the duties of the subjects, which is still valid today (compare the §§ 3–7 AVG), was made. Some duties consist in the payment of money, other duties can only be performed by the obligated person himself. A third category of duties can be fulfilled in a different way than originally intended (eg if the obligated person does not demolish his unlawfully built house, the authority can carry out the demolition and charge the costs to the obligated person). However, these regulations were overshadowed by the paragraph that stipulated that 'corporal punishment' could

[7] Tezner, *Die landesfürstliche Verwaltungsrechtspflege in Österreich vom Ausgang des 15. bis zum Ausgang des 18. Jahrhunderts* (n 4) vol II, 114.

[8] D Capitant, 'Geschichte der Verwaltungsgerichtsbarkeit in Frankreich' in Sommermann and Schaffarzik (n 5) 1335–71, 1344.

[9] Olechowski (n 3) 18f.

[10] *Verordnung des Ministeriums des Innern, mit welcher einige Bestimmungen über die Vereinfachung und Beschleunigung des Geschäftsganges der politischen Behörden kundgemacht werden*, 27 October 1859, *Reichsgesetzblatt* 1859 no 196.

[11] Kaiserliches Patent, 3 September 1803, *Justizgesetzsammlung* no 626.

[12] Kaiserliches Patent, 11 July 1835, *Politische Gesetzessammlung* vol LXIII no 112.

[13] Kaiserliche Verordnung, 20 April 1854 *Reichsgesetzblatt* 1854 no 96.

possibly also be contemplated in the event of 'unlawful behaviour'. For this reason, the ordinance has become known as the '*Prügelpatent*' ('birching patent').[14]

Finally, there was an 1855 regulation which provided guidance on general principles for the administrative authorities. For instance, the regulation mentioned earlier instructed the authorities to justify their decisions and to quote the laws that had informed their decisions. The decision should also itself contain an indication of what legal remedies were available against it and what the deadlines were. However, this official instruction was nothing more than an internal regulation for the authorities: the parties could not refer to it.

III. The Introduction of Modern Administrative Justice in Austria

As in many other German-speaking countries, the jurisdiction of the courts in the early years of nineteenth-century Austria was being increasingly pushed back, and a system that more or less followed the French model was established. It was commonly referred to as *Administrativjustiz*, although critics said this term was inappropriate because it was not about the judiciary in the strict sense of the term.[15] In many cases, they called for a solution based on the English model, in which the ordinary courts should also act in administrative matters ('judicial State solution'). In Austria, the administrative justice system was generally accepted, with only some aspects being challenged. For example, in 1815, Carl Joseph von Pratobevera defended the system prevalent in Austria at the time in an article,[16] but demanded clear legal regulations for this, such as the establishment of deadlines for submissions and complaints. Moreover, approximately 40 years later, in 1858/59, Moritz von Stubenrauch showed his sympathy for *Administrativjustiz* in another essay.[17]

At that time, the dispute between the advocates of *Administrativjustiz* and those of the judicial State in Germany had lost some of its intensity. Both sides had

[14] EC Hellbling, 'Die Landesverwaltung in Cisleithanien' in A Wandruszka and P Urbanitsch (eds), *Die Habsburgermonarchie 1848–1918*, vol II (Austria Academy of Sciences Press 1975) 190–269, 231. Birching was abolished in Austria by an amendment to the penal law of 15 November 1867, *Reichsgesetzblatt* 1867 no 131; cf W Ogris, 'Die Rechtsentwicklung in Cisleithanien 1848–1918' in Wandruszka and Urbanitsch (n 14) 538–662, 566.

[15] L Pahlow, 'Administrativjustiz' in F Jaeger (ed), *Enzyklopädie der Neuzeit*, vol I (Metzler 2005) 79–81.

[16] CJ Pratobevera, 'Ueber die Gränzlinien zwischen Justiz- und politischen Gegenständen und das Verhältniß der Gerichtshöfe zur landesherrlichen Macht' in *Materialien für Gesetzkunde und Rechtspflege in den Oesterreichischen Erbstaaten* 1 (Geistinger 1815) 1–55.

[17] M von Stubenrauch, 'Beiträge zur Lehre von der Administrativjustiz' [1858] Allgemeine österreichische Gerichtszeitung 441–43 and [1859] 133–35. A third part of the article was announced but never published.

apparently recognised the arguments of the other. In 1864, the Hessian lawyer Otto Bähr came up with a compromise formula:

> If... the decisions of the administrative authorities on public rights cannot be considered a judge's verdict, but one does not wish to entrust this verdict to the ordinary courts either, then there is only one option left: to create courts of public law.[18]

In fact, administrative courts had been set up everywhere in the German-speaking region, including Austria. In 1867, the Austrian Empire was transformed into the Austro-Hungarian monarchy, and with the so-called December Constitution, the Austrian part of the dual monarchy was given the basic constitutional framework that existed until it came to an end in 1918. The December Constitution of 1867 was not a uniform document but a bundle of five basic laws.[19] One of them, concerning the judiciary, generically envisaged in its art 15 that whenever 'someone claims his rights have been violated by a decision or order of an administrative authority', he was free 'to publicly raise his claims before the Administrative Court to bring proceedings against a representative of the administrative authority'.

It took almost nine years for the Administrative Court, from 21 December 1867 to 2 July 1876, to come into being.[20] The ministerial official Karl von Lemayer, who was commissioned in 1871 to formulate an implementing law for this basic provision, stated that the Constitution expressly speaks only of a single administrative court, not of a whole system of administrative courts as had been created in Prussia at that time. For this reason, the introduction of modern administrative jurisdiction in Austria did not mean the end of the old *Administrativjustiz*. Indeed, this was kept unchanged, and only after the party had invoked the highest administrative authority could it lodge a complaint against its decision with the Administrative Court. For purely practical reasons, the latter was unable to review the facts of the matter or correct any discretionary decisions. Those before the Administrative Court were purely filing proceedings limited to establishing whether the administrative act issued at last instance was lawful. If it was not, it would be repealed by

[18] O Bähr, *Der Rechtsstaat. Eine publizistische Skizze* (Wiegand 1864) 71.

[19] They were: *Gesetz, mit dem das Grundgesetz über die Reichsvertretung von 1861 abgeändert wird* (an Amendment to the Basic Law on Imperial Representation of 1861), *Staatsgrundgesetz über die Allgemeinen Rechte der Staatsbürger für die im Reichsrate vertretenen Königreiche und Länder* (Basic Law on the General Rights of Nationals for the Kingdoms and Lands Represented in the Reichsrat), *Staatsgrundgesetz über die Einsetzung eines Reichsgerichts* (Basic Law Establishing an Imperial Court), *Staatsgrundgesetz über die richterliche Gewalt* (Basic Law on the Judiciary), *Staatsgrundgesetz über die Ausübung der Regierungs- und Vollzugsgewalt* (Basic Law on the Executive), as well as the *Delegationsgesetz* (Delegation Act, a basic law that governed the affairs common to all lands of the Austrian-Hungarian Monarchy). They all received imperial sanction on 21 December 1867, and were published in the *Reichsgesetzblatt* 1867 no 141–46.

[20] The legislative history is presented in detail by Thomas Olechowski, *Die Einführung der Verwaltungsgerichtsbarkeit in Österreich* (Manz 1999).

the Administrative Court, and the administrative authority would have to issue a new administrative act, whereby it was now bound by the legal opinion of the Administrative Court.

This fundamental provision, which already featured in Lemayer's draft for the later Administrative Court Act of 1875, was significantly supplemented in parliamentary deliberations. The original draft also stipulated that the Administrative Court could revoke a decision and return the file to the authorities if the matter had not yet been sufficiently investigated.[21] However, House of Lords member Baron Franz von Hein stated that the Administrative Court should generally be given the authority to declare that the facts were incorrectly ascertained. The minister responsible, Joseph Unger—presumably encouraged by Lemayer—had worked out a new formulation of the relevant provision:

> However, if the Administrative Court finds that the facts were accepted contrary to the act or that the same needs to be supplemented in its essential points, it has to return the matter to the administrative authority, which has to remedy the deficiencies and then issue a new decision or order. If the Administrative Court finds that essential forms of the administrative procedure have been disregarded, it must cancel the current procedure and begin a new one.[22]

In the course of additional deliberations, the wording of this paragraph was further refined, though this need not be discussed in detail here. It was also essential that the so-called Commission of the House of Lords (*Herrenhaus-Komission*) was able to expressly order that the decision or order of the authority be withdrawn in the event of procedural deficiencies, just as if the content of the decision or order were unlawful.[23]

However, what is of particular interest in the present context is the phrase used by Unger, which also featured in the final text: 'essential forms of the administrative procedure'. What did this mean exactly? Unfortunately, the materials give no information in this regard. MP Ernst von Plener especially emphasised that there are currently 'no regulations, no standards for administrative procedure' and described the current situation as 'completely irregular' and 'left to the pure arbitrariness of the authorities'.[24]

On 2 July 1876, the Law on the Establishment of an Administrative Court came into force. Interestingly, on 14 May, almost two months before, the Austrian Ministry of Education published a decree regulating the principles of

21 ibid 148.

22 *Gesetz betreffend die Errichtung eines Verwaltungsgerichtshofes*, 22 October 1875, *Reichsgesetzblatt* 1876 no 36, para 6.

23 Olechowski (n 20) 150.

24 Speech by Ernst von Plener at the session of the House of Deputies on 18 March 1875, quoted in Olechowski, 'Die Entwicklung allgemeiner Grundsätze des Verwaltungsverfahrens' (n 3) 24.

administrative procedure.[25] This is no coincidence since Karl Lemayer was an official of the same ministry; he probably suggested and drafted the decree personally. From today's perspective, this amounted to an extremely rudimentary regulation of just a few principles. He assumed there was a dichotomy between administrative matters and administrative legal matters. In the latter case, the appeal went to the Administrative Court, so it was vital to pay particular attention to the legality of the procedure. The authority was instructed to always investigate the *material* truth *ex officio* but granted the parties a right to be heard. The question of the admissibility of the resumption of a legally decided matter was regulated in the same way. The decree was soon adopted by other ministries for their area of activity and remained important as an initial orientation for many years.[26]

IV. The Administrative Court's Jurisdiction over Administrative Procedures

The introduction of administrative jurisdiction in Austria was of fundamental importance for the development of administrative procedural law, although the *Administrativjustiz*, the procedure before the administrative authorities, was not changed in any way by the law of 1876. However, in many cases, the Administrative Court revoked the administrative act not for substantive, but formal reasons; for instance, because deadlines had not been observed or parties had not been heard. This is remarkable since there was very little legal regulation of the administrative procedure at that time, which led to the view that the Administrative Court created a law of administrative procedure on its own, a judicial law. However, if we take a closer look at the judgments of the Administrative Court from the period between 1876 and 1925, we may observe that the court never ruled without relying on a legal basis, which would have been utterly unthinkable in the Austrian legal culture of the day. Instead, individual legal provisions or decrees like the one cited above were found, and sometimes very broadly interpreted by the Administrative Court, and, with time, more and more pieces of the mosaic emerged, from which the contours of an administrative procedural law would emerge.[27]

It was Friedrich Tezner, senior lecturer (*Universitätsdozent*) at the University of Vienna and later judge at the Administrative Court, who put the pieces of the mosaic together. He then edited several extensive handbooks,[28] generalising on

[25] *Erlass des Ministers für Cultus und Unterricht an alle Länderchefs und Landesschulräte*, 14 May 1876, *Verordnungsblatt des Ministers für Cultus und Unterricht* 1876 no 20.

[26] Olechowski, 'Die Entwicklung allgemeiner Grundsätze des Verwaltungsverfahrens' (n 3) 25.

[27] For more details, see ibid 26–28; A Ferrari Zumbini, 'Judicial Review of Administrative Action in the Austro-Hungarian Empire. The Formative Years (1890–1910)' (2018) 1 It J Pub L 9–47, 31–45.

[28] F Tezner, *Handbuch des österreichischen Administrativverfahrens* (Manz 1896); F Tezner, *Die rechtsbildende Funktion der österreichischen verwaltungsgerichtlichen Rechtsprechung*, vol IV (2nd edn, Verlag der Österreichischen Staatsdruckerei 1925).

the decisions handed down in individual cases. Thus, he created an astonishingly coherent picture of administrative procedural law. This can be demonstrated by his use of the term *Partei* ('litigant') in administrative proceedings, the right to inspect files, and several other examples. While the Administrative Court was only concerned with remaining consistent in its jurisdiction and terminology,[29] it was Tezner who schematised the knowledge gained from individual cases. He defined terms such as *Partei* or *Recht auf Akteneinsicht* ('freedom of information') so clearly that they could then be used in every administrative procedure.[30] So this was more a matter of scientific positivism than judicial legal training, insofar as textbooks written by professors determine what positive law is—a common phenomenon in the nineteenth century.

V. *Advocatentag* 1884

However, the jurisdiction of the Administrative Court also showed how incomplete the regulations of the administrative procedure were in many cases and triggered the need for reform. As early as 1884, the aforementioned lawyer Joseph L. Brunstein applied to the so-called *Advocatentag*, an annual meeting of Austrian lawyers, requesting that the latter pass a resolution reforming the administrative procedure. This motion was remarkable as it identified a long-term and a short-term goal. In the long term, the one-tier Austrian administrative jurisdiction would be converted into a multi-tier system similar to the one operating in Prussia.[31] The *Administrativjustiz* was to be replaced entirely by administrative courts of first instance, against whose decision an appeal to the Administrative Court was possible. This demand had already been made several times during the creation of the Administrative Court 1871–75, but the government had refused because it would have meant that an overall reform of the Austrian administrative system would take many years. Brunstein declared that it was indispensable to adhere to this long-term goal of multilevel administrative jurisdiction. However, he too recognised the enormous challenges of such a project and demanded legal regulations for the transitional period as a remedy for the worst grievances. Among other things, questions arose as to how

[29] The Administrative Court emphasised that it only makes its decisions for individual cases and is not bound by its own prior judicature: see the decision of the administrative court of 6 April 1886, in A von Budwiński (ed) *Erkenntnisse des k.k. Verwaltungsgerichtshofes* (Manz 1886) no 2995; cf Tezner (n 28) 15. It was not until 1934 that it was decided that in special cases the five-member Senate was to be supplemented by two additional members. The decisions of these so-called Verstärkter Senat then were binding on the court.

[30] For more details, see Olechowski (n 3) 28–32.

[31] For the Prussian model, see D Merten, 'Geschichte der Verwaltungsgerichtsbarkeit in Preußen' in Sommermann and Schaffarzik (n 5) vol I, 177–301.

parties should be informed, how and whether they could be represented, how a request could be changed, a confession withdrawn, and evidence evaluated, as well as who was allowed to inspect the files and much more regarding legal regulation.[32] The *Advocatentag* finally asked Karl von Lemayer, at that time a member of the Administrative Court, Viennese lawyer Arnold Pann, and a professor at the Czech University in Prague, Jiří (Georg) Pražák,[33] each to express an opinion.

In his report, Lemayer strongly advocated expanding administrative jurisdiction towards a multilevel model, while he attached little importance to the temporary regulations proposed by Brunstein for reforming the procedure. He pointed out that Brunstein's wishes could also be satisfied with an internal administrative regulation.[34] Pann was of a different view, praising his colleague Brunstein for his proposed two-pronged approach, saying: 'The better should not be the enemy of the good and therefore the work on reforming the administrative judiciary does not prevent an immediate reform of the administrative procedure.'[35] He detailed the differences between civil and administrative proceedings and stated that administrative proceedings should never be formalised as strongly as civil ones. For him, the investigation of *material truth* must always be in the foreground in public law, and the administrative body must also 'have a completely free hand' when it comes to determining the facts when deciding a matter of public interest. Consequently, this also applies in particular to the extent to which the authorities are bound by the requests of the parties or whether the parties may nominate experts.[36]

Czech jurist Pražák recalled the great constitutional difficulties that an overall reform of the administrative judiciary would encounter and therefore also welcomed Brunstein's attempt to reform the administrative procedural law within the framework of the currently existing administrative organisation. Nonetheless, he vehemently advocated a 'separation of the representation of public, State, and communal interest from the authority to issue decisions or orders', not unlike the separation of the prosecution and the judge in criminal proceedings. At the same time, Pražák pleaded for the previous regulations on the enforcement procedure to be left largely unchanged, especially since, in his opinion, they were characterised by particular 'mildness'.[37]

[32] 'Antrag des Dr. Josef Ludwig Brunstein über die Reform des Administrativ-Verfahrens' in *Drei Gutachten über die Reform des Administrativ-Verfahrens* (Fromme 1884) 3–9.

[33] cf H Slapnicka, 'Die Lehre des öffentlichen Rechts an der Prager Karl-Ferdinands-Universität bis zu ihrer Teilung 1882' (1973) 14 Bohemia 222–42, 238.

[34] *K v Lemayer*, 'Gutachten' in *Drei Gutachten* (n 32) 10–36, 30, 33.

[35] A Pann, 'Gutachten' ibid 37–85, 38.

[36] ibid 42, 65.

[37] G Pražak, 'Gutachten' in *Drei Gutachten* (n 32) 86–111, 92, 102.

VI. The Appeal Procedure Act 1896

The three reports had no immediate consequences. However, ten years later, in 1894, the government introduced a draft in Parliament, intending to set the deadline for the introduction of appeals against decisions and orders of the political State authorities at four weeks.[38] A committee of the House of Representatives took this as an opportunity to generally regulate the appeal proceedings, claiming that the lack of general provisions led to legal certainty. The subsequent law on appeal proceedings of 12 May 1896[39] can be seen as the precursor of the General Administrative Procedure Act of 1925. Other than that, it failed to bring about a complete regulation of the administrative procedure, but it did clarify some important questions.

These issues concerned, for example, the form in which appeals could be submitted (in writing, verbally, and even by telegram) or questions about deadlines falling on Sundays and public holidays. The appeal had to be submitted to the authority of first instance, but only the higher instance could decide on the admissibility of the appeal. The decisions and rulings had to indicate whether they were still subject to an appeal and, if so, indicate the deadline within which this was to be filed. If this information was incorrect and the party filed its legal remedy belatedly, but within the wrong time limit, the first instance decision or order had to be annulled, and a new one had to be issued, which was then subject to a new time limit.

There were no further reforms until the end of the Habsburg monarchy. The unresolved nationality issue made any change to the Constitution impossible, but this was a prerequisite for any far-reaching administrative reform; the legislature could not limit itself to a modest reform that would only have codified the administrative procedure in the spirit of Brunstein. With the collapse of the monarchy in 1918, Austria's legal system was initially adopted unchanged in the successor States but then gradually developed in different directions.

VII. The Administrative Procedural Laws of 1925

Adoption by the Republic of Austria of a comprehensive constitutional and administrative reform and, in this context, also the codification of administrative procedural law, was ultimately due to exceptional foreign and domestic political

[38] *Beilagen zu den Stenographischen Protokollen des Abgeordnetenhauses, 11. Session* (Vienna 1894) no 989. An ordinance of 1859 stipulated a period of 60 days: *Verordnung des Innenministers*, 27 October 1859, *Reichsgesetzblatt* 1859 no 196; cf Hellbling (n 14) 237.

[39] *Gesetz womit ergänzende, beziehungsweise abändernde Bestimmungen bezüglich des Verfahrens bei Geltendmachung der Rechtsmittel gegen Entscheidungen und Verfügungen der politischen Behörde getroffen warden*, 12 May 1896, *Reichsgesetzblatt* no 101, cf Olechowski (n 3) 37.

reasons. With the Federal Constitutional Act of 1 October 1920,[40] Austria formally became a federal State, but most of the old laws from the monarchy remained in place, so administrative organisation became highly confusing. However, when the Austrian provinces (*Länder*) took over, several authorities that had previously been the prerogative of the State as a whole, a 'duplication' of two different administrative apparatuses arose within the *Länder*.[41]

Austria was only able to bring the catastrophic economic situation in the aftermath of the First World War under control thanks to a loan granted by the League of Nations. In the Geneva Protocols of 4 October 1922,[42] Austria committed itself to a comprehensive restructuring programme, through which the administrative apparatus should have become leaner and less costly. A special Department for Administrative Reform in the Federal Chancellery was commissioned to draw up relevant laws, and just a year later, two ministerial councillors, Egbert Mannlicher and Emmerich Coreth, presented the Federal Chancellor with a corresponding package. As Mannlicher and Coreth later reported, it found 'full approval'.[43] In May 1924, the federal government passed a government bill for a total of six federal laws 'to simplify administration': the *Allgemeines Verwaltungsverfahrensgesetz* (AVG, General Administrative Procedure Act)[44] was designated as the basis of the entire bundle of laws. It was to have been 'decisive for the entire administration'. However, it was not to push the standardisation of the administrative procedure to extremes, especially since the individual administrative matters were very different, which is why the AVG was only to apply in subsidiary form from the outset. Several special laws supplemented the AVG. The *Verwaltungsstrafgesetz* (Administrative Criminal Act)[45] contained not only procedural law in administrative criminal matters but also some general provisions for substantive administrative criminal law. The *Verwaltungsvollstreckungsgesetz* (Administrative Enforcement Act)[46] replaced the birching patent, and the *Verwaltungsentlastungsgesetz* (Administrative Relief Act)[47] reformed some particular areas of administrative law. An introductory law[48] to all the above-mentioned legislation was supposed to contain mainly transitional provisions. Finally, it was recognised that the Federal Constitution itself had to be

[40] *Gesetz womit die Republik Österreich als Bundesstaat eingerichtet wird* (Bundes-Verfassungsgesetz, B-VG), 1 October 1920, *Bundesgesetzblatt* 1920 no 1.

[41] Gerald Kohl, 'Von der Doppelgleisigkeit der Verwaltung zur mittelbaren Bundesverwaltung—ein Überblick' (2021) 11 Beiträge zur Rechtsgeschichte Österreichs 315–29.

[42] *Bundesgesetzblatt* 1922 no 842. Cf H Mayer, 'Allgemeines Verwaltungsverfahrensrecht' in H Schambeck (ed), *Parlamentarismus und öffentliches Recht in Österreich. Entwicklung und Gegenwartsprobleme*, vol I (Duncker & Humblot 1993) 519–49, 522.

[43] E Mannlicher and E Coreth, *Das Verwaltungsverfahren. Mit einer Einleitung, erläuternden Bemerkungen, Materialien, einschlägigen anderen Gesetzen und Verordnungen* (2nd edn, Verlag der österreichischen Staatsdruckerei 1927) XXVII.

[44] *Bundesgesetzblatt* 1924 no 274.

[45] ibid 1925 no 275.

[46] ibid no 276.

[47] ibid no 277.

[48] ibid no 273.

modified in detail. The Federal Constitutional Act was amended[49] so that the administrative procedural laws could stand on a secure basis.

The *Erläuternde Bemerkungen* (official explanation of government bills)—presumably written by Mannlicher and Coreth—were characterised by reluctance and emphasised the need to standardise and simplify administrative procedural law, while constantly strengthening party rights.[50] In the National Council, the bills were assigned to a five-member committee consisting of members of all political parties. It is a remarkable detail in the legislative process that one of the committee members, the Christian Social MP, Dr Rudolf Ramek, was elected chancellor before joining in the negotiations, so a substitute, Franz Schumacher, had to be elected for the committee, and he took on the role of rapporteur.[51] This report was exceptionally long (107 pages) but only changed some details. On 21 July, the laws were adopted by the plenary session of the National Council and came into force on 1 January 1926.

It may be seen as a sign of the legal quality of these laws that shortly afterwards, other European States created very similar legal regulations. The Czechoslovak governmental decree of 13 January 1928 and the Polish ordinance of 22 March 1928, deserve special mention here. They were followed two years later, on 9 November 1930, by the Yugoslav law on general administrative procedure.[52] They were all in line with the Austrian laws not only in terms of basic idea and structure but also to the letters in many areas. This is not surprising: after all, Czechoslovakia, Poland, and Yugoslavia had at least partially emerged from the old Habsburg monarchy and the Imperial-Royal Administrative Court had had jurisdiction there, so here too, at least in part, administrative practice had long been codified. As the new regulations extended far beyond the territory of the former Habsburg monarchy, the *Orbis iuris Austriacus* was significantly expanded again around ten years after the disintegration of the empire.

[49] ibid no 268.

[50] *Beilagen zu den Stenographischen Protokollen des Nationalrates, 2. Gesetzgebungsperiode* (Wien 1924) no 116.

[51] *Beilagen zu den Stenographischen Protokollen des Nationalrates, 2. Gesetzgebungsperiode* (Wien 1925) no 360.

[52] H Slapnicka, *Österreichs Recht außerhalb Österreichs. Der Untergang des österreichischen Rechtsraums* (Verlag für Geschichte und Politik 1973) 36f.

4

The Structure and Main Features of the Austrian General Administrative Procedure Act (AVG)

Stefan Storr

I. Principal Reasons for the AVG of 1925

The structure of the AVG of 21 July 1925[1] reflected three principal motives: first, it had to close a gap in the mosaic of the constitutional State. There was broad consent among legal scholars that a statutory administrative procedure offers protection against arbitrariness by authorities and creates legal certainty. The earlier regulation called *Amtsinstruction* 1855[2] already provided some instructions for the actions of administrative authorities; however, it considered the citizen more as 'objects' of administrative activity than as participants endowed with subjective rights.[3] This situation was unsatisfactory as it allowed authorities the 'most boundless arbitrariness'.[4]

Although the previous jurisprudence of the Supreme Administrative Court on the requirements for the legality of administrative proceedings[5] was highly esteemed by practitioners and legal scholars, the legal principles developed by the Supreme Administrative Court had no general validity. Moreover, the Supreme Administrative Court modified the judicially developed legal principles if a case required it. Legal principles developed by a court could not convey rights under

[1] Federal Administrative Act (*Bundesgesetz vom 21. Juli 1925 über das allgemeine Verwaltungsverfahren—Allgemeines Verwaltungsverfahrensgesetz—A. V. G.*), BGBl 274/1925.

[2] Section 92 Regulation on instructions in the administration (*Verordnung der Minister des Innern und der Justiz, wirksam für alle Kronländer, mit Ausnahme des lombardisch-venetianischen Königreiches und der Militärgränze, womit die Amtsinstruction für die rein politischen und für die gemischten Bezirks- und Stuhlrichterämter erlassen wird*), RGBl 52/1855.

[3] E Mannlicher and E Coreth, *Das Verwaltungsverfahren* (2nd edn, 1927) Verlag der Österreichischen Staatsdruckerei, XXV.

[4] I von Plener, *Stenographische Protokolle des Abgeordnetenhauses*, 133. Sitzung der VIII. Session am 18. 3. 1875, S. 4677.

[5] For an overview, see A Ferrari Zumbini, 'Judicial Review of Administrative Action in the Austro-Hungarian Empire—The Formative Years (1890–1910)' (2018) 1 It J Pub L 9.

Stefan Storr, *The Structure and Main Features of the Austrian General Administrative Procedure Act (AVG)* In: *The Austrian Codification of Administrative Procedure*. Edited by: Giacinto Della Cananea, Angela Ferrari Zumbini, and Otto Pfersmann, Oxford University Press. DOI: 10.1093/oso/9780198867623.003.0004

constitutional law if the issue required normative regulation, as in the case of appeal proceedings.[6]

The codification of the administrative procedure was also driven by the expectation that in the future, the authorities would have to pay more attention to procedural aspects and, above all, examine their competence more rigorously than in the past.[7] It seems significant that, in the past, administrative procedural law received little attention even in authoritative books on general administrative law.[8] Also today, administrative procedural law in Austria is rather understood as a separate legal field than as a part of general administrative law.[9]

Second, although the Appeals Act came into force in 1896,[10] it provides little guidance. Instead, it was so rudimentary that the responsible sections of the ministries established their own procedural requirements depending on the legal matter. According to Mannlicher, one of the minds behind the AVG 1925, these procedural differences were considerable and objectively nonsensical. They were perceived as very distressing by executing authorities and legal practitioners.[11] Therefore, one objective was the creation of harmonised rules for administrative proceedings which would apply throughout Austria. In particular, the AVG 1925 would also apply to proceedings on matters for which legislative competence lay with the provinces (*Länder*). Granting the federal state the competence to regulate the provinces' administrative procedure posed a constitutional and a substantial problem:[12] The AVG 1925 had to apply to as many administrative procedures as possible. It had to be generally applicable, so it had to typify yet be abstract. It could not absorb the specifics from the relevant laws it would be applicable to.

Finally, it was essential to keep administrative procedures as simple as possible.[13] Before the AVG 1925 came into force, there had been considerable doubt whether all the administrative authorities—especially the municipalities—were in a position to understand and implement the rulings of the Supreme Administrative Court due to the highly varying degrees of legal knowledge of the employees

[6] E Mannlicher, 'Die österreichischen Verwaltungsverfahrensgesetze vom Jahre 1925' in R Bedall, *Vorträge von Dr. Egbert Mannlicher aus der Zeit seines Altersruhestands (1947–1973)* (2005) 149, 150.

[7] Committee Report to the Federal Administrative Act (*Ausschussbericht zum Bundesgesetz vom 21. Juli 1925 über das allgemeine Verwaltungsverfahren*) 7.

[8] See A Merkl, *Allgemeines Verwaltungsrecht* (Springer 1927) 213f; but there were monographs, for example, by Friedrich Tezner, *Handbuch des österreichischen Administrativverfahrens* (Manz 1896); R Herrnritt, *Das Verwaltungsverfahren* (1932).

[9] For example, E Schulev-Steindl, *Verwaltungsverfahrensrecht* (6th edn, Verlag Österreich 2018); B Raschauer, *Allgemeines Verwaltungsrecht* (5th edn, Verlag Österreich 2017); C Grabenwarter and M Fister, *Verwaltungsverfahrensrecht und Verwaltungsgerichtsbarkeit* (4th edn, Verlag Österreich 2014).

[10] Appeals Act (*Gesetz, womit ergänzende, beziehungsweise abändernde Bestimmungen bezüglich des Verfahrens bei Geltendmachung der Rechtsmittel gegen Entscheidungen und Verfügungen der politischen Behörde getroffen werden*), RGBl 101/1896.

[11] Mannlicher (n 6) 151.

[12] On the problem of creating constitutional competence for the federation: Explanatory notes on the laws concerning administrative reform (*Erläuterungen zu den Gesetzen betreffend die Vereinfachung der Verwaltung*), 116 d Beilagen NR II. GP, p 1.

[13] Mannlicher and Coreth (n 3) XXXV.

there.[14] Furthermore, many laws on specific matters were considered complicated. Thus, the AVG 1925 had to contain as few provisions as possible, and these laws had to be understandable for all administrative officials.[15]

II. The Structure of the AVG 1925

A. The (Court-like) Procedure

The legislator intended administrative procedure to contribute to administrative unity. However, the law did not—as the title implies—regulate a comprehensive procedure for the entire administration and its activities. The administrative procedures were just too diverse—laws on the specific matters thus provided for divergent procedures (usually justified by particular circumstances).

First, the AVG 1925 contained procedural provisions, which only applied when other laws did not contain more specific provisions.

Second, the AVG 1925 was limited to basic regulations, to make room for diverse administrative activities, and to consider specific subjects and matters. Legal principles were codified only for essential procedural issues.[16] Mannlicher stressed the importance of maintaining a 'wise approach' to find the 'right balance between uniform regulation and enabling special regulation in the specific administrative laws'.[17]

In addition, the law did not apply to all administrative authorities but only to those mentioned in a specific introductory law.[18] On this basis, the AVG 1925 was principally applicable to all general federal and regional authorities, only individual matters like fiscal administration and civil servants' service law were exempted.[19]

Finally, the AVG 1925 only concerned 'public' administrative activities (*Hoheitsverwaltung*— 'official tasks'),[20] excluding administrative activities under private law (*Privatwirtschaftsverwaltung*—'private administration').

The model for standardising administrative procedural law was the Code of Civil Procedure, which indicated a 'path' for creating a norm according to the rules of a higher legal level[21]—in the sense of the Austrian legal theory of the

[14] D Koropatnicki, *Kommentar zum Allgemeinen Verwaltungsverfahrensgesetz* (Buchhandlung Altes Rathaus 1927) 9.

[15] Committee Report (n 7) 8.

[16] Explanatory notes (n 12) 3.

[17] Mannlicher (n 6) 157.

[18] Article II Introductory Act to the Administrative Procedure Acts (*Bundesgesetz vom 21. Juli 1925 zur Einführung der Bundesgesetze über das allgemeine Verwaltungsverfahren, über die allgemeinen Bestimmungen des Verwaltungsstrafrechtes und das Verwaltungsstrafverfahren sowie über das Vollstreckungsverfahren in der Verwaltung—Einführungsgesetz zu den Verwaltungsverfahrensgesetzen—E. G. V. G.*), RGBl 273/1925.

[19] ibid art II(5)–(6).

[20] ibid art II(1).

[21] Explanatory notes (n 12) 3.

Stufenlehre.[22] In fact, the AVG 1925 was conceived as a law focused on investigation procedure (s 37 AVG 1925) and saw the 'settlement' (closing—*Erledigung*; s 18 AVG) as the completion of the procedure. The explicit purpose of the investigation procedure—under section 37 AVG 1925—was 'to ascertain the facts relevant for processing an administrative matter' but also 'to enable the parties to claim their rights and legal interests'.

The term 'party', which referred—and still refers—to those involved in administrative proceedings had existed in Austrian administrative procedural law long before the AVG 1925 came into force.[23]

The concept of 'party' (see IIIA.), referring to plaintiff and defendant, was already familiar from civil court proceedings, even if the legal relationship between citizen and state authority is not necessarily one of opposition.[24] The reliance on the Code of Civil Procedure as a model reflected in statutory provisions on submissions (s 13 AVG 1925), summons (s 19 AVG 1925), oral hearings (ss 40ff AVG 1925), and taking evidence (ss 45ff AVG 1925). However, it should be emphasised that administrative proceedings differed from civil court proceedings.

B. Major Legal Principles of the AVG 1925

The legal principle to initiate a proceeding *ex officio* (*Offizialmaxime*) generally applied unless special statutory exceptions prevailed. It did not apply in appeal proceedings and for reinstatements. Nevertheless, the *ex officio* principle did not exclude the applicant's possibility to initiate a proceeding (s 13 AVG 1925). Surprisingly, a relatively informal approach was adopted—submissions, applications, information brought against a person, complaints, and other reports could be filed in writing or by telegraph (not telephone) and even orally if appropriate.

The *ex officio* principle included the jurisdiction of a certain legally defined authority. The AVG 1925 did not permit a *prorogatio fori*. The parties were thus not authorised to determine another than the legally defined authority's jurisdiction by agreement.[25] The law provided a distinction between jurisdiction in the subject matter and territorial jurisdiction. It further included a rule covering the eventuality of disagreement over jurisdiction among authorities. Respective conflicts were to be resolved by the higher authority with jurisdiction over the subject matter.[26]

[22] Merkl (n 8) 214; for another perspective, see Herrnritt (n 8) 1: 'The process is not to create law, but to protect law'.

[23] For example, Royal Chancellery Decree (*Hofkanzleidekret*) of 18.4.1807, Politische Gesetzessammlung Band 28, Nr 48.

[24] But see Herrnritt (n 8) 51: 'in confrontation with the authority', even though he speaks of a 'dual position' on the part of the authority.

[25] AVG 1925, s 6(2).

[26] ibid s 5.

Regardless of whether the procedure began upon application or *ex officio*, the concrete design of the proceeding rests with the competent authority ('Amtswegigkeit') (s 39(2) AVG 1925). 'To the extent that the administrative rules and regulations do not contain any provisions thereon, the authority shall proceed ex officio and determine the procedure of the investigation in accordance with the rules and regulations contained in this part.' In particular, it might 'order ex officio or upon a motion that a hearing will be held in accordance with paras 40 to 44' (AVG). One example is that only an authority itself or a higher authority could assess a conflict of interest in an administrative body. No party had the right to ascertain a conflict of interest.[27] Another example is that an authority had to summon *ex officio* those persons whose appearance was necessary; respective request by parties were not binding on the authority.

The AVG 1925 further stipulated the principle of efficiency and rapidity of procedure (*Grundsatz der Raschheit des Verfahrens*; s 39(2) sentence 3 AVG 1925): 'In all these procedural provisions the authority shall consider as a guideline maximum efficiency, speed, minimum of complications and cost-effectiveness.' Further manifestations of this legal principle could be found in other provisions: if an authority was approached in matters over which it has no jurisdiction, it had to forward the application without undue delay, at the applicant's own risk, to an authority with jurisdiction or refer them to that authority.[28] If the person whose submission initiated the proceeding missed the hearing, it could be held even in his absence.[29] If appropriate, the authority could proceed orally or by telephone (the law no longer exists in this form).[30] Separate appeals against procedural orders were not permissible. One could challenge them only by appealing against the administrative decision on the matter.[31]

The legal principle of substantive truth (*Grundsatz der materiellen Wahrheit*, s 37(1) AVG 1925): 'The purpose of the investigation procedure is to ascertain the facts relevant for processing an administrative matter'. This required an adequate fact-finding process, and if the facts of the case were not clear, even the competent authority was not allowed to release a (correct) decision. Only facts already known to an authority and facts assumed by law needed no further evidence (s 45(1) 1 AVG 1925; also s 56 AVG 1925). Prior investigations in the event of a 'mandate decision' (*Mandatsbescheid*) constituted an exception to this principle. Under section 57 AVG 1925, a mandate decision could be issued if money was charged as established by law, statutes, or a tariff, or in the case of measures that could not be postponed because of imminent danger. An authority could then issue an administrative decision with no prior investigation procedure.

27 Mannlicher and Coreth (n 3) XLII.
28 AVG 1925, s 6(1).
29 ibid s 42(3).
30 ibid s 18(1).
31 ibid s 62(2).

Another legal principle was the free judgement of facts (*Grundsatz der freien Beweiswürdigung*; s 45(2) AVG 1925). An authority could freely assess whether a fact could be assumed to be substantiated or not by considering the outcome of the investigation.

The last major principle to mention here is the parties' right to be heard (*Grundsatz des Parteiengehörs*; s 37(2) Alt. AVG 1925): 'to enable the parties to claim their rights and legal interests'. This legal principle relates to evidence: 'The parties shall be allowed to be apprised of the result of the evidence taken and comment on it' (s 45(3) AVG 1925). The right to be heard was an important legal principle of administrative procedural law, and any violation rendered the procedure and subsequent administrative decision unlawful.[32]

III. Main Features of the AVG 1925

A. Persons Involved and Parties (*Beteiligte*; *Parteien*)

Section 8 AVG 1925 states that the 'persons involved' are those who use the services of an authority or are affected by it, and, to the extent that they are involved in the matter on the grounds of a legal title or a legal interest, they are parties.

The legislative process considered this provision as 'one of the most important provisions', forming the basis for its entire further development by offering the possibility of precisely distinguishing the position and the standing of the party from that of the person involved in all details of the procedure. In doing so, a theoretically and practically elusive procedural differentiation between matters of administration and administrative litigation (party) shall not be made.[33]

However, there was also considerable criticism—the inconsistent application of the concepts 'party' and 'person involved' were considered as the 'greatest weakness' of the AVG 1925)[34] as it could only be determined during proceedings whether a person was a party or a person involved. In the end, this criticism did not prevail, and the provision is still in force today. However, it is true that the distinction between legal title and legal interest no longer exists.

The concept of party had already been developed by the Supreme Administrative Court and legal scholars[35] before the AVG 1925 came into force. The AVG 1925 guaranteed specific procedural rights to the party, for example, the right to inspect files (s 17 AVG 1925),[36] the right to request a settlement (s 18(3) AVG 1925), the

[32] W Antoniolli, *Allgemeines Verwaltungsrecht* (Manzsche Verlags-und Universitätsbuchhandlung 1954) 224.
[33] Explanatory notes (n 12); see also Committee Report (n 7) 10.
[34] Koropatnicki (n 14) 10.
[35] E Bernatzik, *Rechtsprechung und materielle Rechtskraft* (Manz 1886) 183ff.
[36] This right dates back to the Royal Chancellery Decree (n 23).

right to claim rights and legal interests (ss 37, 43(2) AVG 1925), and the right to submit and evidence all aspects pertaining to the subject matter. Parties could also request witnesses and experts to ask questions and comment on the facts presented by other persons involved or witnesses and experts, facts treated as evident, motions filed by others, and the result of investigations by the authorities (s 43(3) AVG 1925). Parties also had the right to ensure an authority remained within its legal competence.[37] They had to be informed of the result of the evidence taken and comment on it (s 45(3) AVG 1925). Experts who were not officially appointed could be rejected by a party if prima facie evidence was presented, casting doubt on impartiality (s 53 sentence 2 AVG 1925). If requested by a party, a written copy of the administrative decision could be pronounced orally (s 62(3) AVG 1925). A party could appeal against an administrative decision (s 63(5) AVG 1925), apply for a proceeding to be reopened (s 69 AVG 1925), for reinstatement to the previous legal position (s 71 AVG 1925) and, in the event of inaction by an authority, request devolution to the next higher authority (s 73(2) AVG 1925).

Under section 8 AVG 1925, a party was a person involved in the matter on the grounds of legal title or legal interest. The law thus referred to legal positions to establish party status, which depended on the person. The distinction between legal title and legal interest dates back to Bernatzik: in his view, legal entitlement referred to the legal position based on guaranteed rights. A legal entitlement constitutes a subjective right that can be granted to State institutions and affect individuals (eg operating a licensed trade, paying a pension).[38]

On the other hand, a legal interest implies that an institution had the right to assert that interest in a certain procedure; one speaks of legal interest because the living conditions protected by the legal system constitute only relationships of interests. Only through an administrative decision following a proceeding they become *legal* relationships (enforcement; res judicata).[39]

This concept of legal interest reflected the fact that the individual could not demand a particular type of decision because the legal relationship was 'complicated',[40] and an authority had to balance different interests.

It was necessary to draw a distinction between legal interests and factual interests, whereby the latter do not confer a right—in particular, no right to be a party in the proceeding: 'rights confer a title to a specific type of official activity; legal interests confer a title to a specific proceeding, and factual interests confer no title at all'.[41]

[37] Mannlicher and Coreth (n 3) xlv.
[38] Bernatzik (n 35) 185; see also Mannlicher and Coreth (n 3); AVG 1925, s 8.
[39] Bernatzik (n 35) 186.
[40] ibid 185.
[41] ibid 186.

The distinction between legal right and legal interest was based on the idea that there could only be formal rights for a specific procedure but not a substantive right to exercise discretion in a specific way.[42]

Cogent criticism of the distinction between 'legal right' and 'legal interest' was articulated in the 1920s already.[43] However, the corresponding discretionary doctrine is no longer valid today. As Mayer stated, it is now 'an integral part of constitutional legal dogma that substantive entitlements exist even in the case of discretionary decisions',[44] which is why the distinction between 'legal right' and 'legal interest' mentioned in section 8 AVG 1925 remains obscure[45] and 'anachronistic'.[46]

B. The Oral Hearing (*mündliche Verhandlung*)

The oral hearing constituted an important part of the investigation proceeding (ss 40–44 AVG 1925). This procedural step, which had not yet been stipulated under constitutional law, showed that civil court proceedings were the model for the AVG 1925. Further, the oral hearing served an essential function of administrative proceedings, namely that of finding a 'consensus-oriented' decision. The term consent decision (*konsentierter Bescheid*) still exists in Austrian administrative law, eg in construction law. The oral hearing not only enabled all parties to present their points of view but also gave the authority an opportunity for legal discussion and induced greater acceptance of the subsequent administrative decision.

However, an authority was not obliged to hold an oral hearing; it could decide whether to do so or not. The 'diversity' and the 'complexity' of administrative tasks demanded a certain degree of authority discretion. A general obligation or an obligation in specific matters would misrepresent the reality and diversity of the questions to be dealt with.[47]

Unlike in civil court proceedings, oral hearings were not public. During the legislative process, there was much debate on whether a public hearing considered a significant achievement of civil court proceedings should be implemented in administrative proceedings. Eventually, an oral hearing in which at least the parties involved could participate was established.[48]

42 See J Hengstschläger and D Leeb, AVG Section 8 (Stand 1.1.2014, rdb.at) rec. 2; Bernatzik (n 35) 186.
43 Herrnritt (n 8) 54.
44 H Mayer, 'Der Parteibegriff im allgemeinen Verwaltungsverfahren' [1977] ZfV 485, 487.
45 G Ress, 'Das subjektive öffentliche Recht' in F Ermacora and others (eds), *Allgemeines Verwaltungsrecht, FS Antoniolli* (Orac 1979) 105, 129.
46 Mayer (n 44) 488.
47 Mannlicher and Coreth (n 3) xli.
48 ibid xlii.

Therefore, section 43(6) AVG 1925 determined an important obligation of the officer in charge of the hearing. The latter was called upon to strive towards a settlement of claims in accordance with the public interest as well as the interest claimed on the part of other persons involved.

If an authority decided to conduct an oral hearing, all persons involved and all witnesses and necessary experts had to be notified. If the oral hearing was to be combined with a judicial inspection, it would preferably be held on site, otherwise at the office of an authority or in the place deemed best suited to the situation (s 41 AVG 1925).

The statutory requirements for scheduling an oral hearing were strictly formal: all persons known by the authority had to be notified personally. If further persons were to be involved, the hearing had to be publicly announced on the official bulletin board of the municipality and published in the newspaper where official announcements of the authority were published.

If the oral hearing was scheduled correctly, i.e. announced on the official bulletin board of the municipality and published in the newspaper used for official announcements by an authority, a party that did not attend the hearing and did not raise an objection lost party standing. No loss of party standing occurred if the latter raised an objection during the hearing or, at the latest, on the day preceding the hearing but prior to the hearing's opening prevented the preclusion of the objecting person (s 42(1) AVG 1925). Whereas, objections raised on the day of the hearing but prior to the hearing's opening did not prevent the preclusion of the objecting person. This rule was justified by the fact that the officer in charge for the hearing might already be on his way to the oral hearing outside the authority. Therefore, the objection would not be included in the file, and the officer in charge would not be aware of it when commencing the oral hearing.

The so-called quasi reinstatement (*quasi Wiedereinsetzung*) did not exist at that time, but was introduced in the AVG 1925 later and allowed the reinstatement into the previous legal position if one of the parties could not present its objections in time without fault.

Also, the provisions of the oral hearing were obviously inspired by civil court proceedings. The officer in charge had to open the hearing and check the identity of the persons appearing, their capacity as a party or other person involved, and any power of attorney. He had to explain the case and ensure that the right to be heard was guaranteed, and other persons involved were allowed to contribute to ascertaining the facts of the case. Persons not involved were not allowed to speak at the hearing. The executive officer in charge determined the order of sequence in which the parties were to be heard, the evidence to be taken, and the results of earlier taken evidence to be presented or discussed. Minutes had to be taken in writing at each oral hearing.

C. Taking Evidence (*Beweisaufnahme*)

The AVG 1925 established detailed rules on taking evidence in sections 45–55 AVG 1925 (contra Koropatnicki, who argues that the rules were rather cursory).[49] As already explained, the legal principle of substantive truth and the legal principle of the free judgement of facts constitute the foundations of this chapter.

Generally, anything suitable for ascertaining the relevant facts of the case and feasible in the circumstances of the particular case shall constitute evidence (s 46 AVG 1925). Nevertheless, the AVG 1925 specifically regulated five kinds of evidence.

These included public and private deeds. The AVG 1925 referred to the Code of Civil Procedure to assess the cogency of proof. Public deeds thus gave full proof of what an authority officially decreed or declared; however, proof of the inaccuracy of the witnessed event or fact—or incorrect notarisation—was permissible. On the other hand, private documents only provided full proof that the therein contained declarations originated from the issuers.

Some people were not eligible to give evidence, such as clergymen, executive bodies, and officials of the federal administration, provinces, and municipalities, as well as officials from other public law entities if the content of their statement was subject to official secrecy and they had not been released from such obligation (s 48 AVG 1925). A witness could refuse to answer questions that would result in prejudice, criminal prosecution, or discredit himself or a relative (s 36a AVG 1925). A witness might also refuse to testify as a person authorised to represent parties professionally.

In principle, similar rights, such as not having to testify or even refusing to do so, also applied to persons involved.

In addition, the AVG 1925 provided rules for appointing experts, distinguishing between officially appointed (and other) experts (s 52 AVG 1925). Officially appointed experts were considered more credible as they were attributed to an authority (s 53 AVG 1925). Parties had the right to refuse a non-officially appointed expert on the grounds of partiality.

Lastly, the AVG 1925 envisaged the possibility of judicial review (s 54 AVG 1925).

D. The Administrative Decision (*Bescheid*)

The AVG 1925 introduced the concept of the *Bescheid* (administrative decision) as a specific form of administrative action; it is still a feature of Austrian administrative law and its present-day jurisprudence. Before the AVG 1925

[49] Koropatnicki (n 14) 10.

came into force, other terms such as *Entscheidung*[50] ('ruling') or *Verfügung* ('order')[51] were used, albeit not consistently (*Entscheidung* meant a declaratory finding of rights, ie it did not create or confer rights such as granting a concession or approval, which was done though a *Verfügung*).[52] The introduction of the term *Bescheid* meant that uniform and simplified terminology could be used from then on.[53] A trend towards standardisation had begun to develop with an amendment to the Federal Constitution of 1925, which also reflected in the new concept of *Bescheid* (administrative decision).[54]

The administrative procedure ended (and still does) with the administrative decision. Following the investigation of the facts of the case and their assessment from a legal point of view, official measures are taken and handed down in an administrative decision. The AVG 1925 listed seven requirements for an administrative decision, not all of which had to be fulfilled.

1. Obligation to Expressly Name an Administrative Decision as Such

Administrative decisions had to be named as such (as *Bescheid*; s 58(1), Alt 1 AVG 1925). The naming of the decision as a *Bescheid* served to complete the procedure and explain the content and scope of the binding ruling (*Spruch*) to the recipient; it served legal certainty.[55]

However, it was not unlawful to not explicitly refer to an 'administrative decision' in all cases. According to the Supreme Administrative Court, this was not mandatory if the administrative decision addressed a specific person and contained the name of the authority, the ruling, and the signature of a civil servant. Also, referring to a decision as 'administrative decision' could be refrained from if the normative character of an individual act, issued by an authority, was evident.[56]

2. The (Normative) Ruling

The ruling had to be contained in the operative part of the administrative decision (s 58(1), Alt 2 AVG 1925). This requirement served two purposes. First, a ruling was normative: it stated duties or rights. It had to cover the full scope of the subject

[50] Regulation on instructions (n 2) s 92.

[51] See also Appeals Act (*Gesetz, womit ergänzende, beziehungsweise abändernde Bestimmungen bezüglich des Verfahrens bei Geltendmachung der Rechtsmittel gegen Entscheidungen und Verfügungen der politischen Behörde getroffen werden*), RGBl 101/1896; Section 129 para 1 Federal Constitutional Law (*Gesetz vom 1. Oktober 1920, womit die Republik Österreich als Bundesstaat eingerichtet wird (Bundes-Verfassungsgesetz)*, StF: BGBl. Nr. 1/1920).

[52] Herrnritt (n 8) 7.

[53] Explanatory notes (n 12) 58.

[54] Federal Constitutional Law Amendment 1925, art 129 (*Bundesverfassungsgesetz vom 20. Juli 1925, betreffend einige Änderungen des Bundes-Verfassungsgesetzes vom 1. Oktober 1920, BGBl Nr. 1—Bundes-Verfassungsnovelle*), BGBl 268/1925.

[55] VwGH 28 January 2004, 2000/12/0311.

[56] ibid 16 May 2001, 2001/08/0046.

of the hearing as well as all motions by parties concerning the main issue and the administrative decision on costs (if applicable) in brief and precise wording, quoting all the legal provisions applied (s 59 sentence 1 AVG 1925). Second, the procedure had to be concluded as mentioned before: any objections to the request to institute a proceeding were also to be dealt with through an administrative decision (s 59 sentence 2 AVG 1925).

3. Statement of Reasons

Administrative decisions had to include the reasons. In fact, this obligation was already part of the *Amtsinstruction* of 1855.[57] In this regard, two requirements were of relevance. First, whenever the party's point of view was not fully shared, or administrative decisions were taken on the objections or submissions of the persons involved, the reasons had to be stated in the administrative decision (s 58(2) AVG 1925). The authority was not obliged to write unnecessary and unsubstantiated statements of reasons.[58] Second, the statement of reasons had to summarise the results of the investigation procedure and the considerations relevant to the assessment of the evidence as well as the respective legal question clearly and succinctly (s 60 AVG 1925). The reasoning explained what had informed the authorities' decision.[59]

One alternative that had not been included in the AVG 1925 but came up in the lawmaking process was that the authority was not obliged to provide a statement of reasons if it could exercise discretion.[60] This is a surprising argument because the rule of law nowadays appears to require the opposite.[61] A statement of reasons is of particular relevance when a decision is necessary because otherwise, it is impossible to know why an authority reached an administrative decision and whether it thereby exceeded its margin of discretion. This was the position of the Supreme Administrative Court even before the AVG 1925.[62] Lastly, the recipient and the appellate court also had to be able to verify the correctness of the administrative decision.

4. Information on Appeals

Administrative decisions had to contain information regarding appeals (s 58(1), Alt 3 AVG 1925). This requirement was initially not part of the legal proposal during the lawmaking process. An administrative decision was not necessarily unlawful because information on the right of appeal was missing, incomplete, or

57 Regulation on instructions (n 2) s 92.
58 Former decrees of ministers regulated simplifications: Tezner (n 8) 203.
59 VwGH 29 November 1982, VwGH 82/12/0079.
60 Explanatory notes (n 12) 7.
61 VwGH 29 November 1982, 82/12/0079.
62 ibid 29 March 1924, A 386/23.

incorrect. If this information was missing, the administrative decision had to be reissued due to a formal error, amounting to 'completely superfluous work and much writing', which would never have obtained the people's consent.[63] In the original proposal, a uniform appeal period of two weeks was included; it could reasonably be assumed that every citizen was aware of this provision.[64]

However, the proposal was not accepted. Instead, the law required (and still does) that the administrative decision indicates whether an appeal may be filed against it. The instructions also had to clarify the nature of the content and form the appeal must take, the authority to which it had to be submitted, as well as the deadline for doing so (s 61(1) AVG 1925).

5. Obligation to Name of the Authority, the Date of Approval, and the Name of the Approving Officer in Charge

Any matter processed in writing had to state the name of the authority, the date of approval, and the name of the approving officer in charge. Only the names of the issuing authority and the approving officer in charge were required to complete the proceeding;[65] the absence of an approval date did not render an administrative decision void or unlawful.[66]

E. Errors and Legal Effectivity (*Fehlerfolgen*; *Rechtskraft*)

The consequences of errors differed depending on whether an administrative decision was issued at the end of an improper procedure or whether specific requirements relating to administrative decisions were not met.

Under the AVG 1925, five 'groups of consequences' of errors were known: the administrative decision could be a non-decision (1), void (2), (only) unlawful (3), the error could be cured or the law would set out the consequences of specific errors (4), or the error was irrelevant (5).

A non-decision (1) in the sense of nullity (*nullum*) occurred if an authority action could not be qualified as an administrative decision in any way. This could happen, for example, if the ruling of an administrative decision was absent. In that case, one would speak of a 'non-binding administrative decision'.

An administrative decision could be declared void (2) *ex officio* by the higher competent authority in exercising its right of supervision if one of four situations arose:

[63] Explanatory notes (n 12) 7: 'völlig überflüssige Arbeit und Vielschreiberei, für die die Bevölkerung nie Verständnis aufbringen konnte'.

[64] Explanatory notes (n 12) 7.

[65] VwGH 20 January 2011, 2010/22/0218.

[66] ibid 17 December 2001, 2001/14/0209.

- the administrative decision was issued by a non-competent authority or by a panel whose membership was not correctly formed (in this case, an appeal may only be brought within three years of notification);
- the administrative decision would result in a situation contrary to criminal law;
- the administrative decision was impossible to implement; or
- the administrative decision was affected by an error expressly sanctioned with nullity by a provision of the law.[67]

Nobody had—nor has—a right to insist that an authority exercises its power to modify or remedy an administrative decision when reviewing a lower authority.

However, the most common consequence (3) of an unlawful administrative decision was that of (ordinary) illegality (*Rechtswidrigkeit*). An unlawful administrative decision could be revoked or amended by appeal (s 63 AVG 1925). The AVG 1925 regulated the appeals procedure—and still does today. The next higher authority had to carry out the appeal decision. Appealing was possible as long as the decision was not legally effective, becoming so when the time limit for appeal expired. Although this doctrine of legal effectivity was criticised as an 'anti-social absurdity',[68] it is—with good reason—still law.

In some cases (4), an authority might correct errors *ex officio* at any time. Section 62(4) AVG 1925 authorised administrative bodies to correct typing or calculating errors or inaccuracies within administrative decisions at any time. The AVG 1925 also provided error consequences if an administrative decision did not contain instructions on the right to appeal, wrongly stated that no appeal was permissible, or indicated no or a shorter appeal period than established by law. In this case, an appeal was considered filed in due time if it was filed within the legal time limit (s 61(2) AVG 1925). If the administrative decision indicated a longer period than permitted by law, an appeal filed within the period declared was considered filed in time (s 61(3) AVG 1925).

The AVG 1925 also contained provisions for cases in which an administrative decision omitted to indicate, or wrongly indicated, to which authority an appeal was to be filed to. In such a case, an appeal was considered correctly lodged if filed either with the authority that issued the administrative decision or with the designated authority (s 61(4) AVG 1925).

Lastly, also irrelevant errors could occur, such as the absence of an approval date when issuing an administrative decision.

[67] AVG 1925, s 68(4)–(5).

[68] F Tezner, *Das österreichische Administrativverfahren* (2nd edn, Österreichische Staatsdruckerei 1925) XIII.

F. The Appeals Procedure (*Berufung*)

As mentioned, the procedure for appeals had been regulated by the 1896 Appeals Act before the AVG 1925 came into force.[69] The appeal established in the AVG 1925 was initially the principal remedy against an administrative decision. The provisions on appeal contained new law and were considered to have the 'deepest' and 'most tangible' impact on administrative procedure.[70]

Since one of the main objectives of the AVG 1925 was to unify the appeal procedures, the concept of appeal (*Berufung*) could not be interpreted strictly. Remedies regulated by special laws were seen as an appeal under section 63 AVG 1925 if they had the function of a comparable legal remedy.[71]

Because this form of legal protection was incompatible with the European Convention of Human Rights (ECHR),[72] a 1991 law set up independent administrative bodies[73] to ensure legal protection in accordance with the ECHR. After the introduction of the EU Charter of Fundamental Rights, administrative courts of first instance replaced the independent administrative bodies; at the same time, administrative appeals became considerably less important.[74]

In the AVG 1925, no appeal was permissible if the party expressly waived the right of appeal after receipt or pronouncement of the administrative decision. Otherwise, two weeks were available for appeal (s 63(5) AVG 1925). When that period had elapsed, and none of the parties had brought an appeal, the administrative decision came into legal force (*Rechtskraft*). This provided a degree of consistency and legal certainty. Section 68(1) AVG 1925 fundamentally determined that submissions by persons involved requesting modification of an administrative decision not (or no longer) subject to appeal should be rejected. However, there were exceptions, either because nobody would obtain any rights as a consequence of an administrative decision because an amendment or a repeal of an administrative decision was justified by major public interest, or the administrative decision was declared void (s 68(2)–(4) AVG 1925).

[69] Appeals Act (n 51).

[70] Mannlicher and Coreth (n 3) xlii.

[71] Mannlicher and Coreth (n 3); AVG 1925, s 63.

[72] ECHR, art 5 allows deprivation only by a court, and art 6 provides jurisdiction of civil rights and obligations of criminal charges performed by an independent and impartial tribunal established by law. Neither the Supreme Administrative Court nor the Constitutional Court fulfilled these conditions in all aspects. The Supreme Administrative Court did not have full powers of review because it had to accept the facts presented by the administration; the Constitutional Court decided constitutional lawfulness only.

[73] Federal Constitutional Law Amendment 1988 (*Bundesverfassungsgesetz vom 29. November 1988, mit dem das Bundes-Verfassungsgesetz in der Fassung von 1929 geändert wird—Bundes-Verfassungsgesetz-Novelle 1988*), StF: BGBl Nr 685/1988.

[74] Administrative Jurisdiction Amendment (*Verwaltungsgerichtsbarkeits-Novelle* 2012), StF: BGBl I Nr 51/2012.

Appeals were permitted against administrative decisions but not against procedural orders. Such orders could be notified only in the appeal against the administrative decision deciding the matter.[75] The appeal could contain new facts or evidence.

If the appeal was not rejected as impermissible or late, the appellate authority would always decide the matter directly. It was authorised to overturn the opinion of the lower instance authority expressing its own opinion concerning the administrative decision and the reasons given. It could modify the contested administrative decision accordingly in any way it saw fit (s 66(4) AVG 1925). The appeal authority could not decide directly when the facts of a case presented before it were so incomplete that implementation or repetition of an oral hearing was deemed unavoidable. Then the appellate authority could remand the subject matter to a lower instance authority for a new hearing and issue a new administrative decision.

Admissible appeals filed on time had a suspensive effect; the competent authority could exclude the suspensive effect with an administrative decision.[76]

G. Obligation to Decide (*Entscheidungspflicht*)

The provision on the obligation to decide was 'entirely new'.[77] Unless otherwise stated in the administrative rules and regulations, the authorities had to issue an administrative decision on the submissions of parties and appeals without undue delay, and in any case no later than six months after receipt.[78]

If an administrative decision was not issued on time, the party could request that jurisdiction for the decision be passed to the appellate authority (in a request for transfer of jurisdiction). The request would be rejected if the delay was not principally due to a fault of the deciding authority.[79]

The competent parliament committee foresaw that the provision would be particularly important in questions of public liability since, at that time, there was no possibility of bringing an action before the Supreme Administrative Court due to the inactivity of an authority. However, it was evident that this provision would 'not miss its effect' thanks to the disciplinary and parliamentary accountability associated with it.[80]

[75] AVG 1925, s 63(2).
[76] ibid s 64.
[77] Committee Report (n 7) 21.
[78] AVG 1925, s 73(1) sentence 1.
[79] ibid s 73(2) sentences 1 and 3.
[80] Committee Report (n 7) 21.

IV. Summary

This chapter only introduced and discusses one part of the AVG 1925. Some rules were omitted, such as the service of documents, which was part of the AVG 1925. The serving of documents was regulated 'too broadly' by 11 regulations, as the Committee Report mentioned.[81] In 1982, a law on the serving of documents came into force. [82] Interestingly, the motives were similar to those leading to the AVG of 1925, namely overcoming the fragmentation of rules on serving documents and creating uniform rules to simplify the serving of documents for the postal service.[83]

Even before the AVG 1925 came into force, various administrative procedural regulations had been in place alongside the case law of the Supreme Administrative Court, in which it had developed administrative legal principles. The AVG 1925 sought to provide a uniform and simple procedural law that would enable authorities to apply it as comprehensively as possible.

At the time of its enactment, the AVG 1925 was both innovative and remarkably practice-oriented. It undoubtedly consolidated the concept of persons as parties and transformed the citizen from being the object to the subject of administrative proceedings. The success of the AVG can probably also be recognised insofar as the law was—and still is—a model for the procedural laws of other countries. Further, many fundamental changes introduced by the AVG 1925 have been maintained to this day with many regulations remaining unchanged.

[81] ibid 14.

[82] Service of Documents Act (*Bundesgesetz über die Zustellung behördlicher Dokumente—Zustellgesetz—ZustG*), StF: BGBl Nr 200/1982.

[83] Explanatory notes on the Service of Documents Act (*Erläuterungen zum Bundesgesetz über die Zustellung behördlicher Dokumente*), RV 162 AB 1050 p 8.

PART II

THE DIFFUSION OF ADMINISTRATIVE PROCEDURE LEGISLATION IN EUROPE (1920–1970)

National Reports

5

The Austrian Model and the Codification of Administrative Procedure in Liechtenstein

Emanuel Schädler

I. Introduction

This chapter provides an overview of how administrative procedure developed in Liechtenstein over the course of the last century, with a focus on the influence exerted by the 1925 Austrian General Administrative Procedure Act. The starting point is the legislation adopted in 1922. Its context is then considered. This is followed by discussion of the legal sources of administrative procedure. Next, some particular procedural requirements are examined in more detail.

II. The 1922 Administrative Procedure Legislation in Context

A. The 1922 *Landesverwaltungspflegegesetz*

Liechtenstein's law of administrative procedure[1] (*Landesverwaltungspflegegesetz* (LVG)) was published and enacted in its primary version[2] (*Stammfassung*) on 12 July 1922. From its enactment in 1922 until 1970, the LVG underwent 26 smaller amendments[3] with no substantial change. A hundred years on, the 1922 LVG is still in force and has remained—despite its critics and numerous efforts at reform[4]—largely unamended. Its full title may be translated as the 'law of general state administration (the administrative authorities and their auxiliary organs, the procedure in administrative matters, administrative enforcement procedure

[1] *Gesetz vom 21. April 1922 über die allgemeine Landesverwaltungspflege (die Verwaltungsbehörden und ihre Hilfsorgane, das Verfahren in Verwaltungssachen, das Verwaltungszwangs- und Verwaltungsstrafverfahren)*, LGBl 1922/24 [primary version].

[2] The primary (and current) version is accessible online at <www.gesetze.li> accessed 15 January 2022.

[3] The amendments are, chronologically: nine by LGBl 1925/8 (adaptation to the formation of the *Staatsgerichtshof* [Constitutional Court]); six by LGBl 1938/16; one by LGBl 1949/11 (adaptation to the formation of the *Verwaltungsbeschwerdeinstanz* [Higher Administrative Court]); one by LGBl 1963/18; nine by LGBl 1966/24 (adaptation to the law on official liability).

[4] For a detailed treatment, see E Schädler, 'Die Reformbemühungen um das Landesverwaltungspflegegesetz (LVG) in den Jahren 2014 bis 2018: Eine Falldokumentation' (2020)

Emanuel Schädler, *The Austrian Model and the Codification of Administrative Procedure in Liechtenstein* In: *The Austrian Codification of Administrative Procedure*. Edited by: Giacinto Della Cananea, Angela Ferrari Zumbini, and Otto Pfersmann, Oxford University Press. DOI: 10.1093/oso/9780198867623.003.0005

and administrative crime procedure)'. It therefore combines not only procedural and organisational law but also administrative procedure and proceedings of appeal. The code combines administration itself with administrative constraint, enforcement, crime, and their respective procedures. From the very beginning, it has sought to be the only basic law—a codification in the strict sense[5]—in Liechtenstein's general administration, to be supplemented with specific laws in areas of special administration.

B. The Legislative Intent: A Single Codification

Liechtenstein's administration is—contrary to those in its neighbouring states—a single-level administration with competence divided between the *Landesverwaltung* (state administration) and the *Gemeindeverwaltung* (communal administration).[6] The national administration essentially prevails and is in charge; communal administration only comes into play insofar as specific tasks are reserved or explicitly delegated to it.[7] However, with regard to the law of proceedings (and that of appeals), the LVG is applied as the *sedes materiae*. By way of exception, a special law in an area of special administrative law, which requires specialist knowledge (for example, taxes) or is politically highly sensitive (for example, real estate with trade and construction), can partly instate a procedure that deviates from the rules of the LVG. This especially concerns the organisational side of appeals rather than the procedure itself. Nevertheless, this partial deviation must be stated explicitly (and thus legislatively particularly justified), although all the principles and many other non-derogated procedural rules of the LVG always remain applicable in such divergent special cases.

The intention of the legislator to design the LVG as a codification of administrative law and procedure is one reason why it also became an especially detailed—in

<www.liechtenstein-institut.li/application/files/4815/9341/9788/Schadler_LVG-Reform_2014_bis_2018.pdf> accessed 14 August 2020.

[5] cf W Beck, 'Kommissionsbericht und Begründung zum Gesetzesentwurfe über die allgemeine Landesverwaltungspflege' (Von Dr. Beck) [20 pages; LI LA {Liechtenstein State Archive} DS 94/1922-1 A or DS 094/1922-001 A + B], 9: '*eine umfassende Regelung*'—a comprehensive regulation.

[6] According to art 1(1), first sentence of the Constitution, Liechtenstein consists of two regions with a total of 11 municipalities. See *Verfassung des Fürstentums Liechtenstein vom 5. Oktober 1921*, LGBl 1921/15 [primary version].

[7] For the communal competence under current legal situation, see art 4 (*Autonomie*, 'autonomy'; English translation: Within their own sphere of activity, the municipalities organise and manage their affairs independently under the supervision of the State. They perform tasks of the State within the delegated sphere of activity); art 12 (*Eigener Wirkungskreis*, 'own sphere of influence') and art 13 (*Übertragener Wirkungskreis*, 'delegated sphere of influence') *Gemeindegesetz (GemG) vom 20. März 1996*, LBGl 1996/76, LR 141.0. For the former legal situation in the time frame of the present investigation, see §§ 4–6 *Gemeindegesetz vom 24. Mai 1864*, LGBl 1864/4, and arts 4–6 *Gemeindegesetz vom 2. Dezember 1959*, LGBl 1960/2.

parts even casuistic—law. It is the most extensive administrative procedure law of the German-speaking countries,[8] consisting of 172 articles totalling about 35,000 words, so we might say that each article averages approximately 200 words. This is noticeably higher than Liechtenstein's other procedural laws: the Liechtenstein Code of Civil Procedure (*Zivilprozessordnung*) of 1912,[9] for example, consists of 616 paragraphs with about 48,800 words overall, meaning that on arithmetical average each article contains (in comparison: only) 80 words.

C. The Historical, Political, and Institutional Context

As was usual at that time in Liechtenstein, due to its generally limited state resources, the LVG of 1922 was mainly drawn up by one person and passed the legislative procedure with no noteworthy changes. Its creator was Wilhelm Beck[10] (1885–1936), a famous lawyer, politician, and publicist who influenced several important pieces of legislation at the time. Although the LVG was substantially an unquestioned, but even today not deeply clarified,[11] collection of foreign (mostly Austrian) drafts, law, and jurisprudence, the 1922 LVG became—from a merely chronological viewpoint, as Benjamin Schindler points out[12]—the first code of administrative procedure to be enacted in a German-speaking country. The Austrian General Administrative Procedure Act (AVG) 'followed' in 1925, with Switzerland in 1968, and Germany in 1976. Thus, the LVG is—so to speak—a paradoxical case of 'antecedent receipt' of (as mentioned above: even today not yet thoroughly clarified) Austrian (and other) sources by its creator Wilhelm Beck (for details, see Section IV.B below).

When the LVG was enacted in 1922, the Principality of Liechtenstein, with its 160 square kilometres, had around 9,000 inhabitants and was predominantly an agricultural State. The economy had stagnated, and the national budget was in deficit. Inflation had hit the Austrian Krone, which was also the national currency in

[8] A Kley, *Grundriss des liechtensteinischen Verwaltungsrechts* (LPS 23, VLAG 1998) 318.

[9] Austria's famous *Civilproceßordnung* of 1895 by Franz Klein was the model for the Liechtenstein *Zivilprozessordnung* of 1912, see E Schädler, *Prozessökonomie in der liechtensteinischen Zivilprozessordnung von 1912, Rezeption, Ausgestaltung und Konzept prozessökonomischer Mechanismen aus rechtshistorischer Sicht* (LPS 55, VLAG 2014).

[10] For biographical information, see G Leipold-Schneider, 'Beck, Wilhelm' eHLFL (version 31 December 2011) <https://historisches-lexikon.li/Beck,_Wilhelm> accessed 14 August 2020.

[11] For further detail, see Emanuel Schädler, 'Zur Herkunft des Landesverwaltungspflegegesetzes: eine überprüfende Rekonstruktion' in Liechtenstein-Institut and Historischer Verein für das Fürstentum Liechtenstein (eds), *Geschichte erforschen—Geschichte vermitteln, Festschrift zum 75. Geburtstag von Peter Geiger und Rupert Quaderer* (LPS 59, VLAG 2017).

[12] B Schindler, 'Die Kodifikation des Verwaltungsverfahrens in der Schweiz' (2013) 35 ZNR 1/2, 33, 35 (with fn 12) and 39 (with fn 47)—also referred to in Emanuel Schädler, *Für ein historisch-kritisches Verständnis des Verfahrensrechts, Versuch einer Apologie anhand von Beispielen aus dem Landesverwaltungspflegegesetz* (Arbeitspapiere LI 54, LI 2016) <https://www.liechtenstein-institut.li/application/files/2215/7435/3621/LIAP_54_Schadler_Verfahrensrecht.pdf> accessed 14 August 2020, 52 fn 280 with further information.

Liechtenstein at the time. Throughout the 'long' nineteenth century, Liechtenstein was connected—not least because of the proximity of its reigning princely house with the Habsburg dynasty—to Austria-Hungary in terms of foreign affairs, its economy (eg through their 1852 customs treaty), and even culturally. The formation of political parties in Liechtenstein after 1914 catalysed domestic controversies regarding the modernisation of the State, and, in the aftermath of the First World War, Liechtenstein realigned itself with Switzerland (with a diplomatic legation in Bern from 1919 to 1933, and 1944 to 1969, as well as a customs treaty in 1924, and the de facto use of the Swiss franc as its national currency).[13]

The years after the First World War were marked by debate regarding a new constitution: the one in force at the time was still the *Konstitutionelle Verfassung* of 1862, which was, in many respects, outdated. For example, it contained only a 'symbolic concession' (Andreas Kley) of fundamental rights without justiciability,[14] appeals were brought before foreign (ie Austrian) courts in Vienna and Innsbruck;[15] and the reigning prince was the 'personified executive', exclusively regulating the administration through princely decrees and appointing a foreigner as *Landesverweser* ([Princely] State Administrator) to lead the administration in situ on his behalf as *Fürstliche* Regierung (*Princely* Government).[16] The *Konstitutionelle Verfassung* of 1862—despite much progressive wording—did not yet establish Liechtenstein as a fully independent State. It lacked effective democratic elements and real legal protection.

After much political wrangling,[17] these criticisms eventually resulted in the new Constitution[18] of 1921 (known simply as the *Verfassung* (LV)), which was published and enacted on 24 October 1921. It is, following a constitutional amendment of 2003, still in force today. Its famous core, in art 2, with its 'doubled' sovereignty (Prince and People), states:

> The Principality [of Liechtenstein] is a constitutional, hereditary monarchy on a democratic and parliamentary basis [. . .] the power of the State is embodied in the Reigning Prince and the People and shall be exercised by both under the conditions set forth in the provisions of this constitution.[19]

[13] For the previous paragraph: Schädler (n 12) 16–17.

[14] For a historical overview, see Andreas Kley, 'Geschichtliche Entwicklung der Grundrechte in Liechtenstein' in Andreas Kley and Klaus A Vallender (eds), *Grundrechtspraxis in Liechtenstein* (LPS 52, VLAG 2012) especially 20–23 for the *Konstitutionelle Verfassung* of 1862.

[15] See H Wille, 'Liechtenstein' in Werner Daum (ed), *Handbuch der europäischen Verfassungsgeschichte im 19. Jahrhundert, Institutionen und Rechtspraxis im gesellschaftlichen Wandel, Band 3: 1848–1870*, 1057–59.

[16] ibid 1054–55.

[17] For the whole historical context of the enactment of the 1921 Constitution, see the in-depth investigation by R Quaderer-Vogt, *Bewegte Zeiten in Liechtenstein, 1914 bis 1926*, vol 2 (Chronos and VHVFL 2014) 221–324.

[18] See (n 6) for the full citation.

[19] In the original wording:

The LVG followed one year after the Constitution, in 1922, and was the first law of many to fill the new constitutional framework[20] with national legislation. The 1921 Constitution set up some requirements for the LVG's prospective administrative procedure, some of which were restatements from the *Konstitutionelle Verfassung* of 1862 (which should now, in 1921 and in the future, also be realised in practice), while others were totally new so as to transform Liechtenstein into a modern '*Rechtsstaat*'[21] with particular focus on basic procedural rights.

III. Sources of Law for Administrative Procedure

After illustrating the background, the main sources of administrative procedure will be considered. Arguably, the principle of *Rechtsstaat* is at the centre stage of both the Constitution and the legislative framework governing remedies against public authorities.

A. Constitutional Principles and Requirements

Adopting almost the same wording as para 19 in the previous *Konstitutionelle Verfassung* of 1862, the 1921 Constitution restated a right to appeal in art 43 LV. However, whereas under the *Konstitutionelle Verfassung* this right was a *lex imperfecta* and of merely symbolic importance, art 43 of the 1921 Constitution became the core of the new comprehensive legal protection for every Liechtenstein citizen according to the *Rechtsstaat* (for further details, see Section V below):

> The right of complaint shall be guaranteed. Every citizen shall be entitled to lodge a complaint regarding any action or procedure on the part of a public authority that is contrary to the constitution, the law, or ordinances and that is detrimental to his rights or interests. Such complaint may be addressed to the immediate superior authority and may, if necessary, be pursued to the highest authority, to the extent that the stages of recourse are not limited by law. If a complaint thus submitted is rejected by the superior authority, the superior authority shall be required to disclose to the complainant the reasons for its decision.[22]

> Das Fürstentum [Liechtenstein] ist eine konstitutionelle Erbmonarchie auf demokratischer und parlamentarischer Grundlage [...] die Staatsgewalt ist im Fürsten und im Volke verankert und wird von beiden nach Massgabe der Bestimmungen dieser Verfassung ausgeübt.

[20] Beck (n 5) 4.

[21] Wilhelm Beck starts the legislative commission report for the LVG with the words (in English translation): 'The new constitution reflects the spirit of the "Rechtsstaat"' Beck (n 5) 1.

[22] In the wording of the primary version of the Constitution:

> Das Recht der Beschwerdeführung ist gewährleistet. Jeder Landesangehörige ist berechtigt, über das seine Rechte oder Interessen benachteiligende verfassungs-,

This far-reaching[23] right to appeal, supplemented by a requirement to state reasons at the end of the wording (see Section V.C below), required different organisational and procedural modifications in order to become a *lex perfecta* in the future.

One change in the 1921 Constitution was the provision—in terms of nationalisation and national independence—that all courts (art 101(1) LV)[24] and authorities (art 108 sentence 2 LV)[25] would now be transferred to Liechtenstein and would no longer be located in Vienna or Innsbruck. The structural composition of the government remained unchanged, with one head of government (now the *Regierungschef* instead of the former *Landesverweser* ([Princely] State Administrator) and two Members of the Government Council (*Regierungsräte*), plus one deputy each (art 79(1) sentence 1 LV).[26] Subject to exceptional approval by Parliament, the *Regierungschef* and his deputy had to be native to Liechtenstein (art 79(1) sentences 3–4 LV).[27] In addition, again subject to exceptional approval by Parliament, citizenship of Liechtenstein was a condition of employment in the Liechtenstein civil service (art 107 LV),[28] and the majority of appointments to collegial authorities were to be held by Liechtenstein citizens (art 108 second sentence LV).[29]

Furthermore, the principle of legality was enshrined in the 1921 Constitution through art 92(2) LV:

> The entire State administration in general must remain within the limits of the Constitution and other laws; even in those matters where the law grants

> gesetz- oder verordnungswidrige Benehmen oder Verfahren einer Behörde bei der ihr unmittelbar vorgesetzten Stelle Beschwerde zu erheben und dies nötigenfalls bis zur höchsten Stelle zu verfolgen, soweit nicht eine gesetzliche Beschränkung des Rechtsmittelzuges entgegensteht. Wird die eingebrachte Beschwerde von der vorgesetzten Stelle verworfen, so ist diese verpflichtet, dem Beschwerdeführer die Gründe ihrer Entscheidung zu eröffnen.

[23] See T M Wille, 'Beschwerderecht' in Andreas Kley and Klaus A Vallender (eds), *Grundrechtspraxis in Liechtenstein* (LPS 52, VLAG 2012), especially 507–09, for the history of the origin of art 43 LV.

[24] In English translation: 'In the first instance, jurisdiction is exercised by the Princely First Instance Court in Vaduz, in the second instance by the Princely High Court in Vaduz and in the third instance by the Princely Supreme Court'.

[25] In English translation: 'All authorities must be relocated to the country'.

[26] In English translation: 'The government consists of the head of government and two government councillors and as many deputies in case of prevention'.

[27] In English translation:

> Both [the head of government and his deputy] must be native Liechtenstein citizens. A deviation concerning the head of government is only permissible if the Parliament decides in favour of it by a three-quarter majority vote.

[28] In English translation:

> For employment in the Liechtenstein civil service, Liechtenstein citizenship is required, regardless of more extensive provisions of this constitution; exceptions may be made only with the consent of Parliament.

[29] In English translation: 'collegial authorities must consist of at least a majority of Liechtenstein citizens'.

free discretion to the administration, the limits set by the laws must be strictly observed.[30]

Art 81(3) 3 LVG refers to this explicitly: 'as with all other decisions or orders, the authority must comply with the provisions of the constitution, laws and regulations in force (*article 92 of the constitution*)'.[31]

As a task of the State, the Constitution stated in art 27(1) LV *expressis verbis* that:

> [t]he State shall ensure that proceedings and enforcement proceedings are conducted expeditiously and in a manner that protects the substantive law, and that administrative justice is administered in accordance with the same principles.[32]

The second half of the last sentence on administrative justice, at the end of art 27(1) LV, was decisive from the viewpoint of the *Rechtsstaat* and comprehensive legal protection. Perhaps this is why this wording was placed so conspicuously at the end of the paragraph. This was a crucial new point. Instead of the previous *Verwaltungspflege* (administration) and the mere symbolic right to appeal, a *Verwaltungsrechtspflege* (administrative justice (by authorities or special units)) and even a *Verwaltungsgerichtsbarkeit* (administrative jurisdiction (by independent courts)) in the form of a sequence of instances had now been created.

B. Levels of Appeal

The levels of appeal in administrative matters set up by the 1921 Constitution reflect and manifest the interplay of all the above-mentioned constitutional principles and requirements of the *Rechtsstaat*.

[30] In the wording of the primary version of the constitution:

> Die gesamte Landesverwaltung überhaupt hat sich innerhalb der Schranken der Verfassung und der übrigen Gesetze zu bewegen, auch in jenen Angelegenheiten, in welchen das Gesetz der Verwaltung ein freies Ermessen einräumt, sind die demselben durch die Gesetze gezogenen Grenzen strenge zu beobachten.

[31] 'wie auch bei allen sonstigen Entscheidungen oder Verfügungen hat sich die Behörde an die Vorschriften der Verfassung, der Gesetze und gültigen Verordnungen zu halten (*Art. 92 der Verfassung*).' See the same constitutional reference at the end of art 81(4) LVG, concerning the exercise of discretion by the authorities.

[32] In the wording of the primary version of the Constitution:

> Der Staat sorgt für ein rasches, das materielle Recht schützendes Prozess- und Vollstreckungsverfahren, ebenso für eine den gleichen Grundsätzen angepasste Verwaltungsrechtspflege.

The ordinary sequence of appeals[33] in administrative matters is generally organised in three stages. The deciding authority is a municipality, the government or, later, an independent office of the government. An appeal can be lodged against its decision with the government or, later, a special appeals commission on the government's behalf. If this decision is challenged, the case is referred to the Higher Administrative Court [of Appeal] (*Verwaltungsbeschwerdeinstanz* (VBI))[34] as the highest *ordinary* court in administrative matters. As an independent administrative court, the VBI was a crucial innovation in the 1921 Constitution.[35] Thus, art 97(1) LV required that '[u]nless the law provides otherwise, all decisions or orders of the government are subject to appeal to the *Verwaltungsbeschwerde-Instanz* to be established'.[36]

In the sequence of appeals, this was followed, from 1925,[37] by the *extraordinary* jurisdiction of the Constitutional Court (*Staatsgerichtshof* (StGH) which—from the 1921 perspective and according to the wording of the Constitution (arts 104–106 LV)—was also to be established in the future. The StGH had some special administrative court functions (art 104(2) sentence 2 LV), but its main purpose was to protect constitutionally guaranteed rights (art 104(1) LV) and to review the constitutionality of decrees (art 104(2) sentence 1 LV).

IV. The Relevance of Austrian Ideas and Institutions

When considering administrative procedure legislation, both Austrian legal culture and institutions have been of relevance. The first aspect is relatively well known, the second less so.

A. The Influence of Kelsen's Theory

As far as understanding the sources of law is concerned, in the first half of the twentieth century, Liechtenstein's legal system was profoundly influenced by two concepts formulated by Austrian jurist Hans Kelsen (1881–1973): the *Stufenbau der Rechtsordnung* (staged structure of the legal system) and an overall corresponding

[33] For the levels of appeal according to the current legal situation, see Emanuel Schädler, *Tafeln zum Landesverwaltungspflegegesetz (LVG) samt Gliederung des LVG im Anhang* (LI 2018)<www.liechtenstein-institut.li/application/files/2315/7435/5600/Schadler_Emanuel_Tafeln_zum_LVG.pdf> accessed 22 August 2020, table 1 '*Instanzen*'.

[34] In 2003, the VBI was modernised and renamed '*Verwaltungsgerichtshof*' (abbreviated: VGH).

[35] Beck (n 5) 3 and 5.

[36] 'Soweit das Gesetz nichts anderes bestimmt, unterliegen sämtliche Entscheidungen oder Verfügungen der Regierung dem Rechtsmittel der Beschwerde an die zu errichtende Verwaltungsbeschwerde-Instanz.'

[37] See *Gesetz vom 5. November 1925 über den Staatsgerichtshof*, LGBl 1925/8.

legal positivism.[38] (Maybe also for this reason, in 1929, Kelsen was appointed as an expert and gave a written expert opinion in a dispute over the interpretation of the Liechtenstein Constitution based on a conflict regarding the 'political' staffing of the VBI.)[39]

Liechtenstein's Constitution of 1921 was drafted in strict adherence to a positivistic *Stufenbau der Rechtsordnung*. The highest-ranking Constitution defines the binding framework[40] for the simple lower laws (*Gesetze*) enacted by Parliament, assigning them their compulsory tasks; the laws do the same for the lower government decrees (*Verordnungen*). The authorities and/or the courts complete the legal order at the lowest stage with administrative acts or judgments.[41] Together, they form a consistent and complete legal system composed of written, 'positive' law. Besides this, there is no other (noteworthy) source of law. This was the prevailing view in the period covered by this study. (As a reference point for comparison, only in the late 1970s did the StGH very cautiously begin to develop as key constitutional content a modern interpretation of fundamental rights, gradually abandoning the purely positivist viewpoint that had prevailed over previous decades.)[42] In terms of administrative procedure, this means all the provisions mentioned in the Constitution and, based on this, in the LVG (see Sections III.A–B above)—but only written positive provisions—were relevant. Apart from this, there were no other sources of law for administrative procedure.

B. Austrian and Domestic Administrative Procedure Legislation

An informative legislative commission report[43] written by its president Wilhelm Beck has survived, the first part of which was also published in the local newspaper.[44] Here, he initially states that in drafting the LVG:

> [i]t was intended to include only good and proven material, especially from German single state, Swiss and Austrian circumstances and in a manner suitable

[38] See for example (published systematically later on, in 1934) H Kelsen, *Reine Rechtslehre, Einleitung in die rechtswissenschaftliche Problematik* (1st edn, Deuticke 1934) 1 (first sentence: '*Die Reine Rechtslehre ist eine Theorie des positiven Rechts*.' English translation: 'The pure legal doctrine is a theory of positive law'; cf ibid 38: '*Die Reine Rechtslehre ist die Theorie des Rechtspositivismus*'. English translation: 'The pure legal doctrine is the theory of legal positivism') and 74–82 (legal stages).

[39] See P Bussjäger, 'Hans Kelsen und der Verfassungsstreit in Liechtenstein' in Clemens Jabloner and others (eds), *Das internationale Wirken Hans Kelsens* (Schriftenreihe des Hans-Kelsen-Instituts 38, Manz 2016), with a printed version of the expert opinion itself.

[40] Thus, literally, Kelsen, *Reine Rechtslehre* (n 38) 94–95.

[41] ibid 79–80 and 98.

[42] E Schädler, 'Die EMRK in der Grundrechtsgeschichte Liechtensteins' [2018] LJZ 125.

[43] See Beck (n 5).

[44] *Oberrheinische Nachrichten* of 12 April 1922, 1 [= 1–5 of the commission report].

for our authorities and the country; foreign laws, drafts and administrative decisions have been taken into account.

Regarding Austria, Beck mentions only Rudolf Herrmann von Herrnritt's *Grundlehren des Verwaltungsrechtes mit vorzugsweiser Berücksichtigung der in Österreich (Nachfolgestaaten) geltenden Rechtsordnung und Praxis* (Tübingen 1921, 555 pages)[45] adding *usw* (ie and so on). No more precise information about sources can be found either in Beck's published writings or in his documentary bequest. Consequently, we rely on circumstantial evidence. At least there is an indication that Wilhelm Beck was specifically influenced by Austrian administrative procedure and doctrine as a model when drawing up the LVG. The bequeathed volumes of his library include—besides the said Herrnritt's *Grundlehren*—Friedrich Tezner's *Handbuch des österreichischen Administrativverfahrens*,[46] and *Das österreichische Administrativverfahren, Dargestellt aufgrund der verwaltungsgerichtlichen Praxis*[47] as well as some later books by Tezner and a later Austrian administrative law collection.[48] In chronological terms, at least the first-mentioned and perhaps also the second book may have been used by Beck in drafting the LVG in 1922. As Tezner systematically recorded and presented in his books the rich judicature and case law of the Austrian Administrative Court since 1876, which at that time also served as a replacement for a missing corresponding codification, Beck may well have taken these works into account.

C. A Preliminary Austrian Draft?

Due to this situation, the dominant (and long unchallenged) opinion among scholars was that the LVG was largely Wilhelm Beck's adaptation of one of the several preliminary drafts for an AVG in Austria before the First World War—thus solving the chronological paradox (Liechtenstein 1922 versus Austria 1925) of antecedent receipt. While (further) work on the AVG in Austria was delayed because of the war, Liechtenstein enacted the LVG based on Austria's preliminary works. However, a review[49] of this plausible opinion shows that things are not so simple. Among the preliminary drafts in the Austrian State Archives in Vienna (ie credited to leading figures: 1913 Erwin von Schwartzenau; 1914 Edmund

[45] Beck (n 5) 3.
[46] Vienna 1896, 533 pp.
[47] Published in Vienna (Österreichische Staatsdruckerei, 1922), 788 pp.
[48] E Mannlicher and E Coreth (eds), *Die Gesetze zur Vereinfachung der Verwaltung, Verwaltungsverfahrensgesetze und Verwaltungsentlastungsgesetz* […] *Nach dem Stande vom 30. September 1925* (Österreichische Staatsdruckerei 1926) [744 pp].
[49] For details, see Schädler (n 11), 164–74.

Bernatzik; 1918 Maximilian Schuster von Bonnot; and 1919 Robert Davy), there are no neutral elements of procedure (concept of party, assessment of evidence, right to be heard, access to file, and information on remedies) that completely provide a basis of receipt of the LVG. On the contrary, considering their conformities, the Code of Civil Procedure (the Austrian one by Franz Klein in 1895 and that of Liechtenstein by Gustav Walker in 1912) can also be considered as an additional basis of receiving. The striking fact remains that much of the wording of the LVG corresponds to the Austrian AVG of 1925.[50]

A retired administrative expert repeated the assumption he had heard: the LVG, in the version that was enacted, was still the largely unamended draft that Wilhelm Beck had rapidly put together as a patchwork. Maybe Beck's own wording takes up more space than may be imagined; in the legislative commission report, he mentions that he tried to turn existing administrative practice into legal regulations, to *legalise* it.[51] The urgency of the LVG's enactment supports the assumption of the unamended draft. As the (resigning) *Regierungschef*, Josef Ospelt objected in a newspaper article *ex post*: 'It is certain that hardly anywhere else in the world would a law of this importance and scope be passed with such haste and without the reliable participation of experts.'[52]

D. Judicial and Academic Attitudes

It should be recalled that the national jurisdiction of the newly established domestic courts had to start from zero in the light of the 1921 Constitution. No special reference can be found to the Austrian[53] AVG or its principles in cases before the VBI and the StGH. Perhaps strict and exclusive reliance on Liechtenstein's domestic law represents an attempt by the courts to assert and present themselves emphatically as operating in an independent legal system proper to Liechtenstein.

In the period of interest here, there were no universities or comparable institutions teaching or researching Liechtenstein law. Nor did any important publications exist except for a few dissertations[54] from foreign universities; however, they do not concern the Austrian AVG specifically.

50 For a listing, see Kley (n 8) 22 with fn 21.

51 Beck (n 5) 4, highlighting in the original.

52 See *Liechtensteiner Volksblatt* of 17 May 1922, 1.

53 Whereas there are some references to Swiss teaching and case law in the later period: see for example StGH 1947/17 of 18 September 1947 or VBI 1965/31 of 23 November 1965.

54 Worth mentioning are: OL Marxer, *Die Organisation der obersten Staatsorgane in Liechtenstein* ([University of Innsbruck] 1924) [95 pages]; K Ritter, *Die Ausgestaltung der Verwaltungsgerichtsbarkeit im Fürstentum Liechtenstein* ([University of Bern] Buch- & Verlagsdruckerei Vaduz 1958) [159 pp].

V. The Main Procedural Requirements

Administrative procedure legislation in Liechtenstein not only includes—but also emphasises and divides into 'fine ramifications'—the following four elements:[55] (1) completeness of the preliminary investigation and fact finding, (2) the right to a hearing, (3) the giving reasons requirement, and—importantly—(4) the organisation of remedies.

A. Completeness of the Preliminary Investigation and Fact Finding

In the (regular) investigation procedure, the LVG aims at a thorough or exhaustive investigation of the facts[56] (art 27(1) letter a LVG) and contains detailed rules in arts 54–77 (*A. Das Ermittlungsverfahren [Instruktionsverfahren]* concerning the investigation procedure [instruction procedure]). The investigation procedure, according to art 54(1) LVG:

> is aimed at the precise investigation of the parties involved, the identification of possible points of dispute, the clarification of the factual and legal circumstances of an administrative matter, the collection and gathering of evidence by the official in charge of the proceedings (chief negotiator) which is requested or deemed necessary for the taking of a decision or issuing of an order.[57]

Therefore, art 58(2) LVG (marginalia: '*Beschaffung des Prozessstoffes*', procurement of the process material) establishes the (essentially prevailing) principle of investigation,[58] and para 3 repeats the aim of the procedure regarding its leading actor from this viewpoint:

> 2) Insofar as the investigations required to clarify the facts of the case are required by official duty to safeguard interests to be protected by law and to ensure that they are satisfied under the purpose and law, they shall be carried out

[55] For an orientation based on a (German) keyword list, see E Schädler, *Index zum Landesverwaltungspflegegesetz* (LI 2018) <www.liechtenstein-institut.li/application/files/5815/7435/5613/Index_LVG_def2.pdf> accessed 11 September 2020.

[56] 'gründlich[e] oder erschöpfend[e] Erhebung des Sachverhaltes'.

[57] 'bezweckt die genaue Erforschung der Beteiligten, die Feststellung der allfälligen Streitpunkte, die allseitige Abklärung der tatsächlichen und rechtlichen Verhältnisse einer Verwaltungssache, die Sammlung und Erhebung der beantragten oder zur Fällung einer Entscheidung oder Erlassung einer Verfügung von amtswegen nötig erachteter Beweismittel durch den prozessleitenden Beamten (Verhandlungsleiter).' cf § 37 AVG.

[58] Whereas para 1 of the same provision correspondingly states a (moderate) principle of negotiation within the limits of public law.

by official channels and independently of applications, confessions, acknowledgements or waivers by the parties. (*Principle of investigation*)[59]

3) The official in charge of the hearing shall, while observing [paras 1 and 2], endeavour to ensure that the facts are clarified and that the parties make appropriate requests to that effect.[60]

B. The Right to a Hearing

Regarding the right to a hearing, there are two important provisions in the LVG in the section on the regular[61] administrative procedure. Article 64(3) LVG (marginalia: '*Parteiengehör*', parties hearing) states that:

> [e]ach party must be given the opportunity to express its views on all facts and circumstances relevant to the settlement of the subject of the proceedings, facts and circumstances brought forward by other parties, by witnesses and by experts or officially questioned, as well as on requests made by other parties, experts and witnesses, and to protect its rights and interests.[62]

And art 81(1) LVG (marginalia: '*Schranken für die Entscheidung*', limitations to the decisions) mirrors this statement from the authority's perspective:

> In the final proceedings, the government may not base its decision on facts and evidence of which the persons concerned have not been informed and have not been given the opportunity to make their views known, either in the preliminary proceedings or in the final proceedings.[63]

Two more provisions in the section of the appeal procedure extend this right to a hearing, mainly due to the broad admissibility of novenas, also to the appeal stage.

[59] '2) Soweit die zur Aufklärung des Sachverhaltes erforderlichen Erhebungen durch Amtspflicht zur Wahrung von gesetzeswegen zu schützender Interessen und zur zweck- und gesetzmässigen Art ihrer Befriedigung gefordert werden, sind sie von amtswegen und unabhängig von Anträgen, Geständnissen, Anerkenntnissen oder Verzichten der Parteien zu pflegen. (Untersuchungsgrundsatz).'

[60] '3) Der die Verhandlung leitende Beamte hat unter Beobachtung [von Absatz 1 und 2] darauf hinzuwirken, dass der Sachverhalt vollständig geklärt wird und von den Parteien hierauf gerichtete zweckdienliche Anträge gestellt werden.'

[61] For the administrative coercion procedure, see art 145(4)–(5) LVG.

[62] 'Jeder Partei muss Gelegenheit geboten werden, sich über alle für die Erledigung des Verhandlungsgegenstandes massgebenden, von andern Parteien, von Zeugen und Sachverständigen vorgebrachten oder von amtswegen zur Frage gestellten Tatsachen und Verhältnisse, sowie über die von andern Parteien, von Sachverständigen und Zeugen gestellten Anträge zu äussern und überhaupt ihre Rechte und Interessen entsprechend zu wahren.' cf (with a similar wording) § 43(3) 3 AVG.

[63] 'Die Regierung darf im Schlussverfahren ihre Entscheidung nicht auf Tatsachen und Beweismittel stützen, über die den beteiligten Personen nicht Kenntnis gegeben und nicht Gelegenheit zu ihrer Äusserung, sei es im Ermittlungsverfahren oder sei es im Schlussverfahren, geboten worden ist.'

Article 99(4) LVG (marginalia: '*Neue Tatsachen und Beweismittel*', new facts and evidence) explicitly refers to the right to a hearing according to art 64 LVG: 'if the [VBI] wishes to base its decision on a substantially new fact not yet discussed with the parties, it may use this only after hearing them (art 64)'.[64] And art 106(6) LVG (marginalia: '*Die Nichtigerklärung [Kassation]*', the annulment [cassation]) stipulates that the parties must be heard before a new decision is taken and must be informed both of the decision and annulment.[65]

C. The Duty to Give Reasons

The general starting point for the 'requirement to give reasons' is the Constitution. In art 43 sentence 3 LV (see Section III.A above), at the end of the right of complaint, is a 'mirrored' statement of reasons requirement: 'If a complaint thus submitted is rejected by the superior authority, the superior authority shall be required to disclose to the complainant the reasons for its decision.'[66] Although—strictly speaking—the wording merely lays down an obligation for the appeal instance to state reasons (only) in the event of rejection, a general obligation to state reasons is derived from it and generally accepted; for the citizen it is a justiciable right.[67] Specifically for the Liechtenstein courts and their judges, art 99(2) sentence 2 LV[68] of the Constitution additionally states: 'They [the courts] shall include grounds with their decisions and judgments'.[69]

For the (regular) administrative procedure, art 83 (marginalia: 'More detailed provisions on the content of the decision')[70] paras 3 and 4 LVG specify:

> 3) The requirement to state the reasons for the decision is only satisfied if the decision indicates the legal principles applied by the authority in the case decided, and if the reasons show the intention to justify in a convincing manner the decision taken.[71]

[64] 'Die Beschwerdeinstanz darf, wenn sie ihrer Entscheidung einen wesentlich neuen, bisher mit den Parteien nicht erörterten Tatbestand als massgebend zugrunde legen will, diesen Tatbestand nur nach deren Anhörung (Art 64) benutzen.'

[65] 'Die Beteiligten sind vor Erlass einer neuen Entscheidung zu hören und sowohl von dieser Entscheidung als auch von der Aufhebung zu verständigen.'

[66] 'Wird die eingebrachte Beschwerde von der vorgesetzten Stelle verworfen, so ist diese verpflichtet, dem Beschwerdeführer die Gründe ihrer Entscheidung zu eröffnen.'

[67] See on the whole topic, TM Wille, 'Begründungspflicht' in A Kley and K A Vallender (eds), *Grundrechtspraxis in Liechtenstein* (LPS 52, VLAG 2012).

[68] cf the same wording in art 95(2) sentence 2 LV in its current version.

[69] 'Sie [die Gerichte] haben ihren Entscheidungen und Urteilen Gründe beizufügen.'

[70] 'Nähere Bestimmungen über den Entscheidungsinhalt'.

[71] '3) Dem Erfordernisse der Begründung der Entscheidung ist nur dann genügt, wenn darin die von der Behörde in dem entschiedenen Falle zur Anwendung gebrachten Rechtssätze angeführt sind und wenn die Begründung die Absicht erkennen lässt, die getroffene Entscheidung in überzeugender Weise zu rechtfertigen.' cf § 60 AVG.

4) In particular, the reasons for the decision must indicate the considerations on which the authority has based its assessment of the evidence.[72]

In the LVG, some further and specifying provisions in the context of the requirement to give reasons concern types[73] of procedure other than the regular administrative procedure. Noteworthy among these is the appeal procedure, with these provisions: in the case of an *Amtsbeschwerde* (official complaint), the representative of public law, for example, has to state the reasons for lodging the complaint (art 92(3) LVG).[74] A special presentation of the reasons for a decision may only be omitted if—and to the extent that—there is agreement on these points between the appeal instance and the lower instance, which must be expressly mentioned in the decision (art 101(4) LVG).[75] In response to a request for leniency or a report, the intervening person must be given a reasoned explanation (art 109(4) LVG).[76]

D. The Organisation of Remedies

As described above, the 1921 Constitution established multilevel legal protection on administrative matters, including the VBI independent administrative court and the extraordinary jurisdiction of the StGH. This organisational side was complemented by a procedural side, with three tendencies corresponding to the ideas of a complete (in retrospect: rather exuberant) *Rechtsstaat*: first, a wide range of remedies; second, greater legitimacy of complaints; third, a comprehensive cognition of the courts.

In a comical turn of phrase, instead of *Rechtsstaat*, Liechtenstein was also called a *Rechtsmittelstaat* by former VBI President Gregor Steger, ie a state of remedies. Indeed, in Section IV (on the review procedure [appeals])[77] (arts 89–109 LVG), the LVG contains a wide range of remedies[78] as shown in Table 1.

[72] '4) Insbesondere muss aus den Entscheidungsgründen hervorgehen von welchen Erwägungen die Behörde sich bei der Beweiswürdigung hat leiten lassen.' cf § 60 AVG.

[73] See for the administrative coercion procedure, art 117(7) LVG; for the administrative crime procedure, see art 148(4)–(5), art 153(5), and art 159(1) LVG.

[74] 'unter Angabe von Gründen'.

[75] 'Eine besondere Darstellung […] der Entscheidungsgründe darf nur dann entfallen, wenn und insoweit eine Übereinstimmung in diesen Punkten zwischen der Beschwerdeinstanz und der Unterinstanz obwaltet, was in der Entscheidung ausdrücklich zu erwähnen ist.' cf art 43 sentence 3 LV ('if […] rejected'); cf also *e contrario* § 58(2) AVG.

[76] 'Auf ein Nachsichtsgesuch oder eine Anzeige ist der einschreitenden Person eine begründete Erledigung zu geben.'

[77] 'IV. Abschnitt: Das Überprüfungsverfahren (Rechtsmittel).'

[78] See also Kley (n 8) 275–83.

Table 1 Appeals/Remedies in the LVG

	Rechtsmittel/Rechtsbehelf	*Appeal/remedy*	*Article LVG*
A.	*Die Vorstellung* (Remonstration)	Presentation (remonstration)	89
B.	*Die Verwaltungsbeschwerde (Rekurs)*	Appeal (recourse)	90–103
C.	*Die Wiederherstellung (Wiedereinsetzung und Wiederaufnahme)*	Restoration (reinstatement and reopening)	104–105
D.	*Die Nichtigerklärung (Kassation)*	Annulment (cassation)	106
E.	*Die Einstellung (Sistierung)*	Abatement (suspension)	107
F.	*Die Erläuterung*	Explanation	108
G.	*Nachsichtsgesuche. Anzeigen*	Requests for leniency. Notifications	109
–	*Aufsichtsbeschwerde*	Supervisory appeal	23, 136(2)
–	*Einspruch/Einsprache*	Opposition	50, 149

The appeals-related terms vary in the LVG; sometimes there are common abbreviations of *verba legalia* ('*Beschwerde*' for '*Verwaltungsbeschwerde*'), synonyms ('*Nichtigerklärung*' or '*Kassation*') or differentiations (slight, but meaningless, between '*Vorstellung*' and '*Remonstration*'; confusion between '*Wiederherstellung*' and '*Wiedereinsetzung*' respectively '*Wiederaufnahme*'). It is also impossible to state clearly whether these are informal legal remedies (*Rechtsbehelf*) or a formal appeal (*Rechtsmittel*) or a mixture of the two.[79] This is further complicated by the sometimes opaque competitive relationships between the various forms, which are often cumulative. For example, art 89(5) LVG states [regarding cumulation: i–v] that:

> In addition to the [i] presentation an [ii] objection and an [iii/a] appeal ([iii/b] supervisory complaint), [iv] requests for leniency, which invoke the kindness of the higher authority, or [v/a] applications for postponement of enforcement or [v/b] similar can be submitted.[80]

Some other articles[81] contain similar cumulative explanations with no clarification regarding all the possible combinations.

79 See ibid 275.

80 'Mit der Vorstellung können ausser dem Einspruch und der Beschwerde (Aufsichtsbeschwerde), Nachsichtsgesuche, welche die Güte der Oberbehörde anrufen, oder Gesuche um Aufschub der Vollstreckung oder ähnliches eingebracht werden.'

81 See for example art 89(1) LVG, art 90(3) LVG, or art 109(2) LVG.

Based on the (strongly positivistic) principle of legality as it was enshrined in the 1921 Constitution by art 92(2) LV[82] (see Section III.A above), this multiplicity of remedies/appeals and their differentiation are perhaps also an effect of the influence of pure legal doctrine and especially what Adolf Julius Merkl (1890–1970), a student of Hans Kelsen's, recorded under the concept of the *Fehlerkalkül*[83] (error calculus). In brief, the legal system determines when an act does not meet its qualitative requirements; it determines what legal consequences this has and whether/how this can/must be remedied. The error calculus—according to Merkl—also expresses itself through the introduction of legal remedies to remove defective acts[84] whereby the provision of positive legal remedies, if they contain an error calculus, already achieves actual remedial effect.[85] The Liechtenstein legislator developed this approach quantitatively with a variety of remedies. And the legal figure of subjective public rights, which was also booming in the jurisprudence in 1922 and formed an echo of the discussions on administrative jurisdiction at the end of the nineteenth century, served as his catalysing legal policy background.[86] Again, among Wilhelm Beck's bequeathed library there is a copy (unfortunately with no personal notes or markings) of Georg Jellinek's *System der subjektiven öffentlichen Rechte* (Tübingen 1919, 366 pages), which is the second edition from 1905 as a reprint from the year 1919. Unsurprisingly, in the legislative commission report, Beck mentions and thus emphasises the *subjektive Rechte* (ie the subjective [public] rights [as justiciable rights]) at the very beginning.[87] Subjective public rights as justiciable rights of the citizens were now to be developed under the regime of the 1921 Constitution to reflect the new[88] administrative court organisation, after they had previously been granted only to subjects on a declaratory basis under the 1862 Constitution. Perhaps, therefore, Wilhelm Beck wanted to enshrine a quantitative maximum degree of legal protection of subjective public rights in the LVG.[89]

[82] 'The entire State administration in general must remain within the limits of the Constitution and other laws; even in those matters where the law grants free discretion to the administration, the limits set by the laws must be strictly observed.' In the wording of the primary version of the constitution: 'Die gesamte Landesverwaltung überhaupt hat sich innerhalb der Schranken der Verfassung und der übrigen Gesetze zu bewegen, auch in jenen Angelegenheiten, in welchen das Gesetz der Verwaltung ein freies Ermessen einräumt, sind die demselben durch die Gesetze gezogenen Grenzen strenge zu beobachten.'

[83] A [Julius] Merkl, *Die Lehre von der Rechtskraft entwickelt aus dem Rechtsbegriff, Eine rechtstheoretische Untersuchung* (Deuticke 1923) 277.

[84] ibid 298: 'Soweit sich der Fehlerkalkül in der Eröffnung von Rechtsmitteln zur Beseitigung fehlerhafter Akte ausdrückt.'

[85] ibid fn 1 (highlighting in the original left out here): 'daß im Grunde nicht erst der Gebrauch eines Rechtsmittels, sondern schon seine positivrechtliche Beistellung—wofern darin ein Fehlerkalkül zum Ausdruck kommt—den eigentlichen Sanierungseffekt erzielt.'

[86] See Schädler (n 12) 47–48.

[87] Beck (n 5) 1–2.

[88] As mentioned above (Section III.B), art 97(1) LV in its primary version of 1921 required: Unless the law provides otherwise, all decisions or orders of the government are subject to appeal to the *Verwaltungsbeschwerde-Instanz* to be established.

[89] See Schädler (n 12) 48–50.

To ensure these rights were realised, a comprehensive catalogue of different legal remedies and appeals was needed. This offered the individual a suitable procedural approach for every conceivable constellation—thus bringing about remedial hypertrophy. The following offers an outline of the individual remedies/appeals.

The *Vorstellung*[90] (presentation) is submitted to the authority that has made the decision; the *Vorstellung* applies for modification or withdrawal of the decision as faulty, unlawful, or somehow incomplete (art 89(1) LVG). The authority can treat a filed *Beschwerde* (appeal) as a *Vorstellung*[91] (art 89(4) LVG).

The *Beschwerde*[92] serves as a prototype and standard of the appeal procedure (art 90(2) LVG), from whose viewpoint the LVG states any possible deviations in the other remedy/appeal procedures and defines special kinds of *Beschwerden* like the *Säumnisbeschwerde* (art 90(6a) LVG) or *Amtsbeschwerde* (art 92(3) LVG). (For the *Aufsichtsbeschwerde* [supervisory appeal] see below.) The *Beschwerde* is normally addressed to the VBI (Higher Administrative Court) and directed against all terminating administrative acts (art 90(1) LVG). It seeks the modification or withdrawal of an administrative act (art 90 para 8 LVG) due to unlawful action and settlement, injuring or disadvantaging legally recognised interests, or their directly inappropriate or unfair treatment (art 90(6) LVG). It must be filed within a time limit of 14 days[93] (art 91(1) LVG). The appeal procedure is underpinned by the principle that the submission of new facts and evidence is broadly admissible: in single-party procedures without restriction until the date of the decision (art 83(5) LVG); in two-party (or more) procedures in the notice of appeal and its supporting evidence[94] (art 99(1)–(2) LVG).

The procedural *Wiedereinsetzung*[95] (reinstatement, ie *restitutio in integrum*) directed against an omitted and therefore predicted procedural act, and the *Wiederaufnahme* (reopening) of a procedure already concluded, refer to the provisions of the *Zivilprozessordnung* (Code of Civil Procedure) and their application by analogy (art 104(1) LVG). A *Wiederaufnahme*[96] can also, without party application, be initiated officially by the deciding authority/court if there is misappraisal or ignorance of facts or evidence and a serious breach of binding public interests (art 105(1) and (3) LVG).

Nichtigerklärung[97] (annulment) is to be pronounced (partially or fully) by the VBI *ex officio* in serious cases such as grave violations of public rights or interests or lack of competence of a deciding authority (art 106(1)(a) and (c) LVG).

[90] cf § 63(1) AVG.
[91] cf ibid § 68(2)–(3) and (7).
[92] cf the *Berufung* ibid §§ 63–67.
[93] cf two weeks according to ibid § 63(5).
[94] cf ibid § 65.
[95] See ibid §§ 71–72
[96] ibid §§ 69–70.
[97] cf ibid § 68(4).

Through *Einstellung* (suspension), the VBI can prohibit the authority from serving or executing an administrative document/act to prevent unlawful and improper infringements of binding public (party) rights or interests (art 107(1)–(2) LVG).

With the *Erläuterung*, the party can, if a legally binding administrative statement is obscure, ambiguous, or contradictory, ask the authority for an explanation (art 108(1)–(2) LVG).

A party may apply, in a *Nachsichtsgesuch* (request for leniency), to the authority for fair and equitable full or partial relief from the consequences of an order/decision (art 109(1) LVG) without contesting it. With an *Anzeige* (notification), a party can, without embarking on an appeal procedure, highlight in a somewhat informal manner the violation of, or disregard for, essential rules or public interests to a deciding authority (art 109(2) LVG).

The disciplinary *Aufsichtsbeschwerde* (supervisory appeal), addressed at the next higher level, is directed against the refusal to perform official duties or against the refusal to, or delay in, performing an administrative act by a certain authority (art 23(1) LVG).

By means of *Einspruch* (opposition), a party can request a hearing in a procedure that would not normally require a hearing, ie the result is a change to ordinary proceedings including a hearing (art 50(1) LVG).

E. The Extent of Complaints and Cognition

The plurality of remedies/appeals is complemented by a tendency to extend the legitimacy of a filing beyond party status. Article 92(1) LVG states:

> Save as otherwise provided, any person has the right to appeal who, whether or not that person has been involved in the procedure at first instance, considers himself to be directly affected (injured or disadvantaged) in his rights or legally acknowledged interests or interests, which the administrative authority is called upon to protect.[98]

In addition, there is a corresponding comprehensive cognition, namely by the VBI, which extends to questions of law, questions of fact, and the exercise of discretion: The VBI has the 'competence and duty of a full authority […] (unlimited review)'[99]

[98] 'Beschwerdeberechtigt ist, abgesehen von besonderen Bestimmungen, jeder, der sich in seinen Rechten oder rechtlich anerkannten oder von der Verwaltungsbehörde zu schützenden Interessen unmittelbar als beschwert (verletzt oder benachteiligt) betrachtet, er mag am Verfahren vor erster Instanz beteiligt gewesen sein oder nicht.'

[99] 'Zuständigkeit und Pflicht einer vollen Instanz […] (Unbeschränktheit der Überprüfung)'. cf § 66 AVG.

as formulated in art 100(1) LVG. Therefore, the VBI also has the power to make reformatory decisions, ie to decide the merits of the case anew[100] (art 101(2) and art 102 LVG).

VI. Hypothetical Cases

Following the questionnaire, some hypothetical cases will now be considered, including authorisations, disciplinary measures vis-à-vis civil servants, expropriation, and administrative planning.

A. Authorisations and Licences: The Opening of a Pharmacy

The relevant legal bases for this case[101] are the *Sanitätsgesetz*[102] (health law; LGBl 1945/3; abbreviated: SanG) and, based on this law, the *Apothekerverordnung*[103] (regulation on pharmacists; LGBl 1948/23).

The competent authority is the *Sanitätskommission* (health commission) consisting of three members (two physicians and one member of the government) appointed by the government for four years (art 2 and art 3(1) and (4) SanG). This commission has to implement the laws and regulations regarding health and directly supervise the matter; it is the permanent (enforcement) authority in this respect (art 2 SanG). However, the government remains the supreme authority in health matters (art 1 SanG). A person who wants to run a public[104] pharmacy must obtain a concession from the health commission (art 6(1) and art 30(1) SanG). Mr Schultz must therefore apply to the commission in writing for a concession, setting out the circumstances of his pharmacy project. The necessary, but not sufficient, conditions for granting such a concession are that the applicant (here Mr Schultz) must prove that (i) he holds a diploma from a recognised university as a qualified pharmacist; (ii) he has at least two years' experience (art 30(2) SanG); further,[105] (iii) he has to be a citizen of Liechtenstein (art 1 *Apothekerverordnung*); and if judged necessary by the commission (iv) must also provide proof of good repute and/or trustworthiness (art 2 *Apothekerverordnung*). For the rest, since it is a concession, the health commission has a wide margin of discretion as does the government, and they have the

[100] cf ibid § 66(4).

[101] The StGH had to decide in 1950 on a case about a pharmacy, see StGH of 20 April 1950 (ELG 1947–54, 203–37).

[102] *Sanitätsgesetz vom 19. Januar 1945.*

[103] *Verordnung vom 15. Dezember 1948 zum Sanitätsgesetz (Apothekerverordnung).*

[104] As opposed to a private pharmacy in a doctor's surgery.

[105] For exceptions, see art 1 *Apothekerverordnung*.

authority to issue directives regarding public interest and need, market saturation, the factual and legal situation in the two (nearby) neighbouring countries Austria and Switzerland, and so on.

The commission decides in a regular administrative procedure according to arts 27–88 LVG. If it denies the application it can be appealed by Mr Schultz with *Rekurs* (recourse) to the government, whose decision may be appealed—basically the same despite different wording—by a *Beschwerde* to the VBI (expressly art 6(2) SanG). Both of these are appeal procedures under arts 89–109 LVG, specifically qua *Beschwerde/Rekurs* (LVG, arts 90–103). This is the main appeal form, which is mandatory (and clarifying in the light of the many various remedies/appeals) *ex lege*, in this special case of refusal to grant a pharmacy concession.

The fundamental procedural rights relevant to the present case as stated in the Constitution (and judicially recognised[106] within the time frame of the present investigation) are:

- the right of access to the ordinary court (art 33(1) LV), according to which no one may be deprived of access to an ordinary court, and special courts may not be instituted;[107]
- the right of appeal (art 43 LV) (see Section III.A above) including the requirement to give reasons (detailed in Section V.C above).

In addition, the LVG specifies as follows regarding regular administrative procedure:

- besides the mentioned (see Section V.B above) right to a hearing (art 64(3) and art 81(1) LVG) and especially a right to an oral hearing (art 50 LVG);
- adherence to the sequence of appeal stages (art 2 LVG);
- independence of judges (art 3 LVG);
- rejection of a public official on the grounds of bias (arts 7, 11, and 12 LVG);
- prohibition of reporting (official secrecy) (art 22 LVG);
- *Armenrecht* (legal aid) according to the Code of Civil Procedure (art 43(1) LVG);
- right of access to the files (art 46(3) and art 60(6) LVG);
- basically[108] the right to a written copy of the order/decision (art 80 and especially arts 82 and 83 LVG).

[106] The StGH had not yet established the following constitutional rulings at that time: the ban on the formal denial of justice, the ban on delaying justice, and the ban on exaggerated formalism.

[107] 'Niemand darf seinem ordentlichen Richter entzogen, Ausnahmsgerichte dürfen nicht eingeführt werden.'

[108] However, see art 46(5) LVG (waiver of rights) and, for example, art 82(2) LVG (the written copy may be omitted if the parties agree to waive it).

Lastly, the overall regular administrative procedure should be process-economical, therefore quick, simple, and inexpensive (art 55(2) LVG).

For the appeal procedure the LVG adds:

- right of access to files (art 94(1) LVG);
- basically (with restrictions)[109] the right to submit new facts and evidence (art 99(1) LVG).

Both a *reformatio in melius* (art 120(1) LVG) and a *reformatio in peius* (art 120(2) LVG) are admissible in the appeal procedure.

For completeness, it must be mentioned that after all the procedures described, Mr Schultz could bring an appeal before the StGH as an extraordinary (constitutional) jurisdiction for the infringement of constitutional rights. This applies in particular to fundamental procedural rights in the Constitution mentioned above. Among the fundamental material rights, freedom of trade and commerce may also be considered (art 36 LV), though these are not very promising.

B. The Dismissal of a Civil Servant

The LVG only states that civil servants have a criminal, civil, and—relevant *in casu*—disciplinary responsibility (art 19(1) LVG).[110] The LVG only states that civil servants have a criminal, civil, and—relevant *in casu*—disciplinary responsibility (art 19(1) LVG). Further, according to the LVG, disciplinary responsibility is governed by the relevant legislation (art 19(2) LVG). The legal basis for the case of Caius, therefore, is the *Beamtengesetz*[111] (civil service law; LGBl 1938/6; abbreviated: BeamtenG), especially its art 8. In cases of breach of duty, negligence, or other conduct incompatible with the performance of their duties or service, as well as unsatisfactory performance, the salaries of officials like Caius may be reduced or, in serious cases and after fruitless warning, they may be dismissed at any time without compensation (art 8(1) BeamtenG). The competent authority in such scenarios is the government through its administrative supervision.

This case concerns a disciplinary procedure, but the BeamtenG does not provide for any specific disciplinary procedure. Thus, the regular (not criminal) administrative procedure and the appeal procedure of the LVG and their procedural rights relating to Caius must apply: especially the right of appeal, including the giving

[109] See ibid art 99(2).

[110] The VBI had to deal with a case—albeit with a different approach—concerning the removal from office of a forest and forestry supervisor in VBI 1930/002 [21 September 1930] and VBI 1933/003 [14 July 1933].

[111] *Gesetz vom 10. Februar 1938 betreffend das Dienstverhältnis und die Besoldung der Staatsbeamten, Staatsangestellten und Lehrpersonen.*

reasons requirement, the right to a hearing,[112] the right of access to the files, etc. (detailed above in Section VI.A). This has to be applied in a subsidiary manner in this kind of disciplinary procedure in the absence of specific rules and, *mutatis mutandis*, with regard to the special legal relationship of the civil service.

The government must first give Caius a reasoned and substantiated warning with the threat of dismissal. If his conduct does not improve, the government may, as a disciplinary penalty, dismiss him with an order. However, before doing so, the civil servant must have the opportunity to give a statement and provide an explanation regarding the accusations (art 8(2) BeamtenG). In addition, the dismissal order must contain information on legal remedies (art 85 LVG). For Caius, as complainant, these include the *Vorstellung* (presentation) to the authority that issued the order, otherwise—instead of it or later, if the *Vorstellung* is rejected—a *Beschwerde* (appeal) to the (next higher) administrative court. They each have to be filed within 14 days (art 91(1) LVG). These basically have a suspensive effect (art 100(1) and art 116(1) LVG), so Caius will probably be exempted from official duties during the appeal proceedings. Under certain circumstances, this could be lengthy as Caius could bring an appeal before the StGH for infringement of (procedural) constitutional rights.

C. Expropriation of a House for a Railway Line

Article 35 LV of the 1921 Constitution states that:

> 1) Where demanded for public welfare, property of any kind may be subject to assignment or encumbrance in return for indemnification that is reasonable, or if in dispute as determined by a judge.
> 2) The procedure for expropriation shall be determined by law.[113]

This special law to determine the expropriation procedure is called the *Expropriationsgesetz*[114] (expropriation law; LGBl 1887/4; abbreviated: ExprG). It had already been in force for 30 years when the 1921 Constitution was enacted, and had originally been based on Austrian[115] law under the *Konstitutionelle Verfassung* of 1862.[116] In art 1, the ExprG pre-formulates the constitutional provision

[112] Worth mentioning is a passage in VBI 1930/002 (n 110), 3 (English translation): 'The divergent views of the parties, whether *in casu* it is a simple administrative procedure or a disciplinary criminal [*sic*] procedure, are irrelevant in this context [. . .] because in both cases the person concerned must be given a fair hearing' (art 64 LVG and art 33(3) of the Constitution).

[113] '1) Wo es das öffentliche Wohl erheischt, kann die Abtretung oder Belastung jeder Art von Vermögen gegen angemessene, streitigenfalls durch den Richter festzusetzende Schadloshaltung verfügt werden. 2) Das Enteignungsverfahren wird durch das Gesetz bestimmt.'

[114] *Gesetz vom 23. August 1887 über das Verfahren in Expropriationsfällen.*

[115] Hence the ExprG is numbered with '§' and not 'article'.

[116] H Wille, *Liechtensteinisches Verwaltungsrecht, Ausgewählte Gebiete* (LPS 38, VLAG 2004), 96.

mentioned above and declares with regard to *formelle Enteignung*[117] (expropriation) that forcible confiscation of property is only permissible against indemnification, and only where it is in the best general interest.[118] The construction of a railway line and the related expropriation of land belonging to Mrs Sempronia are undoubtedly covered by this condition according to case law and doctrine—provided that (but not to be examined further here) all substantive legal requirements and factual circumstances are fulfilled.

The expropriation procedure is a very unusual and complicated 'composite procedure', which combines acts of all three (legislative, executive, and judicial) State powers and is neither an administrative nor a court procedure but a hybrid of the two.[119] However, it is essentially considered administrative, which is why the LVG is complementarily applied in the absence of specific rules.[120] The procedure is two-staged: (i) after informal preliminary proceedings, the necessity of the expropriation must first be ascertained, and then, (ii) only if affirmed, the compensation.

(i) In the run-up to the actual expropriation procedure, correspondence and discussions are conducted, and information exchanged, between a representative of the government and all those involved, such as Mrs Sempronia and any further organisations with an interest. Mrs Sempronia will instruct a lawyer to represent her interests in such an unusual case. If, after these preliminary proceedings, the project is pursued further, the actual expropriation procedure begins. As the ExprG, being a special law, sets up a procedure but establishes no particular or additional procedural rights, those of the LVG (see Section VI.A above) are to be applied *mutatis mutandis* in addition to the procedural rights already in force under the Constitution.

Whether or not expropriation is necessary in a given case must be decided case by case by the *Landtag* (Parliament), referring to its own[121] (and not the LVG's)[122] rules of proceedings in closed session,[123] on the basis of a submission from the government (§ 2 ExprG). This is because Parliament's decision should be made in the same way as a law, to provide special legitimacy for massive interference in fundamental rights through expropriation. It is questionable whether the persons concerned may challenge Parliament's decision on the reason for expropriation before the *Staatsgerichtshof*. At the time of interest here, this seems not to be the case as it was a later remedial development introduced by the StGH judicature.[124] However,

[117] See (from a 2004 perspective) ibid 94–130 ['*formelle Enteignung*']; see (from a 1950 perspective) Ivo Beck, *Das Enteignungsrecht des Fürstentums Liechtenstein* ([Vaduz] 1950).

[118] 'Die Expropriation, d[as] i[st] die zwangsweise Entziehung des Eigentums, ist nur gegen angemessene Schadloshaltung und nur in solchen Fällen zulässig, in welchen es das allgemeine Beste erheischt.'

[119] Wille (n 116) 118.

[120] ibid 119.

[121] See for example *Geschäftsordnung vom 23. Mai 1969 für den Landtag des Fürstentums Liechtenstein*, LGBl 1969/28.

[122] See Wille (n 116) 120.

[123] See *Geschäftsordnung 1969* (n 121) § 21.

[124] Wille (n 116) 118–19 with further references.

there is a general right of petition to Parliament according to art 42 LV, which Mrs Sempronia and/or other legal entities or organisations could use in this case:

> The right to petition Parliament [...] shall be guaranteed; not only individuals whose rights or interests are affected but also municipalities and bodies shall be entitled to have their wishes and requests brought before Parliament by a member of Parliament.[125]

Through the right of petition, the focus could—not so much in legal, but in political and factual terms—be shifted away from the 'object of dispute' of expropriation to other aspects, such as changes in the planned routing of the railway.

(ii) If Parliament approves the expropriation, the government decides on the extent of the property to be expropriated and how this shall be done in greater detail (§ 3 ExprG), including determining the compensation to be paid (§ 4 ExprG). The government will negotiate with Mrs Sempronia to reach an agreement. If this fails, the government makes a written order regarding the compensation to be paid and notifies Mrs Sempronia, informing her that she can object within 14 days (§ 6(1) ExprG). In the event of objection, the government will send the files (possibly alongside an interim procedure for provisional measures) to the *Landgericht* (First Instance Court), which arranges a valuation of the asset to be expropriated in accordance with the provisions of the court order (§ 7 ExprG). Thus, the proceeding changes from administrative to judicial due to the wording at the end of art 35(1) LV, which requests a judicial assessment of the compensation to be granted *in the event of a dispute about it*. Mrs Sempronia is therefore entitled to all party rights under the Code of Civil Procedure in these civil proceedings. The *Beschluss*[126] (court ruling) on the amount of compensation must be served *ex officio* on both parties (§ 8(2) ExprG), ie to Mrs Sempronia and the government. Both can appeal through *Rekurs* (recourse) according to the Code of Civil Procedure (and not the LVG) to the *Obergericht* (High Court) and then to the *Oberster Gerichtshof* (Supreme Court)[127] (and *not* to the VBI). Thereafter, Mrs Sempronia could—as an extraordinary, ie constitutional referral—bring an appeal before the StGH for infringement of her procedural and material constitutional rights (in this case mainly the freedom of ownership (art 34(1) LV) in connection with expropriation (art 35 LV)).

[125] 'Das Petitionsrecht an den Landtag [...] ist gewährleistet und es steht nicht nur einzelnen in ihren Rechten oder Interessen Betroffenen, sondern auch Gemeinden und Korporationen zu, ihre Wünsche und Bitten durch ein Mitglied des Landtages daselbst vorbringen zu lassen.'

[126] There is no independent appeal against the court approval of the valuation or all the court orders concerning its execution; however, any complaints may be lodged in the *Rekurs* against this court ruling, by which the executed valuation is accepted in court (§ 8(1) ExprG).

[127] Wille (n 116) 119.

D. Administrative Planning: Building a New School

In Liechtenstein, constructing school buildings is basically the responsibility of the municipalities.[128] The special law in this case is the *Baugesetz*[129] (construction law; LGBl 1947/44; abbreviated: BauG), and every municipality may additionally enact a municipal building code (art 3 BauG). The competent authorities are the government with the *Bauamt* (office for construction) and the local municipal administration, ie the municipal council (art 2(1) BauG). The *Bauamt* is the supreme supervisory office for all public and private buildings requiring approval; it examines building applications submitted to it by the municipal council and issues building permits (art 2(2) BauG). In the absence of specific rules in the BauG and its ancillary decrees, the LVG with its basic provisions for every administrative procedure regarding parties, their rights, modalities of remedies, etc. is applied complementarily. For the rest, the *Baubewilligungsverfahren* (building permit procedure) is as follows.

A building application, addressed to the *Bauamt* and using the forms provided, must be submitted to the municipal administration (art 72(1) BauG). This must then inform the neighbours and other interested parties of the building project in writing with confirmation of receipt, informing the parties that they may raise objections within 14 days[130] (art 72(2) BauG). During this period, the construction plans are available for inspection by interested parties at the municipal government offices (art 73 sentence 2 BauG). It is in the very field of construction law that the extensive party concept of the LVG—continued and even extended by its interpretation of the right of appeal (see Section V.E above)—has often been further developed and refined. Article 31(1) LVG states at the end that 'in case of doubt, the status of a party (beneficiary, interested party, etc) must be determined with regard to the subject matter and on the basis of the applicable laws'.[131] In other words, in the event of uncertainty, the term should generally be interpreted as a rather *wide* circle of people, who should be informed from the very beginning. Any objection raised by one of these individuals is to be dealt with by the head of the municipality through mediation. If he or she fails to settle it amicably, which is often the case, the building applicant or the objection raiser can sue through the *Landgericht* (First Instance Court) within a further 14 days (art 72(3) and art 4(2) BauG). The latter may also request provisional measures to suspend the commencement of construction. The building permit procedure is suspended during this civil dispute.

[128] cf *Gemeindegesetz vom 2. Dezember 1959*, LGBl 1960/2, art 25(1) letter e: the municipal assembly must be convened when the construction of a larger building, such as a school building, is involved. See also (n 7) for the municipal *eigener Wirkungskreis*.

[129] *Baugesetz vom 10. September 1947*.

[130] Objections after the expiry of the time limit are still possible, but become liable for damages (art 72(5) BauG).

[131] 'Die Eigenschaft als Partei (Berechtigter, Interessent usw.) ist im Zweifel mit Rücksicht auf den Gegenstand und auf Grund der anzuwendenden Gesetze zu bestimmen.'

If the civil court finds in favour of the building applicant, the *Bauamt* either issues a building permit, provided that the regulations have been met, or refuses to allow the construction work to be carried out altogether, stating the reasons for refusal and giving information on legal remedies (art 75 BauG). Appeals against orders of the *Bauamt* or decisions of the local council can be made to the government within 14 days through *Beschwerde*, and the government's decision may be challenged before the VBI (art 4(1) BauG). Thereafter, there is the possibility of appeal before the StGH for infringement of constitutional rights. The right of appeal is available to anyone with (broadly interpreted) party status (art 31(1) LVG). Further, it is available to other persons whose (perhaps only factual) interests are directly affected, injured, or disadvantaged (art 92(1) LVG, see Section V.E above).

VII. The Personal Factor

Finally, in order to ascertain the importance of the Austrian model, adequate attention should be paid to the role played by both individuals and networks. From the first point of view, it can be interesting to consider the work of Josef Peer. From the other viewpoint, reference will be made to judges in general.

A. Josef Peer

Josef Peer (1864–1925) was deeply rooted and experienced in the Austrian bureaucratic tradition (albeit with a modern outlook). Peer spent part of his youth in Liechtenstein and studied in Innsbruck (Dr. iur. 1887), opening a law firm in Feldkirch (near the Liechtenstein border) in 1894. He was mayor of Feldkirch from 1901 to 1909 and member of the Vorarlberg State Parliament—and from 1917 to 1925 Hofrat at the Administrative Court in Vienna. At that time, he also played a decisive role in the disputes over a new Constitution for Liechtenstein. After politically troublesome years of party wrangling over the modernisation of the State of Liechtenstein, in September 1920 the reigning Prince Johann II appointed Peer as special Head of Government for six months. This was based upon the *Schlossabmachungen* (pacifying agreement)—a milestone on the way to a new constitution—between the prince and the political parties. Peer prepared a draft constitution, which was eclectic, moderate, and mediating. It maintained elements of the *Konstitutionelle Verfassung* of 1862, combined them with elements from different neighbouring legal systems (Swiss cantonal, Austrian), and integrated the political postulates of the *Schlossabmachungen* (which had been based on a very progressive draft constitution by Wilhelm Beck, who later created the LVG (see Section II.C above) as one of Peer's political opponents and a radical social democratic innovator). The main features of Peer's draft were eventually included in the new Constitution of 1921. In particular, Peer is credited with having promoted the Austrian model and developing a constitutional jurisdiction through the establishment of a *Staatsgerichtshof*.[132]

B. Austrian Judges

As seen above, the 1921 Constitution attached great importance to staffing courts and authorities mostly with Liechtenstein citizens. The political–polemical 'battle cry' was: '*Los von Wien!*'[133] (Away from Vienna!). But the fathers of the Constitution also knew the remaining minority had to be appointed from unbiased Austrian and Swiss experts to maintain a knowledge transfer from both countries into Liechtenstein's legal system. The substantial degree of replication from the legal systems of both of these neighbouring countries made it vital for Liechtenstein to thus expose its jurisdiction (namely its administrative jurisdiction)[134] to a certain degree of foreign (namely Austrian) influence. The minority of foreign judges, without questioning the independence of the Liechtenstein legal system and jurisdiction itself, contributed their expert knowledge from their home countries.[135] Although this form of received law is difficult to detect, it must nevertheless be taken into consideration.

C. *Hofkanzlei* and *Landesverweser*

Finally, from the institutional viewpoint, one should not underestimate the influence of Austrian administrative tradition and practice originating with the Princely House of Liechtenstein and its *Hofkanzlei* (Princely Court Chancellery) in Vienna. The latter, as the supreme princely office, was responsible for all the affairs of the Princely House of Liechtenstein. Under the *Konstitutionelle Verfassung* of 1862, the chancellery conducted official business between the government and the prince. By 1871, it was also the *Politische Rekursinstanz* (Political Court of Appeal, ie an administrative court) and *Appellationsgericht* (Court of Appeal) in civil and

[132] For the previous paragraph: R Quaderer, 'Peer, Josef' eHLFL (version 31 December 2011) <https://historisches-lexikon.li/Peer,_Josef> accessed 1 September 2020.

[133] The headline of a newspaper article (*Oberrheinische Nachrichten* of 12 April 1919, 1 and *Oberrheinische Nachrichten* of 16 April 1919, 1) calling for national independence by transferring all court instances from Austria (Vienna and Innsbruck) to Liechtenstein.

[134] For the foreign judges in Liechtenstein during the Second World War, see A-C Perrez, *Fremde Richter, Die Rechtsprechung im Fürstentum Liechtenstein unter dem Einfluss schweizerischer und deutsch-österreichischer Richter 1938–1945* (Chronos and VHVFL 2015) especially 43–44 and 210–15 for the VBI and Swiss judges/presidents.

[135] See for the perspective of the Princely Supreme Court, A Dürr, 'Die Beteiligung Österreichs an der Justizpflege des Fürstentums Liechtenstein' in H Schumacher and W Zimmermann (eds), *90 Jahre Fürstlicher Oberster Gerichtshof, Festschrift für Gert Delle Karth* (Sramek 2013) especially 149–51.

criminal matters. Afterwards, these offices became formally independent, but—and crucially—its staff remained identical, with (in part noble) administrative or legal experts appointed by the prince as civil servants who had been educated and had gained experience in the Austrian administration or courts. The same applies *mutatis mutandis* to the *Landesverweser* ([Princely] State Administrator) in Vaduz. Although the *Konstitutionelle Verfassung* of 1862 formally separated the State administration of Liechtenstein from the administration of the princely domains in Liechtenstein, until 1918 the *Landesverweser* remained also the head of their administration in Liechtenstein; it took until 1945 to finally and de facto separate the two administrations.[136]

The influence of the Austrian administrative tradition, represented and practised by the *Hofkanzlei* and the *Landesverweser*, spread as far as Liechtenstein. This way of thinking was met by the cry '*Los von Wien!*' or 'Away from Vienna!' because the population often felt that foreign officials treated them as subjects rather than as citizens with their own independent national administration.[137] However, as described above, throughout the long nineteenth century, a certain administrative dependency on Austria had been established, and this could not suddenly be overcome in the new era of formal administrative independence under the 1921 Constitution. It took many decades for Liechtenstein to establish its own administrative culture. To this day, reminiscences (including linguistic usage) of the Austrian origins of administrative procedure and Liechtenstein's proximity to it can still be identified.

[136] For the previous paragraph: F Frommelt, 'Domäne' eHLFL (version 31 December 2011) <https://historisches-lexikon.li/Domäne> accessed 2 September 2020; K Kindle, 'Hofkanzlei' eHLFL (version 31 December 2011) <https://historisches-lexikon.li/Hofkanzlei> accessed 1 September 2020.

[137] Beck (n 5) 1–2.

6
Administrative Procedure Legislation in Czechoslovakia

Lukáš Potěšil and Filip Křepelka

I. Introduction

The following text deals with the influence of the *Allgemeines Verwaltungsverfahrengesetz* (Austrian Code of Administrative Procedure adopted in 1925; BGBl No 274/1925, hereinafter 'AVG') on the legal regulation of administrative procedure in former Czechoslovakia (now Czechia and Slovakia) from 1920 to 1970.

This period was mainly influenced by two factors. The first is a common heritage. The territory of Czechia (and former Czechoslovakia) was part of the Habsburg monarchy. The second factor relates to Socialism and its impact on the legal system (with intentional discontinuity with the previous system) and isolation through the Iron Curtain from 1948. Unfortunately, for this research, both factors led to the conclusion that it is not easy to identify Austrian AVG influence.

II. Background: History and Legal Culture

The 1928 Code of Administrative Procedure emerged in a similar period as the Austrian APA, which may raise questions concerning whether the Austrian APA influenced it. After the Second World War and during the Communist regime (from 1948), three frameworks emerged in the space of 12 years because the laws addressing National Committees were recodified as Soviet-style units of regional and local government. The last of these (the 1967 Code) was in effect for the longest time.

A. The First Period: 1928–1945

The Czech Republic has had a long tradition of recodifications of rules on administrative procedure since 1928. However, there was (and still is) a specific procedural framework for, among others, taxation. Simultaneously, many administrative law

Lukáš Potěšil and Filip Křepelka, *Administrative Procedure Legislation in Czechoslovakia* In: *The Austrian Codification of Administrative Procedure*. Edited by: Giacinto Della Cananea, Angela Ferrari Zumbini, and Otto Pfersmann, Oxford University Press. © Lukáš Potěšil and Filip Křepelka 2023. DOI: 10.1093/oso/9780198867623.003.0006 statutes provide specific procedural rules applied together with the general legal regulation of administrative procedure.

Czechoslovakia adopted the Code of Administrative Procedure, the *Vládní nařízení č. 8/1928 Sb. o řízení ve věcech náležejících do působnosti politických úřadů (správní řízení)*, ie the Cabinet Regulation on Proceedings in Matters Subject to Competences of Political Authorities (Administrative Proceedings) on 13 January 1928. Like its successors, it did not take the form of a parliamentary statute until 1967. It was a Cabinet Decree implementing the law regulating the organisation of State administration. This Code of Administrative Procedure emerged as 8/1928 Coll (referred to as the '1928 Administrative Procedure Code').

This Code represented the first codification of rules for administrative procedure and was effective from 1 July 1928 to 30 June 1955. This regulation, written in a clerical style, was therefore widely applicable. The Code was applied without substantial change during Nazi occupation, after liberation, and after the Communist coup in 1948.

B. The Second Period: 1945–1970

From 1 July 1955, the *Vládní nařízení č. 20/1955 Sb., o řízení ve věcech správních (správní řád)*, ie. the Cabinet regulation on proceedings in administrative matters/the Code of Administrative Procedure), hereinafter 'Code of Administrative Procedure 1955' was in force. Five years later, from 1 July 1960 this legal regulation was hastily replaced by the *Vládní nařízení č. 91/1960 Sb., o správním řízení* (Cabinet Regulation on Administrative Proceedings), hereinafter 'Code of Administrative Procedure 1960'). These Codes were still in the form of a decree adopted by the Cabinet. Both Codes accompanied the laws regulating the regional, district, and local levels of administration by elected National Committees, emulating Soviets.

In 1967 the new *Zákon č. 71/1967 Sb., o správním řízení (správní řád)*, the law on Administrative Procedure (the Administrative Procedure Code), hereinafter 'Code of Administrative Procedure 1967') was adopted. It was adopted by Parliament (the National Assembly) and came into effect on 1 January 1968. This Code was in effect in Czechia until the end of 2005. It has applied in Slovakia to the present time.

C. The Institutional and Political Context of the APA

Czech territories were part of the Habsburg monarchy/Empire from 1526 to 1918. We mention that Czechoslovakia covered not only lands that belonged to the Austrian part of the Empire but also territories that belonged to the Kingdom of

Hungary.[1] Czechoslovakia emerged after the collapse of the monarchy at the end of the First World War.

The long history of the monarchy was not always one of peaceful cohabitation. Therefore, Czechoslovakia had mixed relations with interwar Austria. There were also tensions relating to numerous Germans living in areas that bordered on Austria and Germany which were oriented more to these countries. Austria (and Hungary as well) symbolised reactionary Habsburg monarchy and some oppression of Czechs, Slovaks, and Ruthenians. Nevertheless, these attitudes did not exclude differentiation between the Habsburg monarchy and early republican Austria, which ousted the dynasty as Czechoslovakia repudiated its heritage.

First of all, interwar Czechoslovakia embraced legal continuity (the proclamation of independence of 28 October 1918 contained an explicit provision to that effect). Significant reforms stabilised the country at a time of revolutions and turmoil elsewhere.

Czechoslovakia developed its first codification of procedural rules for administration in the same period as the interwar Austrian Republic. Officials, experts, and scholars studied at the same faculties of law. We identify similar arguments in both countries. Both codifications were meant to provide efficient administration respecting individual rights. The officials, experts, and scholars behind the Code of Administrative Procedure 1928 had the same legal education in prewar monarchy as their Austrian counterparts. Indeed, these included Austrians, albeit Czech-speaking ones.

Another issue is linguistic asymmetry, which reflected not only the language situation in the late Habsburg monarchy but also the prominence of German in central Europe. Perhaps some (German-speaking) Austrian experts understood Czech. On the other hand, all Czech experts and scholars mastered German, as knowledge of the language was indispensable. They could thus communicate with their German–Austrian counterparts. Cross-border communication during the interwar period flourished. Austrian researchers would be informed as to whether Czech (Czechoslovak) experts and scholars contributed to the reflection of administration and its law in the interwar period.

Indeed, we could describe this situation as due to the influence of Austrian 1925 legislation. Nevertheless, it seems to be more of a parallel development, relying on common heritage.

First of all, it is possible to mention the repeatedly criticised absence of any unifying legal regulation of administrative procedure.[2] The contemporary literature

[1] Bohemia, Moravia, and Silesia (now the Czech Republic) were autonomous territories (provinces) of the Austrian part, also known as Cislajthania. Slovakia and Carpathian Ruthenia were formed from northern Hungary. This situation led to the existence of duality in legal regulation from 1918 and was abandoned in the 1950s.

[2] K Čížek, *Obrys řízení správního* (J Mercy-ho sklad v Praze 1888) 77; J Pražák, *Rakouské právo veřejné. Rakouské parvo správní* (Eduard Baštýř 1905) 147; F Weyr, *Československé právo správní, část obecná* (Právník 1922) 78.

critically pointed out that several regulations, as well as internal instructions, regulated administrative procedure, which appeared insufficient and outdated.[3] The case law of the *Verwaltungsgerichtshof* in Vienna filled the gap. This was the administrative judiciary (established with *Gesetz bettreffend die Errichtung eines Verwaltungsgerichtshofes*, RGBl No 36/1876). The administrative judiciary revealed shortcomings in the absence of a unifying procedural norm. If the Administrative Court in Vienna could annul an administrative act because the principal forms of the procedure were violated when it was issued, it was not entirely clear what constituted essential requirements. The foundations of the judiciary laid at this time served both Austria and Czechoslovakia. Moreover, preparations for the unification of administrative procedure started before the First World War in association with further efforts to reform public administration.[4] They would be applied later.

The mentioned shortcomings persisted in the Czechoslovak Republic, which reciprocated the existing regulations (Act No 11/1918 Coll). At the same time, Czechoslovakia was aware of the importance of the administrative judiciary. *Zákon č. 3/1918 Sb., o nejvyšším správním soudě a o řešení kompetenčních konfliktů*, ie the Law on the Supreme Administrative Court and the Solution of Competence Conflicts established the *Nejvyšší správní soud*, ie the Supreme Administrative Court in Prague five days after the proclamation of independence. The Supreme Administrative Court partly personally, as Ferdinand Pantůček and Emil Hácha mentioned later, and mainly procedurally followed its Austrian predecessor. The Supreme Administrative Court adjudicated according to the slightly amended Act No 36/1876 Coll.

According to Act No 286/1924 Coll, On Austerity Measures in Public Administration, art 3, s 1:

> the Cabinet is required to submit a draft law on uniform regulation of administrative proceedings by 31st December 1925, following the above principles.

This legal regulation established the form of a law. However, in the end, the Code of Administrative Procedure 1928 was adopted in connection with art 10 of Act No 125/1927 Coll, On the Organisation of Political Administration. The article stated that:

> Cabinet regulations shall unify and regulate the regulations on procedures in matters falling within the competence of political authorities—including execution procedure—with a view to the effective simplification and acceleration of procedure.

[3] These were Imperial Decree No 96/1854 Coll, Regulation No 52/1855 Coll, Regulation No 196/1859 Coll, Regulation No 124/1868 Coll, Act No 101/1896 Coll.

[4] J Pražák, *Rakouské právo veřejné. Rakouské parvo správní* (Eduard Baštýř 1905) 147.

Lastly, the government resorted to a decree to facilitate enactment without challenging negotiations in a fragmented parliament. It relied on decades of practices, according to which other administrative regulations also took the form of government regulation (ie by-laws and implementing regulations) and regulations governing public administration.

As mentioned, the 1928 Code of Administrative Procedure was replaced in 1955. Political and social conditions in Czechoslovakia changed significantly after 1948. The regime deemed it necessary to adopt new regulations confirming changes that took place after 1948. Legal regulation came from the new Socialist environment and its approaches.[5] The 1955 Code of Administrative Procedure implemented Act No 13/1954 Coll on National Committees.

The 1955 Code of Administrative Procedure was replaced by the Code of Administrative Procedure of 1960 (Government Decree No 91/1960 Coll), which implemented Act No 65/1960 Coll., on National Committees. This framework faced sharp criticism because of its shortness and vagueness. The Code contained a mere 36 provisions, while the 1928 Code of Administrative Procedure contained 137. The idea of simplifying administrative procedure and opening it up to the working class influenced this development. This legal regulation was marked by the then ideas about society as a unified organism of a new type and emphasising the social-organisational and educational role of State administration.[6]

The 1967 Code of Administrative Procedure was a parliamentary statute embracing so-called Socialist legality. This Code accompanied the new *Zákon č. 69/1967 Sb., o národních výborech*, ie the Act on National Committees. Scholars appraised the 1967 Code of Administrative Procedure positively.[7] This appraisal resulted in its application after the collapse of Socialism in Czechia until the recently applicable recodification with the *Zákon č. 500/2004 Sb., správní řád*, ie Law—Administrative (Procedure) Code. The Code is still effective in Slovakia.

We can add that the 1967 Code of Administrative Procedure 1967 survived, albeit substantially amended after the so-called Velvet Revolution in 1989, the restoration of the administrative judiciary in 1992, its reform in 2003, and accession to the European Union on 1 May 2004.

If we compare all these Codes, we can conclude that the 1967 Code of Administrative Procedure is closer to the 1928 Code than the 1955 and 1960 ones. It may be surprising to note that the Code of Administrative Procedure of 1967

[5] For example the term 'parties' used in the Code of Administrative Procedure of 1928 (and in the Austrian APA of 1925) was intentionally replaced by the term 'participants'. The main purpose was to show the possibility of participation in administrative procedure and State administration.

[6] J Staša, 'K pozapomenutým padesátinám jednoho zákona' (2018) 1–2 Správní právo 89.

[7] J Kaucký, 'Historie přípravy správního řádu' in J Rajchl (ed), *Správní řád 10 let v praxi* (Univerzita Karlova 2016) 11.

(adopted in the Socialist era) had stronger ties to the 1928 Code of Administrative Procedure than with the Codes adopted in 1960 and 1955. The Administrative Procedure Codes of 1955 and 1960 were of inferior quality.

D. Unity and Differentiation

Until 1968, Czechoslovakia was a unitary State. Federalism was adopted from 1969 to the end of 1992. Nevertheless, the administrative rules were always uniform. It applied to the Code of Administrative Procedure 1967. Since dissolution, the Code of Administrative Procedure 1967 became national statutes in both Czechia and Slovakia and were subject to different amendments.

The Code of Administrative Procedure of 1928 did not apply to all administrative authorities and procedures. It applied to the tasks of direct State administration. Particular legal frameworks of a different nature addressed the rest. For example, the Code of Administrative Procedure of 1928 did not (intentionally) regulate proceedings relating to civil servants and the proceedings related to administrative sanctions.[8] Therefore we can conclude that the jurisprudence of the Supreme Administrative Court rather than the Code of Administrative Procedure 1928 filled the gap. On the other hand, it is necessary to appreciate the unification brought by the Code of Administrative Procedure 1928.

The 1928 Administrative Procedure Act started being applied to the municipalities and their administrative proceedings during the Second World War.[9]

The Code's position as a *lex generalis* strengthened when its application extended to other administrative bodies and administrative proceedings in 1955 and subsequent years.

The tax law procedure and administrative enforcement procedure were independent legal frameworks in the 1920–70 period.

E. Constitutional Principles

Czechoslovakia adopted three constitutions between 1920 and 1970. The first one was based on democracy and the rule of law. The later constitutions were more ideological proclamations than genuine legal documents, and many of their provisions were inapplicable in reality.

[8] Only up to 1960, then the legal regulation of administrative offences (Act No 60/1961 Coll) declared the general applicability of the Code of Administrative Procedure including administrative offences.

[9] Order of the Ministry of the Interior No 150/1944 Coll.

The 1920 Constitution (Act No 121/1920 Coll) stipulated the principle of legality and the right to judicial review/control by administrative justice. It remained silent on other principles.

The 1948 Constitution (Constitutional Act No 150/1948 Coll) reflected early Socialist ideology while establishing a unified hierarchical State administration.

The 1960 Constitution (Constitutional Act No 100/1960 Coll) declared that 'Socialism has won in our homeland!', and announced the leading role of the Communist Party. In theory, parliamentary supremacy replaced the traditional division of power into legislative, executive, and judicial branches. The Constitution of 1960 confirmed centralism, embracing the unity of State administration. Article 29 expressed the right of each citizen to be able to bring complaints and requests to any administrative authority.

None of the constitutions fixed the principles of administrative procedure.

F. The Standards Defined by the Courts

Without doubt, Supreme Administrative Court case law was the principal source for the Code of Administrative Procedure of 1928.[10] The Supreme Administrative Court is a general and one-tier court. It closely adhered to the previous case law of the Administrative Court in Vienna. In this respect, the Code of Administrative Procedure 1928 relied on the same traditions and legal environment as the Austrian APA. Some of the conclusions of the case law on administrative procedure are still applicable today, as evidenced by the case law of the contemporary administrative judiciary, which uses them, as well as publications that refer to them.[11]

Other sources were books and textbooks on administrative law,[12] primarily reflecting the relevant case law.

The Code of Administrative Procedure of 1928 did not contain principles of administrative procedure. However, the literature[13] identified the principles of *ex officio* activity, material (objective) truth, the right to be heard, and the principle of proceedings in written form.

Socialist ideology resulted in the preference for collective interests rather than protecting individual rights. Therefore, the Administrative Procedure Act 1928 was a bourgeois and bureaucratic one and not suited to the new era. The sources

[10] J Hoetzel, *Československé správní právo, část všeobecná* (Melantrich 1934) 294.

[11] R Ondruš, *Vybraná rozhodnutí Nejvyššího správního soudu ve věcech administrativních (1918–1948)* (Linde Praha 2001).

[12] K Čížek, *Obrys řízení správního* (Jindř Mercy-ho sklad v Praze 1888); J Pražák, *Rakouské parvo veřejné. Rakouské parvo správní* (Eduard Baštýř 1905); J Hoetzel, *Nauka o správních aktech* (Bursík a Kohout 1907); F Weyr, *Československé právo správní, část obecná* (Právník 1922); J Havelka, *Nástin zásad správního řízení (podle judikatury Nejvyššího* správního soudu) (Všetečka a spol 1927); F Vavřínek, *Stručný přehled zřízení správního* (Všehrd 1928).

[13] Hoetzel (n 10) 307–09.

for the 1955 Administrative Procedure Act and those of 1960 and 1967 were different. On the other hand, the 1928 Code of Administrative Procedure was still an inspiration, especially for the Code of Administrative Procedure 1967, albeit not expressly. The two above-mentioned Codes are similar.

We can claim that the purpose of the principles was the proper interpretation and application of legal regulation containing them. Some principles of administrative procedure emerged with the 1995 Code of Administrative Procedure (arts 3–6). The Code of Administrative Procedure of 1960 anchored them in arts 1–4 and the 1967 Code of Administrative Procedure in arts 3–4, anchoring the principles of administrative procedure in the Administrative Procedure Acts of 1955 and 1960 in Socialist ideology. The tasks of State administration included educating workers as a privileged class. These was not the traditional principles of administrative procedure. The situation changed with the Code of Administrative Procedure of 1967, which contained the traditional principles relating to proceedings, such as the principle of legality, protection of the public interest, cooperation, and the right to be heard, in addition to *ex officio* activity and material (objective) truth. The Administrative Procedure Act of 1967 refrained from ideological proclamations. This neutrality facilitated its smooth application after the Velvet Revolution in 1989 with no significant changes.[14]

III. The Importance of the Austrian APA

A. A Shared Vision of Administrative Procedure

The 1928 Code of Administrative Procedure was adopted in Czechoslovakia three years later than in Austria. Considering that Czechoslovakia separated from Austria-Hungary in 1918, the available sources from 1928 (ie ten years after establishing the independent State) and other (later) years are cautious in acknowledging Austrian inspiration, but it existed. However, we find literature that does focus on the Austrian AVG.[15] Czechoslovak scholars had good knowledge of the situation in Austria and its legislation.[16] When comparing the individual provisions, the Czechoslovak 1928 Code of Administrative Procedure was 20% identical to the Austrian AVG. It should be noted that the structure of the two regulations was also very similar.

Subsequent Codes of Administrative Procedure adopted by the Socialist regime could not, by their very nature, be inspired by the capitalist—and enemy—State.

[14] R Pomahač, 'Základní zásady činnosti správních orgánů' in J Rajchl (ed), *Správní řád 10 let v praxi* (Univerzita Karlova 2016) 55.
[15] Hoetzel (n 10).
[16] A Štafl, *Řádné i mimořádné opravné prostředky v řízení správním: podle vlád. nař. ze dne 13. ledna 1928, č. 8. Sb. z. a n.* (V Linhart 1939) 193.

Despite highlighting Socialist ideology, the Code of Administrative Procedure of 1967 in particular reveals their origins in the previous legal regulation of 1928, as in the Austrian AVG.

Austrian regulation was not directly acknowledged in relation to the circumstances of the establishment of Czechoslovakia. However, the Supreme Administrative Court in Prague relied on the earlier case law of the Administrative Court in Vienna, which it followed. These principles were a traditional part of the scholarship on administrative law and case law referred to them.

B. The Cultural Influence of the Austrian Codification

Professor of administrative law Jiří Hoetzel (1874–1961) referred to the Austrian AVG in a 1928 article, in which he acknowledged the inspiration for the Czechoslovak Code of Administrative Procedure of 1928. He even directly refutes the objection that the Czechoslovak Code of Administrative Procedure of 1928 copied the Austrian one.[17] In the article, he evaluated both legal regulations.

Another case mentioning the Austrian AVG was the 'administrative procedure' entry in the *Dictionary of Czechoslovak Public Law* (1934). We also find remarks in the commentary on the 1928 Code of Administrative Procedure.[18]

On the contrary, from the end of 1938, during the Second World War, and the Socialist era from 1948 to 1989, we find no references to the Austrian AVG.

The requirements and instruments resulted from the jurisprudence of the Administrative Court in Vienna (and later the Czechoslovak Supreme Administrative Court in Prague). These elements were also presented in the literature as well as in the legal regulation of administrative procedure. The Codes of Administrative Procedure of 1928, 1955, 1960, and 1967 made provision for the elements mentioned, but with differing degrees of intensity.

The administrative judiciary was abolished 1952, giving rise to the prosecutor's action. Judicial review of the decision was severely limited to specific cases relating to social security. The civil courts decided on actions.

IV. The Main Procedural Requirements

It is appropriate, at this juncture, to stand back and focus on the main procedural requirements included in the 1928 administrative procedure legislation. Four issues will be considered below (Sections A–C): preliminary investigation and fact

[17] J Hoetzel, 'Nové správní řízení' (1928) 6 Právník 266–76.

[18] J Václav, R Holl and L Jabůrek, *Vládní nařízení o řízení ve věcech náležejících do působnosti politických úřadu* (Praha 1928).

finding; the right to a hearing and the requirement to give reasons; the available administrative and judicial remedies.

A. Completeness of the Preliminary Investigation and Fact Finding

The principle of material (objective) truth is crucial in this regard. While the 1928 Code of Administrative Procedure did not set out any specifics, the later regulations were different. The 1955 Code of Administrative Procedure stipulated a requirement for the most precise and entire determination of the state of facts. This principle was replicated verbatim in the 1960 Code of Administrative Procedure. The 1967 Code included the addition of material truth, obliging the administrative body to precisely and entirely recognise the actual state of facts. It was the same in all cases, namely that an administrative authority was not limited to requests for taking evidence.

The preliminary investigation was not expressly regulated by any of the Administrative Procedure Codes, although in practice authorities tended to refer to it. There were no significant differences between them in this respect.

B. The Right to a Hearing and the Requirement to Give Reasons

The right to be heard is a traditional principle (not only) of administrative procedure. All Codes of Administrative Procedure addressed it. It is crucial at the start of the procedure (with the opportunity to comment) and through access to documents relevant to the decision. It is related with the right to discovery of relevant documents and the rights to comment on same before the decision is handed down.

The requirement to give reasons of the administrative decision was considered in all the relevant regulations of administrative procedure. We can add that the Codes of Administrative Procedure of 1955 and 1960 modified the requirement of proper justification/reasoning on ideological grounds. According to art 25 of the 1955 Code of Administrative Procedure, justification serves to:

> strengthen the confidence of workers in the people's democratic State apparatus and educate them to perform their duties in a voluntary and disciplined manner.

C. The Available Remedies

All the examined Administrative Procedure Codes regulated the (administrative) appeal as an ordinary remedy in administrative procedure. Another traditional measure was the so-called out-appeal procedure (review procedure). The Codes of

Administrative Procedure of 1928 and 1967 also regulated the reopening of proceedings. The Codes of Administrative Procedure of 1955, 1960, and 1967 regulated the actions of the prosecutor, as well as appeals and review procedure. The same administrative authority could make changes, and, if not, the superior administrative authority was competent to decide. It was a measure to safeguard against 'Socialist legality'.

We should remark here that the legal regulation of (administrative) appeals in the 1960 Code of Administrative Procedure was atypical. It did not rely on the traditional two tiers of judgment, but only a different unit or department of the same first instance administrative authority decided on appeals. However, this so-called horizontal approach did not work, and the Code of Administrative Procedure of 1967 returned to the traditional appeal structure.

V. Hypothetical Cases

The following hypothetical cases will be examined below: authorisations and licences (Section A); disciplinary procedures for civil servants (Section B); the expropriation procedure (Section C); administrative planning (Section D).

Some introductory remarks are necessary. We distinguish between the periods before and after 1948. In the period from 1918 to 1948, legal regulation was dual, coming from the previous Austrian and Hungarian laws if no Czechoslovakian legal regulation was adopted 1918. It would have been challenging to answer the questions without a number of uncertainties. This legal dualism was a real problem for the Czechoslovakian legal order and persisted through the entire interwar period. Completely different principles applied for the period of Socialist law after 1948. For instance, individual enterprises were not permitted.

A. Authorisations and Licences

In the interwar period, the legal regulation governing authorisation to open a pharmacy was contained in Act No 5/1907 Coll governing pharmacy. The provincial office granted the authorisation (*koncese*) to operate a pharmacy, and the procedure followed the Administrative Code of 1928.[19] The party to this proceeding had the right to be informed about the procedure and concession. If the provincial office denied authorisation, Mr Schultz could have brought an (administrative) case before the Supreme Administrative Court because there was no superior authority above the provincial political office.

[19] F Vavřínek, *Stručný přehled zřízení správního* (Všehrd 1928) 209.

In 1948, the Socialist regime nationalised industries and services. Private businesses were subject to severe restrictions after 1948, and pharmacies became part of nationalised healthcare.

B. Disciplinary Procedure for Civil Servants

The civil service was regulated by Act No 15/1914 Coll on the Employment of Civil Servants. Due to the art 1 sec 2 of the Code of Administration Procedure of 1928, this Code did not use the procedural matters of civil service.

Act No 15/1914 Coll stipulated rules for disciplinary proceedings. A disciplinary commission decided on disciplinary penalties. Notification of the start of disciplinary proceedings was obligatory, and the official had access to the files. An (oral) hearing would follow. The parties were entitled to know the reasoning behind the decision. The claimant could appeal the decision, but judicial oversight was not admissible under Act No 36/1876 Coll.

After 1948, Act No 15/1914 Coll was replaced by a law regulating the civil service. However, it did not address disciplinary procedure. It was subsequently repealed and replaced by the Labour Code. In this respect, officials enjoyed the same treatment as other employees.

C. The Expropriation Procedure

In this case, Act No 30/1878 Coll on Expropriation for the Purpose of Building Railways and Operating on Them shall be applied. Its Article 14 enshrined the right to object to a published expropriation plan. The so-called political authority conducted the proceedings, applying the Code of Administrative Procedure of 1928. Appeal against the expropriation decision to the Ministry of the Interior was admissible. The decision on compensation for expropriation was left to the court unless an amount was agreed.

D. Administrative Planning

In the case of spatial planning and construction procedure, the legislation was somewhat fragmented for a long time. The regulations governed the so-called position plans. Act No 280/1949 Coll on Spatial Planning was simplified and became clearer. Act No 84/1958 Coll on Spatial Planning (Zoning) later replaced this law.

Planning did not come within the scope of the Codes of Administrative Procedure. A different matter from the planning was a decision on permission to open a school and its construction. Authorities issued a construction permit in proceedings, applying the Codes of Administrative Procedure. Land-use plans took the form of legal regulations, and they could not be opposed. In the case of a building location or a construction permit, there was an administrative procedure in place that allowed appeals.

VI. The Personal Factor

Czechoslovakia engaged the Czechoslovak nationals who had worked as officials and judges with the Austrian authorities to serve the new republic. This applied to Czech judges at the Administrative Court in Vienna. Among others, we might mention Ferdinand Pantůček (judge at the Administrative Court in Vienna before the First World War and the first President of the Supreme Administrative Court in Czechoslovakia), Jiří Hoetzel (expert and professor of administrative law, author of the 1920 Constitution of Czechoslovakia), and František Weyr (professor of theory of law in Brno and author of textbooks on Czech administrative law in the interwar period).

The most important figure (after Ferdinand Pantůček) was Emil Hácha (1872–1945). Emil Hácha was an outstanding expert on administrative and comparative administrative law. After the outbreak of the First World War, he worked as a judge at the Administrative Court in Vienna (1916–18). He went on to work (together with Ferdinand Pantůček) on establishing an administrative judiciary in Czechoslovakia after 1918. He was the President (Chairman) of the Supreme Administrative Court after the death of Ferdinand Pantůček in 1925 until 1938. Thanks to him, the Supreme Administrative Court created the case law that served as the basis for the later adoption of the Code of Administrative Procedure of 1928.

Unfortunately, he gained prominence as the President of Czechoslovakia in its darkest times. The Munich Agreement compelled Czechoslovakia to cede border areas (Sudetenland) to Nazi Germany, and other territories to Poland and Hungary. Emil Hácha became President of the second Czechoslovak Republic. He continued as State President in the Protectorate of Bohemia and Moravia after the German occupation of the Czech lands on 15 March 1939.

Emil Hácha played a tragic role destined to fail. Initially, he cooperated with domestic and foreign resistance movements and used his authority to alleviate Nazi repression. Because of Hácha's poor health since 1942, he had performed the Presidency just on a formal basis. He died in prison briefly after liberation in 1945.

Nevertheless, Hácha's academic and judicial activity is still highly valued. He was an expert on British law, and translated English literature (most notably *Three Men in a Boat* by Jerome Klapka Jerome).

7
The Polish Legislation on Administrative Procedure

Wojciech Piątek

I. Introduction

This chapter provides an overview of how administrative procedure developed in Poland between 1920 and 1970, with a focus on the influence exerted by the 1925 Austrian General Administrative Procedure Act. The discussion will begin with the background, including history and the constitutional framework, which has evolved more than once, during the relevant time frame. This will be followed by an analysis of both the legislative framework governing administrative procedures and their management in some cases.

II. Background: History and Legal Culture

It ought to be said at the outset, for the sake of clarity, that Poland has had general legislation on administrative procedure for almost a century. The first Polish general legislation was enacted in 1928 (in 1922, a single-tiered administrative tribunal had been established following the Austrian model of the *Verwaltungsgerichtshof* in Vienna); a statute on legal remedies against the decisions of the administrative authorities was passed in 1923, and in 1924 a statute on legal remedies against the decisions of administrative authorities in educational matters was enacted. These statutes were also influenced by Austrian law and, furthermore, they partially regulated administrative procedure.[1] The Code of Administrative Procedure (CAP) of 22 March 1928 was legally binding from 1 July 1928 until the close of 1960. On 1 January 1961, the CAP of 14 June 1960 came into force and has been binding ever since.

[1] E Starczewski, 'On the Administrative Proceedings Act' (1926) 12 GAiPP 185.

Wojciech Piątek, *The Polish Legislation on Administrative Procedure* In: *The Austrian Codification of Administrative Procedure*. Edited by: Giacinto Della Cananea, Angela Ferrari Zumbini, and Otto Pfersmann, Oxford University Press.
 DOI: 10.1093/oso/9780198867623.003.0007

A. The First Period: 1928–1945

Following the First World War, there was a pressing need to pass a new law on administrative proceedings that would cover the entire Polish territory and unify the various procedural regulations established by the formerly occupied countries. Before the war, Poland had been occupied by three neighbouring countries (Austria, Prussia, and Russia) with different normative regulations, including those for proceedings before administrative authorities. After the war, these regulations remained binding in the previously occupied parts of Poland. The result was that three different legal orders regulated the same spheres in different parts of the country. There was an urgent need to make administrative procedure uniform and organise administrative authorities more professionally (excessive length of proceedings and the incompetence of administrative officers were regarded as the main weaknesses of public administration at the time).[2] The need was also evident in the jurisprudence of the Supreme Administrative Court (SAC), established in 1922[3] as a consequence of art 73 of the Constitution of 17 March 1921[4] which provided for an administrative tribunal that would be independent from the ordinary courts. The jurisprudence of the SAC was also significant in the preparation and interpretation of the CAP.[5]

In January 1926, the Council of Ministers' commission for preparing the CAP draft was appointed. The commission started its work in February 1926 and held 12 sessions. The commission prepared a draft of the CAP.[6] This was the fruit of discussion among researchers from across the country. Many professors and administrative officers sent their proposals on improving the published draft to the commission. The preparations for the final version lasted two years and were conducted hastily.[7]

The 1928 CAP had binding force until the introduction of the CAP of 1960 (which came into force on 1 January 1961). Nevertheless, after the Second World War, the CAP was gradually interpreted in accordance with—and supplemented by—regulations reflecting the Communist regime, including a separate complaints and requests procedure (from Soviet sources). It was not harmonised with the CAP of 1928.[8] The differences between the CAP and the new regulations (covering the structure of administrative authorities, the basic principles of the new Communist

[2] E Starczewski, 'Draft Law on Administrative Proceedings' (1926) 23 GAiPP 384.

[3] The Act on the Supreme Administrative Court of 3 August 1922, Journal of Laws 1922, No 67, item 600 as amended.

[4] Journal of Laws 1921, No 44, item 267 as amended.

[5] W Klonowiecki, *Party in Administrative Proceedings* (Towarzystwo Naukowe KUL 1938) 27.

[6] It was published in the GAiPP in 1926 (Nos 30 and 31).

[7] For more on the preparation procedure, see R Hausner, 'Origin of the Presidential Decree on Administrative Procedure' (1933) 15 GAiPP 502.

[8] Z Janowicz, *Code of Administrative Proceedings: Commentary* (Wydawnictwo Naukowe PWN 1992) 17–18.

regime, and special procedural regulations) were more significant and effectively limited application of the 1928 CAP.

B. The Second Period: 1945–1960

Preparations for the new CAP began in 1956 and lasted until 1960. It was necessary to introduce a new CAP so as to adapt the administrative procedure to the new institutional and political circumstances in a socialist country.[9] Nevertheless, the procedural regulations set out in this CAP, including the general principles and the organisation of proceedings, were well received by the academic community.[10] In addition to the typical Communist features eliminated in 1990, the CAP of 1960 contained many important procedural guarantees regarding the participation of individuals in administrative procedure, such as the right of objective truth, and, in this connection, the principle of an open system of evidence, the right of a party to participate actively in an administrative procedure, the principle of taking both public and individual interests into consideration, the principle of conciliatorily dispute resolution, and the right to two-tier administrative proceedings. These principles and rights still play a crucial role in the relations between administrative authorities and individuals.

Three further features of Polish administrative procedure legislation must be observed. First, there is no special CAP to supplement the statute passed by the national Parliament. The CAP can be modified only by other statutory provisions (eg construction law, environmental law, and water law) for special administrative proceedings. Central and local government authorities cannot modify statutes; these are of a lower order and must follow the provisions of the CAP. Second, as Poland is a unitary State, there is no such thing as regional legislation on administrative procedure.

C. General and Sector-Specific Rules

The third feature of administrative procedure legislation is that there are no special APAs other than the general CAP. On 22 March 1928, three laws were passed (not statutes but presidential decrees with the force of law): on administrative procedure (Journal of Laws 1928, No 36, item 341), on criminal-administrative procedure (Journal of Laws 1928, No 38, item 365), and administrative enforcement

[9] S Rozmaryn, 'About the Draft Code of Administrative Proceedings' (1961) 4 Państwo i Prawo 631–32.

[10] F Longchamps, 'The Problem of the Durability of an Administrative Decision' (1961) 12 Państwo i Prawo 910; Janowicz (n 8) 19.

procedure (Journal of Laws 1928, No 36, item 342). The CAP was applicable in all proceedings on all administrative law matters handled by administrative authorities and local government units (although the exceptions to this rule were broad and concerned disputes concerning military service, mining authorities, tax proceedings, matters handled by diplomatic missions of the Republic of Poland abroad, disciplinary proceedings, and disputes regulated by criminal-administrative procedure). The second act regulated the procedure for imposing administrative fines. This legislation established the enforcement of administrative obligations not voluntarily fulfilled by debtors. All the statutes mentioned above are regarded as a whole, like the administrative procedure *largo sensu*,[11] while the CAP shapes the administrative procedure *stricto sensu* (it is worth mentioning that three acts on administrative proceedings, administrative fines, and enforcement were also passed in Austria on 21 July 1925. Unlike in the Austrian regulations, no specific act for introducing the three decrees was passed in Poland.

III. Legal Sources for Administrative Procedure

A. Constitutional Principles

As observed earlier, the constitutional framework in Poland has changed more than once. Three constitutions were drawn up between 1920 and 1970.

The first one was enacted in 1921.[12] Article 71 established the right to appeal against decisions issued by public administrative authorities and local government units. The details of this right were regulated in Chapter XIII of the CAP. In art 73, the right to two-instance court-administrative proceedings was created to protect individuals from unlawful administrative acts issued by the State and local government units.

The second constitution was enacted in 1935 (the 'April Constitution' of 23 April 1935, Journal of Laws 1935, No 30, item 227). It contained no principles concerning administrative procedure. In art 70(1)(b), only the SAC was mentioned, specifying its task of exercising control over administrative acts.

The third constitution was passed in 1952 the 'Soviet Constitution' of 22 July 1952, Journal of Law 1952, No 33, item 232). Article 73 expressed the right of each citizen to submit complaints and requests to any administrative authority, which was the object of a separate statute, incorporated into the CAP in 1960. Administrative courts were not reactivated until 1980.

[11] According to Roman Hausner, the connection between these decrees is close; R Hausner, 'Three Laws on Administrative Proceedings' (1929) 8 GAiPP 274.

[12] 'The March Constitution' of 17 March 1921, Journal of Laws 1921, No 44, item 267.

B. Other Legal Sources

Within these constitutional settlements, the sources of the 1928 CAP were:

- the case law of the SAC, established in 1922. Some of the judges were appointed to the commission tasked with preparing the CAP in 1926;
- the case law of the administrative authorities. Selected members from the administrative authorities were the second largest group (after the judges of the SAC), appointed to the commission for the preparation of the CAP;
- academia, namely professors of law and administrative officers who evaluated the draft CAP published in GAiPP (1926, Nos 30 and 31), making suggestions on how to improve the final version;
- the Austrian CAP passed in 1925 after publication of the draft in GAiPP in 1925 (Nos 9, 10, 11, and 13). This CAP was presented as a model for modern administrative procedure 'prepared by outstanding experts in the field of administrative law'.[13] Eugeniusz Starczewski was the president of the commission that prepared the Polish draft CAP. He had no connection with the Austrian education system or culture of law. He was born in 1862 under the Russian occupation and studied law in Moscow. He died in 1927 before the CAP was passed in 1928.

The sources of the 1960 CAP were:

- the general principles of the Soviet regime. The CAP of 1928 was not adapted to these specific circumstances;[14]
- the need to adjust the structure of postwar public administration in Poland to the structural and procedural framework of the CAP;[15]
- academia—professors were much more involved in preparing the new CAP (including participation in the Commission of Administrative Law within the framework of the Association of Polish Lawyers) than in 1928. This meant that the CAP contained the principles and procedural solutions common to modern standards of the rule of law from the outset, providing for the active participation of individuals in specific administrative procedures.

The 1928 CAP did not contain a specific chapter on administrative principles, unlike that of 1960, which set them out in arts 4–12. Nevertheless, the principles of the administrative procedure of 1928 were analysed in the literature and defined as

[13] E Starczewski, 'Draft Law on Administrative Proceedings (1926) 23 GAiPP 385.

[14] S Rozmaryn, 'About the Draft Code of Administrative Proceedings' (1959) 4 Państwo i Prawo 631.

[15] K Jandy-Jendrośka, 'System of Jurisdictional Administrative Proceedings' in T Rabska and J Łętowski (eds), *System of Administrative Law*, vol III (Publishing House of the Polish Academy of Science 1978) 155–56.

general guidelines that would be significant for the construction and interpretation of detailed CAP regulations.[16] The fundamental principles were the following: the *ex officio* activity of administrative authorities, the party's right to be heard, objective (material) truth, the principles of conducting proceedings in writing, the public hearing, and the rule of law.

The nature of the general principles was the subject of controversy in 1960 during preparations for the CAP. On the one hand, these principles were perceived as postulates, general ideas relating to the CAP without force of law. On the other hand, the normative character of the principles was stressed.[17] The second option was adopted in the literature and is still seen in a positive light. The general principles of the CAP are regulations with binding normative force, recognised as fundamental by the legislator and distinguished in the special chapter of the CAP.[18] These principles play a decisive role in interpreting the special provisions of the CAP to this day. In CAP case law, if there is more than one possibility of interpreting the concrete provisions of the CAP, the outcome should comply with its general principles.[19]

IV. The Polish and the Austrian Administrative Procedure Legislation

A. A Long-Standing Influence

There is no doubt in the Polish scholarly literature that the Austrian General Law on Administrative Procedure of 1925 had a role in the legislative process resulting in the enactment of the CAP of 1928. The Austrian tradition also influenced the CAP of 1960, despite the particular circumstances (under the Soviet regime) in which it came into being.

The draft Austrian Code was published in the GAiPP in 1925.[20] Its influence was clear in the fifth version of the draft of the Polish CAP (the former versions were more heavily based on technical matters than on simplifications to the procedure. There were eight versions of the draft altogether).[21] Polish

[16] W Kałuski, *Administrative Proceedings: A Systematic Handbook with the Text of the Current Regulation and Specimens of Applications and Settlements* (Związek Pracowników Administracji Gminnej RP 1929) 19. See also R Hausner, 'Three Laws on Administrative Proceedings' (1929) 8 GAiPP.

[17] For a more detailed discussion, see W Piątek, 'Problems of Reconstruction of General Principles of Administrative Proceedings' in JP Tarno and W Piątek (eds), *General Principles of Administrative Proceedings. Volume II. Part 2* (Wolters Kluwer 2018) 266–68.

[18] Janowicz (n 8) 53. See also S Rozmaryn, 'On the General Principles of the Code of Administrative Proceedings' (1961) 12 Państwo i Prawo 887–88.

[19] J Paweł Tarno, 'Functions of the General Principles of Administrative Proceedings' in Tarno and Piątek (n 17) 57–71.

[20] Nos 9, 10, 11, and 13.

[21] See R Hausner, 'Origin of the Presidential Decree on Administrative Proceedings' (1933) 15 GAiPP 503.

scholars have observed that the basis for the preparatory works in Poland was not the final version of the Austrian CAP but a draft that had been modified during the Austrian legislative process, according to Władysław Czapliński. This explains the differences between the Austrian and Polish regulations concerning the obligation of an administrative authority to provide written explanations for an administrative decision. Unlike the Polish CAP, there were no regulated exceptions to this obligation in the Austrian one. They are derived from the literature but with no concrete legal basis.[22] Nevertheless, Austrian influence was stressed unanimously in the Polish scholarly literature, in addition to other factors impacting on the new law, such as the jurisprudence of the Polish SAC,[23] the practice of the Polish administrative authorities, and former partial regulations on administrative proceedings passed in Poland between 1918 and 1928.[24] Ultimately, the Polish CAP had a similar but more complex structure to the Austrian CAP, with its 123 articles rather than the 80 of the Austrian CAP. According to Professor Hausner, the Polish CAP was around 20% longer than its Austrian counterpart.[25] The similarities between these statutes were regarded as a springboard for analysing Austrian doctrine, including materials from the drafting process, in the interpretation of the Polish CAP. This was also the main reason for publishing the translated version of the Austrian CAP in the GAiPP along with the official explanation (1925) 9 GAiPP 201

During the preparatory phase for the 1960 CAP, there was less evidence of influence deriving from Austrian legal culture and the 1925 CAP than there had been in 1928. The main inspirations were Soviet regulations and reasoning. Nevertheless, involving law professors in the drafting process meant continuing the same line of legal culture. Therefore, the traditional procedural principles and two-tier proceedings were maintained alongside the traditional Soviet institutions, such as proceedings concerning complaints and requests to administrative authorities. Concluding an administrative proceeding with an administrative decision was still a basic way of solving an administrative case. A drawback described in the literature was the lack of an administrative judiciary and the supervision of administrative decisions by an independent and impartial court.[26] As stated above, following the Second World War, the administrative courts were not reinstated in Poland until 1980.

[22] See W Czapliński, 'Socially of Administration and the Duty to Justify Decisions ' (1936) 8 GAiPP 231.

[23] W Klonowiecki, *Party in Administrative Proceedings* (Towarzystwo Naukowe KUL 1938).

[24] S Urbanowicz, 'New Law on Administrative Proceedings' (1928) 24 *Gazeta Sądowa Warszawska* 371.

[25] R Hausner, 'Origin of the Presidential Decree on Administrative Proceedings' (1933) 15 GAiPP 504.

[26] Janowicz (n 8) 19–20.

B. Explicit Jurisprudential and Academic References

The SAC did not cite the Austrian APA in the grounds of its judgments. In contrast to current practice, the grounds of SAC verdicts were shorter but more explicit. The court focused on the circumstances of a given dispute. Reasons from the jurisprudence of the Austrian SAC (*Verwaltungsgerichtshof*) were—but only rarely—presented in support of the final outcome of a judgment.[27] On the occasions when the courts used general principles, they focused on the Polish CAP and national legislation.

As stated above, the Polish translation of the Austrian draft CAP was published in the 1925 GAiPP,[28] and its influence on the Polish CAP was stressed in all the above-cited monographs and papers in law journals, although the references are more general, offering few details. Nevertheless, they appear in almost all publications concerning the CAP of 1928. Polish scholarship fully recognises the influence of the Austrian CAP on Polish legislation and that of the Austrian administrative judiciary on the Polish SAC. Nevertheless, apart from the short texts mainly found in the GAiPP, there is no in-depth analysis of the impact of concrete procedural institutions from the Austrian CAP on the Polish regulation of 1928.

V. The Main Procedural Requirements

It is appropriate, at this juncture, to stand back and focus on the main procedural requirements included in the 1928 and 1960 Polish administrative procedure legislation. They were part of pre–Second World War SAC case law on external remedies that could be submitted to address final administrative acts. Four issues will be considered: preliminary investigation and fact-finding (Section A); the right to a hearing (Section B); the duty to give reasons (Section C); the available administrative and judicial remedies (Section D).

A. Preliminary Investigation and Fact-Finding

As stated above, one of the fundamental principles of administrative procedure was that of material truth.[29]

The obligation of the administrative authority to establish facts relevant to the outcome of the procedure was established in art 44 of the 1928 CAP. The authority

[27] M Baumgart and He Habel, *Law on the Supreme Administrative Tribunal and Law on Administrative Proceedings* (Bibljoteka Prawnicza 1933) 70–71.

[28] See (n 20).

[29] Kałuski (n 16) 23.

could establish the scope of discovery procedure *ex officio*, considering purposefulness, speed, simplicity, and the costs of the procedure. The obligation to establish facts fell to the public authority in question, having the obligation to clarify the substance of the dispute (art 47(1) CAP). Every final decision was considered a statement by an authority, irrespective of the actions of the parties to the proceedings.[30] Under this regulation, the role of individuals was auxiliary. This did not mean that they could not be involved in fact-finding; they had the right to participate actively in a dispute (to be informed and instructed about the course of proceedings and their rights), but the burden of proof was on the administrative authority.

There were two forms of fact-finding: public hearings and closed sessions. The first served to resolve parties' conflicting interests in disputes demanding the examination of facts with the participation of witnesses and experts, or, if the investigation was to be carried out outside the authority which conducted the proceedings, by a separately delegated staff member. Detailed rules for organising and carrying out the hearings were regulated in the CAP. The rights of individuals had to be protected during this process, and, according to the CAP, a public hearing was not obligatory in every case. In particular statutes (ie water law, public industrial law), there were obligations to perform this form of discovery procedure. In addition to such special regulations, public hearings were to be performed in every case if this would assist in fact-finding.[31]

Anything lawful could be used as evidence. An administrative authority was free to evaluate evidence ('free approval'). This latitude was not total and did not exclude review of all the final administrative decisions performed by the SAC, which examined the margins of latitude and procedural issues.[32] Official documents issued by other administrative authorities through the correct procedure were presumed lawful, which meant that a document issued by an administrative authority had to be considered valid and binding in terms of its content. Nevertheless, this presumption was not absolute and could be reversed.

In addition to documents, witness statements, the opinions of expert witnesses, and inspections were regulated under the CAP. The most detailed regulation concerned witnesses. It was obligatory to testify, and penalties would be applied to those who failed to comply. Only three groups of people were free from this obligation, namely, persons incapable of distinguishing information, priests—limited to what had been entrusted to them in the confessional—and officials protecting State

[30] R Hausner, 'Three Laws on Administrative Proceedings' (1929) 8 GAiPP 276.

[31] W Supiński, *Administrative Proceedings: Outline of Theory with Commentary* (Polska Drukarnia Narodowa 1933) 115.

[32] The judgment of the SAC from 6 April 1934, l. rej. 10564/34 published in E Iserzon, *Administrative Proceedings. Criminal-Administrative Proceedings. Compulsory Proceedings in Administration. The Act on Court Administrative Tribunal. The Union Regulations—Jurisprudence* (Księgarnia Powszechna 1938) 41.

secrets known to them, unless granted permission to testify by their superiors. Any witness could also refuse to answer questions if the answer could expose someone to the risk of criminal responsibility, disgrace, or loss of property.

Administrative authorities were free to assess concrete facts (art 50 of the CAP from 1928). This does not mean that their appraisal of evidence was unlimited; at their discretion, they could assign a deciding authority, placing it under the control of a higher administrative body and the SAC.

The fact-finding carried out by administrative authorities could be subject to SAC control. Incorrect procedure (eg if the evidence for the facts was incomplete, inconsistent with collected documents, or gathered unlawfully) was sufficient reason to quash a decision and send the dispute back to an administrative authority for a second examination.[33]

The CAP of 1960 contained a similar regulation on fact-finding and evidence collection. The principle of material truth held, and still holds, a central place in administrative proceedings, obliging administrative authorities to establish the facts *ex officio* during these proceedings; these are initiated by authorities and lead to obligations being imposed on individuals.

B. The Right to a Hearing

The right to be heard was recognised as one of the most significant guarantees of a fair administrative trial. This right was established, in term of a right to defence, in the 1928 CAP, especially concerning proceedings with two or more parties, although administrative procedure is non-contentious.[34]

This right was guaranteed throughout the various stages of administrative proceedings. According to art 47(1) CAP, parties were entitled to recognise evidentiary material and present opinions during the evidentiary proceeding. They were entitled to formulate evidence motions that could be rejected only in extraordinary cases or when they were applied after an established term, or they led to excessively lengthy proceedings (art 47(2) CAP). Parties to the proceedings had the right to take an active part in all the activities performed during the fact-finding stage, including hearing the testimonies of witnesses and expert witnesses or during inspections, as long as doing so did not conflict with the public interest (art 66 CAP). Active participation meant the right to put questions to witnesses and experts, to present opinions, and to formulate motions on how the procedure should be conducted.[35] Each party was to be informed of any appeal brought by another party

33 Supiński (n 31) 118.
34 Kałuski (n 16) 21.
35 Baumgart and Habel (n 27) 36.

(art 89(2) CAP). If the appeal was likely to affect the rights or obligations of another party, the latter would have the right to be heard (art 91 CAP).

The significance of the right to be heard was maintained in the CAP of 1960. An administrative authority was, and still is, required to inform individuals of the possible outcome of the proceeding before issuing a decision based on the evidence (art 8(1) CAP; currently art 10(1) CAP). Individuals had, and still have, the right to participate in every stage of administrative proceedings, above all in evidentiary proceedings.

C. The Duty to Give Reasons

The obligation to set out the grounds for adverse decisions was regulated in art 75(2)–(3) of the 1928 CAP. Besides the general obligation to provide written reasons for a decision in which both the factual and normative reasoning had to be presented, the CAP also provided for exemptions from this duty. Here, the total discretion of administrative authorities when issuing a decision was envisaged, releasing the authority from legal justification. In this case, it was sufficient to present the legal basis for the decision. In cases where discretion was not total, it was only possible to present written explanations when an important public interest was incompatible with providing more detailed grounds. In this, Polish scholarship saw a parallel with the Austrian CAP, which regulated only a general norm concerning the obligation to justify adverse decisions. According to Władysław Czapliński, when issuing discretionary decisions, it was not necessary to take evidence regarding circumstances not provided for in the regulation. In such cases, there was no need to include the results of the discovery proceedings in the *ratio* of a decision. Furthermore, Austrian practice before the Second World War did not seek to justify discretionary decisions based on their factual circumstances.[36]

According to an SAC judgment, the lack of proper justification for a decision was not a ground for quashing a decision because eliminating the fault would not have affected the final outcome of the dispute.[37] This ruling was not unanimously accepted by scholars, who stressed the importance of providing a written explanation of a decision for the protection of individual rights.[38]

In the 1960 CAP, the obligation to prepare written explanations was similar to that set out in the 1928 text. According to the first version of the CAP of 1960, it was only necessary to prepare a written explanation in situations where the decision failed to consider a request by the party into account (in whole or in part), to resolve the disputed interests of the parties, or else imposed/stated an obligation

36 Czapliński (n 17) 232.
37 SAC, 21 March 1931, L rej 4338/29, published in Baumgart and Habel (n 27) 44–45.
38 Supiński (n 31).

regarding a party. Written reasons for a decision could be omitted when the existing statutory provisions indicated that this might be necessary in the interests of national security or public order.

D. The Available Remedies

The 1928 CAP regulated both ordinary and extraordinary remedies. As for ordinary remedies, it was possible to appeal to the next authority in the hierarchy against a first-instance administrative authority decision within 14 days after it was announced or handed down. The appeal served to have the case heard *ex novo* and determine it on its merits. It was not possible to quash the first-instance decision and thus refer the dispute to the first-instance authority.[39] The CAP did not therefore require an appeal to include detailed grounds. Nevertheless, it established grounds for preventing new evidentiary material from being considered. These included excessive length of proceedings and the appearance of new evidence after the first-instance decision had been issued. Another case for exclusion was when the provisions of other statutes stipulated that, under certain circumstances, the administrative or judicial authority competent to decide on the preliminary question had reached a different position on an important point from the stance taken when the decision had initially been issued.

Appeals were not brought directly before the second-instance authority but through the authority that issued the decision. The first-instance body had to refer the appeal to the higher instance authority within seven days. An appeal could be brought during this time provided that a third person would not acquire any rights from a new decision. If there was any risk that the appeal might affect the rights of someone other than the party lodging the appeal, the administrative authority of second instance had to ensure that it would be able to participate.

If a first-tier decision was not enforced before the time limit for lodging an appeal had elapsed, a timely appeal would halt enforcement. Exceptions to this rule were envisaged only in the event of decisions whose immediate enforceability was provided for by law at the request of all the parties to the proceedings or when the parties had waived their right to appeal.

Discovery proceedings before a second-instance authority could be ordered by the appeal authority *ex officio* or upon the parties' request. They could be carried out by an appellate body or the authority of a lower tier. The CAP closely regulated what kind of evidence the second-instance authority was *not* to consider. Such evidence had to be presented during a first-instance procedure, presented only to obtain the extension of a procedure, or to lead to the opening of a new dispute (art

[39] SAC 18 November 1926, L rej 985/24, SAC 25 March 1935, L rej 6886/32, published in Iserzon (n 26) 56–57.

85(2) of the CAP from 1928). In addition to these exemptions, an appellate authority had to consider new evidence.[40]

An appellate authority was not limited by the reason for the appeal or the findings of a body lower down in the hierarchy when issuing its decision. When appropriate, a dispute had to be settled on its merits without referring it to a first-tier body.[41]

The CAP also regulated extraordinary remedies, namely the resumption of proceedings, quashing or changing a correct final decision, and proceedings for rendering a decision void.

The first remedy was a procedural measure that allowed the proceeding to be reopened if significant grounds emerged. These included false evidence, new material circumstances, or new evidence existing when the decision was issued but was unknown to the first-instance administrative authority, and assessment of a preliminary question by a competent authority differing from the one made when the decision was initially issued.

The procedure for finding a decision void did not focus on procedural defects but on grounds constituting an element in a decision. Such grounds concerned the breach of rules regarding competency when issuing a decision, the lack of legal grounds or enforceability, the risk of an offence being committed if the decision were enforced, or defects rendering the decision void due to special regulations.

Under the 1928 CAP, a correct decision too could be changed or quashed. When a decision allowed a party to acquire a right, it could only be altered with its consent.

The scope of ordinary and extraordinary remedies was maintained in the 1960 CAP. However, a second ordinary remedy was added to supplement the appeal, namely a complaint concerning orders issued by first-instance administrative authorities.

The 1928 and 1960 CAPs both established the obligation to inform parties of the right to challenge final decisions before administrative courts. In the 1960 CAP, this became possible with the re-establishment of the administrative tribunals in 1980.

VI. Hypothetical Cases

After describing the main procedural requirements, it can be helpful to consider how they could be applied, with the caveat made earlier that the courts had different margins of manoeuvre in the two sub-periods of our relevant time frame. The following hypothetical cases will be examined: authorisations and licences

[40] Kałuski (n 16) 129.
[41] Supiński (n 31) 157.

(Section A); disciplinary procedures for civil servants (Section B); the expropriation procedure (Section C); administrative planning (Section D).

A. Authorisations and Licences

After the First World War, no statute was put in place to regulate substantive and procedural rights concerning authorisation to open a pharmacy in Poland. On 25 March 1938, a law was passed on practising pharmacy as a profession (Journal of Laws 1938, No 23, item 202 as amended). The act regulated the conditions for practising the profession, stipulating that only a pharmacist with two years' work experience could run a pharmacy. A law on pharmacies was passed on 15 June 1939 (Journal of Laws 1939, No 55, item 346 as amended). It concerned the internal organisation and external responsibilities of pharmacies as self-governing entities. Without normative rules on granting authorisation to open a pharmacy, the regulations of the three occupying countries were binding.[42] Under the law on basic sanitary principles of 19 July 1919 (Journal of Laws 1919, No 63, item 371 as amended), authorisation to open a pharmacy was granted by the Minister of Public Health (art 2 point 13). This act also envisaged regulating specific matters by decree. In 1920, this authority lay with the Minister (Journal of Laws 1920, No 20, item 420 as amended), and, with a special instruction of 1 June 1931 (Monitor Polski 1931, No 136, item 204), it extended to the Polish territories under Russian occupation. Under both acts, authorisation to open a pharmacy took the form of an administrative decision issued in a procedure regulated by the 1928 CAP. Prior to this, Mr Schultz could have adhered to Polish procedural regulations supplemented by those in force in the occupying countries, depending on the territory where he wanted to obtain authorisation. As of 1922 the case law of the newly established SAC supplemented statutory law. Consequently, Mr Schultz would have been able to exercise all procedural rights regulated by the CAP. A party to the procedure could appeal against the first-instance decision, and, after the final decision had been handed down, could turn to the SAC. If it found the decision unlawful, it would have to refer the case to an administrative authority for a second examination.

After the Second World War, the Ministry of Health too could grant permission to open a pharmacy, but the system was nationalised. Pharmacies could no longer be run by private persons but only by special State units. According to art 8(1) of the pharmacies act of 8 January 1951 (Journal of Laws 1951, No 1, item 2 as amended), these units were to run pharmacies within a chain set up by the Ministry of Health. In this legal framework, it would not have been possible for Mr Schultz to apply for authorisation to open a pharmacy.

[42] J Panejko, 'Public Health' in KW Kumaniecki, B Wasiutyński and J Panejko (eds) *Polish Administrative Law in Outline* (Księgarnia Powszechna 1930) 315–17.

B. Disciplinary Procedure for a Civil Servant

According to art 113(b) of the 1928 CAP, the provisions of this act did not apply to disciplinary proceedings unless other statutes provided otherwise. Hence, information concerning the unlawful behaviour of a civil servant constituting a violation of his/her duties was not regulated by the CAP. A person informing a public authority about such an occurrence was not entitled to be a party to the proceedings and would not have been informed of the final result in the case at hand.

The procedure to be followed in disciplinary cases, the competent authorities, and the penalties to be applied were regulated in a statute dated 17 February 1922 on the organisation of the disciplinary authorities and disciplinary proceedings concerning civil servants (Journal of Laws 1922, No 21, item 165 as amended). Criminal rather than administrative procedure was to be applied in disciplinary procedures. The proceedings were confidential, and the details were not to be published. An investigation would be carried out before the disciplinary committee of first instance, during which a civil servant was entitled to present statements. The right to review the evidence was limited to the final findings relating to the facts. A public hearing would be organised as part of an investigation. At first instance, an appeal against the committee could be brought before the highest disciplinary committee, and the final decision was enforceable immediately after pronouncement.

The situation just described did not change with the entry into force of the act regulating the organisation of disciplinary committees and disciplinary procedure involving public officers of 7 October 1932 (Journal of Laws 1932, No 87, item 738 as amended). This decree was binding until 28 May 1984. It was possible to appeal against a first-instance disciplinary committee decision, and both a civil servant and a disciplinary commissioner were entitled to appeal before a second-instance committee. These detailed procedural rules were regulated by an order of the Council of Ministers dated 17 October 1932 concerning disciplinary committees and procedure involving public officers (Journal of Laws from 1932, No 92, item 790 as amended), independently of the CAP of 1928.

The legal framework did not change with the CAP of 1960. Disciplinary procedure against civil servants was a part of the internal public administrative proceedings. It was criminal rather than administrative, and disciplinary commissioners played a crucial role in fact-finding. Civil servants were entitled to a legal defence. The procedure was not open to the public. In matters not regulated by the act, criminal procedure (para 30 of the 1932 text) would be referred to in an auxiliary role. The procedural rights applicable to cases involving civil servants were derived from criminal rather than administrative procedure.

C. The Expropriation Procedure

According to art 171 of the decree on construction law and housing estates of 16 February 1928 (Journal of Laws 1928, No 23, item 202 as amended), the regulations of the three countries that had occupied Poland before the First World War were applicable until a new law on the expropriation of estates was passed. The Polish law pertaining to this area was passed on 24 September 1934 (Journal of Laws 1934, No 86, item 776 as amended) as a 'law concerning procedure in matters of expropriation'. According to art 2 point 2 of this law, expropriation can lead to the deprivation of property, among other things, for building railway lines. The statute of 1934 was applicable on such matters. According to this act, it is also significant that the CAP of 1928 was to be applied in the absence of special regulation (art 4 of the Law). In other words, the Law on procedure in expropriation matters referred expressly to 1928 CAP, so Mrs Sempronia's rights relating to active participation in the expropriation procedure (the right to a hearing, to be fully informed of the findings, and to a two-instance administrative procedure) had its source in the CAP.

Focusing now on the procedural issues arising from the law on expropriation procedure, the procedure can be divided into three stages: the initiation stage, in which a petition led to a voivodeship motion on expropriation; the procedural stage, after which a voivodeship would issue a decision on expropriation (positive or negative); the compensation stage, in which a substantial sum of money to compensate for expropriation would be assessed. According to art 22 para 3 it was possible to enforce a decision on a motion by the investor immediately without waiting for the final and binding effect of a decision in the event of expropriation to build a railway line.

The public hearing was a compulsory element in the procedure. Mrs Sempronia and others with a legal interest in the dispute (landlords, owners of other civil rights associated with the expropriated estate) would need to be informed about the hearing 14 days before the appointed term. If the number of interested parties was higher, it would be possible to inform them in the usual way and in a specific territory. Experts would also be entitled to take part in the public hearing.

The answer to this question would have been the same under the 1960 CAP regulation, minus the role of the administrative court, which did not exist at this time and was only reinstituted in 1980.

To sum up, the expropriation procedure in Poland was—and still is—one of the standard administrative proceedings where a decision about the rights and duties of parties to the proceeding is issued. This was a two-instance procedure, with all the guarantees arising from the right to a hearing, full knowledge of the findings, the right to present documents, but also the duty of the administration to take into serious account the documents presented by the parties and the right to challenge the decision in administrative and court-administrative procedures. Lastly, individuals were entitled to bring a complaint against a final decision to the SAC.

D. Administrative Planning

The answers to the above questions can be found by analysing the presidential decree with force of law on construction law and housing estates of 16 February 1928 (Journal of Laws 1928, No 23, item 202 as amended). First, the school's location would have to be considered in the location plans. Second, a construction permit would have to be issued.

The intention to draw up a location plan would have to be announced in local newspapers and on official noticeboards belonging to the local community. In addition, with regard to the details of the planned investments, including buildings for public use (schools), the announcements would have to state the period within which any interested party could present motions and complaints. The authority competent to establish the location plan would have to consider these suggestions. Local newspapers and public noticeboards were required to announce that the draft plan would be on public view for at least four weeks. Any interested party could formulate complaints against concrete provisions for consideration by the authority that passed this law. The final version of the location plan was the basis for issuing building permits and, if necessary, for expropriation.

A building permit constituted an administrative decision and, in the case of schools, was issued by voivodeships, which could refer this authority to lower local government authorities. Before issuing the permit and any change to it, the authority had to ask the school authority to express an opinion. An appeal could be made to the next-ranking authority. In the first version of the decree concerning appeals, dated 16 February 1928, the regulation of a statute of 1 August 1923 on legal remedies against administrative authority decisions (Journal of Laws 1923, No 91, item 712 as amended) was adopted. This act was replaced by the 1928 CAP, which came into force on 1 July 1928. Following the final decision of an administrative authority, a complaint could be lodged with the SAC.

The decree of 16 February 1928 was repealed by the 31 January 1961 Construction Act (Journal of Laws 1961, No 7, item 46 as amended), which came into force on 14 August 1961. The rule that it was necessary to obtain a building permit before initiating building investments remained in place. Following a decision of a first-instance authority, any interested party (with legal interest) could lodge an appeal. No complaint to the SAC was possible as the administrative courts were only restored in 1980 after its abolition in the aftermath of the Second World War.

VII. The Personal Factor

Among the many lawyers whose views affected procedure and the final version of the 1928 CAP, there were a number of judges of Polish origin at the Austrian *Verwaltungsgerichtshof*. After the Second World War and the restoration of Polish sovereignty, they were subordinate to the Polish authorities and became judges at the Supreme Court (from 1919), some of them joining the SAC from 1922. One of these was Judge Jan Sawicki, the first president of the SAC. His ideas (adopted from the Austrian *Verwaltungsgerichtshof*) strongly influenced the structure and procedure of the Polish SAC. As stated above, the case law of the SAC had a decisive impact on the preparatory works and interpretation of the CAP of 1928.

Jan Sawicki was born in 1859 in Austrian-occupied Brzeżany, a town of approximately 12,000 inhabitants in the Tarnopol district, today in Ukraine, though up to the Second World War it had been part of Poland. In his youth, he attended the Theresianum in Vienna, an exclusive school preparing young people for the civil service. He studied law at the universities of Vienna and Lwów. As he obtained a broad education in administrative law, he started his professional career in public administration as a trainee in the local municipalities in Galicja and the National Tax Directory in Lwów (1887–92). From 1892 he worked at the Ministry of Finance in Vienna. In 1898, he was appointed to the *Verwaltungsgerichtshof* as legal counsel on matters concerning the Galicja region. In the same year, he became a judge of the court. As a judge, he was the president of one of the sections in the tribunal, starting in 1909. After Poland regained independence in 1918, Sawicki made himself available to the Polish authorities, and in 1919 he became a judge at the newly established Supreme Court in Warsaw. At the same time, he became president of the administrative section of this court. He was involved in drawing up the procedure and the structure of the Polish administrative court. Although discussion around the creation of a Polish administrative court was broad, and various concepts were postulated concerning how this judiciary should be shaped (from one to three tiers and from cassation to substantive-oriented adjudication functions), he worked on drafting the law on the 1922 SAC, in which his ideas were adopted and the Austrian model was followed. Despite the conditions in art 73 of the March Constitution, which provided for an administrative court system with more than one tier, the SAC was created as a one-tier court with cassation functions and general jurisdiction. In Sawicki's opinion, there were insufficient specialists in administrative law in Poland to create a judiciary of more than one tier, and it would also have been too costly. Under his leadership, the SAC began operating on 22 October 1922. The new SAC replaced the fourth (administrative) chamber of the Supreme Court. Sawicki, the first president of the SAC, held office until 1928 when he was forced to retire on political grounds. He died in 1940 in Warsaw. He had two sons Jakub and Stanisław. The first became a professor of law at the University of

Warsaw,[43] while the second (with a PhD from the same university) was a translator of German and Scandinavian languages.[44]

Sawicki authored papers on the administrative judiciary.[45] He was a member of the editorial board of the journal *Orzecznictwo Sądów Polskich*. In 1921, he joined the six-person temporary council of the Order of Polonia Restituta. He was awarded the Austrian *Österreichisch-Kaiserlicher Leopold-Orden* and the Italian *Ordine della Corona Ferrea*.

It is worth mentioning that before the Second World War, the majority of the presidents of the Polish SAC (three out of five) were former judges of the Austrian *Verwaltungsgerichtshof* (Sawicki, Rudolf Rużycki, and Włodzimierz Orski). In Poland, with no enduring culture of independence or its own educational system, these judges were the most highly educated group of jurists, and they influenced the entire Polish legal system. Although Judge Jan Sawicki took no direct part in the preparatory works of the CAP in 1928, the jurisprudence of the SAC was of crucial importance for both the content and interpretation of this legislation.

[43] A Zakrzewski, 'Jakub Sawicki 1899–1979' in *Profiles of Scholars. Professors Warsaw University after 1945 S–Ż, Monumenta Universitatis Varsoviensis 1816–2016* (Warsaw University Publishing House 2016) 49–50.

[44] Z Ciesielski, 'Sawicki Stanisław (1907–1944)' in *Polish Biographical Dictionary*, vol XXXV (Publishing House of the Polish Academy of Science 1994) 341–42.

[45] J Sawicki, 'Administrative Judiciary in Poland' (1920) 3 Journal of the Ministry of Justice, Non-Formal Section 178–188 and J Sawicki, *Ustawa o Najwyższym Trybunale Administracyjnym* (Bookshop F Hoesicka 1924).

8

Administrative Procedure in Former Yugoslavia and the Austrian Administrative Procedure Act

Stevan Lilić and Marko Milenković

I. Introduction

This chapter provides an overview of how administrative procedure developed and the influence of the 1925 Austrian Administrative Procedure Act (APA) in Yugoslavia between 1920 and 1970. The 50 years in question cover this dynamic—but also the troubled—period in European and Yugoslav history. In the Yugoslav case, administrative procedure was influenced by contemporary legislative trends, as well as by sociopolitical events and changes of regime.

II. Background: History and Legal Culture

Between 1920 and 1970, two laws on general administrative procedure (LGAP) were adopted in Yugoslavia. The first Yugoslav LGAP was adopted in 1930 in the Kingdom of Yugoslavia, and the second was adopted in 1956 in the (Socialist) Federal People's Republic of Yugoslavia. There was an interim period between 1946 and 1956 during which no law on administrative procedure was in force.

A. The First Period: The Kingdom of Yugoslavia (1930–1945)

The first period was characterised by the adoption of the Law on General Administrative Procedure of the Kingdom of Yugoslavia in 1930 (coming into force in 1931). The Law was among the first in Europe after those adopted in Austria, Poland, and Czechoslovakia. The 1930 Yugoslav LGAP had 176 paragraphs—twice as many as the Austrian 1925 LGAP, as it included numerous provisions typical

Stevan Lilić and Marko Milenković, *Administrative Procedure in Former Yugoslavia and the Austrian Administrative Procedure Act* In: *The Austrian Codification of Administrative Procedure.* Edited by: Giacinto Della Cananea, Angela Ferrari Zumbini, and Otto Pfersmann, Oxford University Press.
DOI: 10.1093/oso/9780198867623.003.0008

of dispute resolution procedure,[1] as well as a comprehensive part on enforcement. Like its Austrian counterpart, the Law was entitled 'General Administrative Procedure' as various divergences from the general administrative procedure were prescribed by sectoral legislation as 'special administrative procedures'. As will be demonstrated in the following section, it can be affirmed that the Austrian 1925 AVG had a significant influence on the Yugoslav 1930 LGAP, with many institutes being transplanted into the Yugoslav system.

Upon adoption of the 1930 Yugoslav LGAP, several commentaries were published with references to the Austrian model. The commentary entitled 'Law on General Administrative Procedure',[2] by Ivo Krbek (a university professor from Zagreb and member of the initial three-man LGAP project team) refers to several Austrian examples and illustrations. On the codification of administrative procedure, Krbek underlines:

> This idea of a separate procedural codification is now also being implemented by our LGAP in the field of administrative law. Two advances have been made from the point of view of legislative technique: not only has a separate procedural law been enacted, but a complete and greater codification has been produced [...] While a small number of substantial legal codifications prevail in the field of judicial law, administrative law has been dissolved by an endless series of small laws. Thus, every major legal codification for administrative law means great progress. In particular, the idea of a separate codification of administrative-procedural law is quite recent. On a larger scale, it came to the fore for the first time, albeit on the basis of a longer work, in the procedural laws of the Republic of Austria of 1925. This example, with more or less individual changes, was followed by Czechoslovakia and Poland, and now Yugoslavia.[3]

In his analysis on special cases for revoking and altering decisions, Krbek underlines:

> This Chapter touches on one of the most delicate administrative law issues: the question of the finality of the decision. It is quite clear that those parties, no longer able to challenge the decision, are bound by it; but the question is whether the government itself is bound by the decision, in so far as it can no longer abolish or change it. In more recent legal theory, it was primarily the Austrian writers who

[1] S Lilić, *ZUP & ZUS—Komentar Zakona o opštem upravnom postupku i Zakona o upravnim sporovima sa komparativnim zakonodavstvom* ['LGAP & LAD—Commentary of the Law on General Administrative Procedure and the Law on Administrative Disputes with Comparative Legislation'] (Savremena administracija, Beograd 1997) 14.

[2] I Krbek, *Zakon o opštem upravnom postupku* ['Law on General Administrative Procedure'] (Naklada 'Obnova' 1931).

[3] ibid 3.

raised this issue and took the principled position of the finality of administrative acts […] In principle, this idea is becoming increasingly prevalent today, which is completely in the spirit of the rule of law and the increasing entry of legal elements into the public administration.[4]

In the Preface to the Commentary of the Law on General Administrative Procedure of 9 November 1930,[5] Franja Goršić (Inspector of the Ministry of Internal Affairs), in his specific wording, notes that:

The circumstance that the first codification of administrative procedural law appeared in Central Europe in 1925—in Austria—can serve as convincing proof that the correct hypothesis that the systematics of the administrative process is a consequence of a well-developed civil litigation law (…) The influence of civil litigation law on our General Administrative Procedure Act is proportionally stronger than the respective civil litigation procedures of Austria, Poland and Czechoslovakia on the codification of the general administrative procedure of those countries.[6]

In the introduction, Goršić provides precious information on the adoption of the Yugoslav 1930 LGAP:

The material needed to compile the Law on General Administrative Procedure was largely obtained in 1929 by the former Commission for the Organization of Administration, to whose agile president, the then Inspector General of the Ministry of the Interior Dr. Otmar Pirkmajer, now Deputy Governor of the Drava Region, we are undisputedly endebted for our Administrative law. With regard to the drafting of the LGAP, the prevailing opinion was that the general administrative procedures of Austria, Poland, and Czechoslovakia should establish a programme that would draw the new administrative process as closely as possible into line with civil litigation without compromising the official maxima of administrative cases initiated *ex officio*, ie, mainly the so-called one-party cases, to which the regulations applicable to the adversarial procedure can only be applied to some extent […] The original project was compiled by Ivo Krbek. It was then reworked by a three-member editorial board in several stages, which, in addition to the project designer, included the Supreme Inspector with the Presidency of the Council of Ministers, Kosta Janković, and the Inspector General of the Ministry of the Interior Aleksandar I. Kuzmanović. The project was passed by the Plenum

4 ibid 170.

5 F Goršić, *Komentar Zakon o opštem upravnom postupku od 9. novembra 1930. godine* ['Commentary of the Law on General Administrative Procedure of 9 November 1930'] (Geca Kon 1931).

6 ibid preface.

of the Supreme Legislative Council on 13–14 October, where it underwent only a few significant changes and additions. The final review fell to Inspector General Aleksandar I. Kuzmanović. The law was passed on 9 November 1930 and promulgated on 25 November 1930 with a *vacatio* of three months after promulgation (Official Gazette, No 271/1930).[7]

B. The Interim Period: The Formal Absence of a Law on Administrative Procedure (1945–1956)

At the close of the Second World War, the postwar government in Yugoslavia issued a decree, the 'Decision on the Disapplication and Annulment of all Legislation Adopted by the Occupiers and their Collaborators',[8] which also covered prewar legislation and by which the 1930 LGAP was formally deprived of legal force in the new (Socialist) legal order. As the Decision did not explicitly repeal the 1930 LGAP, some of its provisions could de facto be applied.[9] As Bogdan Majstorović points out in his 1957 Commentary on the Law on General Administrative Procedure, 'norms which were not contrary to the new political system could be applied', meaning that procedural norms in deciding administrative matters were applicable.[10]

C. The Third Period: The (Socialist) Federal Republic of Yugoslavia (1956–1970)

This period features lesgislation on administrative procedure adopted in a Socialist legislative environment. It is interesting to note that before adopting the new 'Socialist' Yugoslav LGAP in 1956, a new Law on Administrative Disputes was adopted in 1952.[11] As Majstorović argues, the supreme courts in the federal units

[7] ibid 1–2.

[8] Odluka br. 123 od 3. februara 1945 Predsednistva Antifasictickog veca narodnog oslobođenja Jugoslavije o ukidanju i nevažnosti svih pravnih propisa donetih od strane okupatora i njihovih pomaga;ča za vreme okupacije, i važnosti odluka koje su za to vreme donate, o ukidanju pravnih propisa koji su bili na snazi u času neprijateljske okupacije [Decision No 123 of 3 February 1945 of the Presidency of the Anti-Fascist Council of the People's Liberation of Yugoslavia on the abolition and invalidity of all legal regulations adopted by the occupiers and their aides during the occupation, and the validity of decisions made during that occupation, in force at the time of enemy occupation] Službeni list FNRJ, br 4, 13.02.1945.

[9] B Majstorović, *Komentar Zakona o opštem upravom postupku* ['Commentary of the Law on General Administrative Procedure'] (Beograd 1957) 3 (as quoted in: Stevan Lilić, *Komentar ZUP & ZUS sa komparativnim zakonodavstvom* ['Commentary of LGAP and LAD with Comparative Legislation'] (Savremena administracija 1997) 14.

[10] B Majstorović, *Komentar Zakona o opštem upravnom postupku—drugo izdanje* ['Commentary of the Law on General Administrative Procedure—2nd edn'] (Savremena Administracija1959) 5.

[11] Zakon o upravnim sporovima [Law on Administrative Disputes], Službeni glasnik FNRJ, br 23/1952.

and the Supreme Court of Yugoslavia started developing rules of general administrative procedure at that time. This was achieved by examining the procedure for adopting administrative acts and their validity, thus defining general rules to be specifically applied by the courts.[12] Four years later, in 1956, the Law on the General Administrative Procedure of the Federal People's Republic of Yugoslavia was adopted and entered into force on 20 April 1957.[13] Interestingly, after only two years, Majstorović agued that there was already a sizable case law based on the new LGAP.[14] In his 1961 commentary on the law, the author stresses 'the great interest in the law' (by the legal professionals) with numerous challenges being brought by practitioners and academics, noting once again 'the growing case law'.[15] This led the General Administration Secretariat of the Federal Executive Council (ie the federal government) to 'issue a number of official explanations for implementing the law'. As envisaged in art 30 of LGAP, the Secretariat was in charge of implementing this Law.[16]

The 1956 LGAP was amended in 1965 to reflect the constitutional changes of 1963, introducing improvements in the position of the parties in administrative procedure.[17] At the same time, the consolidated version of the Law was published in the Official Gazette (no 18/1965). As Nikola Stjepanović put it in 1963, the Yugoslav LGAP was 'the most comprehensive codification of its sort in the world', also stressing that it 'reflected the current social and political system'.[18]

It should be noted that the second Yugoslav LGAP left a considerable legacy in the post-Yugoslav environment. After the break-up of Yugoslavia in the early 1990s, most of the post-Yugoslav States incorporated the existing Yugoslav LGAP into their legal system before eventually adopting their own new LGAPs. Consequently, the Yugoslav LGAP was 'transformed' into ten new LGAPs now in independent States that had been federal republics or autonomous provinces. Of particular note is Bosnia and Herzegovina, which has four LGAPs (one on the 'State' level of Bosnia and Herzegovina, two on the level of the Federation of Bosnia and Herzegovina and Republika Srpska entities, and one on the level of the Brčko District), all tracing back and sharing the heritage of the Yugoslav LGAP and its Austrian role model.

[12] B Majstorović, *Komentar Zakona o opštem upravnom postupku—treće izdanje* ['Commentary of the Law on General Administrative Procedure—3rd edn'] (Zavod za javnu upravu 1961)6.

[13] B Majstorović, *Komentar Zakona o opštem upravnom postupku—drugo izdanje* ['Commentary of the Law on General Administrative Procedure—2nd edn'] (Savremena Administracija 1959) 3.

[14] ibid.

[15] Majstorović (n 12) 3.

[16] Majstorović (n 12).

[17] B Majstorović, *Komentar Zakona o opštem upravnom postupku—četvrto izdanje* ['Commentary of the Law on General Administrative Procedure—4th edn'] (Službeni list 1965) 3.

[18] N Stjepanović, *Upravno pravo SFRJ—Opšti deo—knjiga II* ['Administrative Law of SFRY—General Part vol II'] (Zavod za izdavanje udžbenika 1964) 41.

D. The Institutional and Political Context: A Synthesis

As noted in the previous section, the time frame in question was marked by two very distinct periods before and after the Second World War. The 1930 Law on General Administrative Procedure was adopted in the following sociopolitical environment:

- Yugoslavia was a newly formed post–First World War unitary State and kingdom;
- Yugoslavia had a capitalist sociopolitical order (with marked disproportions in terms of economic development between its various parts and numbering among the poorest countries in Europe);
- by the time the LGAP was adopted (1930), the king had suspended the 1921 Constitution (the so-called Dictatorship of 6 January 1929);
- the new 1931 Constitution of the Kingdom of Yugoslavia prescribed the king as 'the head of administration in the country' (arts 26 and 27 of the Constitution).[19]

On the other hand, after the First World War, the Law on Administrative Disputes in 1952, and the LGAP in 1956, were legislative acts adopted in the following sociopolitical environment:

- Yugoslavia was reconstructed after the Second World War as a federal 'people's' (Socialist) republic;
- Yugoslavia had a Socialist sociopolitical order under the rule of a one-party Communist system;
- the 1946 Constitution defined Yugoslavia as a federal State comprising six republics (Serbia, Croatia, Bosnia and Herzegovina, Macedonia, Slovenia, and Montenegro) and two autonomous provinces within Serbia (Vojvodina, Kosovo and Metohija);[20]
- the Law on General Administrative Procedure (1956) was adopted after a new Law on Administrative Disputes was adopted in 1952;
- enacting the new LGAP in 1956 meant the 'development and consolidation of our new legal system, our new Socialist law' and had 'great importance as a fostering instrument of administrative action'.[21]

[19] L Kostić, *Komentar Ustava Kraljevine Jugoslavije iz 1931. godine* [Commentary of the 1931 Constitution of the Kingdom of Yugoslavia] (G Kon 1934) 76, 198.

[20] With the 1963 Yugoslav Constitution, two Serbian autonomous provinces gained widespread autonomy, reflected in the legislative powers and separatation of the institutions, including the judiciary.

[21] N Stjepanović, *Položaj gradjana i organizacija u uravnom postupku* ['Position of Citizens and Organisations in Administrative Procedure'] (Savremena Administracija1957) 7.

E. Variety of Legal Cultures

Legislation on administrative procedure in both the prewar kingdom and postwar Republic of Yugoslavia was centralised at the federal level. The administrative units of the Kingdom (*banovine*) were not vested with legislative powers. Although the federal republics of Socialist Yugoslavia had legislative competence, they had no powers to adopt procedural legislation (which was reserved to the federal authorities).

As observed by Ivo Krbek, the 1930 codification of the LGAP allowed the unification of rules that had existed in the early years of Yugoslavia as different areas were parts of different countries and legal traditions.[22] The Kingdom of Yugoslavia was made up of the former Kingdom of Serbia, the Kingdom of Montenegro, parts of the Austro-Hungarian Empire (today's Croatia, Slovenia, Bosnia and Herzegovina, and province of Vojvodina), and the Turkish Empire (today's North Macedonia, parts of Serbia, and province of Kosovo) with a variety of legal traditions (especially in civil, family, and inheritance law).

In Socialist Yugoslavia, all procedural laws were federal, while substantive norms were mostly enacted on the level of federal units. Nevertheless, sectoral legislation normally comprised (and continues to do so) both substantive and procedural norms forming specific administrative procedures in the relevant sectors (eg tax law procedure).

F. Sector-Specific Rules and the General AVG

Throughout the period of interest here, Yugoslav legislation maintained the notion of 'general administrative procedure' as reflected in the titles of the relevant 1930 and 1956 laws. In this we can discern the strong influence of the Austrian role model. However, sector-specific procedural rules existed in various areas such as construction, social security, taxation, etc. The Yugoslav theory furthermore developed the distinction between 'general administrative procedure' and 'special administrative procedures' envisaged by sectoral legislation, which usually contained both substantive and sector-specific procedural norms and the notion of the subsidiary application of general administrative procedure in the absence of specific rules prevails.[23]

In the first commentary of the 1930 LGAP, Krbek indicates the examples of sectoral laws containing procedural rules, recognising the relationship between general and specific rules but seizing the opportunity to underline the importance of the codification of general rules in the 1930 LGAP. Article 1 of the 1930 LGAP

[22] Krbek (n 2) 7–8.

[23] S Lilić, *Posebno upravno pravo (Special Administrative Law)* (Pravni fakultet 1998).

states that the law is applicable for the action of 'general administration' (the administration of the central State), *banovine* (nine administrative units created in line with the constitution of the time with the aim of deconcentrating power and the local municipalities). Article 2 established that the 1930 LGAP was not applicable to authorities not defined by the law ('*na vlasti koje nisu obuhvaćene*') nor to administrative-punitive procedure ('*verwaltungsstraf*') as a separate Law on Misdemeanours (*Zakon o istupima*) was adopted.[24]

III. Legal Sources for Administrative Procedure

A. Constitutional Principles

During the period of interest, Yugoslavia saw a period of lively constitution-making together with a fundamental change in the political system. The constitutions contained norms of particular importance for administrative procedure.

The 1921 Constitution of the Kingdom of Serbs, Croats, and Slovenes provided for the *right to make request* to any authority without difference (art 15).

The 1931 Constitution of the Kingdom of Yugoslavia imposed by the monarch during the '6 January Dictatorship' (1929–31) provided no specific principles of administrative procedure but did, as already mentioned above, establish that 'administrative power' was vested in the king, who would perform it through the ministers responsible (art 27).

According to the 1946 Constitution of the People's Federal Republic of Yugoslavia, citizens had the right to make requests and petitions to authorities (art 39). It further provided for the right to appeal against individual administrative decisions or specific acts by authorised personnel. Importantly, the same article provided that the procedure for filing an appeal was to be prescribed by law, which happened ten years later with the 1956 LGAP. As previously mentioned, the norms of the 1930 LGAP were de facto applied up to 1956 insofar as they 'were not contrary' to the new political system.

The 1963 Constitution of the Socialist Federal Republic of Yugoslavia provided for the equal protection of individual rights in procedures before the courts, administrative and other State authorities, and organisations when deliberating on rights and duties. Furthermore, it stated that the 'community provides conditions for legal aid from attorneys and other forms of legal aid' (art 67). According to the Constitution, everyone is guaranteed either the right to appeal or some other legal remedy against court decisions and those of other State authorities and organisations when deciding on rights or legal interests (art 68).

[24] Krbek (n 2) 4–5.

B. Other Legal Sources for Administrative Procedure

During the period in question, the sources of law included statutes (laws), administrative case law, general principles, and—to a limited extent—academic works. As Laza Kostić (pre-Second World War professor of administrative law and member of the first German-installed occupational government) recalls, in one of the first Yugoslav textbooks of administrative law (1933), the sources of administrative law were generally laws, (rarely) the Constitution, (government) decrees, and other sources, including autonomous statutes and customs.[25]

Analysing the sources of Yugoslav administrative law in 1954, Stjepanović (post-Second World War professor of administrative law and judge of the Constitutional Court of Serbia) distinguishes the following sources: the Constitution, laws (as primary source), other normative acts of State authorities, and customary law (as additional auxiliary source). It is explicitly stated that case law is not a source of administrative law. Stjepanović introduced the distinction between 'general' and 'basic' principles of administrative procedure. General principles include the principle of legality and the right to appeal, while the basic principles include the duty of the administrative authority to assist 'lay' parties in the procedure.[26] Majstorović stresses that, in addition to the norms applied after 1946 (if not contrary to the system of the time), few basic principles of administrative procedure were prescribed by the 1946 General Law on Peoples Councils (Opšti zakon o narodnim odborima, Official Gazette FNRJ, no 43/1946).[27]

IV. The Yugoslav and the Austrian Administrative Procedure Legislation

A. Was There a Legislative 'Reception'?

There is no conclusive evidence that notes to the LGAP drafting group meetings or parliamentary debates were preserved.[28] There are also no written testimonies (eg in the official archives) that the Austrian 1925 LGAP served as a model for the 1930 LGAP.[29] However, by comparing the structure and texts of the Austrian

[25] L Kostić, *Administrativno pravo*—reprint ['Administrative Law—Reprint'] (2000) 28–30.

[26] Stjepanović also states that in accordance with the principle of the 'unity of power', the assessment of constitutionality is performed by the National Assembly. N Stjepanović, *Administrativno pravo FNRJ—opšti deo* ['Administrative Law of FPRY—General Part'] (Naučna knjiga 1954) 34–44.

[27] Majstorović (n 10) 5.

[28] The Archive of Yugoslavia, the Archive of Serbia, and the Parliamentary Archive were mostly closed due to the outbreak of Covid-19, but the available registers of documents do not indicate that any relevant material is available.

[29] It is worthy of note that one of the main authors of the 1930 LGAP, Ivo Krbek pointed out in his Commentary that the Austrian act required a lenghty preparation and that it was followed by a series of laws adopted in Central Europe. Krbek (n 2) 3.

AVG with the Yugoslav LGAP, it is evident that the Austrian model was used. There is a common understanding among administrative law scholars in the former Yugoslavia that there was indeed an influence, and there is one reference in the literature to the Austrian AVG serving as a model (see Section IV.B below). A comprehensive comparison is provided below (Section V.A).

B. Explicit Jurisprudential and Academic References

To the best of the authors' knowledge there were no citations from the Austrian LGAP in the (limited available) case law. However, references to comparative legislation were never common in Yugoslav administrative case law. In Ivo Krbek's commentary, there are indirect indications of Austrian influence on jurisprudence. Analysing the principle of finality of administrative decisions, Krbek concludes:

> It is quite comprehensible that newly created Austrian administrative procedure sought to regulate this problem and to carefully define cases in which the principle of finality of a decision does not preclude a decision from being withdrawn or amended *ex officio*. This approach was followed in full in the new administrative procedure of Poland. Czechoslovak administrative procedure took a different path, only summarily establishing that the previous prerogative of the authorities to annul and change final decisions remained intact [. . .] Thus, the LGAP had to explicitly address this issue, whereby, with few exceptions, it explicitly relied on the said Austrian law and upheld, in principle, the position of the finality of decisions. This approach has already, in principle, entered our positive law, primarily through the jurisprudence of our administrative courts.[30]

Even though the influence of the Austrian LGAP in academic works can be felt to some extent, there are no comprehensive references to the 1925 Austrian LGAP in (the relatively scarce) administrative law articles and monographs. Both before and after the Second World War, there are general references to the Austrian LGAP, but most of them summarily state that it was the first act adopted and that it was followed by other countries, namely Poland, Czechoslovakia, and Yugoslavia.[31]

However, there is a notable exception. Jovan Stefanović (at that time judge at the Administrative Court and later professor of constitutional law at the University of Zagreb), in his 'Commentary of the Law on General Administrative Procedure of

[30] ibid 171.

[31] Krbek (n 29); Majstorović (n 10) (and subsequent editions); Nikola Stjepanović, *Upravno pravo SFRJ—Opšti Deo—knjiga II* ['Administrative Law of the SFRY—General Part, vol II'] (Zavod za izdavanje udžbenika 1964) (and subsequent editions).

9 November 1930',[32] specifically refers to the difference between the 1930 Yugoslav LGAP and the Austrian LGAP, which served as a model:

> Our Law on General Administrative Procedure, in contrast with the Austrian legislation (from 9 July 1925, in force from 1 January 1926), which served as its basis, does not provide definitions or formally clarity the notion of a party. In this, it has followed in the footsteps of the Czechoslovak administrative procedure as a whole, and to some extent that of Poland, where only the concepts of 'interested parties' and 'participants' were defined, while definition of 'party' was left to the regulation of substantive law and practice.[33]

V. The Main Procedural Requirements

It is important, at this stage of our analysis, to understand what administrative procedure legislation was achieving in the practice, as well as whether a 'substantial' influence of the Austrian legislation can be identified. For this purpose, the following issues will be considered: preliminary investigation and fact-finding (Section A); the right to a hearing (Section B); the requirement to give reasons (Section C); the available administrative and judicial remedies (Section D).

A. Preliminary Investigation and Fact-Finding

In terms of structure, the Austrian AVG was clearly taken as a model when the Yugoslav LGAP was drafted in 1930. The LGAP is in nine parts rather than the six of the 1925 AVG, but, albeit with some additions, it adheres to its structure and titles. It consists of the following parts, corresponding to the Austrian model: Part I—General provisions (six sections generally corresponding to the 1925 AVG); Part II—Procedure up to the main decision at first instance (largely corresponding to 1925 AVG Part II on investigation procedure); Part III—The Decision; Part IV—Appeal; Part V—Annulment and modifying a decision in situations not covered by appeal (equivalent to s 2 of Part IV of the 1925 AVG). As underlined above, the 1930 LGAP contained provisions on enforcement (Part VI) and security (Part VII). This is where Yugoslav law deviates and supersedes its model, thus becoming lengthier and more detailed. Lastly, Part VIII—Costs, and Part IX—Temporary and final orders, also share the structure of the Austrian model. In terms of substance, it

[32] Jovan Stefanović, *Komentar Zakon o opštem upravnom postupku od 9. novembra 1930. godine* ['Commentary of the Law on General Administrative Procedure of 9 November 1930'] (1933).
[33] ibid 3.

may be concluded that the drafters of the law have been using the Austrian model, translated and adapted a number of provisions.

Some formulations are very similar with regard to the completeness of the preliminary investigation and fact-finding methodology, in addition to some sections with the same structures. For example, art 70 of the 1930 LGAP (general principles of the investigation procedure) states that 'investigation procedure establishes the facts, which are the ground for the conclusion of an administrative matter, and gives the parties the opportunity to assert or protect their rights and legal interests'. This is strikingly similar to art 37 of the 1925 Austrian AVG. However, it may also be concluded that the authors of the Yugoslav text did not simply take formulations from the 1925 AVG but also adapted and developed several of its provisions. Hence, some sections of the LGAP contain more articles; for example, the specific provision on preliminary issues (art 72). This section also envisages that the authority 'shall aim for the procedure to be purposeful, faster, simpler and cheaper' (art 71) which is similar to art 39(2) of 1925 AVG which provides that the 'authority shall be guided by considerations of possible expediency, speed, simplicity and cost-saving'.

B. The Right to a Hearing

The provisions on oral hearings is one more area in which the 1930 Yugoslav LGAP followed its 1925 Austrian model, with many provisions being transposed into Yugoslav law albeit with certain changes (arts 73–77). These also include the right to a hearing (art 76). In comparison to Austrian law, the Yugoslav LGAP stated in detail that all parties have the right to be present at a hearing and 'duly heard in the matter'. The LGAP further empowers parties to present and explain proposals related to the matter and give statements about all relevant matters. It further provides that the party may respond to claims, legal arguments, proposals, and evidence presented by other parties. Through the authority parties were also permitted to put questions to other parties, witnesses, and experts. Completeness of provisions in the 1930 LGAP allowed for existing rules to remain practically unchanged.

C. The Requirement to Give Reasons

The requirement to give reasons is the important standard established by the 1925 AVG, art 60, envisaging that:

> The statement of reasons shall clearly and concisely summarise the results of the investigative procedure, the decisive considerations in the assessment of the evidence, and the assessment of the legal question based thereon.

However, the 1930 Yugoslav LGAP somewhat deviates from this model. It is envisaged (art 109) that the statement of reasons should include facts, legal reasoning, and, when needed, 'moments that were decisive when judging evidence'. It is further prescribed that the specific statement of reasons is not necessary when a party's request is fully met and there are no objections by any party.

D. The Available Administrative and Judicial Remedies

Lastly, in terms of the (broadly speaking administrative and jurisdictional) remedies available to the parties in administrative procedure, the Yugoslav AVG largely followed its Austrian model. Like the 1925 Austrian AVG, its Yugoslav counterpart also provides for appeal concerning 'the main matter' (art 115) in the Austrian case, 'against an administrative decision settling the matter', with appeals against orders relating only to the proceedings not admissible in either of the laws. Like the 1925 AVG, the Yugoslav 1930 LGAP envisaged the suspensive effect of the appeal. As for other remedies provided under the LGAP, we may mention reinstatement to the previous legal position (art 124, 1930 LGAP). The procedure for reopening the proceedings (art 128, 1930 LGAP) was mostly modelled on art 69 of the 1925 AVG and included the scenario of decisions obtained using forged documents, false testimony, or any other act punishable by law or otherwise obtained by fraud, and new facts or evidence emerging later that could not be presented in the proceedings. The Yugoslav LGAP also provided the possibility of reopening cases when preliminary questions regarding the essential points were subsequently adjudicated differently by the competent administrative or court authority. In addition, the Yugoslav LGAP left a further possibility for the authority to reopen the proceedings 'in the case of a public interest'.

VI. Hypothetical Cases

As a second step to seek to understand whether a 'substantial' influence of the Austrian legislation can be identified, it can be helpful to examine the following hypothetical cases: authorisations and licences (Section A); the expropriation procedure (Section B); administrative planning (Section C).

A. Authorisations and Licences

In this case, it is important to distinguish between two different periods on the basis of the economic and political system in place. On the one hand, the capitalist system of the Kingdom of Yugoslavia (also during Nazi occupation from 1941 to 1945), and the transitional period up to 1949 when the private practice of most of the professions was banned, including pharmacy. In the second period, Mr Schultz would not have been able to open a pharmacy as he would only have been authorised to work in the State-owned pharmacies. During the first period, there was a comprehensive system of licences, and opening a pharmacy was conditional on membership of the Chamber of Pharmacists, established in 1925.[34] As the person opening and running the pharmacy, Mr Schultz would have had to be admitted to the Section of Heads of Pharmacies. In this period, according to the Law on pharmacies and control of the trade of medicines, from 1930 Mr Schultz would have had to apply for a licence to be issued by the head of the administrative unit (*banovina*).[35] Furthermore, every pharmacy was then required to additionally register with the Chamber of Pharmacists (art 9). Detailed rules for issuing permits were set out in articles 10-13, including regulations on how to establish the need for a new pharmacy in a given area (10-11) and an obligatory public selection process for licences (art 12), followed by 'issuance of a permit at the will of the Minister or Ban (head of *banovina*)' to those meeting the professional standard, taking into account the 'length of practice, scientific and moral qualifications, and economic standing' of the candidate.

In the second period, authorisation would have had to be obtained by a legal person of which Mr Schultz was an employee. In both periods, the natural/legal person intending to open the pharmacy was allowed to file a suit and bring an administrative case before the relevant court.

B. Expropriation Procedure

The expropriation procedure, too, must be considered in the context of two distinct periods and political systems. In the Kingdom of Yugoslavia, expropriations were sanctioned by the Constitution. That of 1921 envisaged expropriation in the public interest with fair compensation ('*pravična naknada*') (art 37). The constitution specifically regulated the expropriation of 'large woodland estates ['*veliki šumski posedi*'] in accordance with the Law', but it did not explicitly state the type of compensation due. It also explicitly prescribed that 'large woodland estates' gifted to private owners by 'foreign rulers' were to become public property without compensation. As a Constitution of a newly formed country, it envisaged the abolition of feudal relationships, a legacy of the Ottoman Empire that had previously ruled parts of the new country (art 42). No compensation was envisaged for the owners of 'large

[34] Decree on the Chamber of Pharmacists of the Ministry of Public Health on 31 January 1925.

[35] Article 6 provides details of the conditions pharmacists or 'magisters of pharmacy' had to fulfil in order to be granted a licence. 'Law on pharmacies and control of the trade of medicines' (*Zakon o apotekama i nadzoru nad prometom lekova*), Službeni list, br 285/1931.

feudal estates'. According to the 1931 Constitution of the Kingdom of Yugoslavia, expropriation was permitted upon payment of 'fair compensation' (art 22).

Bearing in mind that the 1946 Constitution of the Federal People's Republic of Yugoslavia was adopted during the transitional postwar period, it still formally guaranteed the right to private property and freedom of entrepreneurship. It provided that private ownership could be limited or a property expropriated when 'required by the public interest but only in accordance with the legislative act' (art 18). However, it was watered down with the provision that the law would determine in what cases and how much compensation would be paid out to the owner. From 1963, under the Constitution of the Federal Republic of Yugoslavia, expropriation became a federal matter (art 161). Considering that practically all businesses were State owned, the Constitution only provides for the expropriation of immovables with 'fair compensation' and in the public interest according to federal law (art 25).

C. Administrative Planning

Currently there are comprehensive codes on planning and building in the countries belonging to the former Yugoslavia. However, from 1920 to 1970, there were no formal requirements to obtain a building permit prior to construction. The comprehensive system of building permits was introduced by various acts of the federal units (republics) in the 1970s and normally assumed that an investor (in this case a public authority) would have to obtain a number of other related permits or other acts prescribing conditions or giving consent for the various aspects of the project. In the period under consideration, the educational investor, which was normally a local municipality, would have to take a decision to build a school on a certain plot belonging to the municipality. If there was a planning document for the city, town, or village, this kind of public building would need to have been envisaged for the building plot concerned. Even though some planning documents existed prior to the Second World War, mostly in larger urban centres, they were adopted more frequently after the Second World War, and they were initially valid for five years, in line with the economic development plans prevailing during that period.

Importantly, from the 1950s a series of legislative acts abolished private property on so-called *buildable land within cities* ('*gradsko građevinsko zemljište*') ie all land within the urban perimeters,[36] leaving owners of properties in a situation in which land belonged to the State, and they were its mere users. This duality affected the position of owners of properties in various aspects of land use, including the change of purpose of (parts) of the building plots on which their properties were erected.

[36] Agricultural land and forests were allowed to remain private property up to certain limits.

VII. A Shared Administrative Culture

Large parts of Yugoslavia were part of the Austro-Hungarian Empire until its dissolution in 1919 (Slovenia, Croatia, Vojvodina),[37] as well as Bosnia and Herzegovina whose annexation by the empire in 1908 triggered political events leading to the 1914 Sarajevo assassination of Franz Ferdinand and the outbreak of the First World War.

Austrian influence was thus strongly present in both the administrative and judicial traditions in much of the newly formed Kingdom of Serbs, Croats, and Slovenes—later the Kingdom of Yugoslavia. This was also reflected in the fact that the majority of civil servants and judges in the country, especially in the pre–Second World War period, were educated in the Austrian tradition. Either they attended the Universities of Zagreb and Ljubljana or went to Vienna and other university centres across the empire before returning and taking up university posts or in administration and the judiciary. This was especially important for the Serbian part of the newly formed State, whose academia (University of Belgrade) and administration were highly populated by former Austro-Hungarian students.

Professor Ivo Krbek of the University of Zagreb was a leading author of the draft of the Law on General Administrative Procedure.[38] Bearing in mind the shared legal tradition with Austro-Hungaria it was only to be expected that the 1925 LGAP would have a decisive influence on its Yugoslav counterpart. In the first commentary to the law and subsequent editions of Krbek's commentaries, he takes no credit for preparing the draft, but Franja Goršić attests that Krbek was indeed the author of the first draft (see Section II.A above).

Lastly, it should be noted that in pre–Second World War Yugoslavia, administrative adjudication took place before administrative courts and the State Council. This points to an interesting blend of a French-style judicial system and Austrian procedural law as a consequence of two major legal systems influencing the country, as most intellectuals attended universities either in Paris or Vienna.

[37] Vojvodina—a northern province of Serbia which in the seventeenth to nineteenth centuries was home to many Serbian intellectuals.

[38] S Lilić, *ZUP & ZUS—Komentar Zakon o opštem upravnom postupku i Zakona o upravnim sporovima sa komparativnim zakonodavstvom* ['LGAP & LAD—Commentary of the Law on General Administrative Procedure and the Law on Administrative Disputes with Comparative Legislation'] (Savremena administracija 1997) 14.

9
The Hungarian Legislation on Administrative Procedure

András Zs. Varga

I. Introduction

Before the dissolution of the Habsburg Empire, Hungary was involved in the development of standards of administrative conduct by the Administrative Court. Hungarian courts have, ever since 1919, exercised control to prevent the abuse of discretionary power. However, in the first part of this chapter's time frame, Hungary did not adopt any general legislation on administrative procedure, while it did so in 1957. The discussion of the domestic legal framework within this chapter will be structured in the following manner. The first section will address the introductory issues considered by the questionnaire, while the second will explain that, though there was no 'reception' of the Austrian administrative procedure legislation, it was known within Hungarian legal culture. There will then be a discussion concerning the similarities and differences of Hungarian administrative procedure legislation with the Austrian one. The fourth section deals with the specific cases included in the questionnaire.

II. Background: History and Constitutional Provisions

As observed initially, while no general legislation on administrative procedure was adopted during the first part of the research's relevant time frame, Hungary (then known as the Hungarian People's Republic) had enacted Act IV of 1957 on General Rules of Administrative Procedure (abbreviated in Hungary as *Et.*). The former law only partially regulated administrative procedure.

A. The Institutional and Political Context of the Administrative Procedure Act

After the First World War—with the disintegration of the Austrian-Hungarian monarchy—a lengthy debate on the feasibility of an Administrative Procedure Act

András Zs. Varga, *The Hungarian Legislation on Administrative Procedure* In: *The Austrian Codification of Administrative Procedure*. Edited by: Giacinto Della Cananea, Angela Ferrari Zumbini, and Otto Pfersmann, Oxford University Press.
 DOI: 10.1093/oso/9780198867623.003.0009

(APA) took place in Hungary (see Section III.A below). Up to the end of the period known as the 'Kingdom without a King' in 1946 and the Communist takeover in 1948, the mainstream position of administrative lawyers (both academic and practitioners) was that despite the Austrian APA of 1925 and the concordance of Austrian and Hungarian administrative behaviour (the K. u. K—Kaiserlich und Königlich, Imperial and Royal—the practice of good administration), adoption of a general APA in Hungary was impossible. During the first years of the Bolshevik-type State administration based on direct and total subordination and hierarchical control, the focus was on institutional reform (introducing Soviet-type local administration to replace the ancient local self-government system, new police, and secret police institutions), centralised administrative planning and management of the economy (nationalisation without compensation, a unified employment system). Quick ad hoc legislative (primarily by decree) and single-case actions were taken. This period was not characterised by legality and predictability: quite the contrary. It was not the time to consider the feasibility of an APA.

After the bloody suppression of the anti-Soviet revolution of 1956, the Communist hegemony felt reasonably secure in its ability to standardise administrative procedures. The goal was, of course, more efficient control rather than substantive legality, still less constitutionality. These were the circumstances in which the APA came into being, but its forerunners included not only Communist leaders but also those who had been reflecting on the APA during the previous decades.[1]

B. The Legal Regime of Public Administration

Since 1920—indeed, since reconciliation with the Habsburg-Lothringen dynasty in 1867—officially after the adoption of Act XXXIII of 1876 on local administration—there has been just one administrative regime in Hungary (between 1849 and 1867, the Austrian regime was in force, and until 1848 there had been autonomous administrative regions, like the Szekler or the Saxon administration in Transylvania).

C. General and Sector-Specific Procedural Norms

The first general APA (*Et.* of 1957) declared that minimal divergence from the general rules was allowed, but, in practice, more and more sector-specific procedural rules appeared in other norms. This was the reason for the official reform of this APA by an amendment, Act I of 1981 (abbreviated in Hungary as *Áe.*). The goal

[1] See A Zs Varga, 'Die Entwicklung des Rechts der öffentlichen Verwaltung' ['The Development of Public Administration Law'] in G Máthé (ed), *Die Entwicklung der Verfassung und des Rechts in Ungarn* ['The Development of the Constitution and Law in Hungary'] (Dialóg Campus 2017) 817–64.

was not achieved over the coming years, and after the political transition (the restoration of constitutionality) of 1990, it was accelerated as dozens of sector-specific rules were adopted. The third APA, Act CXL of 2004 (abbreviated in Hungary as *Ket.*) was controversial in this sense. It was again declared that this is a general APA, but it created a sophisticated system of divergencies (ie excluded sectors regulated entirely by other APAs; partially excluded sectors; privileged sectors not excluded but where wider divergencies were accepted; general regulations that left room for unconditional divergencies). In the end, it had to be admitted that Hungary had an APA that purported to be general, but there were hardly any administrative sectors without divergent or additional regulation.[2]

This led to the fourth and current APA, Act CL of 2016, on general administrative regulations (abbreviated in Hungary as *Ákr.*). The most important innovation in the current APA is that Parliament has learned from the experience of more than half a century and gave up the dream of a truly general and complete regulation of administrative procedures. The current APA is only quasi-general and does not cover all aspects of administrative procedure. It is quasi-general insofar as there are administrative sectors regulated by specific laws (regarding misdemeanours, elections, referenda, taxation, customs, refugees, immigration, citizenship, economic competition, and monetary policy). These sectors had also been regulated separately in the previous APAs. The innovation in the *Ákr.* is that only these exceptions are mentioned in the law, and there are no other formal delegations of sector-specific rules. The APA does not bring about complete regulation of administrative procedure. It contains only regulations compulsory for all sectors (with the exceptions mentioned above) and in any single-case procedure: general principles, parties' rights, evidence, forms of decisions, remedies, and enforcement. All other aspects of the procedure can be regulated by sector-specific rules in accordance with the principles and rules of the APA (*Ákr.*).

D. Constitutional Principles on Administrative Procedure

The Fundamental Law of Hungary rules that the right to the protection of personal data and access to data of public interest is monitored by an independent authority established by a cardinal law (art VI, s 4); everyone has the right to have his or her affairs handled impartially, fairly and within a reasonable time by the authorities; authorities are legally required to give reasons for their decisions; everyone has the right to compensation for damage unlawfully caused by the authorities in the performance of their duties (art XXIV, sections 1 and 2); everyone has the right, alone or with others, to address a written request, complaint or suggestion to any public

[2] See A Zs Varga, 'Tűnődések a Ket. hatályának dogmatikai alapjairól' ['Reflections on the Dogmatic Foundations of Ket'] (2014) 6 Magyar Jog 321–28.

authority (art XV); everyone is entitled to a fair and public hearing by an independent and impartial court for the definition of his/her rights and obligations and any criminal charge against him/her (art XXVIII, s 1); everyone has the right to appeal against a judicial, administrative or other administrative decision that infringes his/her right or legitimate interest (art XXVIII, s 7).

E. Other Fundamental Rules

Before the first APA (*Et.*, 1957) was adopted, laws to partially regulate administrative procedures were in force. The most important was Act XXX of 1929 on the organisation of public administration. This law regulated the election and organisation of local administration, local legislation, the competencies and powers of administrative bodies, remedies against single-case decisions, as well as employment and disciplinary procedures against administrative personnel. Another important law was Act XXVI of 1896 on the Hungarian Royal Administrative Court (in force until 1949), whose case law guaranteed the legality and constitutionality of public administration (the Administrative Court could even take steps to slow down the effects of anti-Semite laws and the later Bolshevik laws).

III. The Relationship between the Austrian and Hungarian Legal Systems

A. Legislation

The said Act XXX of 1929 on the 'arrangement' of public administration was adopted only some years after the Austrian APA. The explanatory note of the Hungarian Act did not mention the Austrian development, but this was due to traditional considerations. During the almost 400 years of coexistence with Austria, the Hungarian doctrine was that Hungary did not give up its independence: the Habsburg dynasty ruled Hungary as Hungarian kings (elected or at least accepted by Hungarians) and not as emperors of the Holy Roman Empire (or later as emperors of the Austrian Empire). This doctrine of *separate country in personal union* was manifested in the existence of the Hungarian Parliament, which was the only source of law in Hungary. Any decree by the king/emperor came into force in Hungary only if accepted/adopted by Parliament. Following this tradition, Hungarian laws refrained from referring to Austrian laws even if these had a particular influence on those of Hungary. Another reason is that the first-instance administrative bodies in Hungary (with general competence) were the elected local councils (in counties and towns). This is one of the unbroken traditions of Hungarian constitutionality. In contrast, Austrian public administration was centralised.

The situation was very different in the academic world. The mainstream opinion was formulated by Győző Concha, who stated in 1905 that a really general APA was not feasible, as public administrative procedures could be regulated only by sector-specific laws.[3] At the same time, there were strong opinions in favour of a general APA: Andor Sigmond (1904), Ede Márffy (1926), Zoltán Magyary (1930).[4] Some of the latter had formulated even private drafts for a general Hungarian APA under the influence of the Austrian APA: József Valló (1937 and 1942), Jenő Szitás (1939), but these drafts had not been presented to Parliament. However, the academic debate was reflected in Act XXX of 1929 and later in the first APA of 1957 (*Et.*).[5]

B. Jurisprudential and Explicit Academic References

Hungarian laws and courts traditionally did not refer to Austrian laws (see Section III.A above). Some general principles such as *secundum legem, extra legem* and *contra legem*, and others (*forum rei sitae, legitimatio ad personam et causam, res iudicata*), were well known and used in Hungarian case law even before 1925. An important monograph set out these principles in 1902.[6] There were also citations of the Austrian APA in academic works such as treaties, monographs, and articles in law journals. Such academic sources are referred to in this chapter.

IV. Similarity and Diversity in Administrative Procedure

The distinction drawn above between the Austrian and the Hungarian legislation did not imply that the fundamental principles of administrative procedure diverged. For our purposes here, the following aspects will be considered:

1. completeness of the preliminary investigation and fact finding;
2. right to a hearing;
3. requirement to give reasons; and
4. the organisation of remedies (broadly, administrative and jurisdictional).

[3] G Concha, *Politika II. Közigazgatástan* ['Politics II. Public Administration'] (Grill 1905) 105.

[4] A Patyi, 'A közigazgatás "rendezése" és a kodifikáció iránti igény ['"Arrangement" of Public Administration and the Need for Legislation'] in A Patyi and A Zs Varga (eds), *A közigazgatási eljárásjog alapjai és alapelvei* ['Fundaments and Basic Principles of Administrative Procedures'] (Dialóg Campus 2019) 77.

[5] ibid 78–79; Varga (n 1) 855.

[6] F Vasváry, *A magyar közigazgatás központi alapszervei* ['Central Institutions of Hungarian Public Administration'] (Politzer 1902) 111–44.

The current APA (*Ákr.*) regulates—and all the former APAs regulated—these institutions.

The APA (*Ákr.*) regulates the duty of administrative bodies to ascertain the facts of a case, the principle of free proof, and the forms of evidence (arts 62–73).[7] The regulation is as detailed as usual for court proceedings. The two main differences are: (1) even if art 62, s 4 declares the principle of free proof ('The authority is free to choose the method of proof and will assess the available evidence according to its own convictions'), the next section imposes a specific limitation: 'In certain cases, a law or government decree may, for overriding reasons of public interest, make use of a document as a means of proof mandatory'; in the case of administrative procedures, recourse to official documents and technical or scientific experts in important testimonies is rare; (2) contrary to court proceedings in administrative procedures, the burden of proof and the duty to establish the facts is not on the parties but on the administrative body, which, *ex officio*, has to gather all the relevant facts, and a formal procedure of proof is ordered only if the results of the preliminary investigation are insufficient.

Any party to an administrative procedure has the right to be heard and to make statements at any stage of the procedure (art 5, s 1), to be assisted by the administrative body in his/her rights and duties (art 5, s 2), to be assisted by an advocate (arts 13–14), and to have free access to the files of the case except formally classified (secret) documents (art 33).

To be given reasons is a constitutional right guaranteed by the Fundamental Law of Hungary (art XXIV, s 1) and repeated by the APA (art 81, s 1). However, in some cases this can be ignored: if there are no opposing parties in the case and the administrative body complies with the request; in the case of formal certificates; if all the parties accept the decision (art 81, s 2).

The general remedy regulated in the APA (art 114) detailed in the 2017 Act I on administrative court procedures is the quashing lawsuit against an administrative decision issued by the Administrative Chamber of the competent (County or Metropolitan) tribunal. This is a novelty of the current APA (*Ákr.*). The former APAs regulated (internal) administrative appeal as a general remedy. Hence an examination of evidence in 2015–16 led to the result that 70% of administrative cases end without appeal, but in 90% of appealed cases, the second-instance decisions are quashed before the courts. Consequently, administrative appeals were shown not to be effective. According to the APA (art 116), (internal) administrative appeal is not general but may be granted by sector-specific laws (as is the case of tax and social insurance cases). Some other forms of remedy are also regulated by the APA—*ex officio* amendment or withdrawal of the decision by the issuing

[7] For an English translation of the APA (*Ákr.*), see: <https://uj.jogtar.hu/#doc/db/62/id/A1600150.TV/ts/20200701/> accessed 15 January 2022.

body or its supervisory body (arts 120–121) or on request from the public prosecutor (art 122)—or by specific law (reopening the case in some economic sectors).

V. Hypothetical Cases

It can be helpful, in order to understand how administrative procedure legislation worked in the real world, as well as whether 'substantial' influence of the Austrian legislation can be identified, to look more closely at the following hypothetical cases: authorisations and licences (Section A); the disciplinary procedure for a civil servant (Section B); the expropriation procedure (Section C); administrative planning (Section D). When reading the materials that follows one should, however, be aware that there could be variations in the intensity of judicial review that could be applied in differing sectors.

A. Authorisations and Licences

According to arts 48–49 of Act XCVIII of 2006 on the general rules for the safe and economical supply of medicinal products and medical devices and the distribution of medicinal products, there is no personal right to open a new pharmacy. A new pharmacy can be opened and operated if the metropolitan or the territorially competent county government office (as designated State health administration body):

- decides to announce a *public tender* to open a new pharmacy,
- the winner of the public tender obtains an *establishment permit*; and
- after establishment, the winner of the public tender obtains an *operating licence*.

If a public tender is announced, the deadline for application is at least 30 days, and the decision is taken after an additional 30 days. The winner of the public tender obtains an *establishment permit ex officio*. Conditions for the *operating licence* laid down by the same body are a previously obtained establishment permit, employing a pharmacist, third-party liability insurance, and a pharmacy room equipped in accordance with legal requirements.

All three procedures (public tender, establishment, operation) are regulated by the APA (*Ákr.*) with some special rules under the said Act XCVIII of 2006 (deadlines, etc.). As the applicant, Mr Schultz, has the right to be heard and to make statements at any stage of the procedures (art 5, s 1), to be assisted by the administrative body regarding his/her rights and duties (art 5, s 2), to be assisted by a lawyer (arts 13–14), and to have free access to the files (art 33). If Mr Schultz's application for an *establishment permit* or an *operating licence* is denied, he may ask the territorially competent Administrative Chamber of the County or Metropolitan Tribunal to quash the administrative decision (art 114 of APA). If the request for quashing is rejected or denied, Mr Schultz may ask the Kúria (the Supreme Court of Hungary) to review the first-instance court judgment under art 115 of Act I of 2017 on administrative court procedure). The Kúria may annul or change the first-instance court judgment. If the Kúria rejects or denies the application for supervision, and Mr Schultz feels that his constitutional rights have been infringed, he may submit a (full) constitutional complaint to the Constitutional Court. The Constitutional Court may annul (but not change) the Kúria judgment. If it does so, the Kúria must pass a new verdict following the decision of the Constitutional Court.

B. Disciplinary Procedure for a Civil Servant

Dismissal of a civil servant is regulated by Act CXCIX of 2011 on public service and Government Decree 31/2012 (III. 7). The APA is not applied. The procedure for dismissal is regulated by labour law rather than administrative law. The head of the office will appoint a disciplinary committee to investigate the case. Caius should be informed about the suspicion of committing a disciplinary offence; he has the right to be heard, offer evidence, make a statement, and be assisted by a lawyer. The procedure should be concluded within 60 days. Caius may challenge the decision on dismissal before the territorially competent Administrative Chamber of the County or Metropolitan Tribunal to have the administrative decision quashed (art 5, s 4 of Act I of 2017 on administrative court procedures). If his lawsuit is rejected or denied, Caius may ask the Kúria to supervise the first-instance court judgment (art 115). The Kúria may annul or change the first-instance court judgment. If the Kúria rejects or denies the application for review, and Caius feels that his constitutional rights have been infringed, he may submit a (full) constitutional complaint to the Constitutional Court. The Constitutional Court may annul (but not change) the judgment of the Kúria. If it does so, the Kúria must hand down a new verdict following the decision of the Constitutional Court.

There is an alternative: the dismissed civil servant may file a complaint with the Civil Service Arbitration Committee, which conducts probative proceedings and holds a hearing, with 60 days for a reasoned decision.

C. Expropriation Procedure

Expropriation has a constitutional background (limitation) in Hungary. According to Article XIII, s 2 of the Fundamental Law, expropriation may only be permitted in exceptional cases: when it is in the public interest, and only in the cases and manner stipulated by an act, under terms of total, unconditional, and immediate compensation. Detailed regulation on expropriation is set out in Act CXXIII of 2007. The procedure is regulated by the APA (*Ákr.*) with some other rules under Act CXXIII of 2007. The list of exceptional cases is regulated by this Act (eg defence, city planning, transport, mining, protection of the environment). Application for expropriation may be submitted to the territorially competent Metropolitan or County Governmental Office by the State, local authorities, or another private or public person who performs at least one activity from the list of the exceptional. The applicant, the owners and other persons whose civil law rights are registered in the official estate register are parties of—and should be notified about—the administrative procedure. Mrs Sempronia enjoys all the rights regarding procedure granted by the APA: she has the right to be heard and to make statements at any stage of the procedure (art 5, s 1), to be assisted by the administrative body regarding her rights and duties (art 5, s 2), to be assisted by a lawyer (arts 13–14), and to have free access to the files (art 33). All the interested parties, Mrs Sempronia among them, may challenge the final decision at the territorially competent Administrative Chamber of the County or Metropolitan Tribunal to quash the administrative decision (art 5, s 4 of Act I of 2017 on administrative court procedures). If her lawsuit is rejected or denied, Mrs Sempronia may ask the Kúria to review the first-instance court judgment (art 115). The Kúria may annul or change the first-instance court judgment. If the Kúria rejects or denies the application for review, and Mrs Sempronia feels that her constitutional rights have been infringed, she may submit a (full) constitutional complaint to the Constitutional Court. The Constitutional Court may annul (but not change) the judgment of the Kúria. If it does, the Kúria must hand down a new verdict following the decision of the Constitutional Court.

D. Administrative Planning

The founding of new schools is regulated under Act CXC of 2011 on national public education. The relevant procedural law is the APA (*Ákr.*). A school may be established and operated by the State, the self-governing body of a national minority, a church, or other private person or body. A new school is established by entry on the register of educational institutions. The administrative body in charge is the territorially competent Metropolitan or County Governmental Office. In some exceptional cases (eg if a university seeks to establish a school for training students), the Education Office, a special body under the supervision of the Ministry of Human Resources. Registration is an administrative procedure following APA (*Ákr.*) regulation. If a private person or body applies to set up a new school, an expert report on the necessity of the new school issued by the Ministry of Human Resources should be attached, and, after registration, the territorially competent Metropolitan or County Governmental Office decides whether to issue an *operating licence*. The operating licence is issued at the request of the registered holder following the 'normal'

APA procedures. Denial of registration or an operating licence may be challenged by the applicant (self-government of a national minority, a church or other private person or body) with the territorially competent Administrative Chamber of the County or Metropolitan Tribunal to have the administrative decision quashed (art 5, s 4 of Act I of 2017 on administrative court procedures). If the lawsuit is rejected or denied, the applicant may ask the Kúria to review the first-instance court judgment (art 115). The Kúria may annul or change the first-instance court judgment. If it rejects or denies the application for review, and the applicant feels that its constitutional rights have been infringed, it may submit a (full) constitutional complaint to the Constitutional Court. The Constitutional Court may annul (but not change) the judgment of the Kúria. If it does, the Kúria must hand down a new verdict following the decision of the Constitutional Court.

VI. A Common Administrative Culture

As observed earlier, before 1920, Hungary was a *separate country in personal union* with Austria. After the First World War, several Hungarian scholars and judges in their native places belonging to other countries (Romania, Czechoslovakia, Yugoslavia) contributed to the spread of Hungarian rather than Austrian administrative law influence (when possible). Nevertheless, the majority of Hungarian scholars and judges from the affected territories moved to Hungary (two entire university faculties). The only difference was the case of Romania, but only concerning private, not administrative, law: the private law in force in Transylvania (part of Romania after 1920) was and remained the General Civil Code of Austria (*Allgemeines bürgerliches Gesetzbuch*) and not the customary Hungarian private law. The only public law element was the land register (based on shared principles and with the same structure in Austria and Hungary). This existed for an extended period after 1920 only in Transylvania.

10
The Austrian Legislation on Administrative Procedure
A View from Germany

Ino Augsberg

I. Introduction

Of course, the relationship between Austria and Germany is an exceptional one. On the one hand, the two countries are closely connected through their common language and centuries-long shared history. On the other, despite these commonalities, they also have very different historically grown traditions, also noticeable in the field of law. In terms of law and jurisprudence, the differences between the systems cannot only be observed from the outside: they are also reflected in internal debate. There is a continuous and even institutionally secured dialogue that does not simply level out the differences but aims to make each nation aware of them. In this respect, the reception of the Austrian Administrative Procedure Act (APA) appears as an almost paradigmatic case for understanding the overall relationship between the two countries and their legal systems.

II. The German Debate on the Codification of an Administrative Procedural Law

In this context, the first question is whether—and if so, under what circumstances and with what considerations and normative justifications—Germany enacted a statute on administrative procedure during the period under review (ie 1920–70). Nevertheless, the answer to this question cannot be a simple 'yes' or 'no'. It has to be both 'yes' and 'no'.

The reason for this seemingly paradoxical answer is the country's federal structure, with its distant historical roots. It does not merely characterise the contemporary structure of the State, tellingly named the Federal Republic of Germany, established under the Basic Law.[1] Federalism was also an essential structural

[1] In what follows, I will focus only on the situation in the Federal Republic of Germany. See, for a concise overview of the history of administrative law in the German Democratic Republic, M Stolleis,

Ino Augsberg, *The Austrian Legislation on Administrative Procedure* In: *The Austrian Codification of Administrative Procedure*. Edited by: Giacinto Della Cananea, Angela Ferrari Zumbini, and Otto Pfersmann, Oxford University Press.
 DOI: 10.1093/oso/9780198867623.003.0010

element of the Weimar Republic and harked back to the atypical construction of the 'Holy Roman Empire of the German Nation' (*Heiliges Römisches Reich Deutscher Nation*). It was only under the rule of National Socialism that this federalistic structure was temporarily abandoned in favour of strong centralisation.[2]

While no APA was enacted at the national level either at the time of the Weimar Republic or in the Federal Republic during the period in question—in fact, no corresponding codification took place at the national level until 1976[3]—successful codifications can be found at the federal State (*Länder*) level. Quite early on, by the late 1920s, a law on administrative organisation was passed for the State of Thuringia. In the years to follow, a similar law for the State of Wuerttemberg was hotly debated but ultimately not promulgated. There is, however, a highly elaborate draft statute.[4]

After the Second World War, a 'State administrative law' (*Landesverwaltungsgesetz*) was passed in Schleswig-Holstein in 1968.[5] Although this statute basically followed a so-called *Musterentwurf* (model draft) of a law of administrative procedure agreed between the federal government and the States as early as 1963,[6] it too went its own way. Regarding the *Landesverwaltungsgesetz*, Schleswig-Holstein not only contained (and indeed still contains) regulations on the State's administrative organisation and administrative procedures, but it also covers a critical area of substantive special administrative law: police law.

The federal structure of both the Weimar Republic and the Federal Republic of Germany was, in both cases, not only a historical fact but also a constitutional requirement. The constitutional decision in favour of sovereignty for both the

'Entwicklungsstufen der Verwaltungsrechtswissenschaft' in W Hoffmann-Riem, E Schmidt-Aßmann and A Voßkuhle (eds), *Grundlagen des Verwaltungsrechts, vol. I: Methoden—Maßstäbe—Aufgaben—Organisation* (2nd edn, Beck 2012) § 2, 63–119, at 103ff and *Public Law in Germany. A Historical Introduction from the 16th to the 21st Century* (OUP 2017) 173ff. Due to the focus on the specific period 1920–70, I also leave out earlier debates, especially in connection with the Administrative Law of the Prussian State (*Landesverwaltungsgesetz*) of 1883, although they certainly still resonate in parts of the later discussion. All translations from German texts are my own.

2 See M Stolleis, *A History of Public Law in Germany. 1914–1945* (OUP 2004) 106ff.

3 More precisely, the law was enacted on 25 May 1976 and came into force on 1 January 1977. On this codification see eg from an American perspective, EJ Eberle, 'The West German Administrative Procedure Act: A Study In Administrative Decision Making' [1984] 3 Penn State Intl L Rev 67.

4 On the historical development in Germany, see M Stolleis, *Geschichte des öffentlichen Rechts in Deutschland. Vierter Band: 1945–1990* (Beck 2012) 257ff; from a contemporary as well as comparative perspective, see F Becker, *Das allgemeine Verwaltungsverfahren in Theorie und Gesetzgebung. Eine rechtsvergleichende Untersuchung* (Kohlhammer/Librairie Encyclopédique 1960) 117ff. From an American point of view, see AH Feller, 'Tendencies in Recent German Administrative Law Writing' (1932–33) 18 Iowa L Rev 144. With specific remarks on the situation in the individual *Länder*, see Stolleis (n 2) 106ff.

5 See in detail W Klappstein and G-C von Unruh, *Rechtsstaatliche Verwaltung durch Gesetzgebung. Entstehung und Bedeutung des Schleswig-Holsteinischen Landesverwaltungsgesetzes für das rechtsstaatliche Verwaltungsrecht* (R v Decker's Verlag, G Schenk 1987).

6 See *Musterentwurf eines Verwaltungsverfahrensgesetzes (EVwVfG 1963), 2. Auflage, mit Anhang 'Münchner Fassung'* (Grote 1968).

State as a whole and the individual federal States, the *Bundesländer*, goes (especially under the Basic Law) hand in hand with the primary competence of these States for both legislation and the execution of laws, ie, for administrative activities. On the other hand, federal competence only extends as far as the German Constitution expressly permits an exception to this rule. Concerning administration, the competence of the States goes even further than their legislative competence, as they are, in principle, also competent and responsible for the execution of federal laws.

Concerning general administrative law, this fundamental division of legislative and administrative competencies means that the federal government does not have its own legislative competency in this particular area. It can, however, make procedural regulations on specific matters of special administrative law in which the Basic Law expressly grants it legislative powers. However, if the execution of these laws is carried out by the *Länder*, these regulations also require the express consent of the Bundesrat as the representative body of the *Länder*. Only in the rare cases when federal authorities also execute federal law does the federal government have an unrestricted right to design procedures and organisations.

While the federal government thus lacks explicit legislative authority to regulate administrative procedure, it does have this authority with regard to administrative court procedure. This divergence of competencies has led to much specific debate. There have been disputes over the relationship between the two procedural regimes, in which the possible character of the administrative procedure as a court-like control procedure has been discussed. In this context, comparison with the Austrian situation played a particular role. However, regarding the situation in the Federal Republic, with an expanded multi-tiered administrative court system, the almost unanimous view is that administrative and judicial proceedings form two distinct areas, so the legislative competency of one area cannot be inferred from that of the other.[7] Only one particular problem has been debated in more detail: whether the so-called preliminary proceedings, ie, opposition proceedings as internal administrative control (*Widerspruchsverfahren*), should be considered administrative and thus be regulated by the *Länder*, or whether, conversely, they could be coordinated by the Administrative Court Rules as a prerequisite for the admissibility of administrative court proceedings. The legislative solution was adopted for the latter, at the same time defusing conflict insofar as this requirement only applies in cases where such an opposition procedure exists. It is therefore up to the *Länder* to abolish this procedure on their own authority (as they have to some extent, but only in recent years).

[7] On the relationship between these two areas of law in general, see H Jochum, *Verwaltungsverfahrensrecht und Verwaltungsprozeßrecht. Die normative Konnexität von Verwaltungsverfahrens- und Verwaltungsprozeßrecht und die Steuerungsleistung des materiellen Verwaltungsrechts* (Mohr Siebeck 2004).

For these reasons, discussion about codifying administrative procedure has always been conditioned on the one hand by the question of how, despite this federal structure, the fragmentation of procedural law into a multitude of different procedural rights could be prevented. On the other hand, due to constitutional requirements, the solution quickly became clear: unification was only possible through a model law jointly agreed upon by the federal and State governments, and all States subsequently adopted it in their legislation. While it was possible to reach an agreement on this procedure for enacting an APA with an identical content relatively quickly, debate on the content of such a model law continued for decades. Both the general idea of such a codification and numerous individual questions, especially that of the possible withdrawal of illegal administrative acts or the revocation of administrative acts, continued to be discussed until the mid-1970s, concluding only in 1976 with the enactment of the APA, which was enacted in a largely identical manner by most States and the federal government.[8]

This lengthy discussion process is astonishing because, on the one hand, there has long been broad agreement in both practice and legal scholarship on the so-called General Part of administrative law, which is not yet defined in general law, although it is already partially to be found in some areas; it is primarily intended to cover questions of procedure, including decisive forms of action and basic organisation. Under the Basic Law, this agreement was further strengthened by the fact that numerous provisions of the General Part were now understood as stemming directly or indirectly from the Constitution.[9] In particular, the principles of the rule of law and democracy served as a starting point for defining the upcoming codification of the General Section as a task determined mainly by constitutional law. This concerned both the 'if' of the codification—which was presented as a consequence of the doctrine of *Gesetzesvorbehalt* (legal reservation)—and the design of the 'how', ie, the question of what the regulations should look like in detail.[10]

[8] For a short overview on the development and the obstacles on the way, see eg H Pünder, 'Administrative Procedure—Mere Facilitator of Material Law versus Cooperative Realization of Common Welfare' in C Waldhoff and H Pünder (eds), *Debates in German Public Law* (Hart 2014) 239–60, 242; in more detail, see Eberle (n 3) 68ff; JP Schneider, 'Chapter 10. Germany' in JB Auby (ed), *Codification of Administrative Procedure. Proceedings of the International Academy of Comparative Law Congress on 'Codification' May 2012* (Bruylant 2014) 203–26. For a contemporary report on the debate in the early 1950s, see O Bachof 'German Administrative Law with Special Reference to the Latest Developments in the System of Legal Protection' [1953] 2 ICLQ 368–82.

[9] For an overview on this interplay of constitutional and administrative law, see eg F Becker, 'The Development of German Administrative Law' 24 George Mason L Rev [2017] 453–76, 465ff.

[10] On the relevance of the rule of law in administrative procedure law see, among others, F Kopp, *Verfassungsrecht und Verwaltungsverfahrensrecht. Eine Untersuchung über die verfassungsrechtlichen Voraussetzungen des Verwaltungsverfahrens in der Bundesrepublik und die Bedeutung der Grundentscheidungen der Verfassung für die Feststellung, Auslegung und Anwendung des geltenden Verwaltungsverfahrensrechts* (Beck 1971) 54ff.

However, it must be emphasised that these requirements cannot be expressly inferred from the Constitution; the wording itself contains practically no explicit references in this regard. However, the Federal Constitutional Court, which played a central role in the concretisation of the Basic Law very soon after its formulation, inferred from the mere reference to the 'rule of law' in the Federal Republic of Germany the idea that the republic was a *Rechtsstaat*. It also referred to the principles of fundamental rights, especially the guarantee of legal protection provided by art 19(4) of the Basic Law,[11] described as the 'keystone of the constitutional State' ('*Schlußstein im Gewölbe des Rechtsstaats*'),[12] a fundamental provision of the Constitution, whereby the citizen now no longer related to the State as a 'subject' but was considered to be on an equal footing. Accordingly, communication between administrative bodies and the citizen had to take the form of dialogue.[13] Starting from this fundamental consideration, the court then established various facets of the concept of the rule of law, such as the protection of legitimate expectations. While these aspects were not explicitly mentioned in the Constitution, they were presented as concretisations of its main principles and fundamental ideas.

In the German debate, this general development was described as the 'constitutionalisation' of the legal order in general, and general administrative law in particular. Recent research has assessed this development to some extent, but with greater scepticism and differentiation.[14] Regarding the period of interest here, however, especially the 1960s, it should be emphasised that although this process of constitutionalisation was based on the decisions of the Federal Constitutional Court, the Federal Administrative Court, and the Supreme Administrative Courts of the *Länder* held a very similar view.

The majority of German legal scholars were of a similar opinion. An example is an essay by Carl Hermann Ule, whose very title succinctly expresses this understanding of the problems: 'Administrative Reform as Constitutional Enforcement' ('*Verwaltungsreform als Verfassungsvollzug*').[15] From this perspective, the specific debate on the question of withdrawal is also merely a question of the appropriate interpretation of the Constitution—in other words, a subset of the application of the law. A concrete problem is (only) reconstructed as a legal problem. Another leading

[11] ibid 148ff.

[12] See R Thoma, 'Über die Grundrechte des Grundgesetzes für die Bundesrepublik Deutschland (1951)' in H Dreier (ed), *Rechtsstaat—Demokratie—Grundrechte. Ausgewählte Abhandlungen aus fünf Jahrzehnten* (Mohr Siebeck 2008) 468ff.

[13] See Bundesverfassungsgericht, in *Entscheidungen des Bundesverfassungsgerichts (BVerfGE)*, vol 45, 297–346, 335.

[14] See L Michael and F Wollenschläger, 'Verfassung im Allgemeinen Verwaltungsrecht—Bedeutungsverlust durch Europäisierung und Emanzipation?' (2015) 75 Veröffentlichungen der Vereinigung der Deutschen Staatsrechtslehrer 131–86 and 187–264.

[15] CH Ule, 'Verwaltungsreform als Verfassungsvollzug' in CH Ule and others (eds), *Recht im Wandel. Festschrift 150 Jahre Carl Heymanns Verlag KG* (Heymanns 1965) 53–89. See also the study by CH Ule and F Becker, *Verwaltungsverfahren im Rechtsstaat. Bemerkungen zum Musterentwurf eines Verwaltungsverfahrensgesetzes* (Grote 1964). On the general problem, see also Kopp (n 10).

figure in these debates, Fritz Werner, who, like Ule, had been a judge at the Higher Administrative Court in Lüneburg from 1949, serving as a chairman of the senate there from 1952 and as vice-president of the court from 1955 and president of the Federal Administrative Court from 1958,[16] had already situated this idea, later known as the 'constitutionalisation' of the entire legal system, into an even more general formula a few years earlier. He spoke of '[a]dministrative law as concretised constitutional law' ('*Verwaltungsrecht als konkretisiertes Verfassungsrecht*').[17]

This intimate connection between the debate on codification and constitutional requirements already suggests that Austrian general administrative law could not play a formative role in those discussions. Where the decisive guidelines for legislation were to be found directly in the Basic Law, it was apparently no longer necessary to draw lessons and experience from comparative law.

The decisive principles of administrative procedure were thus already traditionally present, as norms such as the binding obligation to be heard, the general protection of legitimate expectation, the idea of legal certainty and the like had of course already been recognised. Under the Basic Law, however, these traditional figures were now understood as expressions of a general basic idea of constitutional law. In such a scenario, explicit references to Austrian regulation were no longer necessary, so references to it are quite rare.

III. References to the Austrian Model

However, a closer look at the long preparation of the codification of administrative law at federal and State levels shows that despite the general overview described above, the Austrian experience was referred to time and again.[18]

A. The Background: Commonality and Diversity

In order to understand these references correctly, one must first look at the specific relationship between the two legal systems. On the one hand, what we

[16] See HJ Becker, 'Fritz Werner—Präsident des Bundesverwaltungsgerichts von 1958 bis 1969. Erinnerungen an eine große Richterpersönlichkeit' in P Häberle, *Jahrbuch des öffentlichen Rechts der Gegenwart* (Mohr Siebeck 1987) 105–20.

[17] cf F Werner, 'Verwaltungsrecht als konkretisiertes Verfassungsrecht' [1959] DVBl 527–33; Becker (n 9) 454f; in more detail, see C Schönberger, '"Verwaltungsrecht als konkretisiertes Verfassungsrecht". Die Entstehung eines grundgesetzabhängigen Verwaltungsrechts in der frühen Bundesrepublik' in M Stolleis (ed), *Das Bonner Grundgesetz. Altes Recht und neue Verfassung in den ersten Jahrzehnten der Bundesrepublik Deutschland (1949–1969)* (Berliner Wissenschafts-Verlag 2006) 53–84. On the modern concept of constitutionalisation in general, see GF Schuppert and C Bumke, *Die Konstitutionalisierung der Rechtsordnung. Überlegungen zum Verhältnis von verfassungsrechtlicher Ausstrahlungswirkung und Eigenständigkeit des 'einfachen' Rechts* (Nomos 2000).

[18] See Stolleis (n 4) 257f.

see are two completely independent national legal systems. On the other hand, these two legal systems are much more closely linked than is usually the case with other legal systems. This connection is of course based on the shared history that the German States and Austria can look back on under the umbrella of the Holy Roman Empire of the German Nation. What is more, both States were, and are, united by a common language. Against this background, it is not surprising that Walter Jellinek, in his well-known and highly influential textbook on administrative law—a book which indeed has been called 'the great "summa" of administrative law during the Weimar period'[19]—qualified Austrian administrative law as the 'most closely related' ('*am nächsten verwandt*') to German administrative law.[20]

Furthermore, from the perspective of the sociology of science, there is a unique feature that explains the close connection between legal scholars from Austria and Germany not only through their common history and language but also through their institutional similarities. In 1922, a meeting was held at the behest of Heinrich Triepel, a teacher of constitutional and international law in Berlin,[21] at which the 43 legal scholars present founded the Association of German Teachers of State Law (*Vereinigung der Deutschen Staatsrechtslehrer*).[22] From the very beginning, the 'German' in the name of the 'Association' was not meant to express a particular national identity. It was understood to mean 'German-speaking', as scholars from Germany, Austria, Switzerland, and the University of Prague took part in this first meeting. From 1924 onwards, the *Vereinigung* organised annual meetings for scientific exchange.[23] It focused (and still focuses) on the comparative perspectives of the individual countries from the legal point of view. The Austrian and German professors of constitutional law were, and still are, differentiated by specific references to their respective black-letter law. Certain legal traditions, namely Kelsen's positivism on the one hand and Smend's integration theory and the Schmitt School on the other, certainly had a different impact in Austria and Germany (and perhaps to some extent continue to do so).[24] In particular, Adolf Merkl's *Allgemeines Verwaltungsrecht* has never become the almost canonical reference in Germany that it was in Austria.[25] Instead, in Weimar Germany, reference

[19] Stolleis (n 2) 239.

[20] W Jellinek, *Verwaltungsrecht* (3rd edn, Julius Springer 1931) 111.

[21] On Triepel's life and work in general, see UM Gassner, *Heinrich Triepel. Leben und Werk* (Duncker & Humblot 1999).

[22] See in more detail Stolleis (n 2) 178ff.

[23] On the debates on administrative law in the first meetings, see Stolleis (n 2) 202ff.

[24] On Smend's and Schmitt's influence on the German, see *Staatsrechtslehre* in the first decades of the Federal Republic of Germany, F Günther, *Denken vom Staat her: Die bundesdeutsche Staatsrechtslehre zwischen Dezision und Integration 1949–1970* (Oldenbourg 2004). On the debates with regard to the 'Vienna School', see also Stolleis (n 2) 151ff.

[25] See B Leitl-Staudinger, 'Österreich' in A von Bogdandy and PM Huber (eds), *Handbuch Ius Publicum Europaeum, vol IV: Verwaltungsrecht in Europa: Wissenschaft* (CF Müller 2007) § 62, 195–228, at No 46. Hence an assumption on the possible influence of Merkl's work by AH Feller, made in 1932,

was made primarily to Walter Jellinek's *Verwaltungsrecht*.[26] After the Second World War, Ernst Forsthoff's *Verwaltungsrecht*, of which only the first volume, with the *Allgemeiner Teil*, appeared, became the primary reference.[27]

However, in principle, the *Vereinigung* (a concept that can mean not only 'association' but also 'unification') indicates that the legal scholars in these two countries regard themselves as a joint scientific community. They speak the same language in multiple—not merely literal—ways. Of course, this does not exclude individual differences in technical terminology, but it does clarify that the translation problem, which is usually so crucial in comparative law perspectives, does not arise to the same extent in this context. This is also evident from the fact that common academic work opportunities exist for both German and Austrian legal scholars. In contrast to the otherwise highly nationally introverted scenario, which essentially precludes the employment of foreign scholars or is only available for very narrowly defined particular subject areas, Austrian scholars in Germany and German scholars in Austria are generally considered able to teach the other legal system. Due to the sheer size of the German scientific community and the unique nature of the German State examination as a professional degree, employing Austrian scholars in German universities has nevertheless remained a relatively rare exception; the reverse is likely to be somewhat more frequent.[28]

Both the proximity and distance between the two legal systems are reflected in the traditional approach adopted within the *Vereinigung* to shed light on particular legal questions from the perspective of both the German and the Austrian (or Swiss) legal systems. This form of discussion was favoured by double lectures, typical of the annual conferences since 1924, in which two 'rapporteurs' (*Berichterstatter*) each gave their opinion on the same topic. This system ensured that one side was familiar with the basic structures and relevant discussions within the legal system of the other. On the other hand, this form of juxtaposition also repeatedly revealed the differences between the legal systems and led to academic discussion.

has turned out to be true: 'if one may judge from the fate of other works of Kelsen's disciples, its effect on German thought will be insignificant' (Feller (n 4) 145).

[26] For a short overview of the situation of administrative law in the Weimar republic, see Stolleis, Public Law (n 1) 95ff; Stolleis (n 2) 198ff, and especially on Jellinek ibid 239ff; I Augsberg 'Groß Neues ist ja nicht nachzutragen'. Walter Jellineks '"Verwaltungsrecht" in der frühen Bundesrepublik' in C Krämer (ed), *Die Verwaltungsrechtswissenschaft in der frühen Bundesrepublik (1949–1977)* (Mohr Siebeck 2017) 11–30

[27] See eg O Bachof, who in his report on German administrative law from 1953 (n 8) 369, explicitly stated: 'His *Lehrbuch des Verwaltungsrechts* (Vol. 1, 2nd ed., 1951), may be regarded as the most authoritative account of recent German administrative law'. On Forsthoff's reputation in general, see F Meinel, 'Die andere Seite des Rechtsstaats. Ernst Forsthoff in der Verwaltungsrechtswissenschaft der frühen Bundesrepublik' in Krämer (n 26) 129–48.

[28] On this relationship, see Leitl-Staudinger (n 25) No 46f.

B. Explicit References to the Austrian Model

For this reason, one repeatedly finds accounts in academic discussions where Austrian law is only considered from a German perspective in the context of a more comprehensive comparative law approach that also includes a multitude of other legal systems. However, since the common language, the legal tradition, and the institutional links between the legal systems are so closely linked to the respective national academic discourses, one must also acknowledge the unique, outstanding position of Austrian law.

This does not mean that Austrian regulations have been amply received and discussed. Instead, considering the reception of Austrian general administrative law, certain phases can be distinguished within the basic constellation thus determined, which are naturally also—and above all—influenced by the general historical context. Roughly speaking, the relative neglect of the Austrian situation during the Weimar period is followed by a strangely paradoxical interest during National Socialism, later replaced by a more indifferent attitude under the Basic Law.[29]

First, in the academic debate on the codification of a general APA, references to Austrian legislation have been found repeatedly since the 1920s. These tend, however, to be rather cursory—and were especially so in the early years of the Weimar Republic. The Austrian regulations are mentioned together with the isolated provisions enacted or at least discussed in the individual States, but they are not elaborated on and discussed in greater detail in terms of their individual provisions. An example of this form of reference is the most important textbook on general administrative law of the time, Jellinek's *Verwaltungsrecht*, mentioned above. In the context of the general debate on codification, the volume explicitly mentions the Austrian AVG. However, it is referred to rather casually in the footnotes and only in conjunction with references to other legislative projects in the German States, namely in Thuringia and Württemberg. Jellinek briefly skimmed over the whole discussion. The question of codification was apparently of little interest to him.[30] In fact, he explicitly described it as not very pressing.[31]

Second, it is noteworthy that things took a different turn after the so-called Austrian *Anschluss* to the German Reich. The Austrian side attempted to recommend the General Administrative Law of 1925 as a model for a unified codification of the administrative procedure by the Reich.[32] In particular, legal scholar Hans Spanner[33] made such an attempt in a series of quite prominently placed

[29] See Becker (n 4) 117ff; Stolleis (n 4) 257f.

[30] See W Jellinek, *Verwaltungsrecht* (Julius Springer 1928) 94f; with no substantial changes in this respect, see also Jellinek (n 19) 97f.

[31] See Jellinek (n 30) 95; Jellinek: 'It is difficult to say whether our time has the vocation to further codify administrative law and whether there will be further significant codifications. They would not be absolutely desirable' (n 20) 98.

[32] See Becker (n 4) 120f.

[33] On Spanner's life and work, see M Stolleis, 'Ein solider Jurist. Hans Spanner (1908-1991)' (2017) 50 Kritische Justiz 107–19.

publications.[34] In doing so, he had to transfer the reasons for legislative regulation into the new world view in a very specific way. This transfer was relatively easy to achieve in terms of the basic idea of unification as such since this appeared to be in line with the general preference of National Socialism for a highly centralised, hierarchical architecture of the State. Nevertheless, it was much more difficult to establish with regard to the evidently liberal basic ideas. Basic concepts such as the specific legal status of a *Partei* in the administrative procedure, ie a filing or injured party involved in the proceedings, or the right to be heard, could hardly be preserved without at the same time resorting to the idea of subjective rights, which the National Socialist *Weltanschauung* claimed to have overcome.[35] Spanner thus attempted to explain why these ideas had an objective function that served not only the individual but the individual as *Volksgenosse* (a member of the German people) and ultimately the *Volksgemeinschaft* (the community of the people).[36]

Third, for the first decades of the Federal Republic, however, the Weimar diagnosis was largely valid again.[37] Just as Jellinek's work could be regarded as exemplary for the Weimar period, the standard work on the administrative law of that time can now be used to demonstrate the very same essential attitude for the young Federal Republic. Ernst Forsthoff proceeds in this respect in his highly influential textbook on administrative law in precisely the same way as Jellinek did before him: he mentions the Austrian *AVG*, but only in connection with the other earlier codifications or attempts at codification in the *Länder* and only to a certain extent, *en passant*, literally on the margins of the actual main text, ie in the footnotes.[38]

[34] See H Spanner, 'Die österreichischen Verwaltungsverfahrensgesetze als Vorbild eines Reichsgesetzes über das Verwaltungsverfahren' [1938] Deutsche Verwaltung 676–82 and 'Die Rechtsmittelbelehrung im Verwaltungsverfahren' [1940] Reichsverwaltungsblatt 357ff; R Petz, 'Wertvolles Rechtsgut der österreichischen Verwaltung' [1938] Deutsche Verwaltung 526ff; H Pfeifer, *Rechtsvereinheitlichung und Verwaltungsvereinfachung im Großdeutschen Reich* (Hanseatische Verlagsanstalt 1942); W Antoniolli, 'Die Vereinfachung der Rechtsmittel in der Verwaltung' [1941] Deutsche Verwaltung 74ff.

[35] For a general account of administrative law under National Socialism, see Stolleis (n 2) 249ff; Stolleis, *Entwicklungsstufen* (n 1) 79ff.

[36] See Spanner, 'Die österreichischen Verwaltungsverfahrensgesetze' (n 34) 678f.

[37] Becker (n 4) 117f, stating that:

> despite the close family ties that exist between German and Austrian administrative law, Austrian legislation on administrative procedure has received surprisingly little attention in Germany and has remained largely unknown.

A certain exception to this rule might be found in Ferdinand Kopp's habilitation thesis from 1969, which explicitly intends to discuss the relevance of the rule of law in administrative proceedings in a comparison 'with well-established regulations of other countries, especially Austria.

See also Kopp (n 10) VII. This may, however, not come as a total surprise, given that the book is dedicated to Kopp's academic teacher Hans Spanner (see Kopp (n 10) V). Another early example for a reference to the Austrian model is H von Rosen-von Hoewel, 'Zur Frage der Kodifikation des allgemeinen Verwaltungsrechts' Die öffentliche Verwaltung [1952] 101–03.

[38] See E Forsthoff, *Lehrbuch des Verwaltungsrechts, 1. Band: Allgemeiner Teil* (7th edn, Beck 1958) at 149 and 203. On Forsthoff's life and work in greater detail, see F Meinel, *Der Jurist in der industriellen Gesellschaft. Ernst Forsthoff und seine Zeit* (Akademie 2011).

However, a quite explicit discussion occurred at the 17th meeting of the Association of German Constitutional Law Professors in October 1958, appropriately enough in Vienna.[39] On the topic of 'The Administrative Procedure' (*Das Verwaltungsverfahren*), Karl August Bettermann gave the first and Erwin Melichar the second lecture, respectively, following the procedure of double lectures described above. Bettermann, who had been a judge at the Higher Administrative Court in Münster for a few years in the 1950s followed by two years at the Federal Administrative Court before he took up a chair at the Free University of Berlin in 1956, expounded on the German perspective.[40] In contrast, Melichar, who became president of the Austrian Constitutional Court almost two decades later but was still a full professor at the University of Graz at that time, was speaking from what was decidedly the Austrian perspective.[41] The two reports also testify to the willingness to approach the other side and learn from it. At the beginning of his lecture, Bettermann refers explicitly to the basic ideas of Adolf Merkl, who at the time of the lecture was still a professor at the University of Vienna (in fact, Melichar succeeded him to the Vienna chair in 1963).[42]

Interestingly, both speakers agreed that the codification of administrative procedure is determined by the constitutional context and the will to guarantee a system of legal protection. In fact, Melichar too did not argue directly for a form of regulation following the Austrian model. Indeed, he presented it much more cautiously, not suggesting that corresponding codifications could work under certain circumstances. He emphasised that after almost 30 years of practical experience in Austria, there were no longer any voices either in legal scholarship or legal practice that were fundamentally critical of, or opposed to, this codification.[43]

However, both Bettermann and Melichar also emphasised another interesting point repeatedly mentioned in other debates on the overarching issue, demonstrating that the Austrian codification could not function as a direct role model. In Austria, legal protection in court proceedings is concentrated in a single instance before the Administrative Court, so much administrative law (self) review is shifted over to administrative procedure.[44] On the other hand, the German model has a complete three-tiered system, which allows for a distinction between appeal and review and between the highest administrative courts in the individual States and the Federal Administrative Court. Bettermann had already pointed out the distinction between administrative decisions and court rulings in an influential

39 See Stolleis (n 4) 258.

40 See KA Bettermann, 'Das Verwaltungsverfahren' in *Veröffentlichung der Vereinigung der Deutschen Staatsrechtslehrer* No 17 (De Gruyter 1959) 119–82.

41 See E Melichar, 'Das Verwaltungsverfahren' in *Veröffentlichung der Vereinigung der Deutschen Staatsrechtslehrer* No 17 (n 40) 183–212.

42 See Bettermann (n 40) 121f.

43 See Melichar (n 41) 207.

44 ibid 183ff, differentiating between a system of administrative court control *a priori* and *a posteriori*.

article in the *Gedächtnisschrift* for Walter Jellinek, published in 1955.[45] This model, which, in the prevailing opinion, cannot be derived directly from art 19(4) of the Basic Law, is undoubtedly well supported by its focus on judicial legal protection as a central element of the rule of law and essentially rules out closer alignment with Austrian procedural regulation.[46]

A similar approach, with relatively similar results, was presented at the *Juristentag*, an annual meeting of legal scholars and practitioners at which legal policy issues considered to be particularly urgent were to be discussed together. At its 43rd meeting, in September 1960, both the German and the Austrian sides were asked to present their perspectives.[47] The Austrian side was presented by Hans Spanner, the legal scholar who had promoted the adoption of the regulations of the General Administrative Law during the National Socialist era. While Spanner referred to the positive experiences with Austrian law,[48] the German speaker Fritz Werner once again claimed that since the Austrian regulations also contained '*verwaltungsprozessuale Normen*', ie norms regulating procedure within the administrative court, they could not serve as a model for the German legislator.[49]

Thus, while the Austrian concept was discussed and thus received, its possible function as a model was ultimately set aside due to dogmatic arguments regarding both the constitutional and the general systematic structure of the German legal system.

IV. Administrative Procedure in Germany

At this point, it is worth taking a closer look at the content of German administrative procedural law. Regarding the essential content of administrative procedural law in Germany, the relevant laws of the Federation and the *Länder*, the *Verwaltungsverfahrengesetz*, which finally came into force only in 1977, can also be used as a point of reference for the earlier period of interest here. As mentioned above, this legislation was not intended to implement wholly new ideas for the first time. By contrast, there was widespread agreement that this legislation only put administrative practice into legal form, its essential features having been established

[45] See KA Bettermann, 'Verwaltungsakt und Richterspruch' in O Bachof (ed), *Gedächtnisschrift für Walter Jellinek* (Isar 1955) 361ff.

[46] See F Werner, 'Empfiehlt es sich, den allgemeinen Teil des Verwaltungsrechts zu kodifizieren? Gutachten für den 43. Deutschen Juristentag' in Ständige Deputation des Deutschen Juristentages (ed), *Verhandlungen des dreiundvierzigsten Deutschen Juristentages*, vol I, Gutachten, 2nd part B (Mohr Siebeck 1960) 16.

[47] See Stolleis (n 4) 258.

[48] See H Spanner, 'Empfiehlt es sich, den allgemeinen Teil des Verwaltungsrechts zu kodifizieren? Gutachten für den 43. Deutschen Juristentag' in Ständige Deputation des Deutschen Juristentages (n 46) 5.

[49] See Werner (n 46) 16.

in the Constitution. On the other hand, the concrete individual aspects had been determined by case law and jurisprudence over decades of joint work.

One of these fundamental elements is the principle of the '*Offizialmaxime*', whereby the authority must decide to comprehensively investigate the facts on which its decision is based. Thus, in contrast to civil court proceedings, the authority may not rely solely on the party's submissions. However, not unlike the Austrian model, it is not generally possible to make a full declaration; such a declaration must be appropriately balanced with the need for a rapid decision in the interest of both the public and the citizens specifically concerned.

In any event, the addressee of the administrative measure must also have been allowed to submit his or her comments before the adoption of an onerous administrative act; the general principle of *audiatur et altera pars* is shown here to be an obligation on the part of the authority to be heard, which may be derogated from only in strictly limited exceptional situations, namely in the event of imminent danger.

In principle, administrative acts must be justified. They must also contain legal instructions informing the citizen concerned about how (s)he can seek legal protection against the incriminating measure. Traditionally, this is done first in an internal administrative procedure known as '*Widerspruchsverfahren*', ie opposition proceedings, in which the next highest authority in the hierarchy examines the legality (and in cases of discretionary use also the expediency) of the measure in question in response to a corresponding application by the citizen. If the reviewing authority concludes that the measure was indeed lawful, it rejects the objection and thus confirms the original decision. Conversely, if it considers the measure unlawful, it remedies the objection by annulling the initial decision.

These internal administrative opposition proceedings occur at the same time as a preliminary procedure (*Vorverfahren*), a necessary precondition for administrative court proceedings. This means that if the possibility of such an opposition procedure exists, then a claimant must first have pursued these opposition proceedings unsuccessfully before (s)he can file an action in court. However, the federal and State legislatures may regulate differently whether an opposition procedure exists or not. For some particular matters, namely in civil service law, the procedure is prescribed by special legislation. However, the *Länder* may also abolish the opposition proceedings within the framework of their administrative procedure laws. Indeed, some *Länder* have availed themselves of this possibility in recent years.

In this respect, opposition proceedings, which envisage internal administrative review, are strongly influenced by the general German understanding of the rule of law. Accordingly, rule of law means mainly judicial protection. The very designation of the opposition proceedings as 'preliminary proceedings' confirms this view. It is no coincidence that the guarantee of judicial legal protection, ie the right to judicial review of any measure of State authority that affects the rights of individuals, is the final provision in the first section of the Constitution devoted to fundamental rights. This perspective again underlines why ensuring legal protection has been called the 'keystone' of the German constitutional State.

However, the most heated discussions relating to administrative procedure did not concern questions of legal protection in the strict sense but the more general problem of the annulment of administrative acts outside litigation and thus outside judicial review. In appeal procedures, particularly in opposition proceedings, suspension is not usually a serious problem because opposition typically impedes enforceability and, in any event, the full legal force or validity—*Rechtskraft*—of the administrative act. Therefore, no third party can claim a legitimate expectation that the decision will be upheld during this phase. Nevertheless, this raises the question of whether an administrative act can acquire legal force at all or whether it can only apply to court judgments, and if, since the substantive legal force of the administrative act is affirmed in principle, such administrative acts can still be revoked.

As in the Austrian system, in principle, both questions were answered in the affirmative in Germany, but at the same time, a different solution was found to the question of the circumstances under which it is possible to break the rule of *res judicata*. Whereas a narrowly defined catalogue of specific situations is identified in Austria, the German legislation (§§ 48, 49 *Verwaltungsverfahrensgesetz*), which once again merely reproduced the judicial practice of previous decades, refers to a process of balancing a public interest in annulment against legitimate private interest in the continuation of the administrative act. Therefore, while the underlying considerations and most practical outcomes are very similar, the German laws differ from the Austrian model significantly in terms of the technical implementation of these objectives.

V. Hypothetical Cases

Another way to compare the administrative laws of Europe after the Austrian codification is to seek to understand how the courts exerted control over the legality and fairness of the decisions made by the administration. The following hypothetical cases will be considered: authorisations and licences (Section A); the dismissal of civil servants (Section B); the expropriation procedure (Section C); administrative planning (Section D).

A. Authorisations and Licences

Opening a pharmacy requires an official licence. The conditions for granting such a licence primarily depend on the general provisions of commercial law, especially on two special legal provisions: the *Apothekengesetz* (Pharmacy Law) and the *Apothekenbetriebsverordnung* (Pharmacy Operating Regulation). When the

Pharmacy Act came into force in 1960, it replaced several pre-existing federal laws. However, the new law did not introduce an entirely new set of regulations, merely unifying existing ones. In particular, the basic idea is much older than this specific statute; it can already be found in State-level pharmacy laws at the turn of the nineteenth century.[50] Thus, running a pharmacy is not only regarded as a normal trade: by authorising the supply of medicinal products, which may be supplied only on medical prescription and only through pharmacies, these also fulfil a public service. Specific qualifications are therefore required of the applicant and in relation to local conditions. As regards the person concerned, in addition to the licence to practise pharmacy, a police clearance certificate and a medical certificate of health must be presented. With regard to local conditions, proof is required that the premises comply with the Pharmacy Operating Regulations.

However, there was one crucial new legal aspect that the new regulation of 1960 not only took up but was even the fundamental reason for the reform. In its famous pharmacy ruling of 1958, the Federal Constitutional Court emphasised the relevance of the freedom to practise a profession according to art 12 of the Basic Law. While it did not attack the general idea of compulsory licensing as such, it deduced from the pharmacists' freedom to practise their profession that all other possibilities must be exhausted before using the 'radical means of restricting licensing' (*das Radikalmittel der Zulassungsbeschränkung*), in line with what the court described as a 'German tradition'.[51]

While the substantive conditions for the licence are therefore specific, the procedure, on the other hand, follows the general model. The citizen must submit an application, usually declaring at the same time that the material conditions are met. The authority then checks whether the requirements have indeed been met. If one of the statutory requirements is lacking, it will withhold the permit. If, on the other hand, all the requirements are met, it must grant the permit—since the need for a permit for the activity constitutes a barrier to occupational freedom, which may only be granted by, or based on, laws and not based on administrative initiative. If the authority refuses to grant permission, it must give reasons for its decision and at the same time indicate the opportunities for legal protection in the form of an objection and an administrative court action. Since, in the case in question, an action must be brought to obtain the licence, namely an administrative act in favour of the applicant, the *Verpflichtungsklage* (action for performance) is the admissible form of action. Under the Basic Law, or more precisely, since the Federal Constitutional Court began its work in 1951, there is another option for legal protection. Since refusal to grant an operating licence affects the applicant's freedom to

[50] For a very short overview of the history of the regulation, see K-H Bartels, 'Dichtung und Wahrheit. Zur Geschichte der deutschen Apothekenbetriebserlaubnis' (2000) 145 Pharmazeutische Zeitung 2945–50.

[51] See BVerfGE 7, 377–444, 442.

practise a profession, the applicant may, if all other legal protection measures have been unsuccessful, also file a constitutional complaint (*Verfassungsbeschwerde*) with the Federal Constitutional Court against these unfavourable decisions of the administration and the administrative courts.

B. The Dismissal of a Civil Servant

From the legal point of view, removal from his post would depend on whether Caius is a civil servant or a public employee. The specific legal status of civil servants dates back to the early nineteenth century.[52] The first comprehensive regulation of the legal status of civil servants came about with the Imperial Civil Servants Act (*Reichsbeamtengesetz*) of 31 March 1873. At the time of the Weimar Republic, the status of legal servants was constitutionally established by arts 128–31 of the Weimar Constitution. Thus, art 129(2) expressly states, for example, that civil servants may be temporarily relieved of their duties, temporarily or permanently retired, or transferred to another office with a lower salary only under the conditions and in the manner established by law. A relatively large number of laws, at the level of both *Reich* and the *Länder*, implemented these constitutional requirements. After the National Socialist era, the Basic Law returned to the vision held during Weimar Republic. It also contains constitutional protection of the civil service, the main difference being that a more general protection replaced the more detailed provisions of the Weimar Constitution to uphold the 'traditional principles of the civil service' (*hergebrachte Grundsätze des Berufsbeamtentums*). Once again, this protection is implemented by the civil service laws of the federal government and the individual States.

The norm to be applied concerning specific legal questions thus depends on the public authority under which the civil servant performs his or her duties. The concrete nature of civil service status plays a decisive role in the question of removing an employee from his or her post. In the standard case of civil service for life, ie not for a limited period or a revocable position, there are special provisions in the form of disciplinary rules for permanent removal from the civil service. The competent authority must first investigate the facts internally. Caius must be given a fair hearing before the decision is taken. This right was explicitly mentioned in art 129(3) of the Weimar Constitution, but for this very reason, it can also be regarded as one of the 'traditional principles of the civil service' protected under the Basic Law. However, the actual decision on removal from the civil service is not taken by the employer but by the competent disciplinary court. Caius may appeal against the disciplinary court's decision on points of law.

52 For a short overview, see TI Schmidt, *Beamtenrecht* (Mohr Siebeck 2017) 6ff.

C. Expropriation Procedure

The authority intends to expropriate Mrs Sempronia's house to make way for a railway line. What kind of procedure must be followed? Who must be informed? Who has the right to intervene? What procedural rights does Mrs Sempronia have (right to a hearing, right to have full knowledge of the findings, right to present documents, the duty of the administration to take into serious account the documents presented by the parties, right to challenge the decision about the location of the railway)? If the act of expropriation is actually adopted, who can challenge it? And what kind of remedies can be exercised?

Expropriation can only be carried out as a limitation on the right to property by law or based on a law. This requirement is the consequence of a constitutional safeguard already provided in art 152 of the Weimar Constitution, taken up largely verbatim by art 14 of the Basic Law.[53] Expropriation must therefore be ordered separately by law or be based on a general law that permits it to allow a transport infrastructure project. If the decision is made by law, the only remaining legal remedy is a constitutional referral, as no administrative court protection can be granted against formal laws for the sake of the separation of powers. If the decision amounts to an unlawful administrative act, it can be appealed against and challenged before the administrative courts. If all these appeals are unsuccessful, a constitutional referral (*Verfassungsbeschwerde*) can also be filed.

D. Administrative Planning

The legal bases for building law have changed frequently, but the essential basic ideas were already laid down in the nineteenth-century rules and regulations.[54] In fact, the basic idea of *Baufreiheit*, ie freedom to build on one's own property, was already stated in the *Allgemeines Landrecht für die Preußischen Staaten* from 1764. The legal regulations, however, long remained fragmented because of the fundamental distinction between planning law (*Bauplanungsrecht*) and building regulation law as a sub-form of police law (*Bauordnungrecht*), and responsibility was disputed not only between the *Reich* and the *Länder* but also between the States and the municipalities. It was not until 1950, under the Basic Law, that preparations began for a general, uniform federal building code, which, however, was

[53] For an instructive overview of both the historical and current situation regarding expropriation, see the contributions in O Depenheuer and F Shirvani (eds), *Die Enteignung. Historische, vergleichende, dogmatische und politische Perspektiven auf ein Rechtsinstitut* (Springer 2018); in particular F Shirvani, 'Entwicklung des Enteignungsrechts vom frühen 19. Jahrhundert bis zur Weimarer Reichsverfassung' ibid 25–49.

[54] For an overview of this development, see M Krautzberger, 'Einleitung' in U Battis, M Krautzberger and R-P Löhr (eds), *BauGB. Baugesetzbuch. Kommentar* (14th edn, Beck 2019).

only intended to cover planning law, as regulatory law remained a matter for the *Länder*. In 1960, the Federal Building Code (*Bundesbaugesetz*) finally came into force; it has since been revised several times (and renamed *Baugesetzbuch*, ie Building Code, in 1987), but the basic rules remain the same.

According to these rules, despite the general idea of *Baufreiheit* (which, under the Weimar Constitution as well as under the Basic Law, is considered a consequence of the freedom to hold property), a permit is needed to construct a building complex. As German building law is subdivided into federal regulations determining urban land-use planning law, ie the development potential of an area from the legal point of view, as well as State regulations concerning aspects of building control, the competent authority must observe both sets of regulations.

According to the building planning law, a school is considered a so-called public service facility (*Gemeinwohlanlagen*) under § 5(2) No 2a *Baugesetzbuch* (BauGB), ie a facility intended for the public good. A similar rule already existed in § 5(2) No 2 *Bundesbaugesetz* (BBauG). Such facilities can be explicitly identified in the land-use plan. Depending on whether a development plan (*Bebauungsplan*) was also issued by the respective municipality on the basis of such a land-use plan (*Flächennutzungsplan*), legal development potential, ie the issue regarding the conditions under which building is allowed, is governed by §§ 29ff BBauG (or, today, BauGB).

According to the building code for the *Länder*, schools are generally classified as 'special buildings', for which standard building permit procedure complying with the land-building codes rather than the simplified procedure is required. According to these regulations, the developer must apply to the building supervisory authority responsible, supplying all the necessary documents relating to the building. The building supervisory authority then listens to the local authority and any other bodies prescribed by law regarding the application. It should also notify the owners of neighbouring plots of land if it intends to grant divergences or exceptions and exemptions from any protective measures envisaged in building law.

Those whose subjective rights may be affected by the building measure, usually the owners of neighbouring properties, may challenge the permission to build.

VI. Personal Relations

As already described above, there was, and indeed still is, a scientific community of public law scholars in Austria and Germany, albeit marked by a degree of asymmetry[55] that affects the question of the allocation of academic positions. There are, of course, a few outstanding Austrian legal scholars who have been awarded

[55] See Leitl-Staudinger (n 25) No 45f.

professorships in Germany—the most famous example is undoubtedly Kelsen's chair at the University of Cologne.[56] However, as stated above, due to the much larger German scientific community and the particular features of the German State examination, the process tends to run in the opposite direction, with significantly more German scholars finding employment with Austrian universities than vice versa.

In our context, however, two other prominent Austrian scholars should be mentioned as highly significant exceptions to this general rule. The first one is the most prominent Austrian lawyer in the field of administrative law, Adolf Merkl, who was a professor at Tübingen University from 1943 to 1950.[57] The second prominent scholar, particularly in terms of administrative procedure, is Hans Spanner, already mentioned several times above. In 1956 he moved from his first full professorship in Graz to the University of Erlangen as the successor to Otto Bachof. Having declined an offer from Berlin University in 1959, Spanner accepted one from the Ludwig-Maximilians-University in Munich, and in 1960 he became a full professor of public law, specialising in public commercial and tax law at the same university. Some years later, he also served as the Dean of the Faculty of Law. Among his students in Munich was Ferdinand Kopp, who took up his first professorship at the University of Graz in 1970, where he stayed for eight years and wrote not only one of the first and certainly the most important commentaries on the newly created APA (first published in 1976) but also an equally important commentary on the Administrative Court Code (first published already in 1974).[58]

VII. Conclusion

The result is clear: although the Austrian vision of administrative procedure was relatively well known and discussed, it never attained the status of a concrete role model in the German debate. It was not proposed as such even by Austrian colleagues since the systematic differences between the two legal systems, which both sides saw and recognised, supposedly stood in the way.

[56] See T Olechowski, *Hans Kelsen. Biographie eines Rechtswissenschaftlers* (Mohr Siebeck 2020) 481ff.

[57] For a short overview on his life and work, see H Schambeck, *Leben und Wirken von Adolf Julius Merkl: Vortrag gehalten vor der Niederösterreichischen Juristischen Gesellschaft im Festsaal des Bundesgymnasiums in Wiener Neustadt am 31.1.1990* (Orac 1990).

[58] See FO Kopp, *Verwaltungsgerichtsordnung. Kommentar* (Beck 1974) and *Verwaltungsverfahrensgesetz. Kommentar* (Beck 1976).

11

The Spanish Model of Administrative Procedure (APA 1889/APA 1958)

Javier Barnes

I. Introduction: The Rise of Administrative Procedure in the Nineteenth Century

A. Procedural Requirements for a New and Powerful Administration

The French Revolution produced both the Civil Code and a powerful public administration in continental Europe and its area of influence. A vast administrative machine emerged: it 'provid[ed] for the demands of every individual from birth to death, which no government could perform without the help of a great apparatus of agents'.[1] Since then, the sovereign—ultimately, the State—was no longer a *guardian* as in previous centuries,[2] but an *architect* of the welfare State.

After the French Revolution,[3] inasmuch as the administration had become equal to the other two powers of the State, it could, of its own accord, now dispose of the rights of individuals.[4] Before this development, only a judicial authority could limit, extinguish, or modify these rights.[5]

[1] L Mannori and B Sordi, 'Science of Administration and Administrative Law' in H Hofmann, P Grossi and D Canale (eds), *A Treatise of Legal Philosophy and General Jurisprudence*, vol 9, *A History of the Philosophy of Law in the Civil Law World, 1600–1900* (Springer 2009) 225.

[2] In the seventeenth and eighteenth centuries, the State began to appear as an instrument of social development. However, it involved a matter of verifying a possible wrongdoing and applying a sanction. The heart of every State apparatus continued to be made up of judges. The administration was a particular form of justice.

[3] Mannori and Sordi (n 1) state that at the fall of Napoleon:

> [T]he administrative state had become a definitive acquisition, along with the Civil Code. This occurred not only in the French experience, but also for a large part of continental Europe, which by then looked up to France as an unsurpassed model of state organization.

Public power was no longer expressed only through laws or sentences. These two older means of exercising authority were now joined by a third, which took the name of '*acte administratif*' through which the State was able to unilaterally assert its authority over the citizens in order to satisfy public interests.

[4] ibid.

[5] ibid.

Javier Barnes, *The Spanish Model of Administrative Procedure (APA 1889/APA 1958)* In: *The Austrian Codification of Administrative Procedure*. Edited by: Giacinto Della Cananea, Angela Ferrari Zumbini, and Otto Pfersmann, Oxford University Press. © Javier Barnes 2023. DOI: 10.1093/oso/9780198867623.003.0011

Thus:

> it comes as no surprise that perhaps the most urgent issue that Continental legal culture had to confront during the first half of the nineteenth century was to check, circumscribe, and render socially tolerable the enormous power that executive administrations had succeeded in arrogating to themselves.[6]

'The problem of freedom increasingly becomes more a problem of guarantee'.[7] The emergence of a formidable administrative power inevitably went hand in hand with a struggle to establish new legal guarantees in favour of individual rights and freedoms.[8]

In this context, administrative procedure fortuitously became a useful tool to meet three basic needs that arose with the emergence of the contemporary State in early nineteenth century : (1) the control of administrative power, largely through *administrative* justice, rather than through *judicial* justice; (2) the exercise by the administration, and not by judges, of traditional jurisdictional responsibilities for reasons of ideology or efficiency; and (3) the internal organisation of the public administration, not only in terms of its own staff, but also of its mechanisms and relationships. In other words: control, the drafting of decisions affecting individual rights and freedoms, and the organisation of the work within the administrative apparatus. These three needs require the establishment of specific rules concerning administrative procedure.

However, the three concurrent streams in the formation of rules of administrative procedure are very different in nature. The first two (control and decision-making) are quasi-judicial in character. In these cases, administrative procedure stems from elements characteristic of the judicial process, albeit with the necessary adaptations and greater simplification. On the contrary, the third stream is tied to the administration's organisation and internal structure.

[6] ibid.

[7] ibid.

[8] Mannori and Sordi state:

> In short, at the beginning of the nineteenth century, England and France by now represent two totally antithetical models of management of the administrative space. The former has remained loyal to the foundations of the jurisdictional state, which had constituted the common form of organisation of power in Europe for so long. The second has instead taken the process of simplification begun by Continental absolutism and crowned by the Revolution to its extreme consequences, proclaiming the primacy of executive administration.

ibid 255

On the birth of the administrative tribunals (administrative regime) at the beginning of the twentieth century in the common law world, see HWR Wade and CF Forsyth, *Administrative Law* (11th edn, OUP 2014) 762ff. On the current situation, see P Craig, *Administrative Law* (8th edn, Sweet & Maxwell 2016) 9ff.

B. Old States and Empires: An Accumulated Experiences of 'Administrative Organisation'

The need for procedural requirements to organise and control the powerful emerging administration is experienced similarly in all States. However, this need was felt with greater force, urgency, and intensity in older States, as they had already established extensive administrative apparatuses, that had long before assumed relevant functions and responsibilities. This need became even more evident in the cases that a State also ruled over an empire.[9]

Such accumulated experience may have contributed to the prominent role that administrative procedure has played in Spain since the nineteenth century.

C. The Flowering of Procedural Requirements

By the second half of the nineteenth century, a broad culture of administrative procedure had already been developed in Spain. An administrative procedure regulation of 1888, as stated in its introduction, justified the new norm with reasoning that could well have been written today:

> with the passage of time, administrative procedure may find itself formed without reference to a specific system but as the result of isolated rules decreed in different times in response to the needs of a given time and which may already have been partially satisfied. It is therefore necessary to organise administrative procedure and, at the same time, give it a systematic and rational character, to simplify the handling of cases.[10]

[9] On the one hand, Spain became a modern State at the close of the fifteenth century, with substantially the same boundaries as today. On the other hand, Spanish America, from the start, had been endowed with a remarkable 'administrative apparatus' (regarding the market, commerce, agriculture, mining, defence, public works, education and universities, territorial divisions, justice, and so on), as well as a legal system following the then current norms in European Spain as coequal provinces of the nation, rather than those more associated with a dependent colony of other empires.

John H. Elliot, a well-known British historian and specialist in the field, writes that in less than a century (during the sixteenth century, to be precise), the Spanish Crown had set up a system of government in the New World that various other European monarchs could envy. The creation of the 'State of the Indias' was an impressive achievement from any point of view, especially considering that it appeared to have successfully defied the accepted norms of time and space. The Spanish viceroyalties of the Americas were over 7,000 kilometres away from European Spain, separated by an unfavourable ocean. It could easily take two years for a dispatch from the government in Madrid to reach Lima. In contrast, official communications between Virginia and London might only take four months, but to the English Crown, the system of governance that Spain had created in the New World only affirm the triumphant obedience that the Spanish kings inspired. See John H Elliot, *Empires of the Atlantic World: Britain and Spain in America, 1492–1830* (Yale UP 2006) 205–06.

[10] Regulation on administrative procedure enacted by the Overseas Ministry for Puerto Rico, Cuba, and the Philippines (*Reglamento del Ministerio de Ultramar, Gaceta de Madrid núm. 272, de 28 de septiembre de 1888*).

The laws governing administrative procedures were derived from different legal sources: case law (particularly when legal acts affected individual rights), substantive sectoral laws, sectoral administrative procedural laws, and general procedural laws.[11]

Indeed, during the nineteenth century, national legal systems began to set out procedural rules with different purposes and scope. This can be seen very clearly in Spain. The rights of defence were developed by case law. Some procedural rules owed their origin to the executive itself, which implemented administrative rules to better organise operations and activities; others came from substantive statutes found in various policy areas, in which some procedural rules were incidentally laid down (eg regarding the application for and granting of a licence).[12] Later, special procedural acts would be enacted (such as, for example, the laws on administrative appeals).[13] Finally, in an effort of synthesis and simplification, common and uniform procedural elements were sought for all the different branches of the administration. Thus, general laws of administrative procedure began to develop, which brought together a basic typology of administrative procedures, although their main function was not that of a procedural code (ie a closed catalogue of all judicial processes), but rather that of expressing the administrative culture of a given legal order. At all these levels, Spain produced significant contributions. Here, we will refer only to the first Spanish General Act of Administrative Procedure of 1889 (APA 1889).

D. The General Act of Administrative Procedure of 1889

An act passed by the Spanish parliament on 19 October 1889 (APA 1889), also known as the '*Azcárate Act*' (taking the name of its promoter, interestingly a university professor, rather than a politician), was the first statute that dealt exclusively with general and common administrative procedural rules to be followed when a legal decision has to be made by the state administration. It was not an unplanned act, but the result of numerous debates, commission work,[14] and legislative precedents.[15] The APA of 1889 is the legal precursor to the 1958 APA.

[11] See J Barnes, 'Administrative Procedure' in P Cane and others (eds), *The Oxford Handbook of Comparative Administrative Law* (OUP 2020) 831.

[12] Examples are numerous in fields such as mining, agriculture, trade, or industry. Since the mid-nineteenth century, specific procedural rules have been common in the different sectorial legislations.

[13] For example, on 31 December 1881, a statute on administrative appeals in tax matters was passed. See FG Navarro, *Cincuenta años de procedimiento administrativo en un mundo cambiante* (Iustel-Instituto Andaluz de Administración Pública 2009) 375.

[14] For example, in 1879, a commission was created by parliamentary act to study an administrative procedure act (Act of 16 January 1879, see Gaceta de Madrid núm. 17, de 17 de enero de 1879).

[15] For example, a government decree ordering that within two months internal regulations be drawn up and printed for the handling of the business entrusted to the departments of the State Civil Administration, 14 September 1872 (Gaceta de Madrid núm. 259, de 15/09/1872). In general terms,

The APA of 1889 fulfilled a long-standing aspiration to enact 'codification' for both the executive branch and the administration, just as the judiciary had its procedural law, and Parliament its rules of procedure followed by the chambers.[16]

The 1889 APA laid down a legal framework or common 'bases' (principles and rules), which were to be implemented in further detail through sectoral regulations,[17] according to the specific tasks of each ministry.[18]

The 1889 APA can be regarded as a compromise between the necessary uniformity of certain procedural components and the unavoidable diversity of specific procedures.[19] To this end, the 1889 APA set out a basic structure for authorisation and appeal procedures, and then deferred their completion to distinct ministerial regulations. The 1889 APA also established some basic individual rights (in particular, the right of defence) and provided certain administrative remedies. Regulations were expected to add to the basic framework. The sum of these two components—a common ordinary statute and a diversity of regulations—formed a unified corpus of administrative procedures.[20]

This APA placed special emphasis on streamlining the work of the administration, valuing speed, publicity, and efficiency to process the citizens' applications and requests with a minimum of delay. The procedural rules in this APA not only aimed to protect individual rights, but also to set up a mechanism to streamline administrative work and resolve administrative matters as quickly as possible. Its basic intent is to use administrative procedure as a decision-making process to guarantee the professionalism of administrative personnel, as well as the administration's independence, efficiency, and proximity to the citizen.

since the 1840s, there was already an abundance of separate legal norms on administrative procedure with different scopes.

[16] The introductory explanation of the APA uses this explanation.

[17] The act gives leeway to each ministry to establish specific rules in its procedural regulations. Indeed, the different rules of procedure set out by this APA (types of procedure, deadlines, formalities, communications, requests, appeals, and so forth) essentially lay down a basic framework susceptible to different developments, depending on the functions and needs of each administration.

This political discretion, vested in the various ministers by the act, was used to refine the common principles and rules of the APA. In other words: to evaluate the model of administrative procedure launched by the 1889 APA, it is necessary to also consider the regulations that supplement the system.

[18] In 1890, the first eight regulations (one for each ministry) were already enacted, in accordance with the deadline established by the APA.

[19] In 1940, the dean of Harvard Law School, renowned administrative law scholar James M. Landis, also argued against the uniformity of procedures in agencies with such diverse and heterogeneous functions: it would be absurd, he said, to give the same structure, for example, to a bank as to a train station. It would be equally absurd to insist that the details of the organisation and mode of operation of the Federal Communications Commission and the Federal Reserve, both independent agencies, should be analogous. See JM Landis, 'Crucial Issues in Administrative Law: The Walter–Logan Bill' (1940) Harv L Rev 53, 1077–1102, 1080.

[20] The APA was in force for 69 years, and was superseded by the Act of 1958, which also included a rulemaking procedure.

The APA of 1989 regards administrative procedure as a matter of great concern to the State: the presidency of the Council of Ministers was required to publish annual data concerning the status of administrative procedures throughout the State administration, showing the number of procedures initiated, resolved, and pending in each ministry.

E. A Comparative Overview of the Spanish APA of 1889 and the Austrian APA of 1925

The Austrian APA of 1925 shows a completely different perspective from the Spanish APA of 1889.

The most obvious differences are as follows:

- First, the two APAs express different understandings of the codification of administrative procedures and how they should be performed. The Spanish APA of 1889 strives to unify common elements (procedural principles and structures, time frames, interactions between the individual and the administration and between the different sectors of the administration, among others). The specifics and details to be enacted are relegated to subsequent ministerial regulations in each sector. The Austrian APA 1925 attempts to codify a procedural archetype to be applied systematically across the entire administration.
- Second, the Spanish APA does not focus exclusively on how administrative procedures should be carried out to protect citizens against administrative acts affecting individual rights; it also concerns itself with how the administration should function.
- Third, the most profound difference is that the Austrian APA focuses on individual administrative acts (that potentially affect individuals' rights); it establishes a formal, quasi-judicial structure.[21] And it does this with a high degree of detail and legal technique. The Spanish APA was conceived with a broader purpose in mind.

These differences between the two national models became even more evident in the 1950s. While the 1889 APA was drawn up in the context of a liberal State, concerned with ensuring the administration acted in accordance with the law, the

[21] The influence of procedural law doctrines of and their legacy in the form of a quasi-judicial structure in administrative law are well known, so much so that, at the time, it was considered inherent to the actual procedure. See: E Mannlicher, 'Die österreichische Verwaltungsverfahrensreform des Jahres 1925' [1926] ZöR 357.

This influence of procedural law on the formation of administrative procedure—in a paradigmatic manner in the Austrian model—is principally due to the fact that it focuses on issuing administrative acts affecting individual rights.

1958 APA also sought to shape an administration that would be efficient, speedy, and socially committed.

II. The Spanish APA of 1958

A. The Birth of a New Administrative Procedure Act: APA of 1958

On 17 July 1958, an ambitious Administrative Procedure Act was passed in Spain, superseding the 1889 APA.

The 1889 APA was proposed again by another law professor serving in congress. The APA of 1958 was sponsored by Laureano López Rodó, professor of administrative law, senior civil servant, and prominent politician in the modernisation of the country since the late 1950s. During the act's parliamentary debate process, it was emphasised that this would be a more appropriate APA for a welfare State and that its intent to achieve 'good administration'.[22]

It was an innovative APA, establishing a legal regime of fundamental components, such as the administrative act, principles of administrative action, procedural rights, and some standardised procedures (eg authorisations, appeals, rulemaking). It had enormous influence, contributing to creating what can be called the Ibero-American model of administrative procedure. In Spain, the statutes subsequent to the 1958 APA, namely the APA of 1992, and the current one of 2015, have all followed the same model. Germany implemented an analogous model in 1976, unifying terminology of legal concepts (administrative act, public agreement, procedural principles).

B. The Main Features of the APA of 1958

From its very outset, the APA of 1958 sought to delve deeper into the broad concept of administrative procedure: an administrative procedure is not only a process to be followed by an administration to issue a legal act. It serves also as a directive of conduct (principles that guide the mode of internal performance; the criteria for assigning responsibilities and tasks amongst different administrative units; the mechanisms of gathering, processing, and exchanging information, and so on).

For the 1958 APA, administrative procedure was not merely a tool to apply laws that resemble judicial proceedings. First of all, because administrative procedure has a certain inherent flexibility and simplicity when compared to the

[22] See F González Navarro, *Cincuenta años de procedimiento administrativo en un mundo cambiante, editan Instituto Andaluz de Administración Pública* (Editorial Iustel 2009) 585–87.

judicial process; in addition, there are no consequences for minor procedural infractions.[23] Second, because the 1958 APA established principles of administrative action—such as celerity, simplicity, and efficiency—that do not require a temporally sequenced action in many cases, unlike the judicial process.

The 1958 APA provided for other innovations compared with the 1889 APA:

- First, it instituted more complete and modern regulation of the two main archetypical procedures that the 1889 APA had already established: on the one hand, a general procedure by way of petition and/or authorisation, and, on the other, a procedure for appeals.
- Second, it created new, standardised procedures governing revocation, rulemaking, sanctions, and for collegiate bodies.
- Third, it defined the complete legal regime of the administrative act (concept, typology, validity and efficacy, reason-giving, effects of substantive and procedural infringements).
- Fourth, it laid down system-wide rules applicable to all procedures concerning deadlines, records, and information, interested parties, legal standing, independence and neutrality, and general principles of action.

C. The Dialogue between Acts (1889–1958)

Drafting the 1958 APA entailed a sort of 'dialogue' with the 1889 APA: it aimed to overcome the deficits and problems observed during the long existence of the latter; to give continuity to its achievements; and to update and expand its contents.

On the one hand, the main criticism made towards administrative procedures under the 1889 APA was the unnecessary fragmentation and diversity of some procedural components. With this in mind, the new 1958 APA strove to harmonise certain procedural rules. On the other hand, the 1889 APA did not apply to local authorities, which were regulated separately in the 1920s, and were now considered necessary to include. For these reasons, the first concern of the new 1958 APA would be to avoid unnecessary diversity and promote a degree of unification and uniformity through the fusion of the main types of administrative procedures into a single act.[24]

[23] Its approach implies a less formalist understanding of administrative procedure. The Act, in fact, avoids rigid formalism in favour of a more ends-based interpretation, as well as balanced proportionality in the event of non-observance of certain minor formalities or procedural requirements. Many other later administrative procedure acts have followed such a so-called spiritualist or non-formalistic concept (including the Latin American and German APAs, eg, s 48(2) of the Spanish 1958 APA; ss 44, 46 of the German 1976 APA; ss 47–48 of the Spanish 2015 APA.

[24] It should be pointed out, in fact, that the diversity or fragmentation was not substantial. During the 69 years that the Act was in force, various ministerial regulations were issued, which, depending on the different historical periods, could have been as many as eight.

D. The Search for a Greater Degree of Uniformity in Administrative Procedure: Some Solutions in the 1958 APA

To accomplish these goals, the new APA of 1958 employed four techniques:

- One, in general terms, it was not as minimalist as the APA of 1889: it expanded its content and consequently left less leeway when implementing regulations.
- Two, the implementation of regulations was exercised by the cabinet, not by the ministers, as done previously in the 1889 APA, thus demonstrating once again that administrative procedure is a matter of utmost interest to the State.
- Three, it chose to select and regulate several characteristic procedures (authorisation or petition, appeal or complaint, revocation, sanctions, rulemaking) to establish a general framework, which allowed for necessary adaptations.[25]
- Four, it could be considered subsidiary in regard to some procedural components enacted by local administration and other entities, although such a departure from the APA had to be duly justified.

However, the most subtle strategy of the 1958 APA to unify administrative procedure to what was considered an appropriate and necessary extent consisted in establishing common legal regimes for each of the fundamental components of administrative procedure: one for administrative and other legal acts, another for collegiate bodies, and yet another for the general principles of administrative action. It was the most effective way to implement the cultural unification desired. By doing this, the 1958 APA moved away from the old aspiration—unduly derived from civil codification and judicial procedural codes—to bring all imaginable administrative procedures together in a single act, and it stepped back even more from the idea of reducing the natural heterogeneity of administrative procedures to a uniform pattern.

In short, APAs after 1958 would no longer be acts full of deadlines and formalities (even though they do contain provisions for these): they would be laws containing principles of administrative action and procedural components, with an aim to establish a common administrative culture. Uniformity is more concerned with legal concepts than formalities and legal deadlines. Here lies the essence, in my opinion, of the Spanish APA model, which would later be followed by many other national laws.

[25] The explanatory memorandum of the 1958 APA is quite significant in this regard:

> The APA has avoided ... the rigid and formalistic organization of a unitary procedure in which all those actions are integrated as necessary phases, and consequently, it does not regulate the initiation, organization, instruction and termination as phases or mandatory moments of a procedure, but as types of actions that may or may not occur in each case, according to the nature and requirements of the procedure in question.

E. The Later Spanish APAs: 1992 and 2015

In 1992, a new APA was enacted, replacing that of 1958. In 2015, a subsequent APA (still in force today) was enacted to modernise that of 1992. Both the 1992 and 2015 APAs follow the same scheme as that of 1958, updating their content to account for new concerns (eg information technologies and electronic administrative procedures) or to integrate the experience of administrative praxis and case-law doctrine.

III. A Comparative Perspective on the Austrian APA of 1925 and the Spanish APA of 1958

As mentioned above, the general Spanish administrative procedure acts of 1889 and 1958 were promoted by law professors involved in politics: Gumersindo de Azcárate and Laureano López Rodó, respectively. The main legal journals of the 1940s and 1950s[26] systematically expressed the relevance and necessary centrality of procedures in the field of administrative law,[27] as well as a profound knowledge of comparative law.

The Austrian legislation of 1925 was well known in academic spheres. But the Spanish 1958 Act did not arise from this new legislation, but instead stemmed from the need to reform the 1889 APA,[28] and further develop its own model.

The Austrian model was not considered during the implementation of the 1958 APA. The models, objectives, needs, and times for each legal order were very different, as summarised in the following arguments.

A. Different Historical and Political Backgrounds

The two APAs were passed in different and distant historical periods and circumstances.

The APA of 1925 was enacted after the dissolution of the Austro-Hungarian Empire (1918), essentially when Austria was subjected to postwar Allied impositions and international pressure demanding a radical simplification of its administration, in exchange for financial and economic aid to cope with the postwar crisis.[29] To this end, codification of the legislation on administrative procedure

[26] *Revista de Estudios Políticos* (REP) and, since 1950, above all, la *Revista de Administración Pública* (RAP).

[27] This is true both in general terms and in the specifics: the notification of an administrative act, specialised administrative procedures, procedural demarcations, adverse effects, etc., especially in the RAP since its very foundation.

[28] For example, REP 1949.

[29] H Schäffer, 'El procedimiento administrativo austriaco: evolución, estado actual y perspectivas de futuro' in J Barnes (ed), *El procedimiento administrativo en el Derecho comparado* (Cívitas 1993) 410, 413.

emerged as an appropriate and long-awaited tool, referred to in the 1920 Austrian Constitution itself.

The APA of 1958, decades later, was formulated in the context of the reform and modernisation of the Spanish administration undertaken in the 1950s, a process openly inspired by the requirements imposed by the rule of law. Modern statutes on contentious-administrative jurisdiction had been enacted shortly before, in 1956, and were still in force up to 1998, in addition to regulations for expropriation enacted in 1954, which is still in force today, to name just a few examples from legislation made during this period. These reforms were made possible, again, by a group of distinguished professors of administrative law.

B. Different Statutory Precedents

The Austrian legislation of 1925, without previous statutory precedents, is expressed in a collection of five laws, the main one being the General Act of Administrative Procedure.

Spain, on the other hand, wanted to solve quite different problems, created by the 1889 APA, the main one being the number of special procedures that had arisen from its implementation, and which, albeit following the same structure, diverged into many unnecessary elements, such as confusing names and deadlines for applications or appeals. Spain wanted a single act unifying and simplifying all that was necessary.

C. A Fundamental Difference between the Austrian and Spanish Models: 'Courtroom Procedure-Oriented' Model vs 'Administrative' Approach

Nevertheless, the circumstances mentioned in Sections I–II above are no more than anecdotal: there was, and still is, a substantial conceptual divergence between the two systems, which has only widened with the passage of time.

The Austrian model of administrative procedure, that was born in 1925, strongly resembles the procedures used during a trials. The reason for this ultimately lies in the fact that the model's specific purpose is the issuance of individual administrative acts that affect individual rights. Hence, guarantees analogous to those for a judicial process must be incorporated into the administrative procedure, albeit with the necessary adaptations.

The Spanish model also guides administrative acts enacted since 1889, albeit in a more simplified way. But taking into account that administrative procedure demonstrates the need to fulfil other purposes (such as organising the internal work of the administration) and other legal acts (such as regulations), the structure of administrative procedure must also diversify and cannot always resemble that of the courtroom.

The 1958 APA intended to further broaden the purposes of administrative procedure: from the issuance of administrative acts to rulemaking; from the procedure for collegiate bodies to inter-administrative relations. The Austrian legislation of 1925 could not serve as a model for this.

In short: the Austrian model of administrative procedure is based on procedures resembling those of a trial and is more formalistic. The Spanish administrative procedure model is, in some ways, more 'administrative' and therefore more diverse in structure and object. From the Spanish perspective, the Austrian model would already have been inappropriate in 1958, for being overly formalistic and poorly suited to the unique needs of the Spanish authorities.

D. Differences Concerning the Regulation of Administrative Procedure for Issuing Administrative Acts

Furthermore, if we only examine what both APAs have in common—an administrative procedure for the issuance of singular administrative acts—inevitably numerous differences will be found in the details, reflecting the different legal cultures of the two legal orders. According to the Spanish perspective, already by 1958, the Austrian 1925 APA was far too similar to the civil judicial process, and therefore not adaptable to the singularities of the Spanish administration.[30]

IV. Comparison between APAs

A. Peer Review Comparison or the Finding of Comparable Basic Types of Procedures: Different Sources of Administrative Procedures

An effective comparison of administrative procedures (either within one legal order or between those of different national systems) requires adequate classification methods. This is the only way to compare procedures of equivalent species and nature.[31] It would make no sense to contrast, for example, the (judicial) criminal

[30] It is enough to consider and compare the Austrian regulation of fundamental procedural components, such as administrative bias, legal capacity, and the capacity to act, representatives, transcripts, files notes, administrative penalties (eg when the administrative body conducts a hearing, examination, inspection, or taking evidence), oral hearing, costs, and so forth.

[31] Barnes (n 11) 843; J Barnes, 'Towards a Third Generation of Administrative Procedure' in S-R Ackerman and PL Lindseth, *Comparative Administrative Law* (Edward Elgar 2010); J Barnes (ed), *Transforming Administrative Procedure* (2nd edn, Global Law Press 2015); J Barnes, 'Three Generations of Administrative Procedure' in Ackerman and Lindseth (n 31) 302, 306, 309.

procedure of one country with the (judicial) civil procedure of another since they are not intrinsically comparable. Similarly, administrative procedures of a quasi-judicial nature, such as the administrative procedure to impose sanctions or the procedure to concede licences, cannot be compared with rulemaking procedures.

In fact, the nature and structure of many administrative procedures are very diverse, considering the extraordinary multiplicity of the functions they must perform, the different types of authorities, and even the diverse underlying modes of government (eg cooperative governance vs command-and-control mode) they follow, among other factors, which leads to the coexistence of different generations or species of administrative procedure.

- First, the comparison of administrative procedures must be made between procedures of the same or similar nature (for example, between procedures for the issuance of administrative acts; and within this type of procedure, the distinction may be made between those regarding discretionary administrative acts vs regulated or obligatory ones, or between those issued by a ministerial administrative body or by an independent entity). Administrative procedures in each case fulfil different functions, need different structures, and, therefore, require different laws.
- Second, each legal system presents a complex set of administrative procedural norms arising from a variety of sources. The composite character of administrative procedural laws requires a comparison of the underlying legal systems that looks beyond the general APAs of each (when they exist), to contemplate and consider the entire environment through which the administrative procedures flow. No APA 'codifying' (a misleading term) administrative procedures can exhaust the legal regulation of a State's administrative procedures. A general APA often embodies or expresses a pervasive administrative culture. Nevertheless, a general APA of a given legal order may not be completely representative of its concurrent legal reality, if it is not up to date.[32] A complete and true comparison, in other words, cannot be limited solely to the APAs. In fact, comparisons should be more concerned with the procedural models employed, rather than the types of code enacted.

Consequently, the first premise for a valid comparison lies in finding the basic patterns, according to the appropriate and agreed criteria, that thereby allows for peer review'.

Historically, legal families of administrative procedures have been forged, with their own specialties and singularities for cultural or political reasons (such as the Ibero-American, Austro-Hungarian, North American). However, the greatest

[32] Barnes (n 11) 836.

homogeneity or convergence of factors can very well be found at the generational or species level.

In this regard, on the one hand, the Austrian 1925 APA is a worthy representative of the first generation of administrative procedures, where the administration, in some ways, acts as if it were a judge. The Spanish 1889 APA also belongs to this first generation. Both can therefore be compared, in terms of their content and style. In doing so, it may be noted, for example, through such a comparison, that the 1925 APA is more complete and 'quasi-judicial' than the 1889 APA. On the other hand, the 1925 APA and the 1958 APA could be regarded as no longer belonging to the same generation, insofar as the latter already contains certain components of the second generation (among others, it established second-generation rulemaking procedures).[33]

B. Final Remarks Concerning the Comparison of the 1925 APA and the 1958 APA

- In the history of law, it cannot be assumed that a later statute of one nation is necessarily inspired by an earlier one of another. In the field of administrative procedure, this certainly holds true. The Spanish 1889 APA had no influence on the Austrian APA of 1925. The latter, in turn, had no influence on the subsequent Spanish 1958 APA. As another example, the Italian 1990 APA had no influence on the Spanish 1992 APA, which merely updated the preceding 1958 APA, and so on. This does not mean that the respective precedents were not all well known in each legal community.
- The concepts of civil codification and the codification of judicial proceedings are not equally applicable to the field of administrative procedure. A general law of administrative procedure cannot be equivalent or analogous to a civil code, nor to a judicial procedural code: it cannot bring together in a single code all the administrative procedures of a legal system, still less can it reduce the myriad of procedures existent to a single model. Therefore, the 'codification' of administrative procedure—always limited and in need of constant updating—is not as significant or necessary as some administrative scholars may think, a belief perhaps due to the universally renowned and lauded achievement of compiling the Civil Code—and the enactment of subsequential codified judicial procedural legislation.
- A general APA establishes a foundational administrative culture (a good example can be found in the US APA of 1946). In this regard, the classic titles given to these laws ('of administrative procedure') frequently fall short and do

[33] ibid.

not do justice to their true content, because general administrative procedure laws are, on occasion, more accurately called 'constitutions',[34] defining the interactions between the administration and the individual beyond formal procedures. This is precisely the case of the Spanish APA.

- The existence of a general APA in each legal system is not in itself conclusive to evaluate corresponding institution: there may be a general act which, not being up to date, and therefore ill-suited to address new special procedures, is obsolete and hardly representative of the institution. Conversely, there may be no general act, and yet there is a modern system of administrative procedures implemented de facto. It is also possible to compare legal systems that do not have APAs. The first question of an APA—from a historical and comparative perspective—thus lies in resolving which elements are to be unified and made uniform in an act, and how this is accomplished.
- The Spanish APA of 1958, following the experiences of the 1889 APA, produced an administrative procedure model of great influence, to be renewed in the subsequent APAs of 1992 and 2015 in Spain, and to serve as a model for many other systems.[35]
- The authors of the 1958 APA were familiar with the comparative experiences of other APAs (especially the Austrian APA of 1925 and the US APA of 1946).[36] Nevertheless, they were aware that these were not suitable models for their specific legal culture. Austrian legislation has always been well known in Spain, even before the reforms of 1992 and 2015, but it had never been considered as an adequate option.

[34] It has been said of the US APA 1946 that it is a bill of rights for the hundreds of thousands of Americans whose affairs are controlled or regulated by federal government agencies; and that it serves as a sort of 'constitution' for US administrative law (see KE Hickman and RJ Pierce Jr, *Federal Administrative Law: Cases and Materials* (2nd edn, Foundation Press 2014)).

[35] See the collective work in preparation on administrative procedure in Ibero-America, edited by Giacinto della Cannanea.

[36] See Barnes (n 29).

12
The Austrian 1925 General Administrative Procedure Act

A View from Italy

Mario P. Chiti

I. Introduction

The Italian legal system is usually considered to be characterised by the codification of many areas of law. This is historically justified because both the Civil Code and the Code of Civil Procedure were adopted just four years after political unification in 1861, and the Criminal Code followed in 1889. It should nonetheless be borne in mind that other important areas of the legal system were only codified very recently. One such case is administrative law, for which general administrative procedure legislation was adopted in 1990, while the Code of Administrative Proceedings dates back to only 2010. Moreover, as will be observed later, the legislative provisions governing administrative procedure differ from those enacted elsewhere as they do not constitute a complete code.

Our analysis begins with an overview of the existing general administrative procedure legislation and the external influences it reflects. This is followed by a consideration of the factors that made the Austrian codification of administrative procedure less influential than has been the case in other legal systems. Next comes a description of early attempts to lay down a general legislative framework governing administrative procedure. The chapter concludes with a discussion of the institutional and cultural factors that prevented the adoption of such a legislative framework before 1990.

II. Italian General Administrative Procedure Legislation: An Overview

Parliament passed the first general discipline of administrative procedure in Italy in 1990 (law no 241/1990, *Nuove norme in materia di procedimento amministrativo e di diritto di accesso ai documenti*), two decades after the time frame covered by the research in this book.

Mario P. Chiti, *The Austrian 1925 General Administrative Procedure Act* In: *The Austrian Codification of Administrative Procedure*. Edited by: Giacinto Della Cananea, Angela Ferrari Zumbini, and Otto Pfersmann, Oxford University Press.
 DOI: 10.1093/oso/9780198867623.003.0012

It was a relatively concise law composed of 30 articles, focusing strictly on procedure, and leaving aside the regulation of the administrative act that concludes the proceeding (usually called *provvedimento amministrativo*). Law no 241/1990 has been amended several times since then, with more detailed rules on the same issues and a controversial regulation of the administrative act (with law no 15/2005). However, considered as a whole, it still conserves the character of a law of general principles.[1]

Before this general law, administrative procedure was regulated by various sectoral disciplines, including public expenditure law (1924), urban and planning law (1942), trade law (1971), and banking law (1936). Those sector-specific frameworks were not homogenous, neither sharing the same principles nor following a similar model. The edifice of the administrative system was held in place by the case law of the administrative court (*Consiglio di Stato*).

The Austrian experience of the laws of 21.7.1925 on the *Vereinfachung der Verwaltung* (in particular the *Verwaltungsverfahrengesetze*) had no significant influence on drafting sector-specific rules or general law no 241/1990.

The same was true of other important foreign laws, such as the USA's Administrative Procedure Act (APA) 1946, 'rediscovered' after 1990. Only the German general law of 1970 influenced the direction of Italian legislative proposals on this matter, due instead to the traditional weight of German legal thinking on Italian scholarship rather than the model implicit in the law, a comprehensive 'code' of roughly 300 extremely detailed articles, far removed from our tradition.

We can say that the 1990 Italian general law of administrative procedure is a primarily autonomous product of the national legal culture, ie case law, academic culture, the world of bureaucracy, and more recently, EEC/EC law and the Court of Justice's case law.

III. The Austrian Codification of Administrative Procedure

Soon after coming into force, the Austrian law was known to the scholars of public law who were developing a 'new' administrative law, casting off ties with the 'pandectistic' school and reconsidering the role of the administrative act. However, in the lively debate that took place between 1920 and 1940, the Austrian experience, while often referred to, did not influence academic discussion of new

[1] Among the academic works in English concerning the Italian APA, see G Pastori, 'The Origins of Law n. 241/1990 and Foreign Models' (2010) 2 It J Public L 259 (explaining that little interest was shown in foreign models); D Sorace, 'Administrative Law' in JS Lena and U Mattei (eds), *Introduction to Italian Law* (Kluwer 2002) 125 (for which the APA lays down 'minimal regulation'); G della Cananea, 'The Italian Administrative Procedure Act: Progresses and Problems' [2011] Ius Publicum Network (on the same topic), <www.ius-publicum.com/repository/uploads/12_01_2012_9_44_DellaCananea_EN.pdf> accessed 2 February 2022.

developments, such as the distinction between administrative procedure and the theory of the *atto complesso* (the complex administrative act). Moreover, there is no evidence that a full, or even partial, translation of that law existed until *La procedura amministrativa*,[2] 1964, edited by Giorgio Pastori was published in 1964 by the *Istituto di Studi sulla Pubblica Amministrazione*, with an innovative introduction by Feliciano Benvenuti, the leader of a small group of scholars pressing for quick and consistent regulation of the matter.

The Austrian experience was not an object of study in itself; rather, it was seen as part of broader 'Germanic' legal culture, with the German national lawyers taking the lion's share. This situation is demonstrated by several essays of the period, which addressed administrative procedure in new ways under the direct influence of German literature. Discussion on the legal dimension of administrative procedure long remained the monopoly of scholarship as no proposal for a general regulation governing the matter was raised until the end of the war. Several sectoral laws of the time, in which the main procedural stages are carefully carved, are worth mentioning.

A real turning point in the literature came about in 1940 with the monograph *Il procedimento amministrativo*,[3] by a young scholar just 26 years old: Aldo M. Sandulli. This volume is rightly considered the foundation of modern Italian law on the matter, introducing a new, consistent, and comprehensive approach. It represented the pinnacle of European legal culture in this field in its day.[4]

The positive gap between this volume and the traditional scientific mood of that period can be appreciated by comparing it with the *Procedimento amministrativo* entry written for the *Nuovo Digesto Italiano* by two leading authors.[5] Here, administrative procedure is largely confused with judicial procedure, failing to consider its peculiarities. Even though it was reasonably close to the Austrian model, the essay made no explicit reference to it.

Sandulli's monograph contained a section on both the Austrian[6] and the German experiences, which Sandulli criticised for different reasons: the Austrian one for its lack—in line with the liberal-democratic principles of the time—of independence from general procedural (judicial) law, which meant that it failed to take into account the peculiarities of administrative action. He critiqued the German one due to its limited interest in administrative procedure as distinct from the

[2] G Pastori, *La procedura amministrativa* (Neri Pozza 1964). The book included a long second part with the full translation of the main national regulations of other countries, including Austria.

[3] AM Sandulli, *Il procedimento amministrativo* (Giuffrè 1940), later republished without alterations in 1968.

[4] The 1939–40 period, even if marked by wartime events, saw the publication of other seminal books on administrative law, such as *Il potere discrezionale della pubblica amministrazione*, by MS Giannini (Giuffré 1939), important for our subject too.

[5] O Ranelletti and A Amorth, 'Procedimento amministrativo' in *Nuovo Digesto Italiano* (Utet 1939) X, 527.

[6] Sandulli (n 3).

administrative act. Despite Sandulli's criticism, his interest in this experience gave scholarship new impetus to examine the 'Germanic' disciplines in greater depth as possible models for the Italian legal order.

IV. Early Attempts to Adopt Administrative Procedure Legislation

In 1944, following the liberation of southern and central Italy, the new government, headed by Ivanoe Bonomi, established a commission for the general reform of public administration—one that would be in line with the values of the new State. Its mandate included drafting a general law on public administration. The Commission was made up of leading scholars in newly liberated Italy, working alongside judges and legal practitioners; it was presided over by Ugo Forti, an authoritative scholar at the University of Naples with a particular interest in administrative procedure.

The Commission, supported by the PM, agreed to bring together the main principles of administrative law as crafted by scholarship and the case law of the Council of State (*Consiglio di Stato)* in a single text.

The Commission carried out its mandate quickly, having considered both the main national background and some leading foreign laws. As for administrative procedure, the main reference was the Austrian law of 1925, but the Commission decided unanimously not to follow this precedent, considering it too detailed, long, and generally unsuited to the Italian legal order.[7]

The draft was divided into five titles, the second of which was devoted to administrative procedure, suitably spread over three chapters (starting a proceeding, inquiry, the decision). The rules on the administrative decision were dealt with separately, in a title of their own (Title III). This was the first official normative document to provide a specific reference to administrative procedure.

The Commission concluded its works in 1947, and the report was published in 1948. However, its main findings were also made known to the Constituent Assembly (*Assemblea costituente*), elected in June 1946 to prepare the new Constitution (approved in December 1947 and in force a month later).

In the same period (1945–46), the executive established a second commission to prepare documents and materials for the next constituent Assembly operating by decision of the coalition governing at the end of the war. Its composition was similar to the 'Forti Commission', with a sizeable representation from leading public law scholars, but scholars from other disciplines and experts nominated by the political parties also participated. This made the Commission more political

[7] For further details, see G Miele, 'Italian Administrative Law' (1954) 3 ICLQ 421, 449.

than the first one, if not a technical surrogate of the next Assembly to be elected through a national poll. The Commission's mandate went further than merely reforming public administration, carrying out a 'study of (all) the issues relating to the reorganisation of the State'. Once again, to underline the thread of continuity linking the two executive-appointed commissions, the chair was awarded to Ugo Forti. Since then, the two commissions have been known as 'Forti 1' and 'Forti 2'.

The 'Forti 2' Commission provided a significant number of documents and materials on issues of constitutional importance, including translations of foreign laws and leading essays. According to the records, the Commission did not take the Austrian law on administrative procedure into consideration, acting no differently from the first Forti Commission. Once again, the Austrian law was considered excessively detailed and lengthy.

Unlike the first Commission, the 'Forti 2' focused on the constitutional issues of reorganising the State, leaving aside most administrative law issues. Only a few sessions were devoted to discussing specific proposals for insertion in the Constitution or 'sub-constitutional' laws or some administrative principles such as the right to be heard and the duty of public administrations to give reasons.

The Constitution of 1948 is considered one of the best results of the political and scientific climate of the postwar period in Europe, so it comes as no surprise that it served as a source of inspiration for later foreign constitutions. However, the constitutional regime on public administration has been considered very poor, if not sketchy, for decades. This view is largely inaccurate because the Constitution explicitly emphasises general principles applicable to public administrations, such as the principle of legality underpinning administrative issues, the principles of impartiality, 'good administration' (*buon andamento*), and participation in administrative actions. Second, the Constitution contains comprehensive principles on the full and effective procedural and judicial protection of citizens' rights and interests vis-à-vis the public administration. Third, as rightly pointed out by an (at that time) isolated scholar (Carlo Esposito),[8] the individual rules on administrative action must be considered in the framework of the whole Constitution.

The main reasons for the late interest in a law on administrative procedure before 1990 were:

1. political parties' limited sensitivity to administrative issues, albeit on opposing grounds put forward by the two opposing coalitions;
2. the ongoing ambiguity of Italian administrative law between a subjective or objective approach, as evidenced in the constitutional principles and later legislation (even in law no 15/2005 on administrative procedure). This ambiguity was fully resolved in favour of a subjective approach only in the Code

[8] C Esposito, *La Costituzione italiana. Saggi* (Cedam 1952) 248.

of Administrative Judicial Proceedings (*Codice del processo amministrativo*) of 2010;

3. the lasting influence of the French 'administrative regime' heritage, where the most relevant principles of law develop, and are sometimes created, by the case law of the administrative courts. Also, the alleged risk that a codification for administrative action could freeze its dynamics;
4. many administrative law scholars believed that reforms should focus on administrative organisation rather than on administrative action already disciplined by sectoral rules and covered by the case law of the Council of State (*Consiglio di Stato*);
5. the hostility of the senior civil service towards a law on administrative procedure, which appeared as an intolerable limitation of their discretionary powers.

Many of these issues have only been seriously reconsidered since 1990.

13
Why France Was Unaffected by the Austrian Codification of Administrative Procedure

Jean-Bernard Auby

I. Introduction

While other chapters in this book have shown that the Austrian codification of administrative procedure had a profound effect upon the shape and scope of the legislative provisions adopted by other nations in Central and Eastern Europe, France stands apart in two ways. First, while Austria and other nations decided to accord centre stage to legislative principles and rules governing administrative procedures in the 1920s, only recently has the French Parliament adopted general legislative provisions on controlling the bureaucratic apparatuses of the State, with regard to their dealings with individuals. Little need be said about this change as it has already been examined in various studies. Second, the Austrian 1925 General Administrative Procedure Act (GAPA) has had very little resonance in French administrative law scholarship. Not only has scant attention been given to the codification—with few exceptions—but there has more generally been a reluctance to focus on administrative procedure, a situation that requires further explanation.

II. France up to 2016: Living without a GAPA

The starting point for understanding why the Austrian codification was not followed by French political institutions is a traditional reluctance to adopt one type of GAPA over another. This may be explained in two ways. On the one hand, French administrative law has developed through a very influential and powerful tribunal, the Conseil d'Etat. Therefore, judicial review and its proceedings have always taken precedence over administrative procedure, and the absence of codification has been compensated for by judicial standards. On the other hand, resistance to the codification of administrative procedure has been

Jean-Bernard Auby, *Why France Was Unaffected by the Austrian Codification of Administrative Procedure* In: *The Austrian Codification of Administrative Procedure*. Edited by: Giacinto Della Cananea, Angela Ferrari Zumbini, and Otto Pfersmann, Oxford University Press. © Jean-Bernard Auby 2023. DOI: 10.1093/oso/9780198867623.003.0013

a consequence of the public authorities' wish to hold on to their procedural particularities.[1]

It remains to be said, first, that some procedural requirements have been established through parliamentary legislation, including the duty to give reasons for individual decisions adversely affecting the individual (Loi 79-587 of 11 July 1979) and, second, that this resistance to the codification of administrative procedure has recently diminished. In 2013, Parliament delegated the executive branch to adopt rules to simplify relations between citizens and the public administrations (law No 2013-1005 of 12 November 2013). Codification eventually took place, albeit with relatively timid content, in the form of the *Code des relations entre le public et l'administration*, enacted in 2015.[2]

III. The Austrian Codification and French Legal Culture

While the aspects just mentioned are well known, the lack of interest in the Austrian codification must be considered in more detail.

In the academic literature of the years following the Austrian codification of 1925, I have found just one brief mention of it, in the comparative work of Roger Bonnard, *Le contrôle juridictionnel de l'administration. Etude de droit administrative comparé*, published in 1934.[3]

It also seems that a German-language analysis was translated into French under the auspices of the Institut de Droit Comparé de Paris, but I have not been able to find it, despite the help of the Institut.[4]

In any case, the administrative law textbooks and treatises of the period made no mention of it: neither those of the years immediately following the act nor those dating from wartime: nothing, for example, in the 1938 *Précis élémentaire de droit administratif* of Maurice Hauriou[5] nor in the 1943 *Précis de droit administratif* of Roger Bonnard,[6] in spite of the special interest this author had in Germanic laws and his significant investment in comparative law, especially evident in his said *Le contrôle juridictionnel de l'administration*.

[1] JB Auby, 'General Report' in JB Auby (ed), *Codification of Administrative Procedure* (Bruylant 2014) 27.

[2] Ordinance and Decree 23 October 2015. See, for example G Koubi, L Cluzel-Metayer and W Tamzini (eds), *Lectures critiques du code des relations entre le public et l'administration* (Librairie Générale de Droit et de Jurisprudence 2018).

[3] R Bonnard, *Le contrôle juridictionnel de l'administration. Etude de droit administrative comparé* (Librairie Delagrave 1934) 251.

[4] R Hernritt, *La nouvelle procédure administrative autrichienne* (1932).

[5] M Hauriou, *Précis élémentaire de droit administratif* (Recueil Sirey 1938) 241ff (on administrative decisions).

[6] R Bonnard, *Précis de droit administratif* (Librairie Générale de Droit et de Jurisprudence 1943) 104 (where just a few lines are dedicated to procedural matters in a discussion on administrative legality).

What are the reasons for this silence? In part, it is surely due to some reservations in the scholarship of the time towards Germanic developments (though this does not apply to Bonnard), but that is not the only explanation. What is really significant is that, until recently, French administrative law scholarship was not particularly interested in administrative procedure.

Quite strikingly, for example, in some famous postwar treaties, the chapter on the regime of administrative acts begins with the entry into force of the acts and says nothing about the procedure for their preparation. Examples include André de Laubadère, *Traité élémentaire de droit administratif*, published in 1953,[7] Marcel Waline, *Droit administratif*, published in 1963,[8] both of whom can be said to have been the best-known postwar administrative lawyers.

It was only later that French scholars gradually came to take an interest in administrative procedure. The situation changed a little at a time thanks to publications by lawyers[9] and experts in public administration.[10] Eventually, part of the scholarship even rallied to the idea of a codification of administrative procedural rules.[11]

It would appear that this traditional indifference towards administrative procedure and the Austrian historical model can be explained on at least two grounds.

The first is the omnipresence of litigation. As observed earlier, French administrative law developed in the courts, including a very influential and very powerful tribunal. Judicial review and its proceedings have always therefore taken precedence over administrative procedure. Hence, for example, the fact that in what is probably the most respected general treatise on administrative law of the last 50 years, that of René Chapus, the rules of administrative procedure are analysed in the chapter on litigation, in the section relating to procedural defect as a form of illegality.[12]

The second is the limited presence of a subjective vision within French administrative law. The fact that it is rooted in the objective litigation of legality makes it traditionally somewhat unreceptive to the idea of subjective public rights. Austrian

[7] A de Laubadère, *Traité élémentaire de droit administratif* (Librairie Générale de Droit et de Jurisprudence 1953) 173.

[8] M Waline, *Droit administratif* (Sirey 1963) 457.

[9] Especially J-M Auby, *La procédure administrative non contentieuse* (Dalloz 1956–27); G Isaac, *La procédure administrative non contentieuse* (Librairie Générale de Droit et de Jurisprudence 1968); R Hostiou, *Procédure et formes de l'acte administratif unilatéral en droit français* (Librairie Générale de Droit et de Jurisprudence 1975); P Delvolvé, *L'acte administratif* (Sirey 1983); S Saunier, *Recherche sur la notion de formalisme en droit administratif français* (Presses universitaires d'Aix-Marseille 2007).

[10] Especially Georges Langrod, a very prominent scholar of comparative public administration, who commented on the Austrian 1925 GAPA. G Langrod, 'Procédure administrative et droit administratif' (1948) 64(54e) Revue du droit public et de la science politique en France et à l'étranger 549–556.

[11] See for example C Wiener, *Vers une codification de la procédure administrative* (PUF 1975).

[12] R Chapus, *Droit administratif général* (15th edn, Montchrestien 2001) 1105ff.

law and the subsequent Germanic vision of administrative procedure in general, on the other hand, are based on a largely subjective approach,[13] which remains foreign to the French administrative law tradition, even if it has been possible to observe some shift towards an attenuation of its objectivist orientation in the recent past.[14]

[13] See Z Kmieciak (ed), *Administrative Procedure in the Habsburg Succession Countries* (University of Lodz and Wolters Kluwer Polska 2020).

[14] Association Française pour la Recherche en Droit Administratif, *Les droits publics subjectifs des administrés* (LexisNexis 2011).

PART III
COMPARATIVE REPORTS

14

The Habsburg Empire, the Austrian Republic, and the League of Nations

From the *Damnatio Memoriae* to a Long Overdue Reappraisal

Stefano Mannoni

I. The Rediscovery of the Habsburg 'Mixed Polity'

Never has a heritage been more disputed, challenged, and even reviled than that of the Habsburg Empire. Heritage? No, even before it passed away, we should add. Because prior to its demise, many spectators of the last breaths of empire were fighting among themselves over the meaning of a 500-hundred-year old constitutional edifice. On one side were those who disapproved of its archaism; on the other stood those who reviled the detractors of a very effective concoction of nationalities.

Historians were divided along the same lines: the majority siding with the detractors—until very recently.

An 'ossified carcass', according to AJP Taylor's definition from nearly a century ago.[1] It has not fared much better in some more recent works, where it was labelled 'the sick man of the Danube', following the unflattering depiction by Geoffrey Wawro[2] and John Zametica.[3]

But why should we bother about a legal legacy openly disowned in 1919 when the remains of the empire were shattered and carved up to spawn various brand-new States?

The answer seems straightforward: indeed, not much seems to have been learned from an empire that, at the height of its expansion, spent no less than one-quarter of its budget on carrying the burden of its ubiquitous bureaucracy, one that struggled to govern dozens of restless ethnic groups, ranging from Italians to Poles.[4] Even worse, the same fate would befall the inadequate Republic of Austria, which

[1] AJP Taylor, *The Habsburg Monarchy: 1809–1918* (first published 1948, Penguin 1990) 245.

[2] G Wawro, *A Mad Catastrophe: The Outbreak of World War I and the Collapse of the Habsburg Empire* (Basic Books 2014) 15.

[3] J Zametica, *Folly and Malice: The Habsburg Empire, the Balkans and the Start of World War One* (Shepheard Walwyn 2017) 2.

[4] Wawro (n 2) 34.

Stefano Mannoni, *The Habsburg Empire, the Austrian Republic, and the League of Nations* In: *The Austrian Codification of Administrative Procedure.* Edited by: Giacinto Della Cananea, Angela Ferrari Zumbini, and Otto Pfersmann, Oxford University Press. © Stefano Mannoni 2023. DOI: 10.1093/oso/9780198867623.003.0014

picked up what survived of the German core of the Empire: a tiny State unfortunate and weak as though it were a de facto Italian protectorate.

Historians rarely agree on anything—luckily enough, we might add. We should not, therefore, be surprised to see distinguished scholars painting a very different picture of the Habsburg Empire. The year 2019, for instance, saw the publication of a very insightful article in the *New York Times* entitled 'What the Hapsburg Empire Got Right'.[5] And, indeed, according to the authors, it got a number of things right, so much so that the States that took the place of the old Empire were soon forced to revive the bequest of Vienna: 'Cutting loose from the past was never going to be easy as the nationalists had claimed. In countless ways, the old Empire refused to give up the ghost.'

This article was a rallying call for a powerful *rassemblement* of scholars around the legacy of the Habsburgs.

Bearing witness to this new outlook, to quote only two, are, 'The Grand Strategy of the Habsburg Empire',[6] which shed light on the contribution of Prince Eugene of Savoy to laying the military foundations and pillars of Vienna; and, of course, the seminal work by Pieter M. Judson, *The Habsburg Empire: A New History*.[7] A history that is indeed new to the extent it strives to dispel the myth of a creation so riddled with tensions and contradictions as to be doomed. *Vielvolkerung*, ie an amass of peoples loosely bound by half-medieval institutions? If this is the case, its heirs were even worse off: *Vielvolkerung* was held together by nothing at all. The role played by bureaucracy and the rule of law in keeping disparate nationalities together until 1918 should not therefore be in any way underrated. In the light of such a decisive adjustment of our perception of Franz Joseph's Vienna, it makes sense to conclude that, yes, there was a bequest worth accepting, albeit reluctantly, by the States that took the place of the Empire.

II. Administrative Procedure Legislation after 1925: Austria and Its Neighbours

Coming now to the pivotal point in the present research, we can therefore say that studies undertaken on the impact of the 1925 Austrian Code of Administrative Procedure on Czechoslovakia, Poland, and Yugoslavia do provide support to the increasingly favourable view. In impoverished postwar Vienna, there was still something to be learned, even though the authors of the legislation in these

[5] P Miller-Melamed and C Morelon, 'What the Hapsburg Empire Got Right' *New York Times* (New York, 10 September 2019) <www.nytimes.com/2019/09/10/opinion/hapsburg-empire-austria-world-war-1.html> accessed 3 February 2022.

[6] A Wess Mitchell, *The Grand Strategy of the Habsburg Empire* (Princeton UP 2018).

[7] PM Judson, *The Habsburg Empire: A New History* (Belknap 2016).

brand-new countries were somewhat shy of acknowledging such a politically embarrassing sway due to the unpopularity of the cultural heritage of the old German masters.[8]

But why did so many of those States feel the need to draft legislation of this kind in the midst of domestic and international turmoil?

The answer comes from an institution that, if possible, is even more neglected and undervalued than the Habsburg Empire: nothing less than the League of Nations. We have to thank Angela Ferrari Zumbini for brilliantly revealing that the 1925 Austrian legislation bears the signs of the harsh recovery plan Geneva imposed on Vienna.[9] Shattered by a devastating financial crisis, Vienna had to accept the terms imposed on it, which were so ruthless as to outdo the notorious present-day Troika so familiar to us. Suffice it to say, dispatched by Geneva, proconsul Zimmermann laid off no less than 50,000 Austrian public employees.[10] It comes as no surprise that the demands of the League of Nations also extended to the streamlining of bureaucratic procedures: and it is here that we find the rationale of the administrative procedural code, which owes nothing to Kelsen's highly praised 1920 constitution. Instead, it owed more than a little to the rich and elegant case law developed by the judges before 1914, when they struck a balance between administrative prerogatives and the rights of subjects.[11]

Again, the historical reassessment is more than welcome, embracing both the old Empire and the new League of Nations born in 1919. That the League of Nations might accomplish something like promoting a complex reform comes as something of a surprise: never has an international organisation been dismissed and even despised more than the one that emerged from Versailles in 1919. Yet on this terrain, too, on the same footing as the rediscovery of the Habsburg Empire, historians have worked hard to recalibrate their judgement. During the 1920s, the League was not, in fact, particularly ineffective. Admittedly, the Treaty of Locarno—just to cite one example—was brokered by American bankers, but it was instrumental in bringing Germany into the League in 1926.

Furthermore, the rule of law did acquire a higher status after the infamous Versailles Treaty, thanks to both international oversight and cooperation. The treatment of minorities is enlightening. The new States born in *Mitteleuropa* and on the eastern border were forced to accept the fact that the protection of minorities was embedded in international treaties, a provision they resented enormously,

[8] C Morelon, 'Introduction' in P Miller and C Morelon (eds), *Embers of Empire: Continuity and Rupture in the Habsburg Successor States after 1918* (Berghan 2019) 3.

[9] A Ferrari Zumbini, *Alle origini delle leggi sul procedimento amministrativo: il modello austriaco* (Napoli Scientifica 2020) 85.

[10] P Clavin, *Securing the World Economy: The Reinvention of the League of Nations, 1920–1946* (OUP 2013) 27.

[11] A Ferrari Zumbini, 'Standards of Judicial Review of Administrative Action (1890–1910) in the Austro-Hungarian Empire' in G della Cananea and S Mannoni editors, *Administrative Justice* Fin de Siècle: *Early Judicial Standards of Administrative Conduct in Europe (1890–1910)* (OUP 2021) 41–73.

being a clear encroachment on their sovereignty but which they nonetheless had to enforce.

This *état de grâce* with Geneva did not last very long, unfortunately. It is not fortuitous that Austria was, again, the stage for the change of course in 1931 when the Court of Permanent Justice struck down the proposed customs union between Vienna and Berlin. A dire *faux pas*, pushed through by a small majority, which cost the Hague and Geneva their reputations.

III. Conclusions

However, the sad events just mentioned should not overshadow three significant findings, which can be described as follows.

First, despite the narrative of a break between the imperial past and the new States that succeeded to it, the legacy of the Habsburgs in terms of the rule of law was not lost out in the process.

Second, the context created by an international organisation like the League of Nations was favourable to strengthening the rule of law, as domestic legislation was intertwined with the one mentioned above.

Third, issuing rules to improve bureaucratic efficiency is not at odds with individual rights. A complex society cannot have one without the other.

A lesson may be learned, if I may say so, that is as relevant today in a Europe that is becoming less and less conscious of the benefits of the Union, as it was yesterday, in the aftermath of the bloodiest conflict humanity has ever witnessed.

15

The Austrian AVG

An Underestimated Archetype with Deep Roots and External Factors

Angela Ferrari Zumbini

I. Introduction

This study stems from the diachronic orientation of the CoCEAL research project,[1] which is divided into two connected lines of research.

The first part dwells on the belle époque period of administrative law, focusing on the 20 years between the close of the nineteenth century and the start of the twentieth century to examine the development of the rules of conduct for administrative action in the case law from a comparative perspective.[2] In this context, a study of the case law of the Administrative Court of the Austro-Hungarian Empire between 1890 and 1910 proved particularly fruitful.[3] Although it contains an inestimable wealth of ideas, themes, and reflections constituting the fundamental nucleus for the emergence and elaboration of the concept of administrative procedure and procedural protection of private individuals, this case law is almost forgotten today, not only in Italy and abroad but even in Austria itself.[4] This lack of interest in the case law of the *Verwaltungsgerichtshof* (from now on also VwGH) in the field of comparative studies certainly cannot be justified only by linguistic difficulties (the judgments are drafted in Gothic script) but should be further investigated from the historical and sociological points of view. Now come to light once more, the judgments of the *Verwaltungsgerichtshof* and their systematisation by Friedrich Tezner have revealed the existence of a well-defined and complex

[1] G della Cananea and M Bussani, 'The Common Core of European Administrative Laws: A Framework for Analysis' (2019) 26 Maastricht J Eur & Comp L 217.

[2] G della Cananea and S Mannoni (eds), *Administrative Justice* Fin de siècle: *Early Judicial Standards of Administrative Conduct in Europe (1890–1910)* (OUP 2021).

[3] A Ferrari Zumbini, 'Standards of Judicial Review of Administrative Action in the Austro-Hungarian Empire' in della Cananea and Mannoni (n 2) 45.

[4] During the presentation held in Vienna in March 2019 illustrating the preliminary results of the research on the late nineteenth-century *Verwaltungsgerichtshof* case law, former president of the *Verwaltungsgerichtshof*, Clemens Jabloner stated that this case law is unfortunately now also forgotten in Austria.

Angela Ferrari Zumbini, *The Austrian AVG* In: *The Austrian Codification of Administrative Procedure*. Edited by: Giacinto Della Cananea, Angela Ferrari Zumbini, and Otto Pfersmann, Oxford University Press.
 DOI: 10.1093/oso/9780198867623.003.0015

system of rules of administrative procedure and case law developing on the basis of the recognition that individuals too should enjoy judicially protected procedural rights, starting from the late nineteenth century.

The second line of diachronic research, the results of which are published in this volume, centres on an analysis of the diffusion of the Austrian law of 1925. The term diffusion[5] refers both to the adoption in other countries of a law on administrative procedure that followed the structure and content of the AVG, and to the diffusion of the concept of administrative procedure in addition to some fundamental principles of administrative action, thus allowing the emergence of a common legal heritage of administrative rights in Europe.

This chapter presents an outline and reconstruction of the essential elements and characteristics of the Austrian procedural model (Sections II–VI) followed by an in-depth examination of some comparative scenarios (Section VII) together with a number of reflections of an institutional nature aiming to resolve some apparent contradictions (Section VIII). There then follow some concluding remarks (Section IX).

II. The Case Law of the *Verwaltungsgerichtshof*

The Austrian Administrative Court played a crucial role in drawing up general principles of administrative action. When the law establishing the *Verwaltungsgerichtshof* was passed in 1875, the legislation on administrative matters was antiquated, incomplete, and above all lacking in a general law on administrative action. During the parliamentary debate to approve the law establishing the VwGH, several members of both chambers emphasised the need to codify administrative law since at that time there were 'no guidelines to administrative procedure, which is completely unregulated and left to the arbitrariness of the administrations'.[6]

The legislator gave judges the power to annul acts for 'shortcomings in the essential forms of the procedure' but avoided defining or listing these essential forms, leaving it to the VwGH. Therefore, the court had to define general standards of administrative action to be used as a criterion for assessing the legitimacy of administrative acts in concrete cases. To quote Becker, the Austrian Administrative Procedure Act of 1925 would not have been conceivable without the case law of the

[5] Regarding which, please refer to the introduction to this volume (Chapter 1).

[6] The quoted words are by Ernst von Plener, member of the *Abgeordnete Haus*, pronounced during the session of 18 March 1875, reported in P Gautsch von Frankenthurn, *Die Gesetze vom 22. October 1875, R.G.B. Nr. 36 und 37, Jahrgang 1876 über den Verwaltungsgerichtshof: mit Materialien* (Manz'sche kk Verlag 1876) 170ff. The quotation is from p 175 'keine Vorschriften, keine Normen für das administrative Verfahren. Das administrative Verfahren unserer Behörden ist vollständig regellos, der reinen Willkür der Behörden überlassen.'

VwGH as the AVG in many respects simply transposed the principles developed in the 50 years of the Administrative Court into positive law.[7]

III. The Concept of Procedure and Tezner's Systematisation

Having underlined that the concept of administrative procedure, like the procedural model and structure codified in the 1925 Act, sprang from the drafting formulated from the late nineteenth century by the VwGH, a number of further considerations can be made.

First of all, the concept of administrative procedure emerged in a legal context, the Austro-Hungarian Empire, which, despite having become a constitutional monarchy, could certainly not be defined as democratic in the modern sense. Thus, the proceduralisation of administrative activity, although generally regarded as a phenomenon common to all democratic systems, must be placed historically in an imperial context. At the time of the empire, it was not only a matter of summarily laying down the outlines of a few institutions, but the entire structure, the various stages of the procedure, and the individual institutions were set up, organised, and regulated in an almost complete and detailed manner.

Second, the concept of administrative procedure did not arise solely from the desire to structure a rational and functioning administration, one where procedure was instrumental to the adoption of a decision that can be considered correct in its compliance with the principle of lawfulness. An element that played a fundamental, if not central and primary, role in the development of the rules of procedure was the will to recognise and guarantee procedural rights to individuals. Thus, the watershed whereby individuals came to be recognised as subjects with rights in relation to the administrative activity rather than its mere objects was the factor determining the emergence of the concept of procedure.

Third, it is undoubtedly possible to highlight and reaffirm the centrality and importance of Austrian administrative legal culture. Between the close of the nineteenth and the beginning of the twentieth century, when legal theory and practice both focused almost exclusively on the end product of administrative activity, the measure itself, when German scholarship focused on the *Verwaltungsakt*, as dogmatically reconstructed by Otto Mayer, the Austrians paid greater attention to

[7] F Becker, *Das allgemeine Verwaltungsverfahren in Theorie und Gesetzgebung. Eine rechtsvergleichende Untersuchun* (W Kohlhammer Verlag 1960) 64, but the same concept is also expressed by W Antoniolli, *Allgemeines Verwaltungsrecht* (Manzsche Verlag 1954) 222 and R von Herrnritt, *Das Verwaltungsverfahren: Systematische Darstellung auf Grund der Neuen Österreichischen und Ausländischen Gesetzgebung* (Springer 1932) 10.

procedure. This attention to administrative procedure represents, as Tezner puts it, *eine epochale rechtskulturelle Leistung österreichischen Geistes*,[8] an epoch-making breakthrough in legal culture. Endowing individuals with procedural rights under the seal of judicial protection made it possible to separate and delimit the concept of the individual from that of the community, thus establishing the single–individual legal sphere of the subject as distinct from the general–indistinct one of the community. Karl Freiherr von Lemayer[9]—one of the fathers of the law who established the VwGH[10] and later became its vice president[11]—described this fundamental contribution of the *Verwaltungsgerichtshof* as a *judicium finium regundorum* between collectivism and individualism.[12]

Fourth, having situated the actual genesis of the regulations governing procedure in the first 50 years of activity of the *Verwaltungsgerichtshof*, ie from 1876 to 1925, it becomes possible to perceive more accurately and persuasively the general conception that constitutes its theoretical and cultural antecedent. The *background theory*[13] that emerges is that of the *Verwaltungsgerichtshof* seen as a whole, explicitly manifested by Friedrich Tezner, a member of the VwGH who later became president of the Division and was the first to systematise the regulation of administrative procedure on the basis of the case law of the Administrative Court.[14] Tezner's influence on codification is therefore twofold. On the one hand, he had a profound influence on piecing together the case law through his systematisation. On the other, as a member and president of a Division of the Court,[15] he also participated in creating the procedural rules from case law.

As a theorist of administrative procedural regulation, Tezner is extremely clear on this point. The introduction to the second edition of 1925 of his *Das*

[8] F Tezner, *Die rechtsbildende Funktion der österreichischen verwaltungsgerichtlichen Rechtsprechung, IV. Das österreichische Administrativverfahren. Systhematisch dargestellt auf Grund der verwaltungsrechtlichen Praxis* (2nd edn, Österreichische Staatsdruckerei 1925) *Einleitung*, XLVI.

[9] For an overview of Lemayer's life and work, see the chapter devoted to him in W Ogris, *Elemente europäischer Rechtskultur: Rechtshistorische Aufsätze aus den Jahren 1961–2003* (Böhlau Verlag 2003) 285ff.

[10] The bill to establish the VwGH was drafted by Karl Freiherr von Lemayer, commissioned by Minister Unger in December 1871. See Lemayer's own account in his *Der Begriff des Rechtsschutzes im öffentlichen Recht (Verwaltungsgerichtsbarkeit); im Zusammenhange der Wandlungen der Staatsauffassung betrachtet; Festschrift aus Anlaß der Feier des 25jährigen Bestandes des Österreichischen Verwaltungsgerichtshofes* (A Hölder k k Universitäts-Buchhändler 1902) 206.

[11] Karl Freiherr von Lemayer was appointed to the VwGH in 1881, becoming Senatspräsident in 1888 and vice president in 1894.

[12] This allegory by Lemayer is cited in Tezner (n 8) *Einleitung*, XLVI.

[13] For a comprehensive definition and analysis of the notion of background theory (in its general relationship with both administrative and constitutional law), see P Craig, *Public Law and Democracy in the United Kingdom and the United States of America* (OUP 1991).

[14] Professor Friedrich Tezner was the first to construe an organic systematisation of Austrian administrative procedural law based on the VwGH case law. In essence, Tezner made a systematic collection, divided by subject matter, of the decisions of the VwGH, on which he then founded a dogmatic reconstruction of the institutes: F Tezner, *Das Handbuch des österreichischen Administrativverfahrens* (Manz'sche k u k Verlag 1896).

[15] Tezner was appointed to the VwGH on 1907 and became Senatspräsident in 1921.

österreichische Administrativverfahren[16] is entirely devoted to a radical critique of Kelsen's normativism, highlighting the contrast between a legal positivist vision and the regulation of administrative procedure as developed by the *Verwaltungsgerichtshof*. Tezner opens his volume by stating that:

> the development and effect of administrative procedural law, which has been essentially shaped by the case law of the Administrative Court, is in extreme contradiction with the normative legal theory developed by Kelsen.[17]

Indeed, it is easy to see the incompatibility between a discipline based on reference to the *Natur der Sache*, the 'nature of things', which permits the justiciability of rights not envisaged by a rule of positive law, and a pure doctrine of law which, on the contrary, only recognises the legal value of a pre-existing legal norm adopted according to correct lawmaking in compliance with the practice on sources. Pure legal doctrine aspired to an almost geometric reconstruction and systematisation of law, making it comparable to the other exact sciences. An influence of this conception can be seen in the codification of case law, ie the systematisation and positivisation of an otherwise fragmentary and not entirely orderly case law.

However, it should not be forgotten that codification was primarily adopted[18] to comply with an international treaty to grant loans to Austria as a remedy for its economic and financial situation, and thus for economic reasons—which should have no place in any pure theory of law. In this dialectic between natural law and normativism, Tezner is aware of and—so to speak—resigned to the idea that Kelsen's normativism was by now the dominant doctrine that would shape Austrian law. Nevertheless, perfectly embodying the maxim *Victrix causa diis placuit sed victa Catoni*,[19] he nevertheless remained faithful to his ideals and values, even if history would have it otherwise.

However, although the naturalistic view of the law was fated to concede defeat, as happened with the Austrian law influenced by the normativist *Stufenbautheorie* Tezner's systematisation of the administrative procedural rules survived the profound institutional and philosophical changes of the time.

Following an unusual and unexpected course, the newly born Austrian republic, also founded on the principles of the 1920 Constitution (inspired by Kelsen)

[16] In 1922 Tezner elaborated his systematisation still further and published *Das österreichische Administrativverfahren, dargestellt auf Grund der verwaltungsrechtlichen Praxis*, whose second edition, re-elaborated and enlarged, flows into his monumental work in four volumes *Die rechtsbildende Funktion der österreichischen verwaltungsgerichtlichen Rechtsprechung* (of which it constitutes the fourth and largest volume: the first three concern legal dogmatics, sources of law, and organisation).

[17] 'Die Entwicklung als auch die Wirkung des im wesentlichen durch die Rechtsprechung des Verwaltungsgerichtshofes herausgebildeten Verwaltungsprozessrechtes steht im allerschrossften Widerspruch mit der von Kelsen ausgestalteten normativen Rechtslehre.' Tezner (n 8) Einleitung, XIV.

[18] See Section IV.B below.

[19] Marco Anneo Lucano, *De bello civili, Pharsalia*, Book I, line 128.

adopted the rules of procedure as created and structured by the case law of the *Verwaltungsgerichtshof* during the imperial period. So, in this case, again referring to Lucan's famous phrase, the defeated cause also pleased the victor, not just Cato, even if Tezner was unable to attend the enactment of the law of 21 July 1925, having died just less than two months earlier, on 13 June.

Lastly, it should be emphasised that the importance of procedure in itself, highlighted by Austrian jurists as early as the close of the nineteenth century, was recognised and built upon regardless of the underlying theoretical and philosophical convictions of scholars. Indeed, the emergence and conceptualisation of an autonomous fundamental concept of procedure can be found in two Austrian authors from divergent, if not opposing, schools of thought.

Friedrich Tezner, an advocate of natural law and justice, dedicated a monograph to the concept of *Administrativverfahren* as early as 1896,[20] stressing the fundamental importance of the path that the administrative decision follows as it takes shape. He introduced a clear distinction between production (meaning the production process) and product (*Erzeugungsvorgang und Erzeugnis*),[21] laying more emphasis on the former than the latter since it is in the process that individuals can exercise their rights before the decision is made. Similarly, the normativist Merkl, a follower of the Vienna School and pupil of Kelsen, used the allegory of the path and the target (*Weg und Ziel*).[22]

IV. The Main Factors Leading to the 1925 Codification

As often happens, a law is not adopted as the result of a single determining factor. The law (or rather the laws) of 1925 on administrative procedure are the product of various homogeneous and concordant factors, but with different nuances and profiles.

A distinction can be made between the determining factors that led to the adoption of the first general law on administrative procedure: those internal to the Austrian system and those external to it.

A. Factors Internal to the Austrian Legal System

The parliamentary debates leading up to the establishment of the VwGH show, from a historical point of view, that there was much criticism of the total lack of

[20] Tezner (n 14).

[21] F Tezner, *Das österreichische Administrativverfahren, dargestellt auf Grund der verwaltungsrechtlichen Praxis. Mit einer Einleitung über seine Beziehung zum Rechtsproblem* (Österreichische Staatsdruckerei 1922) 145.

[22] A Merkl, *Allgemeines Verwaltungsrecht* (Springer 1927) 213.

regulation of the administrative procedure with regard to the provision (among the grounds for the invalidity of administrative acts) of lack in the essential forms of the procedure.

At the academic level too, this debate did not end with the introduction of administrative jurisdiction. The case law of the VwGH played a fundamental role in the enucleation and elaboration of the fundamental principles of the administrative procedure, also indicating a basic structure and regulating various essential aspects, such as evidence. This creative power with which the VwGH was vested, wholly comparable to the creative capacity of the more famous French Conseil d'Etat,[23] was noted and appreciated.

However, many exponents of both academia and the government administration, called for a codification of procedural rules. Between the close of the nineteenth century and the beginning of the twentieth century, several works were published arguing for the utility, if not the necessity, of reform (and thus a codification) of administrative procedure. Lemayer, the founding father of the *Verwaltungsgerichtshof*, published his apologetic studies on administrative jurisdiction in 1896;[24] Brunstein's study of 1900 focused precisely on administrative procedure reform,[25] and Tezner drew up a draft law on administrative procedure in 1902.[26]

Legislative intervention was called for (largely) to implement two distinct but coherent fundamental requirements of the rule of law.

At government level, the studies and drafts for an outline of the Administrative Procedure Act were explicitly inspired by what was defined as the primary purpose of any procedural rule, namely legal certainty (*Rechtssicherheit*). At the request of Prime Minister Ernest von Körber, the *Studien über die Reform der inneren Verwaltung*[27] were drafted in 1904. The conclusions stated that the lack of any explicit regulation of procedure constituted a lacuna in the organisation of the administration. In this context, even the best case law, by nature subject to fluctuations, cannot fill this lack and comply with the fundamental principle of legal certainty.[28] In 1911, a draft law was presented at the close of the work of the *Kommission zur Förderung der Verwaltungsreform*, chaired by Schwartzenau, the future president of the VwGH, but it was not approved; first due to the outbreak of war, then because of the need to verify whether, in the new constitutional context, legislative power in this area would be attributed to the *Bund* or the *Länder*.[29]

[23] G Langrod, 'Procédure administrative et droit administratif' [1956] Revue internationale des sciences administratives 5ff.

[24] K Lemayer, *Apologetische Studien zur Verwaltungsgerichtsbarkeit* (Hoelder 1896).

[25] JL Brunstein, *Das Administrativ-Verfahren und seine Reform* (Manz 1900).

[26] F Tezner, 'Praktische Vorschläge zur Reform des österreichischen Administrativverfahrens' (1902) 53 Allgemeine österreichische Gerichtszeitung 51.

[27] On this matter, see the critical analysis by JA Ritter von Grimm, *Zur Reform der inneren Verwaltung: kritische Besprechung der 'Studien über die Reform der inneren Verwaltung'* (Manz 1905).

[28] These conclusions are reported by Becker (n 7) 66–67.

[29] EC Hellbling, *Kommentar zu den Verwaltungsverfahrensgesetzen*, 2 vols (Manz 1953–54) 8ff.

There was also broad academic consensus on the desirability of codifying administrative procedures. In addition to the principle of *Rechtssicherheit*, scholars also based their arguments on the basic principle of making the parties to the procedure subjects of rights by law.

Indeed, various ministries adopted instructions or guidelines dictating certain basic principles of administrative procedure officials were to follow (the said instructions of the Ministry of Education of 1876[30] or the more famous *Prügelpatent* of 1854[31] regulating the administrative enforcement of the decisions of political and police authorities). However, these were internal ministerial acts, service instructions for officials, in which the addressees of the measures were considered 'objects' of administrative activity.[32]

Through its case law, the VwGH had granted an essential series of rights to the addressees of measures. After all, the idea of judicial protection of the rights of individuals in their relations with the public authorities is 'naturally as old as the very concepts of State and law'.[33] However, the growing case law did not allow for a systematic and formal attribution of the status of 'subject of rights' to the parties and did not necessarily guarantee uniform and constant application.[34]

Codification was (also) intended to achieve the goal of formally granting subject-of-rights status to citizens during administrative procedures[35] without the possibility of heterogeneous and diverse application. This purpose is clearly consistent with the complementary principle of legal certainty but not necessarily a consequence of it, since legal certainty could also aim (primarily) to ensure the legality of administrative action, leaving the protection of the individual legal subjectivity in the background.

B. Factors External to the Austrian Legal System: Peace Treaties after the First World War

The final and decisive impetus for adopting a law on administrative procedure stemmed from postwar circumstances. In particular, a decisive factor for the codification of administrative procedure was the so-called *Genfer Reformbeschlüsse*

[30] See Chapter 3 in this volume.

[31] *Kaiserliche Verordnung, wirksam für alle Kronländer, mit Ausnahme des lombardisch-venetianischen Königreiches und der Militärgränze, wodurch eine Vorschrift für die Vollstreckung der Verfügungen und Erkenntnisse der landesfürstlichen politischen und polizeilichen Behörden erlassen wird*, of 20 April 1854, RGBl 96.

[32] E Mannlicher and E Coreth, *Das Verwaltungsverfahren* (2nd edn, Staatsdruckerei 1927) esp XXV; Hellbling (n 29) 3ff; von Herrnritt (n 7) esp 10ff.

[33] Lemayer (n 10) 1, author's translation.

[34] E Mannlicher, *Die österreichische Verwaltungsreform des Jahres 1925* (Springer 1926).

[35] H Schäffer, 'Administrative Procedure in Austria: 80 Years of Codified Procedure Law' (2005) 17 ERPL 871ff.

concluded in 1922 between the defeated Austria on the one hand and victorious United Kingdom, France, Italy, and Czechoslovakia on the other.[36]

In this international treaty, signed after the First World War ended, the new Austrian republic, which had emerged from the ashes of the Austro-Hungarian Empire, was obliged to introduce a law of administrative simplification in order to reduce Austria's expenditure and give it access to loans.

For the sake of clarity, it should be mentioned that, with the end of the First World War, the Treaty of Saint Germain was signed in 1919, laying down, among other things, the conditions for the creation of the new Austrian republic. Among the peace conditions was a ban on unification with Germany (*Anschlussverbot*). In the following years, the economic situation in Austria deteriorated dramatically, and the newly founded republic faced devastating inflation. In May 1922, just under 350 billion Kronen in banknotes (*Papierkrone*) were in circulation, while in July there were almost 600 billion, and in August over 800 billion were in circulation. Wages were paid every three to four days as their purchasing power had already been halved by that time.[37] Meanwhile, in the elections of October 1920, the Christian-Social Party lacked the necessary majority to form a homogeneous government, as it needed the support of the *Großdeutsche Volkspartei* (a party advocating the unification of the German people).

All these factors led to the international treaty known as the *Reformbeschlüsse* in Geneva on 4 October 1922. The United Kingdom, Italy, France, and Czechoslovakia were to act as guarantors for Austria so that it could obtain a loan from the League of Nations totalling around 690 million gold crowns (Goldkronen) over 20 years.[38] In return for these guarantees, Austria undertook a number of obligations.

To qualify for this financing, it was necessary to guarantee a series of economic, financial, and budgetary reforms, but also in the sphere of State administration, as these elements were mutually as far as a stringent and lasting reduction in public spending was concerned, thus making it possible to foresee effective future repayment of the loan.

First, the obligation to remain independent (the *Anschlussverbot*) was restated. Then, an obligation was imposed to carry out a comprehensive financial and budgetary reform to drastically reduce costs. Lastly, and also to reduce expenditure, Austria was required to submit a comprehensive administrative reform

[36] EC Hellbling, *Österreichische Verfassungs- und Verwaltungsgeschichte: ein Lehrbuch für Studierende* (Springer 1956) esp 449ff.

[37] These data are provided by L Kerekes in his article 'Österreichs Weg zur Sanierung (1922)' (1977) 23(1–2) Acta Historica Academiae Scientiarum Hungaricae 75ff, esp 78.

[38] It is not certain exactly what the final amount paid out by the League of Nations was, but it is certain that Austria received at least 650 million Goldkronen. G Strejcek, 'Vor 90 Jahren flossen Österreich aus einer Völkerbund-Anleihe rund 650 Millionen Goldkronen zu. Die folgende Sanierung des Staatshaushaltes brachte aber keine nachhaltige politische Stabilität' *Wiener Zeitung* (Wien, 13–14 October 2012) <www.wienerzeitung.at/nachrichten/wissen/geschichte/493525-Rettungsschirm-des-Jahres-1922.html> accessed 17 February 2022.

project in Parliament aiming to simplify and streamline administration and administrative procedures within the space of two years.[39] To fulfil this duty, Austria submitted a package of administrative simplification laws to Parliament in 1924 (including the General Act on Administrative Procedures), passed in 1925.

As early as the close of 1923, the Department for Administrative Reform of the Federal Chancellery had submitted detailed drafts, later incorporated into the bills drafted in 1924 by Ministerial Councillors Coreth and Mannlicher. The aim to simplify procedures and render them uniform coexisted with, and was balanced by, a constant awareness of the rights of individuals within the procedure.[40] Naturally, the victors of the First World War pursued the sole aim of getting Austria to improve the efficiency of its administrative machinery as a whole,[41] from the point of view of the simplification and acceleration of procedures, with purely economic objectives and motives, and certainly not with the judicial protection of Austrian citizens in mind (after all, relations between citizens and the State fall outside the normal sphere of effectiveness of international treaties).

It should be recalled that the 1925 Act was also enacted in order to fulfil specific international obligations, which represents a fundamental element in the interpretation of the reform, allowing the AVG to be contextualised also from the functional point of view. Thus, the rationale behind a law granting numerous rights to private individuals was mainly economic, aiming to simplify administrative activity and thus make it more efficient. This was not a purely domestic requirement; it was imposed by international agreements.

Of course, this does not preclude the fundamental contribution of other, parallel motivations, namely those of giving full effect to the constitutional principle of legality by introducing a legal regulation of the administrative procedure, and those examined above of guaranteeing legal certainty and the theoretical attribution to individuals of the status of subjects of rights.

V. The *Allgemeine Verwaltungsverfahrensgesetz*: Codification or Innovation?

The *Allgemeine Verwaltungsverfahrensgesetz* is traditionally regarded as an innovative codification, linked to the normativist influence of *Stufenbautheorie*.

[39] The text of the international treaty signed in Geneva on 4 October 1922 is very difficult to find online. A copy may be found in A Feiler, *Das neue Österreich* (Historisches Wirtschaftsarchiv 2015) (unaltered reprint of the original of 1924) 101–18.

[40] Becker (n 7) 67.

[41] For example, among the reforms adopted by Austria to fulfil its international obligations was the reform of the railways, which began in November 1922 with the separation of ownership between the railway network and the railway management service (the latter became a company, an economic body with legal personality, separate from the State apparatus, in 1923). See CS Solvis, *Der Weg zur Neuordnung der Österreichischen Bundesbahnen* (Springer 1933) esp 18ff.

In contrast, a broad correspondence between the structure and principles of the AVG and the previous case law of the *Verwaltungsgerichtshof* has been shown to exist. The dichotomy between a definition of codification as innovative and one with constant law must not be understood in absolute terms; otherwise, both reconstructions may be open to criticism. Any judgement in this regard must be formulated in a more complex way, taking into account the different spirit and multiplicity of influences that have contributed to the creation of the AVG.

On the one hand, the innovative contribution of the Austrian law of 1925 is undeniable, first of all in envisaging the positivisation of the rules regarding public action, perfectly in line with Kelsen's normativism (even if the factors that led to the adoption of the AVG are diverse, as we have seen). Innovativeness can also be seen in the introduction of new concepts, such as that of *Bescheid*, which encompasses the various preceding types of acts and has since dominated the Austrian dogmatics of administrative acts.[42]

On the other hand, it was noted that the principles, structure and many institutions of the administrative procedure codified in 1925 have specific antecedents in late nineteenth-century *Verwaltungsgerichtshof* case law and Tezner's systematisation from 1896, revised in 1922. Signs of processualisation of the procedure could already be found in judges' rulings, and Tezner examined the regulation of evidence extensively in his works. Codification, therefore, largely positivised case law, introducing some significant innovations.

After all, the primary goal of rules of administrative procedure was to protect the rights of individuals faced with the power of the public authorities, whether procedure was understood as a path within which rights were to be recognised, including on the basis of natural law, or whether it was considered as a path within which the rights provided by law were to be guaranteed.[43]

VI. The Austrian Model

The rules of administrative procedure as codified in Austria in 1925 are usually said to be a 'judicial model', in which there is a guarantee of cross-examination in order to ensure the legality of administrative action.[44] This model is often contrasted with

[42] In fact, in the case law in question, it was possible to find the term *Bescheid* as early as the 1916 judgments. However, the concept of *Bescheid* as a unitary category encompassing different types of administrative only came about with the 1925 Act.

[43] For Herrnritt, a follower of Kelsen, '*Der Prozeß hat nicht Recht zu schaffen, sondern Recht zu schützen*', or rather the process—understood in the sense of processus and therefore of path—is not intended to create law but to protect law. See von Herrnritt (n 7) 1.

[44] A Sandulli, 'Il procedimento' in S Cassese (ed), *Trattato di diritto amministrativo—Diritto amministrativo generale*, vol II (2nd end, Giuffrè 2003) 1035ff, esp 1049.

the American *interest representation* model, where broad participation ensures the democratic nature of administrative action.[45]

Perhaps it would be appropriate to re-evaluate this definition. Indeed, an analysis of the law reveals a model that is undoubtedly judicial in nature insofar as its structure is somewhat similar to that of a court hearing, but with two primary and fundamental aims, efficiency and the protection of the rights of the parties. On the one hand, there is a strong drive for simplification (imposed by the Geneva Treaty), but, on the other, there is a codification of the principles developed by the VwGH, based on the *Parteiengehör*. The result is not only the objective protection of the lawfulness of administrative action but also subjective protection of the rights of the parties. Moreover, s 43(2) AVG requires the presiding official of the procedure to conduct the proceedings with constant regard to its purpose (ie to establish the state of facts decisive for the adoption of the measure), without allowing deviations or delays (thus fostering efficiency), but always 'in such a way that the right of the parties to be heard is safeguarded'.

One of the main aims of the law was to establish a uniform and standardised model of administrative procedure, which all public administrations would have to comply with.[46] This objective naturally presupposed that procedural uniformity is possible, even when faced with a multiplicity and variety of substantive law. The aim of drawing up a uniform model is emphasised by Mannlicher and Coreth (fathers of the 1925 laws),[47] who outlined the difficulties, first and foremost those of officials but also those of the subjects involved in disentangling themselves from the very different procedural regulations established by the various authorities.

In order to avoid a single model unduly straightjacketing administrative activities to the detriment of effectiveness and efficiency, the law did not provide for remarkably detailed disciplines but rather the essential rules to be followed in the various stages of the procedure, which could then be applied in different ways by the administrations according to circumstance.

Indeed, in s 1 of Part II of AVG dedicated to the purpose and course of the investigation procedure, the law allowed the authorities ample discretion regarding the practicalities of the investigation so that it could be adapted to various needs (*Grundsatz der arbiträren Ordnung*). In the absence of specific instructions, the administrative authority had to proceed and determine the course of the administrative procedure on its own initiative (s 39(2) AVG). However, the law laid down the principles that the authority had to follow, namely 'expediency, speed, simplicity and economy' (*Zweckmäßigkeit, Raschheit, Einfachheit und Kostenersparnis*).

[45] L Torchia, 'I modelli di procedimento amministrativo' in L Torchia (ed), *Il procedimento amministrativo: Profili comparati* (Cedam 1993) 33ff.

[46] See Chapter 4 in this volume.

[47] E Mannlicher and E Coreth, *Die Gesetze zur Vereinfachung der Verwaltung* (Wien Staatsdruckerei 1926).

The Austrian model is minimal in the sense that the 'skeleton' of the procedure is clearly codified and can thus be adopted in—and adapted to—any type of procedure. These features therefore make it chameleon-like, allowing a comprehensive scope of application. Being regulated in a less detailed fashion makes the model widely applicable. This ensures a uniformity that avoids doubts about interpretation and simplifies administrative activity, not only for the authorities but also the interested parties, who can know with certainty which rights to exercise and which procedures to follow regardless of the type of procedure in which they are involved.

The Austrian model is built on an individual bilateral procedural ideal, where the priority is to protect the rights of individuals vis-à-vis public authorities while ensuring expeditious administrative activity. However, this does not mean that proceedings to adopt general (non-regulatory) or multiple acts were excluded entirely from the scope of application of the Austrian Act of 1925.

The chapter on oral hearings specifies that all known interested parties must be notified that an oral hearing has been scheduled, and, if necessary, a notice must be posted in the town hall or in the newspaper used to broadcast official public information (art 41(1) AVG). In addition, if drafts or other materials are to be presented during the oral hearing, this information must be specified in the notice so that the interested parties can view them and possibly present their objections or other views. It is clear that these provisions refer to proceedings concerning a large number of not necessarily known interested parties, what we would call master plans today.

Lastly, the whole structure of the law follows that of a procedural code, even on the systematic level. The AVG starts by defining the jurisdiction by subject matter and territory, providing for cases of compulsory abstention due to conflict of interest; it then regulates summonses, notifications, and evidence, ending with the allocation of costs. It should be noted that the structure of the procedure modelled on the court hearing (also) derived from the approach of VwGH case law, which, having to find a reference model for the administrative procedure (totally absent in legislation, especially in terms of its complex nature), referred to institutions, principles, stages, and rules for hearings. It is sufficient to glance through the table of contents of Tezner's book to see the intertwining of substantive rules with typically procedural rules such as forms of evidence and the allocation of legal costs.

VII. Comparative Aspects

Having analytically pieced together the genesis and distinctive features, as well as the characteristics and essential elements, of the Austrian procedural model, it may be helpful to dwell on some comparative aspects. In particular, it would be helpful to recall and compare the various paths that this procedural model has taken, crossing and shaping—to different degrees of intensity and with different nuances—the administrative laws of a large part of Central Europe (Section A), followed by a discussion of the lack of interest in Austria shown in comparative studies (Section B). Lastly, the Austrian procedural model will be qualified as an archetype whose importance and centrality should be re-evaluated (Section C).

A. The Diffusion of the AVG in Central Europe

The diffusion and influence of this law today appear unjustly underestimated and neglected. It served as a model for the legislators (and scholars) addressing the question of codifying administrative law and administrative procedure, often, for various reasons (and to varying degrees), taking their inspiration from the AVG.

The legal orders most profoundly inspired by the Austrian codification were those that had been part of the Austro-Hungarian Empire in some way. Although it would have been reasonable to assume that the nation States that emerged from the ashes of the empire would have disregarded the Austrian regulations in order to reassert their conquered independence, this was not the case.

Moreover, the model did not spread to the former imperial territories alone. The Austrian law of 1925 had a profound influence on the Mitteleuropean States, even before its formal adoption. In fact, the draft laws for administrative simplification formed the model for the law on administrative procedure in Liechtenstein.[48] This country, never part of the empire but strongly influenced by it for various reasons (the ruling family was variously interwoven with the Habsburg dynasty, and until 1920 the currency was the Austrian crown), is an example of the early transposition of the law in question, with the draft being transposed even before it was adopted in Austria.

The *Landesverwaltungspflegegesetz* was enacted in Liechtenstein on 12 July 1922,[49] and regulated not only administrative procedure but also the enforcement of administrative decisions and administrative criminal law, just like the Austrian laws. The purpose of the Act was to standardise and codify the work of public authorities, using Austrian draft laws as a model for imitation.[50] This law is still in force in Liechtenstein, albeit with some minor amendments.[51]

The influence of the 1925 Act is particularly evident in the countries that previously fell (even partially) within the empire's territory. A clear and precise

[48] See Chapter 5 in this volume.

[49] *Gesetz vom 21. April 1922 über die allgemeine Landesverwaltungspflege (die Verwaltungsbehörden und ihre Hilfsorgane, das Verfahren in Verwaltungssachen, das Verwaltungszwangs- und Verwaltungsstrafverfahren), Landesgesetzblatt* [LGBl] 1922 No 24.

[50] See Chapter 5 in this volume.

[51] On the amendments and the text currently in force, see E Schädler, 'Die Reformbemühungen um das Landesverwaltungspflegegesetz (LVG) in den Jahren 2014 bis 2018: Eine Falldokumentation' 2020 <www.liechtenstein-institut.li/application/files/4815/9341/9788/Schadler_LVG-Reform_2014_bis_2018.pdf> accessed 17 February 2022.

transposition of the Austrian model can be found in Poland.[52] Poland had previously been divided up and controlled by three different governments, namely the Austro-Hungarian Empire, the Russian Empire, and Prussia, and found it necessary to unify its legislation after the creation of the new State. In order to unify and make the regulations for the newborn nation autonomous, it was decided to adopt the Austrian model. In 1922 a Supreme Administrative Court was established (modelled on the *Verwaltungsgerichtshof*, and whose first president, Jan Sawicki, had been a judge at the Administrative Court in Vienna), and on 22 March 1928, the Code of Administrative Procedure was enacted (together with the Administrative Criminal Law and Law on the Execution of Administrative Decisions). After the Second World War, a new code was adopted in 1961, which, despite changes introduced to adapt the procedural model to the new Communist regime, kept the basic Austrian structure intact. The correspondence was, of course, exclusively formal, but it would seem important to underline the survival of the model even in a non-democratic regime. By way of example, citizens enjoyed rights *vis-à-vis* the authorities (along the lines of the Austrian model) and the Soviet Constitution of 1952 recognised their justiciability. However, administrative jurisdiction was abolished (to be re-established only much later, 1980), and, therefore, the justiciability of rights granted to citizens was envisaged, although there was no court to exercise judicial review.

The sequence of events in Czechoslovakia[53] was very similar to that in Poland. Due to its historical membership of the Empire, the newborn nation created from the ashes of the Austro-Hungarian Empire was well aware of the fundamental importance of the existence of an administrative jurisdiction. As early as 1918, the Supreme Administrative Court was therefore established, which did not merely follow the model of the *Verwaltungsgerichtshof*. Indeed, among the first members of this court were two judges who, until 1918, had been judges of the *Verwaltungsgerichtshof* in Vienna and who became the first and second Presidents of the Czechoslovak Administrative Court respectively: František Pantůček and Emil Hácha brought their cultural background with them, so much so that Czech scholarship is unanimous in its agreement that the Czechoslovak Administrative Court predominantly used the previous Viennese jurisprudence when deciding cases[54] (at least until the 1950s, when the new Communist regime abolished administrative jurisdiction in Czechoslovakia as well).[55]

Like Austria, the Czechoslovak Republic also faced a challenging economic and financial situation; and a law of 1924, dedicated to austerity measures, required the government to submit a draft law for the uniform regulation of administrative

[52] See Chapter 7 in this volume.
[53] See Chapter 6 in this volume.
[54] See ibid.
[55] ibid.

procedure. The Code of Administrative Procedure was adopted in 1928, substantially transposing the Austrian law. However, the influence of the AVG was veiled at the time as the new State intended to assert its autonomy and independence from the previous empire (relations with Austria were, moreover, very different between the territories previously coming under the Austrian Cisleithanian part, such as Bohemia, Moravia, and Silesia, and the Slavic territories previously coming under the Kingdom of Hungary, such as Slovakia).

After the Second World War, references to Austrian law were limited as far as possible and almost eliminated as they reflected a bourgeois and capitalist mentality that the Communist regime rejected. However, after the collapse of the Soviet regime and the re-establishment of democracy, the Czech Republic adopted a new Code of Administrative Procedure in 2004,[56] explicitly inspired by Austrian law (in the 1991 version).

The Kingdom of Yugoslavia also adopted a general law on administrative procedure in 1930, which is unanimously recognised by scholarship as emphasising the Austrian model.[57] The 'procedural' structure of the procedure was particularly appreciated, highlighting the greater technical efficiency and superior appropriateness of the procedural laws. After the law was repealed in 1945 (together with all laws contrary to the new political regime), the new People's Republic of Yugoslavia adopted a general law on administrative procedure in 1956. Despite the amendments necessary to adapt regulation to the new non-democratic regime, this law also echoes the Austrian model, while tempering the protection of citizens' rights (envisaged in the abstract) with the overriding public interest.

A particular case is Hungary, which, for obvious reasons, was inseparably linked to the culture and traditions of the Habsburg Empire but at the same time claimed its autonomy during imperial times: Austria's power was both *Kaiserlich und Königlich*, as the Habsburg dynasty ruled the Hungarian part as kings and not emperors. This circumstance led to a substantial (albeit partial) transposition of Austrian law in Hungary, but in disguised form. Indeed, in 1929, a (non-general) regulation on various aspects of public administration, including procedural profiles, was adopted; it was clearly inspired by the Austrian laws of 1925 but did not mention them in any way.[58] At the close of the Second World War, the administration was profoundly modified to introduce strict hierarchical control and Soviet-like organisation in an institutional framework deemed incompatible with the (even abstract) provision of procedural rights.

[56] R Pomahac, 'Re-codification of the Administrative Procedure in the Czech Republic' (2007) 3 ERPL 691ff. See also T Sever, I Rakar and P Kovac, 'Protecting Human Rights through Fundamental Principles of Administrative Procedures in Eastern Europe' (2014) 5 Law and Economics Review 249ff.

[57] See Chapter 8 in this volume.

[58] See Chapter 9 in this volume.

After the bloody repression of 1956, the Communist regime felt sufficiently secure in its power to reintroduce rules of administrative procedure[59] to make administration more efficient (also in terms of control). With Act IV of 1957, the General Rules on Administrative Procedure were adopted.

There is one more case of the diffusion of Austrian law that emerged from this research that is of particular interest and, again, largely neglected. It concerns the attempt to have an Administrative Procedure Act inspired by the AVG adopted in National Socialist Germany.

The deep interconnection and mutual influence between Germanic and Austrian culture is a given; in the field of public law, this is also apparent in the existence of the *Vereinigung der Deutschen Staatsrechtslehrer*, an association that has brought together German-speaking theorists of statecraft since 1922.[60] In his handbook, Jellinek described Austrian administrative law as being most closely related to German administrative law,[61] although this reference remains isolated, without leading to any careful analysis of the 1925 Act in this respect.

This lack of interest in Austrian law during the Weimar Republic transformed into intense curiosity during the National Socialist period.[62] After the *Anschluss*, numerous Austrian jurists also advocated unifying the rules of administrative procedure by adopting the AVG of 1925 as a model for Germany. One of the leading proponents of this idea was Hans Spanner,[63] who had to find a way to justify adopting a law containing individual rights in a regime where only the collective existed. Procedural rights were thus interpreted and reworked from a collectivist perspective to protect individuals as members of the *Volksgemeinschaft*.[64] Despite interest aroused in the project,[65] it was not approved.

After the defeat of the Nazi regime and the entry into force of the *Grundgesetz*, intense academic discussions took place about the possibility and advisability of codifying the rules of administrative procedure.[66] One of the terms of reference was the Austrian law of 1925, but it was often simply referred to as a historical

[59] On this point see A Zs Varga, 'Die Entwicklung des Rechts der öffentlichen Verwaltung' in G Máthé, *Die Entwicklung der Verfassung und des Rechts in Ungarn* (Dialóg Campus 2017).

[60] F Günther, *Denken vom Staat her: Die bundesdeutsche Staatsrechtslehre zwischen Dezision und Integration 1949–1970* (Oldenbourg 2004).

[61] W Jellinek, *Verwaltungsrecht* (3rd edn, Julius Springer 1931) esp 111.

[62] CH Ule, F Becker and K König (eds), *Verwaltungsverfahrensgesetz des Auslandes* (Duncker & Humblot 1967).

[63] See Chapter 10 in this volume.

[64] H Spanner, 'Die österreichischen Verwaltungsverfahrensgesetze als Vorbild eines Reichsgesetzes über das Verwaltungsverfahren' [1938] Deutsche Verwaltung 676ff. The reference to the *Volksgemeinschaft* is on p 678, as cited by Augsberg in Chapter 10 in this volume.

[65] F Kopp, *Verfassungsrecht und Verwaltungsverfahrensrecht. Eine Untersuchung über die verfassungsrechtlichen Voraussetzungen des Verwaltungsverfahrens in der Bundesrepublik und die Bedeutung der Grundentscheidungen der Verfassung für die Feststellung, Auslegung und Anwendung des geltenden Verwaltungsverfahrensrechts* (Beck 1971).

[66] H Hill and others (eds), *35 Jahre Verwaltungsverfahrensgesetz—Bilanz und Perspektiven* (Dunker & Humblot 2011).

antecedent, and no in-depth analysis was carried out.[67] Indeed, many scholars considered that the protections available to citizens in Austrian law already existed in the German system.[68] In fact, in line with Mayer's theories, many scholars considered administrative case law to be a good source of protection for the rights of individuals against the administration. Even among scholars advocating legislative codification with a broader *Rechtsschutz*, the idea that case law could remedy any procedural failings in favour of the individual's rights was well established. Ule's successful *je-desto*[69] formula summarises the biunivocal relationship between procedural and judicial protection.

As is known, after long and heated debate, the *Verwaltungsverfahrensgesetz* of 1976, which adopted a different model from the Austrian one,[70] was issued. It can therefore be concluded that the Administrative Procedure Act of 1925 dominated the administrative law scene and its dogmatics for at least 50 years in Central Europe.

B. The Lack of Interest in Austria in Comparative Studies

Despite the centrality of Austrian law, as summarised in the previous paragraph, the importance of the AVG (in terms of influence, elaboration of a model, and diffusion) is often underestimated in recent research, but sometimes in older research too.

Until the 1960s, at least in continental Europe, the importance of the Austrian contribution was clearly recognised and highlighted,[71] but over time its centrality gradually diminished for reasons that must also be examined in depth from the point of view of the history of ideas.

Austria is often overlooked in the more recent works on comparative administrative law, even in the most important and impressive works devoted to the codification of administrative procedures.[72]

Austria is often forgotten also in comparative studies from the English-speaking world. Frank Goodnow's first treatise on comparative administrative law,[73]

[67] See, for example, the short reference in E Forsthoff, *Lehrbuch des Verwaltungsrechts*, vol 1, *Allgemeiner Teil* (7th edn, Beck 1958) 149 and 203.

[68] KA Bettermann, *Das Verwaltungsverfahren*, in *Veröffentlichungen der Vereinigung der Deutschen Staatsrechtslehrer*, vol 17 (DeGruyter 1959) 118ff, esp 168.

[69] CH Ule, 'Verwaltungsverfahren und Verwaltungsgerichtsbarkeit' [1957] DVBl 597ff.

[70] JP Schneider, 'Germany' in JB Auby (ed), *Codification of Administrative Procedure* (Bruylant 2014) 177ff. W Hoffmann Riem and others (eds), *Grundlagen des Verwaltungsrechts* (2nd edn, Beck 2012).

[71] AM Sandulli, *Il procedimento amministrativo* (Giuffrè 1940); Pastori (n 5). For Germany, see CH Ule, F Becker and K König (eds), *Verwaltungsverfahrensgesetze des Auslandes*, vol I (Duncker & Humblot 1967) esp 41ff; Becker (n 7).

[72] One recalls the thorough and detailed volume edited by Auby (n 70), lacking any chapter on Austria.

[73] FJ Goodnow, *Comparative Administrative Law: An Analysis of the Administrative Systems National and Local, of the United States, England, France, and Germany* (GP Putnam's 1897).

published in 1897, gave an overview of the national and local administrative systems of the United States, England, Germany, and France.

Of course, in America there is no shortage of scholars who have emphasised the importance and, at times, even the countless merits of Austrian administrative law and its codification, as evidenced, for example, by the reviews of Adamovich's two volumes of the *Handbuch des österreichischen Verwaltungsrecht* published in the *American Journal of Comparative Law*.[74] In both reviews, Austrian administrative law is identified as a shining example to be followed, especially concerning the detailed codification of administrative procedure, emphasising its importance for comparative studies, while that of France appears to be overrated.[75]

In comparative studies, the German-speaking country of choice is often Germany, not only because of its undisputedly great public law tradition. However, Germany has always been bound to the legacy of Otto Mayer, who systematised administrative law based on the concept of the administrative act, since this is the basis for judicial protection.[76] Citizens' rights had long been assured by a system based on case law, so much so that Mayer considered it unnecessary to enact a procedural law. And even when the law was enacted in 1976, it was decided that procedural defects do not lead to the annulment of the act if the substantive content could not have been different, thus demonstrating that the substantive correctness of the act prevails over the formal shortcomings of the procedure.

C. The Austrian Model as an Archetype

Our research shows that not only should the Austrian procedural model be understood for illustrative purposes, but it can also assume the value of an archetype.

The *Allgemeine Verwaltungsverfahrensgesetz* dominated the scene of Central European administrative law for many years after its adoption. The main structure and institutions of the Act were widely and variously disseminated, in different ways and with different aims. The structure of the AVG was adopted in Liechtenstein even before it was formally adopted in Austria and was the primary reference for States emerging after the First World War and beyond. The transposition of the AVG was in some cases somewhat explicit, while in others, it was veiled in order to display autonomy and independence from the old ruler.

Ultimately, the Central European States that adopted rules of administrative procedure in the 50 years following the adoption of the AVG used the Austrian model as a true archetype, conforming to it to varying degrees. This is also because

[74] Both volumes were reviewed by R Parker: the first volume (*Allgemeiner und materiellrechtlicher Teil*) in 1956(1) 146ff; the second volume (*materiellrechtlicher Teil*) in 1954(2) 287ff.

[75] R Parker states that the importance of France is 'much overrated' in his review of Adamovich's second volume (n 74) 288.

[76] O Mayer, *Deutsches Verwaltungsrecht* (3rd edn, Duncker & Humblot 1924).

Austria has shown that the adoption of a general regulation of administrative procedure contributes not only to protecting the rights of individuals but also to making administrative action more efficient.

Over time, Austrian (and other) scholarship has generally agreed on the efficiency of the AVG. This consideration also contributes to understanding and resolving an apparent contradiction, ie why non-democratic and even totalitarian regimes have adopted (albeit with the necessary adjustments) rules of administrative procedure in the wake of the Habsburg heritage.

Thus, the importance of the Austrian model clearly emerges from two angles. First, it constitutes an actual 'model', in the sense of an ideal type to be compared with other procedural models, the essential features of which must be correctly reconstructed. Second, the Austrian Act of 1925 contributed to establishing the idea that a law of procedure favours good administration.[77] In this, as with established principles, when considered individually and as a whole, lies the Austrian contribution to the European legal heritage as far as administrative law is concerned.[78]

This conclusion offers a more nuanced view of reality and deserves greater emphasis, particularly in comparative studies devoted to the influence of specific legal experiences in other legal systems. The AVG should play a central role not only in the study of the codification of administrative procedure—where it is often neglected—but also in the debate on the subject of comparative administrative law and its fundamental concepts.

VIII. Institutional Implications: Dismantling Some (Apparent) Contradictions

Administrative procedure and its regulation have been defined as the epiphany of the State as a way of manifesting sovereignty.[79] They have traditionally and unanimously been considered a variable strictly dependent on a series of elements inherent to each State, namely the imprint of constitutional law,[80] the conception of

[77] On the importance of combining diachronic legal comparison, ie legal history, with the history of legal thought and the history of ideas, see G della Cananea, 'The Regulation of Administrative Procedures in Europe: A Historical and Comparative Perspective' (2020) 1 ERPL 223ff. G Gorla, 'Prolegomeni ad una storia del diritto comparato europeo' (1980) V Foro italiano 12ff is still valid in the assumption that comparative law, meaning the performance of comparison, can be understood as the history of comparative law and as the history of law *tout court*, 12.

[78] On general shared law and the identification of general principles common to all systems, see C Schmitt, *Der Nomos der Erde im Völkerrecht des Jus Publicum Europaeum* (Duncker & Humblot 1950).

[79] F Benvenuti, 'Introduzione ai lavori' in *L'azione amministrativa tra garanzia ed efficienza*, Quaderno n 1/1981 di *Problemi di amministrazione pubblica*, 7ff, esp 9.

[80] CH Ule, 'Verwaltungsreform als Verfassungsvollzug' in CH Ule (ed), *Recht im Wandel. Beiträge zu Strömungen und Fragen im heutigen Recht: Festschrift hundertfünfzig Jahre Carl Heymanns Verlag KG* (Heymanns 1965) 53ff; R Wahl, *Herausforderungen und Antworten. Das Öffentliche Recht der letzten fünf Jahrzehnte* (DeGruyter 2006).

public administration,[81] the prevalence of subjective or objective protection,[82] and the structure of judicial protection.[83]

In the wake of the analysis carried out thus far, many relevant aspects emerge on the institutional level; these offer reflections that may help resolve certain apparent contradictions.

First of all, we have seen that the adoption of a law on administrative procedure does not necessarily coincide with democratic needs and aims. Undoubtedly, the proceduralisation of administrative activity in a democratic system brings numerous advantages and safeguards for the citizens, increasing the democratic index of the system in which citizens can participate (in various ways) in the process of shaping the decisions of public administrations.[84] However, it has been seen that even non-democratic regimes have adopted real laws on administrative procedure (or discussed them anyway) not to grant citizens more rights, but for the sake of efficiency and political control—of politicians—over administrators and citizens.[85] Of course, in non-democratic regimes, the judicial protection of individual rights vis-à-vis the power of the State has been eliminated. However, the proceduralisation of administrative activity intervenes on the structural level of public action but not on judicial protection.

It can thus be deduced that well-structured regulation of administrative procedure is synergistic with a well-functioning public administration, irrespective of the purposes concretely pursued (ie pursuing the public interest through the protection, welfare, and guarantees available to citizens or through their oppression). The Austrian law of 1925 has proven to make public action more efficient, and other States have adopted that model (with the necessary adjustments according to the different political regimes in place), even though they espouse diametrically opposing ideals.

Besides the apparent contradiction between the adoption of the same procedural model in pursuit of divergent goals, such as the democratisation of the system and the oppression of citizens' rights, there is another apparent paradox to the diffusion of Austrian law.

[81] S Cassese, 'Il procedimento amministrativo tra modello partecipativo e modello "neoclassico"' in Torchia (n 45).

[82] S Cassese, 'La costruzione del diritto amministrativo in Francia e Regno Unito' in Cassese (n 44) 1 and ff.

[83] M Nigro, 'Procedimento amministrativo e tutela giurisdizionale contro la pubblica amministrazione. Il problema di una legge generale sul procedimento amministrativo' in *L'azione amministrativa tra garanzia ed efficienza* (n 79).

[84] N Luhmann, *Legitimation durch Verfahren* (Suhrkamp 1969); J Waldron, 'The Rule of Law and the Importance of Procedure' in JE Fleming (ed), *Nomos* vol 50, *Getting the Rule of Law* (New York UP 2011) 3ff.

[85] MD McCubbins, RG Noll and BR Weingast, 'Administrative Procedures as Instruments of Political Control' [1987] J L Econ & Org 243ff; LS Bressmann, 'Procedures as Politics in Administrative Law' (2007) 107 Colum L Rev 1749ff.

Indeed, the break-up of the Austro-Hungarian Empire was followed by the unification of the new States through the transposition of Austrian procedural law. The States that emerged from the ashes of empire were often made up of territories that had previously been under different rule and thus found themselves with different regulations inherited from different previous legal orders (for example, Poland was divided between the Austro-Hungarian Empire, Prussia, and the Russian Empire, but the Kingdom of Yugoslavia too comprised territories previously under the Austro-Hungarian Empire, the Ottoman Empire, and independent kingdoms). The new nations therefore imperatively needed to unify their legal systems. This aim was often pursued (in the specific field of administrative law) through the not-always-explicit transposition of the law that had proved to work well, ie the AVG. Thus, the claim to uniformity, unity, autonomy, and independence in relation to the previous dominations was also achieved by adopting a law originating from a former empire. Liechtenstein, traditionally linked to the Austro-Hungarian Empire in various ways, also adopted the AVG.

It is interesting to highlight two further reflections on the role played by judges by comparing the evolutionary trajectories of two legal systems with a robust judicial imprint in their administrative law.

First of all, the emergence of the notion of administrative procedure took place in Austria thanks to the work of the Administrative Court, which, when deciding on the legitimacy of acts, looked at the procedure followed for its adoption, attributing equal (if not greater) importance to the 'path' than to the final product.

This evolution contrasts with the development of the traditionally better known (at least European) administrative court, the Conseil d'Etat. Of course, in France too,[86] administrative law is rooted mainly in case law,[87] especially as far as general principles are concerned. However, the Conseil d'Etat has always prioritised judicial review, leaving the procedural aspects in the background. Indeed, with some notable exceptions, even French legal scholarship has never placed administrative procedure at the heart of its interests.

In France, the roots of administrative law in case law, which developed in the absence of precise normative regulations, have led to the marginalisation of procedure in favour of the centrality of judicial control. In Austria, in precisely the opposite direction, it has led to the emergence of the concept of procedure, with its consequent regulatory development.

This curious discrepancy can be interpreted in the light of the different approaches underlying administrative law in the two legal systems;[88] in France, it is

[86] Auby (n 70) esp especially the chapter on France. JM Auby and R Drago, *Traité de contentieux administratif* (3rd edn, Librairie générale de droit et de jurisprudence 1984).
[87] G Vedel and P Devolvé, *Droit administratif* (9th edn, PUF 1984).
[88] As Auby's chapter in this volume suggests (see Chapter 13).

substantiated by an objective[89] form of judicial protection, seeking to guarantee the lawfulness of administrative action, whereas, in Austria, a subjective type of protection prevails, aiming to safeguard the rights of individuals vis-à-vis the public authorities.

In any event, it may be noted that the roots of administrative law in case law do not necessarily lead to privileging the *judicial review* aspect over the procedural one and the rights associated with it.

Second, it should be pointed out that administrative judges' 'lawmaking' power led to late codification in France, while in Austria, it brought about the first one.

Thus, it is not necessarily true that a strong and powerful court imposes its principles by opposing codification.

IX. Concluding Remarks

This analysis leads to some concluding remarks concerning at least three features of the AVG.

The first of these is genetic. The roots of the Austrian Administrative Procedure Act of 1925 are embedded in the solid foundations of administrative case law from the imperial era. Indeed, the AVG simply transposed into positive law many aspects of the principles that emerged in the 50 years of activity of the VwGH. However, it should not be forgotten that codification was primarily[90] adopted in order to fulfil an international treaty and allow loans to Austria in order to restore its economic and financial situation—an external imposition for economic reasons.

A genesis so contextualised also allows a complete understanding of the AVG's structural and functional aspects. The objectives of uniformity, simplification, and efficiency contribute to creating a minimal and adaptable model that at the same time affords protection to the rights of the parties involved.

Lastly, the fundamental and distinctive features of the Austrian procedural model thus reconstructed constitute a guideline for interpreting its paths of entry into other legal systems, both in terms of positive law and the history of ideas. These paths of entry showed precisely how the AVG of 1925 dominated the scene of administrative law and its dogmatics in Central Europe for at least 50 years.

[89] É Laferrière, *Traité de la juridiction administrative et des recours contentieux* (Librairie générale de droit et de jurisprudence 1989) (reprint of the first edition 1887–88) states that it is not 'un procès fait à une partie, c'est un procès fait à un acte' vol II, 534.

[90] See Section IV.B above.

16

Procedures vs Principles

Opposing Conceptions of Administrative Law (Austria, France, Spain, and Others)

Otto Pfersmann

I. Introduction

The Austrian Law on general administrative procedure (*Allgemeines Verwaltungsverfahrensgesetz*—AVG) is an interesting legal enigma. Its enactment, in addition to its relation to other legal orders and comparative scholarship, is subject to opposing explanations and evaluations. Sometimes, it is seen as a simple result of external pressure, and sometimes as a complement and achievement of the constitutional design set forth in the Federal Constitution of 1920. It comes late in time and is nonetheless in many ways a precursor. It largely inspires other legal systems but is entirely ignored, not only by French or English lawmakers and scholars but also by Americans lawyers and lawmakers, who also took the initiative of codifying administrative procedure 20 years later in 1946. It seems more complicated with respect to Spanish legislators and scholars who had introduced a first, very short codification in 1889, revising their own codification in 1958, 1992, and then in 2015.

The Austrian conception consisted in explicitly structuring the steps of procedure in one unified and specific piece of legislation, largely unifying the procedures despite a federal conception of the Republic—contrary to Germany, who largely and for a long time maintained a federal structure of administrative procedure—drawing mainly on internal rather than external review and thus disciplining the administration from inside, and articulating this internal procedure with strictly judicial review of legality in a final step. This conception not only differs from what we find in France, Italy, and Spain, or for other reasons in the United Kingdom; it differs also and fundamentally in the way legal normativity is conceived. This may be more difficult to explain and to conceptualise, but it still exercises a strong grip on legal thinking, general legal culture, and comparative law, if considered in its own right. [1]

[1] See for instance M Thaler, 'Vom Wesen und Wert der Verwaltungsverfahrensgesetze' (2009) 64 ZöR 433–59 <https://doi.org/10.1007/s00708-009-0037-3>. This article is particularly interesting as it analyses not so much the well-known—at least to an Austrian public—substance of the Austrian

Otto Pfersmann, *Procedures vs Principles* In: *The Austrian Codification of Administrative Procedure*. Edited by: Giacinto Della Cananea, Angela Ferrari Zumbini, and Otto Pfersmann, Oxford University Press.
 DOI: 10.1093/oso/9780198867623.003.0016

The reasons for the enactment of this very specific legislation are often seen in external factors, as Austria went through a deep financial and political crisis in the years after the First World War, while the former allies sought to prevent the country from adhering to the German State. Stabilising the young republic required important loans, which the League of Nations tied to requests for economic and administrative reform.[2]

Contrary to the still prevailing view in comparative law regarding the Austrian case, I take the view that, (1) context is historically interesting but is not an explanation of legal developments and structural differences, (2) the Austrian case suffers from an ideological comparative disadvantage, (3) while the French system develops a specific administrative common law vested in organic ambiguity largely followed by Italy, remaining scholarly and unable to understand different conceptions it considers irrelevant, (4) the intricate roads of Austrian administrative organisation and scholarly theorisation lead to the structural prevalence of rule-guided procedure over substantive principles, (5) whereas the Spanish legal order responds to a conception of administrative holism, integrating Austrian ideas later inserted into a democratic constitutional environment.

A. The Legal Irrelevance of a Stern Historical Context

While some scholars may see the Austrian Administrative Procedure Act of 1925 mainly as a result of international pressure exercised by the League of Nations,[3] from which the young and poor Republic tries to obtain a loan in order to stabilise its finances and reform its monetary system, others would consider it the result of internal factors of legal development. The Geneva Protocols of 4 October 1922, were a State treaty signed by Great Britain, France, Italy, and Czechoslovakia to

Administrative Procedure Act, but tries to understand and explain its specific value within the legal system. The author generally endorses a strictly positivist view, and comes nonetheless to the conclusion that the statute enhances compliance with legal requirements by administrative authorities. The article is also particularly significant because it is published in the context of the discussion ultimately leading to the replacement of the original conception of internal administrative review with a system of administrative tribunals in 2014.

[2] Geneva Protocols. *Staatsvertrag: Genfer Protokolle vom 4. Oktober 1922*, BGBl 42/1922; Austrian Federal Gazette 842/1922 <https://alex.onb.ac.at/cgi-content/alex?aid=bgb&datum=19220004&seite=00001659> accessed 16 March 2022. Concerning the historical context, see also R Freund, *Die Genfer Protokolle. Ihre Geschichte und Bedeutung für das Staatsleben Deutschösterreichs* (1924, reprint De Gruyter 2020); K Berchtold, *Verfassungsgeschichte der Republik Österreich: vol 1: 1918–1933: fünfzehn Jahre Verfassungskampf* (Springer 1998); K Koch, W Rauscher and A Suppan, *Zwischen Staatsbankrott und Genfer Sanierung*: 11. Juni 1921 bis 6. November 1922 (Verlag für Geschichte und Politik Oldenbourg 1998); S Miecke, *Regelmäßigkeiten der Entstehung einer Kodifikation des Verwaltungsverfahrensrechts in Deutschland und Österreich mit einem Ausblick auf die Europäische Union, Europäische Hochschulschriften Band 4651* (Peter Lang 2008).

[3] This seems to be the view taken in the Spanish and Italian contributions in the present volume—see Chapters 11–12.

set up a loan, guaranteeing Austria's independence and thus prohibiting any possible adherence of the country to the German Republic and committing Austria to a radical financial and administrative reform.[4] While it is certainly true that the League wished for a simplification and clarification of an administrative institution inherited from the monarchy, it was mainly interested in a reform of State finances and a significant reduction in the number of public servants. This issue has, however, very little to do with the particular way in which Austria would reform its administrative *procedure*, even though the creditors would see this enactment as proof of good will. It is therefore by no means evident that the international community expected a particular piece of legislation, which, in any event, required a perfect knowledge of the Austrian legal system and a perfect intuition of the choice to make at that particular juncture.[5] Indeed, the Treaty commits Austria to administrative reform but not to a codification of its administrative procedure, whereas the first statute enacted in compliance with the Treaty by Austria itself imposes on itself a 'simplification and unification of administrative procedure' as an autonomous goal. This is certainly an understandable objective in the dramatic context of financial crisis, but it does not require a codification, nor—obviously—this one. What is interesting and significant, however, is that Austria considers *procedure* to be an essential element of reform. But this links the internal concretisation of protocols to Austria's own conception of legality. And if the statute requires a reduction in the ways of going to appeal in order to bolster more expedient decision-making, it does not itself organise procedure. The law codifying procedure was enacted three years later in 1925.

On the other hand, French and English law on administrative matters were, and are, entirely different from each other and entirely different from Austrian conceptions. Why would France or the United Kingdom or Italy or Czechoslovakia compel Austria to enact exactly *this* legislation in order to comply with the demand for administrative reform? None of these countries had ever thought of going in

[4] See (n 2).

[5] The relevant passage in the Treaty reads as follows (French original)

> d) Le gouvernement autrichien prendra et exécutera toutes les décisions nécessaires en vue de réaliser pleinement le programme d'assainissement, y compris les réformes administratives et les transformations indispensables dans la legislation.
>
> (Protocole III, p 1671)

The Treaty is followed by a federal statute concerning reconstruction, '*Bundesgesetz vom 27. November 1922 über die zur Aufrichtung der Staats-und Volkswirtschaft der Republik Österreich zu treffenden Maßnahmen (Wiederaufbaugesetz)*', BGBl 843/1922. Paragraph 3 reads (my translation):

> § 3
>
> 1) The discharge of the missions of public administration is to be simplified in any respect and managed in the most economical way.
> 2) In particular, the following principles are to be applied:
>   a) a simplification and unification of administrative procedure under the maintenance of the general principles of this procedure;
>   b) a reduction in the minimum of the modes of appeal within administrative procedure.

this direction, and, with the exception of Czechoslovakia, none took up the ideas expressed in the law as an inspiration for their own legal system. The substance of the Austrian legislation is perfectly extraneous to the then main existing models of administrative organisation and law. Instead, sooner or later, a significant number of countries followed the Austrian example to a certain extent. These countries had certainly had links with Austria in the past, but ties were dissolved along with the former Empire, and some of these countries could even consider Austria more as a former enemy then as a close friend from whom to borrow legal ideas. The external explanation is thus a case of confusion between an occasional accelerator and a specific legal development, rooted in structures, conceptions, and problems dating back to the times of absolutism, Enlightenment, and liberal constitutionalism of the late eighteenth century. There is a point where the Austrian system develops into something very different from the French or English models, while these two may later appear to be the reference on matters of comparison. This certainly does not constitute a sufficient justification for the comparative oblivion of the Austrian model. The reasons lie deeper, and they may show that the very nature of 'administrative law' may be conceived of in very different manners, making comparison a real challenge. One can understand that certain choices have not been made in one place; which were made elsewhere, but it is more difficult to explain how these choices operated and how positive law and its doctrinal analysis may have come into play together in certain important moves. And it is still up to the scholar of comparative law to conceptualise what happened. And what happened did not only come about in Austria; it was a result of the neglect of comparative law.

B. The Theoretical Irrelevance of the Scholarly Lack of Interest in Specific Legal Structures

There are, trivially, external causes for the lack of interest in legal developments, which would objectively have deserved closer attention and perhaps even a certain exemplarity. Two main factors are to be considered here: the political importance of a State in the international landscape and the development of comparative legal scholarship. Under both criteria, the neglect of Austrian developments appears to be due to reasons of scientific indifference, interesting only for a better understanding of scholarly errors: comparative scholarship is only marginally interested in small countries, and there were two already dominant models of 'administrative law', or its purported inexistence: France and Great Britain as representative of the common law world.

The first external element consists trivially in the fact that small countries are faced with a disadvantage in comparative law, and even more so in general legal culture. *General legal culture* in this understanding is the sort of knowledge a lawyer trained somewhere in the Western hemisphere has of other systems. Legal studies remain specifically local, and acquaintance with other systems is usually as vague as it is fraught with persistent prejudice. Legal scholarship should correct such shortcomings, but quite often amounts to nothing but prejudice writ large. When Austria appears in comparative literature, it mostly concerns the birth of constitutional review in the European model with the Federal Constitution of 1920 or its supposed link with Kelsen and the Vienna school of legal theory. Such references usually remain superficial, and there it generally ends. It is not without significance that German lawyers often consider their Federal Constitutional Court to be an original contribution, not mentioning its Austrian organic, conceptual, and theoretical precedent.[6] Austria is too small to be interesting from a comparative point of view, and other players seem much more important, especially, perhaps, the players who succeeded in making their legal conceptions prevalent in legal culture and scholarship. Comparative studies focusing on German administrative procedure do not even mention the Austrian precedent.[7] Beyond these external factors, understanding the Austrian problem requires a reconstruction of the view from inside.

The second element of comparative differentiation is thus historical and structural. The French system developed a variety of centralised administrative organisation and administrative procedure in terms of administrative justice (*justice administrative*) by strictly separating administration from civil and criminal justice and introducing special organs for the settlement of 'difficulties', whereas the English conception of administrative law, mainly influenced by Dicey's misunderstanding of the French system, considers that the very idea would be entirely mistaken and contrary to the *rule of law*, which is meant to refer to a system where judges enjoy full independence and where rules are neither codified nor, allegedly, codifiable.[8] Both visions have marked comparative scholarship, as the dominant

6 Jutta Limbach, former president of the German Federal Constitutional Court, never mentions the Austrian precedent and presents her court as having only American and German antecedents. See for instance J Limbach, 'Der Vorrang der Verfassung' 16 November 2000 <www.ueberseeclub.de/resources/Server/pdf-Dateien/2000-2004/vortrag-2000-11-16Professor%20Dr.%20Jutta%20Limbach.pdf> accessed 16 March 2022.

7 See for instance: T Müller, *Die Europäisierung der Verwaltungsverfahrensgesetze in Deutschland und Spanien* (Mohr Siebeck 2019).

8 AV Dicey, *The Law of the Constitution* (10th edn, OUP 1985) 330, famously and misleadingly denied the very existence of administrative law—dubbing it *droit administratif*—as one who understood it to mean such a privilege for public officials that citizens could not apply to ordinary courts for redress, whereas British subjects could always appeal to courts enjoying the independence of common law judges. This view is obviously ideological and is intended to promote and protect the British legal order as he then believed it to be as better than the French—or other similar—systems. He is of course forced to admit that 'administrative authorities' exist even in Britain and that they issue decisions, hence there must be rules to frame their enactment, independently of the ways and methods of review these acts could possibly encounter. It is all the more striking that this conceptual confusion between the differentiation of decision-making and the competence to control normative acts has marked the debate in common law countries for a very long time. In a relatively recent article, a recognised specialist in English administrative law still tries to save Dicey's conceptions as relevant for contemporary scholarship: JA Rohr, 'Dicey's Ghost and Administrative Law' (2002) 34 Administration & Society 8–31. doi:10.1177/0095399702034001003.

possible varieties of legally dealing with administration and both standpoints leave no room for something like the Austrian system. The French and English traditions were established well before the Austrian way clearly introduced a specific alternative. The French system probably gained a more recent and lasting momentum through its integration into the institutional system of judicial review in European law: the ECJ was conceived according to the French model of the Council of State with the advocate general corresponding to the *commissaire du gouvernement*, now the *rapporteur public* in France. Interestingly, the German system of administrative procedure never acquired a similar comparative importance. It ultimately followed the Austrian way but with an important difference: the Federation having no empowerment to unify this domain, whereas it was included in the Austrian distribution of competence as a matter of federal legislation, *if needed.*[9]

The third element consists of a conceptual error concerning the classification of legal systems. The main divide in comparative law is often thought to be the dichotomy between systems where legislation is the starting point and those where judge-made law prevails. In the first group, general rules are usually considered to be mechanically applied to concrete cases, however tricky they may be; in the second group, the idea is rather that there is no relevant legislation at all, or that legislation is not relevant at all and that, even if there were, judges would impose their own solutions and set the principles the legislator is not in a situation to provide.

The Austrian 'general law on administrative procedure' does not quite fit into this purported divide, and the divide does not really explain very much about

[9] Article 11 of Federal Constitution of 1920:

> Art. 11 The Federation is competent for legislation, the Länder for execution (*Vollziehung*) in the following matters:
>
> (7) Administrative procedure and administrative criminal procedure, including execution as well as the general provisions of penal administrative procedure, even in domains where legislation is attributed to the Länder.
>
> [German text]
>
> Verwaltungs- und Verwaltungsstrafverfahren einschließlich der Zwangsvollstreckung sowie die allgemeinen Bestimmungen des Verwaltungsstrafrechts auch in Angelegenheiten, in denen die Gesetzgebung den Ländern zusteht.

Current wording (2022):

> Art. 11 ... (2) In so far as a need for the issue of uniform regulations is considered to exist, administrative procedure, general provisions of administrative criminal law, administrative criminal procedure and administrative execution also in matters where legislation lies with the Länder, are prescribed by federal law; divergent regulations can be made in federal or Länder-laws settling the individual spheres of administration only when they are necessary for the regulation of the matter in hand.
>
> [German text]
>
> 2) Soweit ein Bedürfnis nach Erlassung einheitlicher Vorschriften als vorhanden erachtet wird, werden das Verwaltungsverfahren, die allgemeinen Bestimmungen des Verwaltungsstrafrechtes, das Verwaltungsstrafverfahren und die Verwaltungsvollstreckung auch in den Angelegenheiten, in denen die Gesetzgebung den Ländern zusteht, durch Bundesgesetz geregelt; abweichende Regelungen können in den die einzelnen Gebiete der Verwaltung regelnden Bundes- oder Landesgesetzen nur dann getroffen werden, wenn sie zur Regelung des Gegenstandes erforderlich sind.

administrative law—if at all—elsewhere. The French tradition is not civilian, and the English-speaking tradition rested on a misunderstanding that may not have been entirely overcome even today as defining the common law world. The evolution of the Austrian way may have included a momentum of judicial elaboration of principles, while the whole system always tended towards codification oriented along ideas of general interest rather than the solution of individual cases.[10]

Procedure exists by necessity wherever administration is legally organised, and all legal systems know of some variety of administration whereby the legal situation of addressees is modified through normative acts issued by competent authorities. This may be legally organised with varying degrees of precision and differentiation, with various degrees of articulations between hierarchically organised levels of norm-setting and with more (or less) developed procedures allowing review of the conformity of normative acts with respect to norms of higher ranks, and such procedures may be entrusted to varyingly independent organs. The exact sphere of administration varies according to the configuration of the relevant legal system; the more questions may be left to *consensus*, the more possible acts may be left to legislation or some form of arbitration. As administration legally exists—by definition—as a mode of norm-production, it must be organised legally, but this may be done in different ways with regard to the enactment of decisions and the possibility of challenging them. There may also be quite different ways of analysing those legal structures and integrating them into some variety of legal culture and scholarship. This leaves room for a wide range of different options and requires making choices: (1) normative competence may be vested in administrative bodies themselves, with extensive discretion, or this competence may be restricted and the main choices made under some variety of formal legislation structuring, determining and systematising procedure—and legislation may itself be subject to constitutional or supranational review, (2) whether and to what degree to unify or diversify procedure, (3) leaving some space for internal procedure against external review, and (4) articulating internal procedure and external (judicial or other) review of administrative action.

C. Administrative Common Law in Place of Legislation

The main structural reason why the French model remained irrelevant for Austria lies in its entirely different understanding of norm-production and thus of administrative law itself. France elaborated a system of administrative common law and considers the principles thus emerging as administrative law proper.

10 See, again, the highly interesting reconstruction by Thaler (n 1).

Two main moves have guided the interest of French legal doctrine and politics away from systematic legislation if not from legislation in general: the scope of limiting the power of 'ordinary' judges and a growing and persistent anti-positivist and anti-formalist conception of law generally. It is interesting to observe that this last element of French legal scholarship and thus of general legal culture only emerged at the end of the nineteenth century. Laferrière firmly denies the very possibility of codifying administrative law,[11] whereas public law scholarship progressively considers cases as the most abundant and secure source of administrative law.[12] But this ultimately has its roots in the developments of the Revolution.

The French Revolution had failed in its main objective. It was unable to establish a convincing alternative to the *ancien régime*, which it had furiously overthrown. Many ideas were launched and spread all over the continent, but none of the constitutions or constitutional designs survived, and the constitutions that finally achieved a certain stability, ie those of the Third and Fifth Republics are not revolutionary. The Revolution succeeded, however, in bringing several problems to the floor, and these were less strictly related to the questions it mainly had to address, such as the organisation of government and the representation of citizens.

Besides the point who would *rule* the 'executive', ie who would act at the highest level, one had to answer who would perform concrete normative acts and actions imputable to the State—and how it was all to be systematically related. Of course, these acts and actions had existed before, but the modification of government competence revealed that their volume was constantly growing and could not be simply left outside of the legal realm. The interesting point is that this problem appeared as a structural side concern that would have tremendous consequences for what would become 'administrative law' in Europe.

One heritage of the *ancien régime* was its judicial organs. They had to be reorganised and disciplined. And there were two very specific problems to be considered in the whole new institutional design. One was the registration of the king's normative acts. Even under absolute monarchy this implied the competence for reviewing the act, leaving the monarch less absolute than he considered himself to be. For the Revolution, this had to be strictly abolished, as the new sovereign (the *people*, which is its representatives) should not be limited by anything but itself, ie, the general will, expressed through legislation. This move hindered the

[11] E Laferrière, *Traité de la jurisprudence administrative et des recours contentieux*, vol 1 (2nd edn, Berger Levrault 1896) xii.

[12] Asserting this, Laferrière quotes Serrignys *Traité de l'organisation, de la compétence et de la procédure en matière contentieuse administrative* (Aug Durand 1865) vi, stating:

> La jurisprudence est ici une des sources essentielles de la doctrine, parce qu'elle seule peut faire la part entre les principes permanents et les dispositions contingentes, établir une hiérarchie entre les textes, remédier à leur silence, leur obscurité, leur insuffisance, en s'inspirant des principes généraux du Droit et de l'équité. (xii)

See A-L Girard, *La formation historique de la théorie de l'acte administratif unilatéral* (Dalloz 2013).

establishment of constitutional review in France for centuries and hindered its extension to enacted law even until 2010. The second problem was the tendency of the judiciary to hand over decisions in all areas, including therefore all matters in which the new sovereign intended to act in order to implement the law made by the general will, ie, the representatives of the people. And the third problem surfaced only later at a conceptual and theoretical level, but was of course substantially present: whether the sovereign as actor is bound within the sphere determined by the legislator.

The second problem did not reach constitutional level until 1799, with the institution of the Consulate and the establishment of a progressively authoritarian regime. According to art 52 of the Constitution of Year VIII:

> Under the direction of the consuls, a Council of State is in charge of writing the draft bills and the regulations of public administration and resolving the difficulties emerging in administrative matters.

This determining move closed a conflict resulting in two legislative provisions enacted in the first period of the Revolution, the laws of 16 and 24 August 1790,[13] and the decree of 16 Fructidor of the Year III (2 September 1795): 'It is repeatedly prohibited that the tribunals have in whatever manner cognizance concerning the acts of administration, under the sanctions of the law'. It is not without significance that these provisions are still found in French law today.[14]

What remained after the Revolution is a certain conception of administrative law that largely influenced comparative perspectives: administrative law is the set of decisions handed over by the State Council when faced with 'difficulties emerging in administrative matters'. When a French student is learning 'administrative law', he or she learns decisions collected in casebooks and explained one by one by members of the Council of State. What is to be mastered in this way are principles and concepts of administrative action, elaborated according to a particular common law method, if by common law we understand the progressive construction of normative standards through particular cases, including the normative standards defining the status of the case itself. The common idea that French law belongs to the broader category of the 'civil law system', where this term refers to a systematically codified set of rules that is then applied with some degree of consistency to a variety of cases, is entirely erroneous: even where codifications

[13] *Loi des 16–24 août 1790 sur l'organisation judiciaire*, Article 13:

> Judiciary and administrative functions are and shall forever be separated from administrative functions. Judges shall not trouble, under penalty of abuse of power, in whatever manner, the operations of administrative bodies, nor summon administrators before them for reasons concerning their functions. <www.legifrance.gouv.fr/loda/id/JORFTEXT000000704777/> accessed 16 March 2022.

[14] <www.legifrance.gouv.fr/loda/id/JORFTEXT000000668326/> accessed 16 March 2022.

exist, the law is not conceived as codified but as gradually emerging from judicial sources and is studied and taught accordingly. Where there is no—or only partial and late codification—as in the case of administrative law, the common law conception prevails entirely. French administrative common law is not only different from, but by its very foundation and conception, intrinsically opposed to codification. This can easily be seen from the way in which the canonical presentation of case law sets its own beginning: it is a case of tort and damages, which at the time legally fell under the provisions of the civil code. Nonetheless, the Tribunal of Conflicts decides that administrative matters are framed 'by different standards'.[15] The point is that no legislative source whatsoever sets such standards, which means that they are to be framed by the Council of State as an autonomous para-legislative organ.[16]

At the same time, the French common law concept is fundamentally *ambiguous*. It starts with an attempt to limit the judiciary to civil and criminal matters and ends up with a large set of standards created through decisions by the Council of State. But what is the Council of State?

From the very beginning, the Council of State was, and is, a multifunctional organ, mainly charged with advising the government on draft legislation and collaterally resolving difficulties. Even in the current French Constitution of 1958, the Council originally appeared only as an adviser,[17] it is still not mentioned in a principal judicial function for the French mainland.[18] Even though the Council of State claims to be a jurisdiction—when it acts through its 'Section of Contentious

[15] Case *Blanco*, D. 1873, III, 20, 8 February 1873:

> Given that the principles in the Code civil which regulate the relations between individuals are inapplicable to the possible liability of the state for damage done to individuals by persons employed in the public service;
>
> Given that the responsibility of the State, being neither general nor absolute, is subject to special rules which vary depending on the exigencies of the public service and the need to reconcile the rights of the state with the rights of private persons;
>
> Given that accordingly, under the laws cited above, the jurisdiction to determine such matters is vested exclusively in the administrative authorities.

Translation by Tony Weir, with corrections by the author of this chapter <https://law.utexas.edu/transnational/foreign-law-translations/french/case.php?id=1021>.

[16] This is what the Council of State candidly admits in its own comment on the case: 'Le droit de la responsabilité administrative, depuis l'arrêt *Blanco*, s'est construit sur un fondement essentiellement jurisprudentiel, de façon autonome par rapport au droit civil' <www.conseil-etat.fr/ressources/decisions-contentieuses/les-grandes-decisions-du-conseil-d-etat/tribunal-des-conflits-8-fevrier-1873-blanco> accessed 16 March 2022.

[17] Article 39(2): 'Government Bills shall be discussed in the Council of Ministers after consultation with the Council of State and shall be tabled in one or other of the two Houses'.

[18] The revision of 2008 introduced the new art 66(1):

> If, during proceedings in progress before a court of law, it is claimed that a statutory provision infringes the rights and freedoms guaranteed by the Constitution, the matter may be referred by the Council of State or by the Cour de Cassation to the Constitutional Council, within a determined period.

A judicial function is mentioned only with respect to oversees communities and these provisions were also enacted with later revisions.

Affairs' (*Section du contentieux*), and even though it is considered as such by the European Court of Human Rights or the European Court of Justice, it is not clearly established as such in French law. The formal president of the Council is still the prime minister—while its real president is only its 'vice president'. Even though the Council does not decide as an agency within the administration and as part of the government largely understood, the ties with the active administration have never been entirely and formally dissolved. In its contentious function, the Council is a para-judicial organ concerned with standard-setting for the administration. The French administrative common law has thus set a specific understanding of administrative law itself as an autonomously growing set of heterogeneous principles intrinsically opposed to any form, not only of codification but of lawmaking, by parliamentary assembly in general.

The first element of ambiguity is thus that *administrative* justice need not necessarily be delivered by judges, if by *judges* one understands organs with constitutionally guaranteed independence with respect to whatever instructions related to the cases to be decided, with respect to carrier and position, a strictly legal discipline in handling cases and a respective duty of strict impartiality. Whereas such guarantees are explicitly granted to 'judges' in the French Constitution,[19] the term 'judges' in this context does not refer to the members of administrative jurisdictions, including the Council of State. Their constitutional protection, if any, results only from two decisions of the Constitutional Council, related to the separation of the administrative and judicial authorities. In the Austrian conception, the Administrative Court is an element of the 'Guarantees of the Constitution and the Administration'.[20]

This is also relevant for the competence they respectively exercise. Besides controlling administrative decisions, the French review authorities also set general norms through principled decision, and they do it independently of statutory norms possibly stating the contrary. This would be entirely unthinkable in the Austrian conception, where the distribution of competencies also frames the status of norms produced by whatever organ. In other words, the hierarchy of norms is not organised, even though the dominant scholarship claims the contrary. The reason is as simple as it may be surprising: the theory of the hierarchy of norms is nearly unknown in France, and when a hierarchy is invoked, it is naively the idea

[19] Article 64(4): 'Judges shall be irremovable from office'. While a member of the Council of State will be part, according to a revision of the Constitution dating from 2008, of the High Council of the Judiciary (art 65), this authority will not be competent with respect to members of administrative tribunals or the Council of State itself. The presence of members of the Council of State is conceived of as a counterweight with respect to a too corporatist composition of the High Council of the Judiciary.

[20] The introduction of administrative tribunals as organs of *judicial* review of administrative decisions has also been operated through constitutional revision (BGBl. I Nr 51/2012) in 2012—like the previous introduction of the 'independent bodies administrative decision' in 1988, which those tribunals replaced. These bodies were 'tribunals' in the meaning of the ECHR, but not in the stricter understanding of the Austrian Constitution, whereas the present administrative tribunals qualify as courts in the strict sense.

that superiority conditions validity with no criterion for what may be 'superior' and with no conception of derogatory force.[21]

The French conception of administrative common law which largely also permeated EU law is based and premised on the constant growth of a set of norms with a high degree of generality and indeterminacy, called 'principles', elaborated and publicised through jurisprudential considerations. It draws attention to heterogeneous issues of substance where the reasoning may be guided by considerations external to positive law and the structural hierarchy within the system. The Austrian system is not less mindful of principles but considers them in their structural relations and constructs the administrative act (*Bescheid*) with respect to a strict calculus of deficiency: if one of the necessary elements lacks, there is no legally valid act; if other elements fail, the act is valid, but review may correct it according to the rules of procedure. A central question remains thus for both legal orders and conceptions, how exactly general interest is conceived of and conceptualised and how the degree of discretion is identified and controlled. French administrative scholarship develops *theories* with respect to unilateral administrative acts. And their evolution is complex and hesitant. They remain bound up with the idea that the administrative act is one of *will* set by a competent authority. This indeed captures an element of the positivist definition of normativity as the 'meaning of an act of will directed at a set of actions to be performed by its addressee', but the point is that the French conception speculates about a psychological datum, whereas positivist theory tries to locate the objective elements of meaning contained in the formulation of the norm.[22] The nature of the will constitutes the main focus of the French reflection and theory, which first seems to endorse a German conception where the State is a person imposing its 'will' on its subjects. These views are subsequently harshly criticised as expressing German imperialist warmongering and enhance an anti-positivist stance observable to the present day. And instead of analysing the normative structure of the 'administrative act' in order to grasp its concept, the effort lies in the *construction* of a concept able to determine its nature in and of itself.[23]

[21] See O Pfersmann, 'Carré de Malberg et la "hiérarchie des norms"' (1997) 31 Rev Fr Dr Const 481–509; O Pfersmann, 'La production des normes: production normative et hiérarchie des normes' in M Troper and D Chagnollaud (eds), *Traité international de droit constitutionnel*, vol 2 (Dalloz 2012) 483–528.

[22] See O Pfersmann, 'Le statut de la volonté dans la définition positiviste de la norme juridique' (1999) 28 Droits 83–98. The problem with Kelsen's definition of the norm consists mainly in the fact that expressions of will remain psychological; that is, they are not data that could be empirically identifiable whereas the actual problem remains the analysis of the meaning of those propositions that could be identified as stating obligations, prohibitions, or permissions. In other words, from a normativist standpoint, 'will' is nothing but a distinctive aspect of deontically modified propositions in which the psychological element is reduced to imposing a duty, whereas in the German and the French—and in most civil law systems—discussion of the psychological nature of public entities is at the heart of the considerations.

[23] See again, the excellent reconstruction of these intellectual debates in Anne-Laure Girard's thesis (n 12).

D. Regulating Administrative Law through Procedure

The Austrian approach shared some elements with the French historical evolution but remains extraneous to the idea that 'principles' could be set outside a constitutionally defined catalogue of normative forms. Its history is rather well known among German-speaking legal scholars and excellently presented in this volume by Thomas Olechowski.[24] Knowing the evolution of the system is fundamental, but it does not in itself say very much about the relationship—or absence of a relationship—with other systems.

The problem of organising a specific procedure of litigation concerning administrative matters has known of many different solutions dating back to the days of Maria Theresa. It was only at the end of the eighteenth century that Austrian absolutism clearly sought to provide an autonomous sphere of action for administration and to free it from formerly existing possibilities of judicial litigation on these matters, as the public interest should be pursued 'out of the most noble public judgement'.[25] At this stage, the parallel with French revolutionary developments is striking. However, and even though there were attempts to introduce a Council of State,[26] the French example was not followed in this respect. A second important step consisted in the abolition of the last feudal prerogatives in the wake of the revolution of 1848: this meant that the judicial competence of the feudal lord disappeared again to the benefit of the administration, a question that was obviously absent from the French evolution, despite the restoration of the monarchy and the authoritarian turn following the *coup d'état* of Napoleon III.

After overcoming absolutism and neo-absolutism, the Constitution of 1867 would effectively set a new turning point, with the promise of the institution of an administrative court competent in cases with no relevance in terms of civil rights and for which civil litigation would be available, but where one purports to have been harmed in relation to 'one's' other 'rights'. This jurisdiction was finally instituted by statute in 1876. The law provided that the Court would also have jurisdiction in matters relating to 'essential matters of administrative procedure'.

This specific competence in turn paved the way for its codification, on which the principles elaborated by the Court had an important impact, but most probably also the generalising systematisation elaborated by Friedrich Tezner in his handbook of Austrian administrative procedure.[27] Tezner's contribution is mainly

[24] See Chapter 3 in this volume; see also his chapter 'Die Entwicklung allgemeiner Grundsätze des Verwaltungsverfahrens' in M Holoubek and M Lang (eds) *Allgemeine Grundsätze des Verwaltungs-und Abgabenverfahrens* (Linde 2006) 13–40. I largely follow this very careful, complete, and documented historical reconstruction.

[25] See Olechowski (n 25) 18.

[26] As Olechowksi recalls.

[27] *Handbuch des Österreichischen Administrativverfahrens* (Manz 1896) and *Das österreichische Administrativverfahren. Dargestellt auf Grund der verwaltungsgerichtlichen Praxis* (Österreichische Staatsdruckerei 1922, 2nd edn, 1925).

recognised for his interest in the principles of procedure, especially the rights of parties, the principle of the administrative obligation to act in view of the public interest and its legally organised elaboration of a legal settlement. This element is indeed central in the context of an ongoing legislative debate, permanent scholarly discussion, and the evolution of case law. Tezner's work crystallised a synthesis without which the following steps cannot really be understood. But he also had to provide a conceptual framework.

And it appears that besides the substantive issues, extracted from the case law, conceptual problems were essential to understand the choices and developments followed in different systems. If we look at the historical moment in which Tezner wrote his handbook, a succession of quite different structures had operated in Austria, as in other countries, where administration was linked to some kind of jurisdictional settlement of litigation as under the reign of Maria Theresa, where structures of administration action and justice proper (criminal and civil) were entrusted to the same authorities at first instance (the so-called mixed district authorities or *Gemischte Bezirksämter*[28] between 1853 and 1867), and structures in which no such articulation occurred. Prussia had instituted bodies of administrative litigation dubbed 'jurisdictions',[29] France had introduced a model of *administrative justice*, entrusted to authorities that would not have been considered strictly judicial and for which the theory of the minister as judge (*ministre-juge*) prevailed even after the Council of State had been authorised to decide in its own right,[30] for the question indeed regards what kind of authority decides according to which rules of procedure.

A conceptual problem thus arises precisely because the very nature of 'administrative procedure' is unclear or rather was obscured in the existing scholarship at the time, even though this was due to structural ambiguities rooted in the slow and hesitant blossoming of administrative law itself.

The first point of confusion concerns *contentious* administrative matters as opposed to other administrative questions and the frequent idea that what is contentious must be settled by *jurisdictions* and that jurisdictions were the courts that settled civil and criminal matters.

The second problem concerns the very nature of what is to be termed 'jurisdiction', as in German the word *Rechtsprechung* simply means 'to say the law', and

[28] RGBl 1853, IV. Stück, Nr 10 <https://alex.onb.ac.at/cgi-content/alex?apm=0&aid=rgb&datum=18530004&seite=00000065&size=45>.

[29] See C Bornhak, *Geschichte des Preußischen Verwaltungsrechts*, 3 vols (Springer 1884–86), especially the last volume.

[30] It is generally considered that the view that the minister is, as such, judge of first instance was abandoned with the law of 24 May 1872 and the decision of the State Council 66145 (*Cadot*) of 13 December 1889, stating that the Council was competent to decide on all requests for annulment against whatever decision of an administrative authority, except if a statute explicitly provides otherwise. What is again interesting in this case is the request that the application itself denied: the scholarly reconstructed meaning of the decision consists in the—legally not grounded—generalisation of the Council's affirmation of competence.

saying the law may be done through various forms of authoritative pronouncements, and those forms are unable to say anything about the procedural and organic nature of the authority in charge of issuing the pronouncement.

The third question concerns the essence of the relevant authority. Bernatzik, dedicating an entire monograph to *Rechtsprechung* (*ius dicere*, 'saying the law') insists that the main question is not whether an authority is 'judicial' or not, as the use of the qualification 'judicial' is blurred to the point of being undecidable. In his text, he largely discusses French scholarship, showing that even such authors as Aucoc, Durcrocq, or Batbie use a terminology they do not explain and for which they provide no clear criteria.[31] The main point, for Bernatzik, then, is that *decisions* are handed down after a set of legally separate steps—the *procedure*—with normative effects (force of law *Rechtskraft*) on the addressees. At the same time, Bernatzik appears rather sceptical concerning the organic criteria of jurisdiction as they were considered then and now, namely independence and impartiality—which he tends to relativise, arguing that the judges can be partial and administrative authorities impartial, and that it is all a question of degree. This may appear surprising in relation to the present, as well as to the standards of the times in which he wrote, even within Bernatzik's own conceptions. He was a member of the Imperial Court (*Reichsgericht*), which later became the Constitutional Court under the republic, and he seemed to favour a development towards a more judicialised system of review, all the while presenting this as a political option, as he clearly did not want to contaminate his legal analysis.[32] This stance shows an analytical and critical approach to legal concepts and substantive conceptions, for which procedure and the legal nature of decisions are the main focus in the development of administrative law.

When Tezner tried to systematise the case law of the Administrative Court with respect to procedure and its main principles, he seemed to be largely indebted to Bernatzik, with whom he clearly shared the view that *procedure itself* makes administration a legal object long before, and rather than, punctual substantive pronouncements. Both Bernatzik and Tezner polemicise against the leading German scholarship in public law, and German-speaking scholarship seems to close the horizon of Tezner's critical assessment of the state of the art as he visibly does not read and thus does not quote scholarship written in other languages. However, the inheritance of Bernatzik and Tezner was later strengthened and enriched by the Vienna school of legal theory, known for its decisive contribution to the theory and practice of constitutional justice, yet drawing for this very reason on the focus of procedure in all domains of normative production—and destruction (annulment). In the period that separates the systematisation of the case law of the Administrative

[31] E Bernatzik, *Rechtsprechung und materielle Rechtskraft* (Manz 1886) 26f.

[32] Bernatzik considers the fact that regulations cannot (yet) be reviewed with legal force as a deficiency of the Austrian system of the time (ibid 290f).

Court from the codification of administrative procedure, one can understand that this was indeed the main interest in Austrian public law scholarship.

This conception stands in marked contrast to that taken by the French, Italian, and Spanish.

E. Administrative Organisational Holism: Codification

The Austrian and Spanish conceptions have some elements in common but differ in the overall design and scope of codification.

The Spanish codification seems to have begun prior to the Austrian developments, with a short statute enacted in, reformed, and extended by different steps until most recently. It is a codification of procedure, regulating both the production of administrative acts and their contestation. There are, however, two main differences. First, the scope of the codification is much broader than in Austria, as it includes the entire organisation of public administration. Second, this domain may also appear more limited; its more recent sphere of competence regards common rather than general rules, which means that procedural unification is not one of the constitutive purposes of this legislation.

The most significant difference, however, consists in the legal context in which both codifications arise. In Austria, it all began with a constitutional reform instituting the Administrative Court and a concretising statute missioning this new institution with judging, among other questions, 'essential matters of administrative procedure'. Whereas no codification was enacted in the decades to follow despite intense scholarly discussion, the republican Constitution created a special federal competence for general legislation on administrative procedure, but it also designed a highly innovative structure of judicial review in which the Administrative Court is integrated under the heading 'Guarantees of the Constitution and the Administration' (Chapter VI), and which links the review of constitutionality and the review of legality both objectively and in terms of a right to petition one or the other Court according to the level of the norms disputed. While taking the subjective rights of the citizen into account, the Spanish law of 1958 operates in a legally authoritarian environment, while many provisions concerning administrative organisation and norm-production would have to be inserted into the Constitution in Austria. It was only after the adoption of the democratic Constitution of 1978 that similar questions are also discussed and decided in Spain.

There is also a highly interesting plurality of opinions concerning Spanish interest in the Austrian codification. Whereas for some scholars the Austrian experience had no relevance to the Spanish debate, others highlighted the determining reception of the works of the Vienna school of public law and legal theory and seem to mean that the Spanish reform of 1958 might have been largely advanced by a strong reception of Adolf Merkls and Hans Kelsens writings. As Marcos Vaquer Caballería explicitly quotes endorsing Merkl: 'All administration is administrative procedure, and administrative acts present themselves as mere products of administrative procedure'.[33] He underscores the fact that the main influences were Austrian and to a lesser extent, Italian. Again, with Merkl, he takes the view that judicial procedure is very different from administrative procedure and that in this latter domain it is the purpose of legislation to ensure that all persons may obtain the same guarantees and application of the law.

It was probably even more important in the then authoritarian setting that procedure warranted equality of treatment in combination with the possibility of challenging the legality of an administrative act.

The reception of Austrian administrative theory sheds some light on the way an explicit set of procedural norms could be a trigger for the advancement of legal values in anticipation of constitutional reform, as the Austrian experience shows how the strengthening of the rule of law under constitutional structures was considered incomplete without a codification of administrative procedure.

[33] 'La codificación del procedimiento administrativo en España' (2016) 42 Revista General de Derecho Administrativo <http://laadministracionaldia.inap.es/noticia.asp?id=1506243> accessed 16 March 2022.

17

Austria and Germany

Procedure and *Rechtsstaat*

Dian Schefold

Reading the excellent study by Ino Augsberg on the influence of the Austrian legislation on administrative procedure in Germany with its extensive documentation,[1] I fully agree with the arguments presented in his chapter here, but I shall try to systematise them, focusing on the development of Prussian administration and the realisation of the concept of *Rechtsstaat*, the rule of law, presented in the study.

Three categories of arguments strike me as important: (1) opposition to the *Reine Rechtslehre* (pure theory of law) and its founder Hans Kelsen in the German debate; (2) the limited power of the central State over administration and especially administrative procedure, and (3), most importantly, the development of administrative structures, theories on self-government, and administrative process in Prussia. This third point requires especial attention on the development before the First World War.

I. Opposition to Kelsen's Theory

To understand the debate on the Administrative Procedure Act, one has to go back to the Austrian Federal Constitution (B.-VG., of 1-10-1920), with its broad understanding of the principle of the rule of law, expressed in art 18(1).[2] This article, according to Kelsen's pure theory of law, defines the rule of law establishing the principle of the reserve of the law for all administrative activity, based on the democratic legitimation of all the laws (art 1). Therefore, it seemed necessary to draft an Administrative Procedure Act regulating the workings of the Federation (*Vollziehung, 3. Hauptstück*, arts 60–94), including administration (*Verwaltung*, arts 60–81), and jurisdiction (*Gerichtsbarkeit,* arts 82–94). Since judicial process in administrative and civil and criminal matters obviously had to be ruled by law, the previous administrative procedure—as a condition for appealing to the

[1] See Chapter 10 in this volume.

[2] Bundes-Verfassungsgesetz (B.-VG.) of 1-10-1920, BGBl. Nr 1/1920. See F Ermacora (ed), *Österreichische Bundesverfassungsgesetze* (Böhlau Verlag 1989).

Dian Schefold, *Austria and Germany* In: *The Austrian Codification of Administrative Procedure*. Edited by: Giacinto Della Cananea, Angela Ferrari Zumbini, and Otto Pfersmann, Oxford University Press.
 DOI: 10.1093/oso/9780198867623.003.0017

Administrative Court—was subject to this ruling too. Although its independence was guaranteed by the Constitution, jurisdiction was a part of the *Vollziehung* and thus within the scope of this law. All this was in line with the theory of Hans Kelsen, the father of the Austrian Constitution.

Nevertheless, this does not mean that the Austrian Administrative Procedure Act may be Kelsen's work. As Angela Ferrari Zumbini has elaborated,[3] Austria had, since 1875, its Administrative Court (*Verwaltungsgerichtshof*), which developed a fruitful and rich jurisprudence, searching for answers to questions of administrative law in the growth of modern administration. Friedrich Tezner,[4] judge and Head of Section of the Court, studied these developments, and published, starting in 1896, several works on administrative procedure.[5] He was therefore qualified to influence the Administrative Procedure Act, and he underlined his contribution to it. What is more, he opposed the influence of Kelsen's theory, the *Reine Rechtslehre*, on the law enacted in 1925, pointing out its roots in the jurisprudence of the Administrative Court.[6] According to Tezner, the rules on administrative procedure established by the act are nothing more than a codification of the jurisprudence of the Administrative Court.[7] Thus, there was a similar development to that taking place in Germany, where the Administrative Procedure Act of 1976 was considered a codification of the jurisprudence of the Federal administrative courts, in explicit contrast to Italian Law No 241 which required a reform of the public administration.[8]

Obviously, a theoretical approach like the *Reine Rechtslehre* cannot determine the detailed regulations of administrative procedure, and consequently, the experience of jurisprudence may have been more relevant. But the connection between the concept of *Rechtsstaaat* (with its democratic basis), the protection of rights by an administrative court, and the regulation of the previous administrative procedure, resulting from the Austrian Constitution of 1920, cannot be contested either.

At least from the German point of view, this aspect prevailed, and it was opposed to the prevailing traditional German ideas. Therefore, there was some scepticism about regulating administrative procedure. German administrative law was determined by the difference between executive and judicial power. While the latter was subject to legal regulation—for civil and criminal jurisdiction at *Reich* level from

[3] A Ferrari Zumbini, *Alle origini delle leggi sul procedimento amministrativo: Il modello austriaco* (Editoriale Scientifica 2020) on the Administrative Court, see 27ff.

[4] On his work, see ibid 20, 55ff.

[5] See the bibliography ibid 165f.

[6] ibid 116–18.

[7] ibid 106ff.

[8] For a comparison between the German and Italian scenarios, see D Schefold, 'Riforme amministrative, riforme del procedimento amministrativo e il ruolo della dirigenza pubblica: il modello tedesco' in S Gambino (ed), *Dirigenza pubblica e innovazione amministrativa* (Maggioli Editore 1992) 95ff, 105ff.

the 1870s—administration was, in principle, left to the discretionary power of the constitutional monarchy and its bureaucracy until 1918, in the republican State legitimated by democratic principles, but without broadening the field of reserve of the law:[9] laws regarding limitations of fundamental rights (liberty and property) were necessary, but not for public services, payments, and organisation. In these fields, legislation was possible and often used, but not as a general principle determining all administrative activities. While Kelsen criticised this independence of administrative authority, most German scholars did not follow his line of thinking and preferred to protect State authority, sometimes even with anti-Semitic tendencies. Therefore, Kelsen remained—during the Weimar Republic and throughout its controversies over methods and schools of public law (the *Methoden- und Richtungsstreit*)—the defender of a theoretical orientation, but he went against the prevailing schools. It took a long time, even after the Second World War, for this leading theory to be reconsidered.

II. The Limited Power of the Central State over Administration and Administrative Procedure

As mentioned above, a crucial problem of the regulation of administrative procedure in Germany is the division of power between the central State and its members, the *Länder*. Whereas civil and criminal law procedure was transferred to the power of the central State after German unification in 1871, its legislative authority on administrative matters remained very limited: the (few) areas of federal administration and some special powers explicitly enumerated in the Constitution. All the rest, and especially the administrative execution of federal laws, remained in the hands of the *Länder*. The central State could thus legislate on its own administrative procedure but not that of the *Länder*, which required more administrative regulation. As a matter of fact, the central State, competent in this regard, passed special acts on administrative procedure relating to national insurance (*Reichsversicherungsordnung*, 1911) and tax law (*Reichsabgabenordnung*, 1919) but nothing on general administrative procedure.

Under the Weimar Constitution, which extended federal powers, national legislation, rather than that of the *Länder*, could have regulated administrative procedure,[10] but the importance of this power was contested, and there were no

[9] Typical of the position prevalent in the first quarter of the twentieth century, seeF Fleiner, *Institutionen des deutschen Verwaltungsrechts* (6th–7th edn, JCB Mohr–Paul Siebeck 1922) 5ff, 121ff. For the dogmatic reasoning, based on Otto Mayer's theory, see *Deutsches Verwaltungsrecht*, vol I (3rd edn, Duncker & Humbolt 1923, reprint 1969) 7, 54ff, 70ff; K A Bettermann, 'Verwaltungsakt und Richterspruch' in *Gedächtnisschrift für Walter Jellinek* (Isar Verlag 1955) 361ff.

[10] Weimar Constitution, art 14, see G Anschütz, *Die Verfassung des Deutschen Reichs* (14th edn, Verlag von Georg Stilke 1933) note 1 to art 14.

projects to enact a general law of administrative procedure. The focus was therefore on the *Länders*' legislation, very well presented in Ino Augsberg's contribution to this volume.[11] Thus, Thuringia enacted its own law, and, in Württemberg, a project was presented and discussed, but not enacted. Even the plans to unify a law on administrative procedure based on the Austrian model in the unitarian State of the Nazi period produced no results.

III. Administrative Structures, Self-Government, and Administrative Process in Prussia

To understand this hesitation, it may be necessary to consider the special scenario of Prussia, decisive for Germany, because it comprised approximately two-thirds of the territory and population of the German Empire and, therefore, the most important solutions for administrative procedure. As a result of the State's remarkable growth, first following the Congress of Vienna (1815) and subsequently the wars with Denmark (1864), Austria, and the *Deutsche Bund* (1866), then later with France (1870–71), reform and unification of administrative structures, especially in the conquered territories, seemed necessary, and as far as the principle of local self-government was concerned, a law in line with the principle of the rule of law was required.

Rudolf Gneist played a determining role in preparing the bill in question.[12] This lawyer, a professor in Berlin, a liberal at the beginning of his career, had studied the British system of self-government intensively and found its core in the honorary functions of the justices of the peace and other officials belonging to the local gentry and nominated by the Crown, working as counterparts of the civil service (whose influence, which had grown in the British nineteenth-century reforms, he underestimated). He transferred these principles to Prussia and promoted his ideas for a new system of local self-government, combined with administrative jurisdiction regarding the concept of the rule of law in numerous essays and proposals, and lastly in a book published in 1872 (2nd edn, 1879) entitled *Der Rechtsstaat und die Verwaltungsgerichte in Deutschland* ('The Rule of Law and the Administrative Tribunals in Germany').[13] It is not a huge volume, but it extensively describes the historical forms of protection of rights by the courts in the Holy Roman Empire,

[11] Chapter 10.

[12] See M Stolleis, *Geschichte des öffentlichen Rechts in Deutschland*, vol 2 (Beck 1992) 385ff. On Gneist's role in the respective Prussian legislation, see ER Huber, *Deutsche Verfassungsgeschichte seit 1789*, vol 4 (Kohlhammer 1969) 353ff. For my point of view, see Dian Schefold, 'Selbstverwaltungstheorien: Rudolf Gneist und Hugo Preuß' in D Lehnert and C Müller, *Vom Untertanenverband zur Bürgergenossenschaft* (Nomos 2003) 97ff.

[13] R Gneist, *Der Rechtsstaat und die Verwaltungsgerichte in Deutschland* (Springer 1872, 2nd edn 1879, reprint 1958).

and it argues in favour of a typical German solution from these experiences, opposing—in a nationalist tone—French ideas of administrative jurisdiction.[14]

On the one hand, the Prussian State needed State functionaries at the local level, with authority on matters of State administration, especially the police. To this end, the second tier of local government, the *Kreise*, were administrated by a *Landrat*, a civil servant working for the State administration, and the chief of police in the towns was nominated by the State authorities.

On the other hand, Gneist insisted on an honorary element of the local administration. He therefore proposed the contribution of State-nominated citizens, with the participation of local representatives. They would decide on important matters such as commissioning (*Kreisausschuss*), in conjunction with the *Landrat*. This would occur when administrative acts were challenged, like an administrative tribunal, and in similar ways for important and formalised procedures for deciding some specific matters (*Beschlussverfahren*). Administration and (administrative) jurisdiction were connected, but in legal cases, the *Landrat* acted independently of any directives from his superiors, and the honorary members of the commission were, by definition, independent too. With these guarantees, according to Gneist, the independence of the commission as an administrative tribunal respected the principles of the rule of law. It was possible to appeal against the decisions of these administrative tribunals before similar administrative tribunals of appeal (*Bezirksausschuss*), established at government district level (*Regierungsbezirke*), with honorary members operating alongside the State's functionary. The Prussian Superior Administrative Court (*Preußisches Oberverwaltungsgericht*) in Berlin headed this organisation from 1875.[15]

This was the model for the bill presented to the Prussian Parliament, first in 1869, and, following very controversial debates, enacted with a law of 13.12.1872.[16] It was completed by the law on the Superior Administrative Court (*Preußisches Oberverwaltungsgericht*, 1875) and other laws on administrative organisation. Lastly, a law on the administration of the State of 30.7.1883[17] (*Landesverwaltungsgesetz*) codified and harmonised the subject matter. It had enormous influence on the development of the Prussian administrative law and remained, albeit often amended, in force until the Second World War, and some parts remained in form up to the 1970s.

The legislation was originally a very controversial compromise.[18] The Prussian nobility, represented in the First Chamber, opposed, and then accepted the new

[14] ibid ch VII, 158ff: '*Die Negation des Rechtsstaats in dem Staatswesen Frankreichs*' ('The negation of the rule of law in the French State').

[15] The parallel with Austria, where the Administrative Court was also founded in 1875, as mentioned previously, is worthy of note.

[16] *Preußische Gesetzessammlung* (PrGS) 661.

[17] ibid 195.

[18] For details, see Huber (n 12) 352ff.

regulation only after pressure was applied. On the other hand, for the defenders of local self-government, the influence of the State on the local bodies was too strong; Gneist's concept of self-government protected a social group, but not the local corporate entities, in line with the ideas of Hugo Preuß,[19] and placing a State functionary locally, which the government deemed necessary to protect the general interest, appeared unsatisfactory. Furthermore, the independence of the administrative jurisdiction seemed weak, although the jurisprudence of the Prussian Administrative Court was very important for the development of German administrative law.

Precisely for these reasons, however, the influence of the law was strong.[20] It contained, above all, regulations for the authorities of the administrative jurisdiction, as well as the administrative process and the conditions for appeal to the courts, in addition to the formalised decisions of the commissions. Elements of administrative procedural regulation therefore existed. An additional law on administrative procedure seemed less urgent, and its introduction would have raised all the associated problems in the conflict between the powers of the central State and the *Länder* once again. Consequently, in the Weimar Republic, only administrative jurisdictions for the central State and the *Länder* were protected by the Constitution,[21] but without concretising the details, the more comprehensive laws on administrative procedure remained limited in *Länder* outside Prussia.

During the Second World War, administrative jurisdiction was practically eliminated, and after German defeat and division into zones of occupation, Prussia was dissolved by Law No 46 of the Allied Control Council of 25-2-1947. The reconstruction of the rule of law required new reflections, and after the totalitarian experience, the protection of fundamental rights by the judicial power, now including administrative jurisdiction whose independence would be more strongly protected, was a priority. So, the characteristic elements of the *Rechtsstaat* were seen from a new perspective. The choice was to reject a form of administrative procedure related to an administrative process along the lines of the Austrian AVG and, albeit in another context, the Prussian *Landesverwaltungsgesetz*, opting for judicial control of administrative action. This line, set out in the *Grundgesetz* (arts 19(4), 92, 95) was followed by the institutionalisation of a new administrative jurisdiction, culminating in the Federal Administrative Court (since 1953), and then a law on administrative justice (*Verwaltungsgerichtsordnung*, 1960), with its impact on administrative procedure. Debate on a separate law on administrative procedure

[19] For the opposed concepts, see Schefold (n 12) 97ff.

[20] Emanuel Schädler's analysis of the Liechtenstein law in the volume raises the question of Prussian influence (see Chapter 5).

[21] Article 107, see Anschütz (n 10) note 1 to art 107, defending special administrative tribunals, while there was a large tendency in favour of the power of ordinary courts. See D Schefold, 'Ungelöste Probleme der Verwaltungsreform und der Verwaltungsgerichtsbarkeit in Preußen' in D Lehnert (ed), *Hugo Preuß 1860–1925* (Bohlau 2011) 213, 223ff.

appeared secondary, with the above-mentioned complication of the shared legislative power between central State and *Länder* in this field. Nevertheless, it is worthy of note that the first law on administrative procedure in a German *Land* after 1945, in Schleswig-Holstein, was influenced by its Prussian tradition and was enacted as the *Landesverwaltungsgesetz* in 1967[22]—tellingly bearing the same title as the Prussian law of 1883.

The question arose whether, in the light of judicial protection, legal regulation of administrative procedure would follow, or, in accordance with the separation of powers, defence of the public interest would require action not regulated in detail by law. This was the topic of debate of 1958, well described by Ino Augsberg, between German constitutionalists supporting the conceptions of Karl August Bettermann, defending the free action of administration, controlled by the judiciary on the one hand, and that of Erwin Melichar, defending the Austrian solution on the other hand.[23] As we can observe, the latter, supported by the Hochschule Speyer under the influence of Carl Hermann Ule, finally prevailed. But its long history and controversy help to understand why, in Germany, the final administrative procedure laws at Federation and *Länder* levels were enacted only in 1976.

[22] *Landesverwaltungsgesetz* of 18.4.1967, *Gesetz- und Verordnungsblatt* 131.

[23] KA Bettermann, 'Das Verwaltungsverfahren' in *Veröffentlichungen der Vereinigung der Deutschen Staatsrechtslehrer*, vol 17 (de Gruyter 1959) 118ff, and E Melichar 'Das Verwaltungsverfahren' in *Veröffentlichungen der Vereinigung der Deutschen Staatsrechtslehrer*, vol 17 (de Gruyter 1959) 183ff.

18
The Austrian Legacy

Giacinto della Cananea, Angela Ferrari Zumbini and Otto Pfersmann

I. Presentation of the Research Findings

This concluding chapter contains some observations on the results obtained in the course of our comparative research, which seeks to ascertain whether, in a relatively wide area of public law,[1] namely administrative procedure,[2] a multinational 'common core' exists, also noting the many differences. Naturally, the coherence between the initial research choices and the results, and also their intrinsic relevance, is for the reader to assess. Accordingly, only a few general remarks will be made here.

The first concerns the 'agonizing question often prompted by social science research';[3] that is, whether the research did not merely demonstrate the obvious because there are new elements, including new methodology or the observation of phenomena or aspects hitherto relatively unknown, thus leading to the advancement of knowledge.[4] Leaving aside the methodology, discussed in the introduction,[5] the new findings regard the reasons why the Austrian administrative procedure legislation was adopted and its diffusion into other legal systems.

The second general remark concerns the significance of the findings of this research. It was observed in the introduction that the term 'influence' is inadequate to make sense of the interaction between legal systems. Hence the conjecture that the concept of 'diffusion' may be more appropriate for identifying and formulating elements of similarity and dissimilarity.[6] The findings of the research confirm that Austrian administrative procedural legislation was important in itself thanks to its innovative and systematic character. They show that such legislation was also of fundamental importance for a group of legal systems that may conventionally

[1] RB Schlesinger, 'Introduction' in RB Schlesinger (ed), *Formation of Contracts: A Study of the Common Core of Legal Systems* (Oceana 1968) 2 (pointing out the 'too narrow topic' often chosen by previous comparative research).

[2] The reasons have been illustrated elsewhere: G della Cananea and M Bussani, 'The Common Core of European Administrative Laws: A Framework for Analysis' (2019) 26 Maastricht J Eur & Comp L 217.

[3] Schlesinger (n 1) 41.

[4] For further remarks on the goals of the research in terms of the advancement of knowledge as opposed to the definition of a body of precepts, see della Cananea and Bussani (n 2) 221.

[5] See Chapter 1, Section IV.

[6] ibid Section III.

Giacinto della Cananea, Angela Ferrari Zumbini, and Otto Pfersmann, *The Austrian Legacy* In: *The Austrian Codification of Administrative Procedure*. Edited by: Giacinto Della Cananea, Angela Ferrari Zumbini, and Otto Pfersmann,
Oxford University Press.
DOI: 10.1093/oso/9780198867623.003.0018

be designated *Mitteleuropea*. What emerges is not just that there was—in roughly quantitative terms—a vast area of agreement around certain general principles of administrative procedure among them, but that qualitatively the area of agreement was even more remarkable than had hitherto been thought. The reasons for this diffusion will be examined, but there will also be a discussion of the institutional and cultural factors hindering this propagation within other legal systems.

Lastly, these findings have interesting implications for our research on the common core of European administrative laws. In this respect, while they help belie our initial conjecture about the emergence of a common core, they bear out previous expectations only in part. It emerges that the connection between the regulation of administrative procedure and liberal democracies is less uniform than is generally believed.

II. The Originality of the Findings

Both the first wave of studies, between the 1920s and the 1930s, concerning Austrian legislation on administrative procedure, and the second wave in the 1950s and the 1960s, highlighted the innovative features of the Austrian legislation, noting its complete and systematic regulation of administrative procedure and its significance for some neighbouring legal systems.[7] Our findings confirm these results from previous studies. At the same time, some innovative elements emerge; first, the factors determining legislative change were more complex than had been thought; second, the spread of Austrian ideas and institutions in *Mitteleuropa* was even more rapid and significant than had been understood; third, the legislation on administrative procedure was kept in place notwithstanding huge political and constitutional change.

A. The Levers of Change: Reconsidering Legislative Intent

It was already well known that Austrian administrative procedure legislation was preceded and prepared for by the judicial elaboration of general principles, along with their systematisation by academics such as Friedrich Tezner, and

[7] See S Urbanowicz, 'New Law of Administrative Procedure' (1928–29) 1 Rev Polish L & Econ 150, 152 (affirming that 'the first source on which the authors of the proposal could base themselves was the Austrian law'). See also G Langrod, 'La codification de la procédure administrative non contentieuse en Pologne' (1960) 13 R Adm 533, 534 (for the remark that Poland and other nations regulated their procedure 'à l'instar du modèle autrichien'); G Pastori, 'Austria' in G Pastori (ed), *La procedura amministrativa* (Neri Pozza 1964) 99 (same remark); G Isaac, *La procedure administrative non contentieuse* (LGDJ 1968) 109 (same remark); F Becker, *Das allgemeine Verwaltungsverfahren in Theorie und Gestez. Eine rechtsvergleichende Untersuchung* (Kohlhammer Verlag 1960) (which included Czechoslovakia, Hungary, Poland, and Yugoslavia in the same group of legal systems).

that it was characterised by a high technical level and thorough systematicity. What was not known is that the factors or levers of change were not only domestic or national.

The standard account is that between the judicial definition of procedural requirements and primary legislation, there was not only a fundamental continuity but also a sort of natural progression. There are two aspects to consider. One is that between 1875 and 1925 the Austrian Administrative Court defined and refined a range of procedural requirements, including the right to be heard, the duty to give reasons, and the right to have access to certain documents held by public authorities. The other aspect concerns legislative intent. The legislator, so the argument goes, turned to the question of whether legislation should be required in the framework of institutional reforms, at the heart of which lay the new Constitution, which was heavily influenced by the ideas of Hans Kelsen. In other words, the legislative intent was to generalise and thus reinforce the procedural requirements drawn up by the Administrative Court. In this argument, there is much that is significant about the institutional and intellectual foundations of Austrian administrative procedure legislation: first, the idea that parliamentary intervention was coherent with the principles previously elaborated by the Court; second, that its intervention was to a certain extent necessary because procedural requirements lacked generality; third, the influence played by a prestigious school of thought, that of Kelsen and Merkl. Their influence was particularly noticeable in requiring 'the entire public administration shall be based on the law'.[8]

However, the argument from legislative intent should be viewed with caution for two related but distinct reasons. A concealed premise underlying the argument is that, in a democracy, the parliamentary process operates in such a way that Parliament is either the direct initiator or the controller of all that emerges formally as primary legislation. But comparative legal analysis has shown that the reality is different as most of what becomes legislation comes from the bills introduced by the executive. It is, however, amended as it goes through the parliamentary stages. Moreover, the argument from legislative intent is weakened in a more specific manner. It is predicated upon the assumption that Parliament simply did what it wished to do. For some, it did so principally intending to simplify administrative action, which might have contained public expenditure.[9] This assumption does not, however, fully accord with the facts. What the facts tell us is that the inclusion of administrative procedure legislation within the necessary reforms was

[8] Article 18(1) of the Austrian Constitution (in the original text: 'die gesamte staatliche Verwaltung darf nur auf Grund der Gesetze ausgeubt erlassen'). On Kelsen's conception of democracy, see his essay 'Foundations of Democracy' (1955) 66 Ethics 1 (where he criticised the Soviet theory of democracy). On the importance of Merkl's ideas, see H Schambeck, 'The Development of Austrian Administrative Law' (1962) 28 IRAS 215, 226 and, from a theoretical viewpoint, SL Paulson, 'How Merkl's Stufenbaulehre Informs Kelsen's Concept of Law' (2013) 21 Revus 29.

[9] Pastori (n 7) 97.

also influenced by external pressure. It was one of the conditions for delivering the loan requested by Austria.[10]

This is a healthy caveat against the belief that there is a necessary correlation between judge-made law and legislation, in that the latter codifies the former. As observed in the next section, such a belief does not withstand scrutiny. Moreover, to the extent that Austrian administrative procedure legislation was influenced by external pressure, this indicates that we should be ready to consider a broader range of factors. This is not to detract from the importance of policy processes within representative institutions but to observe, first, that some qualifications are necessary and, second, that the influence played by external factors is not entirely new. This may help us, for instance, to consider more cautiously the wave of studies, especially with regard to the European Union, that takes it for granted that before 1950 States enjoyed full sovereignty and that representative institutions exercised it. This may have been true of only the two or three States that retained a dominant position worldwide, not all.

There is a further difficulty with the argument from legislative intent. It concerns the legislators of the other legal systems, which adopted general legislation on administrative procedure between 1921 and 1930. In contrast with the assumption that public law is structured around rules that differ to some extent from one nation to another, so that each one bears a distinctive imprint, there is evidence that this was not so for at least some legal systems. This circumstance deserves separate treatment in the following section.

B. The Rapid Diffusion of Austrian Ideas and Institutions

The second noteworthy aspect emerging from our analysis is the rapid diffusion of Austrian ideas and institutions.

Their 'diffusion' was very rapid. Lichtenstein adopted Austria's innovative administrative procedure legislation even before the Austrian Parliament passed it. Schädler's analysis[11] acknowledges that the legal precepts enacted by Lichtenstein bore more than a mere similarity with those included in the draft legislation submitted to the Austrian Parliament. Moreover, the findings point to a pattern of diffusion that diverges from Walter Gellhorn's observation that 'new societies ... are unlikely to be instantly attentive to the niceties of administrative procedure'.[12] This remark reflected practical necessities, meaning that when many decisions need to be taken in a short time, policymakers are particularly concerned about what they perceive as bureaucratic formalism. But the new democracies immediately

[10] This is highlighted in Chapters 14–15 in this volume.
[11] See ibid Chapter 5.
[12] W Gellhorn, 'Protecting Citizens against Administrators in Poland' (1965) 65 Colum L Rev 1133.

took up Austrian principles and rules. Czechoslovakia and Poland did so in 1928, followed by Yugoslavia two years later, in 1930. A spatial and temporal cluster thus emerged,[13] which implied that the Austrian ideas and institutions applied to various nations previously part of the Habsburg Empire, though not to all (Hungary, for example).

Conversely, they applied not only to those parts of Yugoslavia that had been absorbed by the empire but also, paradoxically, to Bosnia, whose independence had been at the heart of the Great War. In contrast with Gellhorn's assumption, it could be argued that it is precisely when new institutions are being set up that policymakers are particularly keen to learn from more advanced legal systems. Piątek adds in his chapter that Poland needed to adopt uniform legislation for territories that had been subject to Austrian, German, and Russian rule before the Great War, and the choice fell on Austrian legislation.[14]

Interestingly, all national reports show that while Lichtenstein, Czechoslovakia, Poland, and Yugoslavia made no formal *renvoi* to Austrian administrative procedure legislation, it was not a mere source of inspiration for all those legal systems but was actually regarded as a model. There were, of course, some adaptations to the national contexts, as often happens in these cases. But the basic fact—legally and politically significant—is that within a decade, the Austrian legislation was regarded as a model and amply imitated by a group of countries. Accordingly, even though national rulers made their own decisions without any form of cooperation, let alone coercion, a sort of interdependence emerged as a consequence of their choices.[15] The implications of this first wave of administrative procedure legislation movement are extremely important and deserve separate treatment in the next section.

C. The Durability of Administrative Procedure Legislation

There is yet another aspect worthy of note that emerges from the national reports. It concerns the durability of the procedural requirements established during that decade. In Austria, leaving aside the *Anschluss* period (1937–45), the administrative procedure legislation has remained substantially unchanged for almost a century. Only some modifications were adopted in 1991.

But what is perhaps more striking is the survival of these procedural frameworks despite the regime changes in Czechoslovakia, Poland, and Yugoslavia in the years that followed the end of the Second World War. We use the term 'regime

[13] See Z Elkins and B Simmons, 'On Wavers, Clusters, and Diffusion: A Conceptual Framework' (2005) 35 Annals Am Acad Pol & Soc Sci 33.

[14] See Chapter 7 in this volume.

[15] See Elkins and Simmons (n 13) 35.

change' descriptively to briefly describe the adoption of 'Socialist' constitutions, replacing the previous 'bourgeois' constitutions within the countries that came under the control of the USSR and only regained full independence after 1989.[16] The point of overall interest is that the general legislation on administrative procedure adopted through national patterns in the 1920s diverged in some respects. The administrative procedure legislation adopted in the 1920s was maintained in Czechoslovakia, although its interpretation gradually changed to accommodate new Socialist values. Although the new rulers formally abolished such legislation in Yugoslavia, judges and lawyers continued to regard it as a frame of reference for solving issues that arose between citizens and the public authorities. In Poland, the legislation enacted in 1928 was replaced by a new one in 1960; this was more consistent with Socialist values, though some procedural safeguards remained.

A first explanation is that administrative procedure legislation was viewed as part of the accepted order of things, so it became socially undesirable to abrogate it, even after an important change in the form of government. Another one is that the correlation between democracy and administrative procedure legislation, which is often taken for granted, must be reconsidered, in the light of the experience of those countries of Mitteleuropa. There are two more case to be considered from this angle: Hungary and Spain.

D. A Correlation between Administrative Procedure and Democracy?

As observed earlier, Hungary is one of Austria's neighbours which did not adopt a legislative framework for administrative procedure soon after 1925. The reasons the Hungarian rulers decided to do so after the Soviet invasion of 1956 are complex.[17] But some things are clear, at least: first, they could not look to the legal system of the USSR, where no such legislation existed[18] (nor, incidentally, does it exist today in the Russian Federation); second, they could refer to the laws of the other Socialist countries, which were variably influenced by the Austrian legislation; third, the provisions of the Act were general but were not meant to be comprehensive; fourthly, all individuals were given the opportunity to participate in the procedures affecting them, though, as one commentator later observed, the Act could not be suitable adapted to the perceived necessities of the *Rechtsstaat*.[19] This

[16] See H Kupper, 'Evolution and Gestalt of the Hungarian State' in S Cassese, A von Bogdandy and P Huber (eds), *The Max Planck Handbook in European Public Law: vol. I The Administrative State* (OUP 2017) 310 (discussing administrative law under Socialism).

[17] See Chapter 9 in this volume.

[18] See W Gellhorn, 'Review of Administrative Acts in the Soviet Union' (1966) 66 Colum L Rev 1051, 1054 (noting that a draft code was prepared on the eve of the Second World War, but was put aside).

[19] Kupper (n 16) 325.

confirms that the administration and administrative law of Communist countries was an area in which considerable variation existed.[20]

In the same years, a new law on administrative procedure was adopted in Spain. The Act, adopted when Spain was under Franco's authoritarian regime, replaced that of 1889, known as the '*Azcarate* Act', which had been adopted under a liberal regime.[21] Nevertheless, the focus in 1958 was the need to improve administrative procedures and aspects of judicial review (legislation was adopted for the latter in the same period). Interestingly, although some of its accomplishments included the essential principles of fair administrative procedure, including the individual's right to be heard and assurance of publicity for rules affecting the public, the Act guaranteed a degree of flexibility in administrative proceedings. Accordingly, not all procedural infringements implied the annullability of individual acts and measures.

On the most general level, the correlation between liberal democracy and administrative procedure legislation is more complex than it may appear. Legislation of this kind was adopted by liberal democracies, such as Austria in 1925 and the USA in 1946. But it was kept or adopted by political regimes that differed from liberal democracies in various ways. A first tentative explanation for this takes inspiration from the retrospective analysis elaborated by a French specialist of administrative law, Jean-Marie Auby, with regard to the *détournement de pouvoir* ('misuse of power') and the other techniques for reviewing the acts of the executive, which were defined and refined by the Conseil d'Etat between 1850 and 1870. Auby observed that it might be 'surprising' that such techniques saw the light 'under a political regime stamped with authoritarianism',[22] and the answer he gave was not limited to the French leader of that era, Napoléon III. He argued that 'imperial leaders ... conscious of the popular reactions that the reduction of political liberties might lead to... wished, as a counterpoise, to accord citizens the satisfaction of having a government respectful of law and free of arbitrariness', a sort of 'safety valve' policy.[23] In other words, procedural requirements could be viewed as a compensation for the loss of political freedom. Auby added another plausible reason, more internal to the administrative and political system, namely that the statement of general rules—in the French case, in the jurisprudence of the Conseil d'Etat—served to centralise the control of government officers, especially at local level. These are differing explanations, and the latter may be associated with

[20] For this remark, see S Lubman, 'Book Review of Z. Szirmai, Law in Eastern Europe' (1964) 64 Colum L Rev 1364, 1366.

[21] See Chapter 11, Section II in this volume, where the author explains that the APA of 1889 was the precursor of that of 1958. Whether 'authoritarian' regimes are to be distinguished from totalitarian ones is an interesting question, that requires separate treatment: they are regarded in the same terms by K Kovacs, 'Avoiding Authoritarianism in the Administrative Procedure Act' (2020) 28 Geo Mason L Rev 573.

[22] JM Auby, 'Abuse of Power in French Administrative Law' (1970) 18 AJCL 549, 551.

[23] ibid.

a broad conception of the rule of law, while the former is only compatible with a narrow one. Nevertheless, both can be helpful for a better understanding of the various functions that can be performed by administrative procedure. Although it is normally associated with efficiency and procedural fairness,[24] administrative procedure can be, and often is, used as an instrument of political control.[25] In a similar vein, Martin Shapiro argued that, though appeals are viewed either from the perspective of due process or from that of ensuring uniformity, they can, and often do, serve to impose centralisation.[26]

III. The Significance of the Findings from the Perspective of the 'Common Core'

The discussion in this section is more wide-ranging and has distinct objectives. First, when a legislative framework, such as a constitution or a code, is regarded as a model and thus adopted, copied, or imitated by other countries, as happened with the French and German Civil Codes in a number of countries, the question that arises is whether they do so because of its intrinsic quality or for other reasons. Second, while it is evident from the preceding argument that the Austrian administrative procedure legislation has been taken as a model, the nature of the relationships between the various legal systems requires closer examination, given the concept of 'diffusion' discussed in the introduction. Last but not least, our analysis also has another purpose: to explain why other neighbours, including Germany and Italy, did not make a similar choice.

A. Distinctive Traits of the Austrian Legislation

In comparative studies, there is sometimes an inclination to emphasise which legal system adopted a specific solution for the first time, be it a general principle, a set of rules, or a legal institution. This is understandable but is of relative importance, because it is now always the case that the first is also the best. That having been said, it is fair to say that the Austrian administrative procedure legislation was not the first, as it was preceded by the *ley Azcarate* adopted in Spain in 1889. However, unlike its Spanish antecedent, it was effective because there was no need

[24] See P Craig, 'Procedures and Administrative Decision making: A Common Law Perspective' (1993) 1 ERPL 56.
[25] For this line of reasoning, see MD McCubbins, RG Noll and BR Weingast, 'Administrative Procedures as Instruments of Political Control' (1987) 3 J L Econ & Org 243 (1987) (from a principal–agent perspective).
[26] M Shapiro, 'Appeal' (1980) 14 L & Soc Rev 629. See also PH Solomon Jr, 'Review: Courts and Judges in Authoritarian Regimes' (2007) 60 World Politics 122, 135 (noting the use of administrative courts to provide a fire-alarm model of oversight within authoritarian states).

for governmental secondary legislation. It was an innovative and systematic legislative framework, two decades before the US Administrative Procedure Act (APA) 1946 and 50 years before the German one (1976). It was regarded as a model by other nations, and there is more than one reason why this was so. First, it reflected the general principles defined and refined by the *jurisprudence constante* of the Administrative Court,[27] which was one of the most important specialist courts in Europe and set out these principles in a clear and helpful manner. Second, the principles formed a coherent whole. Third, it defined a sort of archetype for all administrative procedure.

As the features of Austrian legislation have been treated extensively by other contributions in this volume,[28] suffice it to briefly mention some of the principles defined by the legislator, particularly in the general law on administrative procedure. One such principle was the prohibition of bias or impartiality. Interestingly, these legislative provisions dealt with both family and political ties and contained a default rule concerning the 'other important reasons that are likely to cast doubt on their impartiality' (s 7). Needless to say, this was a problem widely felt at the time, given the growing influence exerted by mass parties, as distinct from the political patronage of the relatively small political organisations of the liberal period. The second principle was the individual's right to be heard before a public authority could take a decision that might adversely affect his or her interests. While this principle was shared, at least since the belle époque, by other legal systems, in the Austrian legislation it was not only clearly stated, but there was also one important distinctive trait; that is, participants' submissions could also be oral (s 13), in which case they could 'be recorded in transcripts so as to convey their essential content' (s 14) and, therefore, be kept. The generalised solution was more advanced than those of other legal systems at that time and is still so with respect to more recent legislative frameworks, where there is only an exchange of documents between citizens and public authorities. Third, the files kept by the competent administration were open to access by the party concerned ('inspection', in the terminology of s 17) many years before the 'government in the sunshine' laws of other Western countries. Fourth, the content and form of the administrative decision were regulated in detail. To borrow Martin Shapiro's subtle distinction,[29] there was not just a giving-reasons requirement in its simplest or purely procedural version; that is, an obligation to furnish some reason of any kind for the choice made by a public authority exercising its discretionary power. There was, instead, a requirement to provide reasons 'if the position of the party [was] not fully taken into account or if

27 See Chapter 3 in this volume; A Ferrari Zumbini, 'Standards of Judicial Review of Administrative Action in the Austro-Hungarian Empire' in G della Cananea and S Mannoni (eds), *Administrative Justice* Fin de siècle: *Early Judicial Standards of Administrative Conduct in Europe (1890–1910)* (OUP 2021) 45.

28 See Chapter 4 in this volume.

29 M Shapiro, 'The Giving Reasons Requirement' (1992) Un Chicago Legal Forum 175, 186.

objections or applications of the participants [were] rejected' (s 58). There was thus a sort of dialogue requirement, in the sense that the public authority was obliged not only to justify its choices but also to do so in the light of the arguments and evidence adduced by the individual. From a comparative perspective, it is interesting to add that the Austrian legislation neither imposed a procedure for rulemaking nor set out general standards governing it. In this respect, it differed from the US APA (1946), which prescribed notice and comment requirements.

Considered as a whole, these provisions were based on the idea that administration, in the operational sense, should not differ substantially from the judicial function. This is evident at the level of general principles, such as neutrality and independence, and in the language of legislation, for example, when it uses the term 'parties', which is typical of judicial proceedings. Moreover, it is evident in the recognition and protection of the right to be heard, as a protection from any Kafkaesque and dehumanising series of events that would give the individual no possibility of interaction with those who wield public authority.[30]

Two brief remarks are appropriate at this stage. First, these and other requirements were unlikely to solve all the problems that beset the discharge of administrative functions and power, nor do they assure the substantive justice of the final outcome. However, they can help to prevent the use of discretionary power in an arbitrary way. On the other hand, the same may be true of a judicial trial. Second, that each case must be adjudicated by an independent umpire is clearly appealing, but it should not be forgotten that a governmental agency also has the task of implementing policies. From the comparative perspective, this is important to understand the significance of the American norms on rulemaking.

B. The Diffusion of the Austrian Model

The opening chapter of this book cast doubts on the adequacy of the concept of 'influence' and suggested that another one, 'diffusion' could be used as a working hypothesis.[31] In this respect, the research findings show four or five points of general interest. The first is that there was indeed a diffusion of Austrian ideas and institutions, but it was uneven. It was more robust in some nations that adopted some kind of administrative procedure legislation, namely Lichtenstein, Czechoslovakia, Poland, and Yugoslavia.[32] It was much weaker in other neighbours, such as Italy,

[30] Franz Kafka's *Der Process* was written between 1914 and 1915, but was published posthumously, in 1925. The divergence between the Austrian and the Spanish administrative procedure legislation is described by Barnes (see Chapter 11, Section I.E.

[31] See Chapter 1 in this volume.

[32] See ibid Chapters 6–8. These findings are confirmed by other recent studies, including B Bugaric, 'Post-Communist Slovenia: Between European Ideals and East European Realities' (2016) 22 Eur Pub L 25 (affirming that the Yugoslav APA 'was categorically modelled upon' the Austrian APA) and J Stasa and M Tomasek, 'Codification of Administrative Procedure' (2012) 2 TLQ 59 (affirming that the Czech Republic's regulation of administrative procedure 'stems directly' from the Austrian tradition).

where no general legislation was adopted, although the Austrian codification generated interest among public lawyers. It was practically absent in legal systems, such as those of Germany and France. There is thus a mixture of commonality and diversity that makes legal comparison interesting. The following remarks focus on commonality, while diversity will be discussed further in (Section D).

The second point of general interest is that our case involves a plurality of legal systems, unlike many other cases where there is a bilateral relationship between a donor country and a recipient one. A group of legal systems responded to like conditions in a similar way, adopting basically similar principles and institutions. Nevertheless, they did so asymmetrically as the principles and institutions elaborated in Austria were taken as a model by the other legal systems, with a view to modernising their administrative institutions. Finally, they did so without any sort of formal coordination.

The third point of general interest concerns the pathways of reform. Clearly, in this case, diffusion was not coerced. It was thus very different from the colonial context[33] and what occurred after the Second World War when Germany and Japan adopted new constitutions.[34] The pathways to reform were also less indirect than we saw in our previous enquiry into the judicial elaboration of general principles of administrative law from 1890 to 1910. For example, the English model of judicial review of administration was considered by both German and Italian liberals, also with an eye on the Belgian institutions. Conversely, in this case, there was a direct one-way transfer from Austria to its neighbours.[35] However, 'transposition' of Austrian law did not occur. Instead, its ideas and principles were developed within the other legal systems. This probably explains the success of the attempts to innovate domestic legislation and its durability.[36]

The fourth point of general interest concerns the instruments used by reformers. Everywhere, formal instruments have been used to adopt administrative procedure legislation. The predominant choice in both Poland and Yugoslavia, similarly to

[33] On colonial institutions, see RB Seidman, 'Administrative Law and Legitimacy in Anglophonic Africa: A Problem in the Reception of Foreign Law' (1970) 5 L & Soc Rev 161 (1970); RJ Daniels, MJ Trebilcock and LD Carson, 'The Legacy of Empire: the Common Law Inheritance and Commitment to Legality in Former British Colonies' (2011) 59 AJCL 111 (referring to path dependency theories).

[34] For further analysis, see CJ Friedrich, 'Rebuilding the German Constitution' (1949) 18 Am Pol Sc Rev 461, 462 (1949) (arguing that the basic law was 'resultant of constitutional ideas partly German, partly French, partly English, and partly American'); HS Quigley, 'Revising the Japanese Constitution' (1959) 38 Foreign Aff 140 (for a very critical assessment of the 'foreign imposition not wholly suited to a people of very different legal and social tradition', such as that of Japan). But see also J Williams, 'Making the Japanese Constitution: A Further Look' (1965) 59 Am Pol Sc Rev 665 (1965) (for whom more recent studies have brought additional information showing that the Japanese side supported innovations).

[35] This expression is borrowed from W Twining, 'Social Science and the Diffusion of Law' (2005) 32 J of Law & Soc 205.

[36] For further analysis on this point, see D Berkowitz, K Pistor and JF Richard, 'The Transplant Effect' (2003) 51 AJCL 163, 167 (suggesting that 'countries that have developed their formal legal order internally have a comparative advantage in developing effective legal institutions over countries on which' such institutions were imposed externally).

Lichtenstein, was to act by way of parliamentary legislation, while Czechoslovakia proceeded by way of executive regulation. But there was always a formal adoption of the framework governing administrative procedure. However, the success of the Austrian model largely depended on the fact that it was not perceived as foreign law,[37] despite the dissolution of the Habsburg Empire. It was supported by jurists and judges who had worked within the Habsburg institutions and shared the same culture, legally and linguistically.[38] Legally, the primary justification for the requirements of procedure was the ideal of *Rechtsstaat* and its corollary; that uncertainty about the procedure to be followed and disregard for the pre-established order make errors more likely, the outcome of administrative action less (or not at all) predictable and, last but not least, can undermine public confidence in the fairness and propriety of the decision-making process. Linguistically, German was the lingua franca for all those lawyers and judges. The process by which ideas and legal institutions spread beyond Austria through this group of nations was thus qualified by the existence of *vicinitas* and *affinitas* (vicinity or proximity and affinity) to borrow the concepts used by Gino Gorla,[39] reinforcing those ties. As a specialist of the Habsburg Empire, Robert Evans, observed at the end of his book on the making of the commonwealth that what had once been united could not be entirely dissolved.[40] Hence Stefano Mannoni's remark that this commonwealth was a laboratory for multinational coexistence and should, therefore, be reconsidered not only because of the authoritarian and Communist regimes that replaced it.[41]

C. A Vast Area of Agreement between Legal Systems

While the major administrative systems of that time had very few general legislative provisions governing administrative procedure, Austria opted for a complete and systematic body of legislation and was followed in this by other legal systems. In the group of legal systems which constituted *Mitteleuropa*, there was a vast and significant area of agreement around the conception of administrative procedure

[37] Piątek observes that the Austrian law on administrative procedure was translated and published in the Polish Official Journal (Chapter 7 in this volume). For further remarks on the uses of the laws of other polities, see RB Schlesinger, 'The Past and Future of Comparative Law' (1995) 43 AJCL 477, 479 (pointing out that when the dominant focus was on foreign law, those engaged in comparative law were 'compelled to emphasize differences rather than similarities').

[38] See Chapter 7 in this volume (observing that other Polish statutes, including the statute governing judicial review of administration, were influenced by the Austrian legislation).

[39] G Gorla, 'Il ricorso alla legge di un "luogo vicino" nell'ambito del diritto comune europeo' (1973) 96 Foro it 89.

[40] RJW Evans, *The Making of the Habsburg Monarchy 1550–1700: An Interpretation* (Clarendon Press 1979).

[41] See Chapter 14 in this volume. See also J Mathews, 'Minimally Democratic Administrative Law' (2016) 68 Adm L Rev 605 (discussing the role of the duty to give reasons and of judicial review within modern 'minimally democratic' regimes).

and certain general principles governing it. This diffusion from remarkable from the twin perspectives of space and time. A cluster thus emerged.[42] The relevance of this area of agreement can be appreciated both quantitively and qualitatively. In rough quantitative terms, there was a vast area of agreement around the enactment of a general legislative framework containing principles to be followed by public authorities, with the exception of Hungary, where the Act of 1957 did not define general principles. Qualitatively, that area of agreement between Austria and its neighbours was even more interesting than had been thought—from a twofold point of view. On the one hand, the concept of 'administrative procedure' was regarded as distinct from the innumerable forms of administrative proceeding provided for and governed either by sector specific rules or by practice and custom. On the other hand, it is possible to identify an area of agreement not just in terms of generic values and ideals such as justice and good governance, but in terms of principles and precise rules.

Of note is the power to collect factual evidence and assess it. The general approach of Austrian law was that public authorities had to find the relevant facts and give an assessment of factual findings resulting in a record of the procedure. In a strikingly similar manner, the other legal systems provided that: (1) a public authority had to conduct a thorough and exhaustive investigation of the facts;[43] (2) fact-finding had to be complete;[44] (3) administrative authorities were required to establish the facts relevant for the final decision, though interested parties were entitled to give their contribution;[45] (4) the 'investigation procedure establishes the facts, which are the ground for the conclusion of an administrative matter'.[46]

Another fundamental principle of Austrian legislation was the individual's right to be heard. This principle, too, was shared by the other legal systems that adopted general administrative procedure legislation. In Liechtenstein, not only were individuals entitled to make their case but each party had the right to 'express its views on all relevant facts and circumstances', including those 'brought forward by other parties' and experts.[47] The Czechoslovakian legislation, too, recognised the right to a hearing[48] The Polish legislation recognised the individual's right to be heard, in terms of a right to defence, which included the power to contest the evidence produced by the administration.[49] The Yugoslav APA did not simply recognise the right to a hearing, but went one step beyond, requiring parties to be 'duly heard'.[50]

[42] Elkins and Simmons (n 13) 35.
[43] Liechtenstein LVG, art 27: see Chapter 5 in this volume.
[44] Czechoslovakian APC, arts 48–65: see ibid Chapter 6.
[45] Polish CAP, art 44: see ibid Chapter 7.
[46] Yugoslav LGAP, art 70: see ibid Chapter 8.
[47] Liechtenstein LVG, art 64(3): see ibid Chapter 5.
[48] Czechoslovakian AC, art 45: see ibid Chapter 6.
[49] Polish CAP, art 47: see ibid Chapter 7.
[50] Yugoslav LGAP, art 76: see ibid Chapter 8.

Lastly, in Hungary, where the right to be heard was not recognised as such, it was protected by the rules concerning the collection and assessment of elements of fact.[51] Interestingly, if more than one person was involved in the same procedure, the official responsible could hear them at the same time, so that a sort of 'dialogue' could emerge. On a more general level, all these legislative provisions rested on the acknowledgement that the final decision could not be reached by the application of rules and had to give the individual some kind of hearing.

There was still another fundamental requirement; that is, the duty to give reasons. The Austrian solution was followed, once again, by other legal systems. In Lichtenstein, the administration was required 'to justify the decision taken in a convincing manner', though this applied directly to decisions adversely affecting the individual[52] The Czechoslovakian legislation established a general requirement to give reasons.[53] On the other hand, the Polish legislation established a more limited requirement to give reasons only for adverse decisions, and the public authority enjoyed greater discretionary powers with regard to the exceptions.[54] The Yugoslav norm partially differed from the Austrian one in that it required the decisionmaker to give a statement of reasons concerning the 'decisive' aspects and provided an exception if the party's request was fully met.[55] Conversely, when Hungarian administrative procedure legislation was adopted, it followed the Austrian model in that it required the administration to set out the relevant elements of both fact and law.[56] While all this confirms that there was an area of agreement in terms of principles and rules, it also shows that there were differing aspects within such agreement; these concerned the contents of the duty to give reasons, as well as the exceptions.

After comparing administrative procedure legislation, the next step, allowing an assessment of the relevance and significance of the area of agreement, is to consider whether sector-specific rules were consistent with the general principles examined thus far. That it is necessary to take both provisions into account may appear a truism, but it has seldom been considered in previous comparative studies. In our research, four issues were selected, the first of which concerns the internal functioning of public authorities, especially disciplinary measures against civil servants, while the others regard some important 'external' decisions, including authorisations and licences, expropriation, and urban planning. Nevertheless, these issues obviously do not give an exhaustive picture of the whole field of administrative procedure. For example, the picture does not include sanctions, which

[51] Hungarian Act, arts 17(2) and 22: see ibid Chapter 9.
[52] Liechtenstein LVG, art 83: see ibid Chapter 5.
[53] Czechoslovakian AC, art 45: see ibid Chapter 6.
[54] Polish CAP, art 48: see ibid Chapter 7.
[55] Yugoslav LGAP, art 109: see ibid Chapter 8.
[56] Hungarian Act, art 39: see ibid Chapter 9.

were regulated in Austria and elsewhere by particular provisions. However, they allow legal solutions for comparison of these issues.

To begin with, let us consider the dismissal of a civil servant, which provides a good test for understanding the extent to which the power of the State is limited and structured. Interestingly, in all the legal systems that formed part of the cluster, the State had discretionary power to dismiss its servants. However, this power had to be exercised within the strictures of administrative procedure. Moreover, the State had to respect the procedural requirements illustrated above, including the right to be heard and requirement to give reasons.[57] Let us consider now the opening of a pharmacy. Although freedom of trade was recognised by all these legal systems, it was subject to administrative authorisation, and the power to issue was clearly discretionary, sometimes including an assessment of technical expertise,[58] and sometimes 'good reputation and trustworthiness' too.[59] However, this authority had to be exercised in a regular administrative procedure, in the course of which the applicant had the right to an oral hearing[60] and then, in the event of an adverse decision, judicial remedies could be used in the courts. Together with the freedom of trade, the right to property was the other fundamental economic right protected by Western constitutions and civil codes. However, they allowed private property to be seized, only in the public interest and provided that compensation (sometime a 'fair' one) was paid, though there were some exceptions.[61] Inevitably, the rules concerning private property changed with the advent of 'Socialist' constitutions. Before that, there was nothing akin to any procedural protection equivalent to the 'due process clause' in the US Constitution. Some protection was provided by legislative rules. For example, if building a railway line required the expropriation of both land and houses owned by an individual, a particular procedure—sometimes a legislative one[62]—had to be followed in the course of which the person concerned could intervene and receive legal assistance.[63] Lastly, urban planning was an increasingly important manifestation of administrative power. We propose a hypothetical case concerning the building of a new school. Amid various differences concerning the nature of authority (again, after the advent of 'Socialist' constitutions) and its allocation, at least before 1945, a certain procedure had to be followed everywhere, in the course of which neighbours had to be informed;[64] and in some cases, appeals could be brought before higher administrative authorities.[65]

[57] See ibid Chapter 5, Section VI.B; Chapter 6, Section V.B; Chapter 7, Section VI.B; Chapter 8, Section VI.B.
[58] ibid Chapter 8, Section VI.A.
[59] ibid Chapter 5, Section VI.A.
[60] ibid; Chapter 6, Section VI.A; Chapter 8, Section VI.A.
[61] See Chapter 8, Section VI.C (concerning foreigners).
[62] Chapter 5, Section VI.C.
[63] ibid; Chapter 7, Section VI.C; Chapter 8, Section VI.C.
[64] Chapter 5, Section VI.D; Chapter 6, Section V.D; Chapter 7, Section VI.D; Chapter 8, Section VI.D.
[65] Chapter 7, Section VI.D.

D. The Significance of Negative Findings

Thus far, we have considered the positive results of our comparative research, that is, those that support the initial hypothesis and verify it. But these are not the only ones that matter from the scholarly point of view—for two reasons, one of a general nature and the other more specifically concerning our enquiry into the 'common core' of European administrative laws. The negative results, which do not support the hypothesis and in some sense disprove it, are also significant. They provide a better understanding of the topic because they limit and qualify the relevance and significance of the positive results. Moreover, on the basis of our research, there is a strong belief that both common and distinctive features between national legal systems are important and must, therefore, be considered and explained.

To begin with, not only the United Kingdom, where there has thus far been no comprehensive and systematic collection of legal rules concerning administrative procedure, but also the principal administrative systems of continental Europe in the first half of the twentieth century, those of France, Germany, and Italy provided an interesting contrast to the *Mitteleuropean* countries. They provide a contrast because they did not follow Austria in adopting administrative procedure legislation during our relevant time frame.[66] And the contrast is interesting because their private law was codified at that time. Moreover, they adopted general administrative procedure legislation at a later stage. The case of Spain is different because it did adopt administrative procedure legislation as early as 1889 and subsequently in 1958, but with the differing features illustrated by Barnes in this volume.

A first and somewhat obvious explanation is that the legal systems that looked at Austrian general administrative procedure legislation were 'new' and had previously been either partially or wholly included in the Habsburg Empire. Quite the contrary, both England and France, and to a lesser extent Germany and Italy, had stabilised their administrative systems, which, as is often the case, were risk-averse. Deviation from the status quo—essentially based on the judicial elaboration of general standards of administrative conduct—was, therefore, much more challenging. For example, in the 1950s, German scholars were still highlighting the effective judicial protection provided by the courts.[67]

A second and more specific explanation concerns both France and Italy. They had special administrative courts, which did not just adjudicate the disputes between citizens and the institutions entrusted with the discharge of public functions and powers but also had advisory functions vis-à-vis the executive branch. In short, those institutions were both adjudicators and lawmakers.[68] It is not

[66] See Chapter 10 in this volume (observing that the Austrian legislation 'could not play a formative role'); ibid Chapter 12; ibid Chapter 13.

[67] O Bachof, 'German Administrative Law with Special Reference to the Latest Developments in the System of Legal Protection' (1953) 2 ICLQ 368, 373.

[68] JP Gilli, Review of Isaac (n 7) 661; P Weil, 'The Strength and Weakness of French Administrative Law' (1965) 23 CLJ 242, 256.

surprising, therefore, that their members expressed scepticism about the necessity of administrative procedure legislation and concern about the risk of 'crystallising' the safeguards for the individual.[69]

Third, primary and judicial regulation are not the only potential means of defining general standards of administrative procedure. There is another one: executive regulation. The rationales supporting this mode varied from one legal system to another: between 1922 and 1943, Italy had a markedly authoritarian regime, while France was a democracy. However, especially under the Constitution of the Fifth Republic (1959), the French executive was vested with significant normative powers.[70] One brief but apposite example will serve as an illustration. Eighty years after the Austrian legislation, when the French Parliament decided that the time was ripe for adopting a legislative framework governing the relations between citizens and public authorities, it delegated the executive to adopt it. Another explanation concerning Germany is discussed by Schefold in this book.[71] He observes that under the Weimar Constitution, the federation (*Bund*) had limited legislative competence, which did not include the regulation of administrative matters.[72] Nor was there such a thing as a due process clause or one concerning the rule of law, which is now enshrined in the *Grundgesetz*. However, even after 1949, when such a clause existed, few steps were taken to lay down a general framework governing administrative procedures.

It would thus appear that there was broad disagreement between the legal systems compared. However, we should ask ourselves whether there is a risk of superficiality in confining legal comparison to the level of 'positive law'.[73] Well before the beginning of our comparative enquiry, it had been pointed out that the area of disagreement among the legal systems of Europe is considerably narrowed if one takes into consideration not only legislative provisions but also other sources, including the general principles defined and refined by the courts, government guidance to public authorities and administrative customs.[74] Even the supposed contrast between the United Kingdom and France was found, upon closer examination, to be much less significant than had been believed. In all those legal systems, the general principles including legality, due process of law, and publicity served to prevent misuse and abuse of power by public authorities.[75] It cannot be ruled out a

[69] M Letourner, 'Récension à G. Langrod, La doctrine allemande et la procedure administrative non contentieuse' (1962) 14 RIDC 222.

[70] French Constitution, art 37. For further remarks, see D Baranger, 'Executive Power in France' in P Craig and A Tomkins (eds), *The Executive and Public Law: Power and Accountability in Comparative Perspective* (OUP 2005) 157. See also G della Cananea, 'The Growth of the Italian Executive' ibid 243.

[71] See Chapter 17 in this volume.

[72] See the Weimar Constitution, arts 6–7, which included, for example, judicial procedure and expropriation.

[73] For this caveat, see Schlesinger (n 1) 42.

[74] JB Auby, 'Introduction' in JB Auby (ed), *Codification of Administrative Procedure* (Bruylant 2014) 27 (for a discussion about 'living without an APA'); P Craig, 'Perspectives on Process: Common Law, Statutory and Political' (2010) 55 PL 27.

[75] See della Cananea and Mannoni (n 27).

priori, therefore, that the law on administrative procedure that can be found in the countries that have opted for one type of general legislation or another may not be very different from the law that exists in the absence of such legislation.

The research findings show that although all the legal systems examined laid down the same well-known general principles of procedural fairness, in some instances those principles were implemented through different rules. The three procedural requirements considered previously are revealing. Let us first consider fact-finding within administrative procedure, which was of increasing practical relevance due to the increase in the regulatory role of public authorities. The rule followed by Austria and its neighbours was that administrative authorities had the power and the duty to collect information. But this rule was mitigated by the provision of 'oral hearings', which had to be held with the participation of all interested parties.[76] In France, Germany, and Italy, by contrast, there was no general duty to allow the interested parties to participate.

Second, the general rule established by the Austrian legislation corresponded to the *audi alteram partem* maxim, with two important specifications; that is, the general statement about the orality of the procedure (s 13) and the possibility of recording oral submissions (s 14). Similar provisions were adopted by the other legal systems that opted for general legislation on the Austrian model. Conversely, in other countries, the breadth of the *audi alteram partem* maxim was limited in a number of ways, and there was no general requirement of an oral hearing. In the United Kingdom, though the *audi alteram partem* maxim was recognised and enforced during the nineteenth century, the years between 1915 and 1960 saw the courts' increasing reluctance to exert an intense review on the respect of procedural requirements.[77] Things changed only, and partially, with the decision of the House of Lords in *Ridge v Baldwin*, which was generally regarded as a revival of the principles of natural justice.[78] In Germany, again in the early twentieth century, Otto Mayer asserted that there was no general duty to provide a hearing, thus contrasting with the established rule of law governing court proceedings.[79] In a similar vein, 50 years later, Otto Bachof observed that there were uniform rules for 'the procedure in administrative tribunals', but there were no general rules concerning administrative procedure, particularly with regard to the right to be heard.[80] He added that it was 'obvious' that in certain cases 'a hearing before the act would be impracticable'.[81] In Italy, additionally, the lack of an oral hearing still

[76] Austrian APA, s 40. On the rules of the other legal systems, see Section II.B above.
[77] W Wade, 'Recent Trends in the Administrative Process in England' (1960) 13 Admin L Rev 27, 29; P Craig, *Administrative Law* (5th edn, Sweet & Maxwell 2003), 411.
[78] W Wade, *Constitutional Fundamentals* (Stevens & Sons 1980) 63.
[79] O Mayer, *Préface de l'édition française* in *Le droit administratif allemand* (Giard & Brière 1905, French translation by the author).
[80] Bachof (n 67) 370, 372.
[81] ibid 373.

affects procedural protection of the individual's rights and interests except in few cases, such as disciplinary procedure within the civil service.

Third, an area of divergence can be found with regard to the giving reasons requirement. As observed earlier, the Austrian legislator did not content itself with laying down a general requirement to give reasons; it also established a sort of dialogue requirement, meaning that reasons had to be given if the position of a party was 'not fully taken into account' or its objections were rejected (s 58). In England, although the Franks Committee had recommended the giving of reasons in 1958, as far as tribunals were concerned, there was no general duty in English common law, though an obligation to furnish reasons was imposed by statutory provisions in particular cases.[82] In Germany, in the absence of any general duty to provide reasons, the administrative courts required that reasons be given for acts imposing duties on individuals.[83] Italian administrative tribunals gradually did so regarding all measures adversely affecting individual rights.[84] In France, a duty to give reasons was recognised by administrative transferred in similar terms and, again in 1979, when Parliament eventually adopted legislation in this respect, it confined its scope of application to some cases, including sanctions and measures limiting the exercise of fundamental rights.[85]

To sum up, a line can be drawn between the legal systems that adopted general legislation on administrative procedure in the first period of our relevant time frame and the major European administrative systems of the day. A discernible dividing line also exists with regard to what the French call '*le fond du droit*'. Even though the same general principles of procedural fairness and propriety are adhered to in all the legal systems selected for our comparative research, it turns out that the rules adopted and the results differ. Interestingly, the observed differences do not follow the traditional distinction between civil and common law.

E. The 'Common Core': An Evolutionary View

The research findings have various implications from the perspective of our broader comparative enquiry into the 'common core' of European administrative laws.

The first is methodological. It concerns the utility of legal comparison. Dicey's attack on administrative law in the Victorian period, when he argued that in the United Kingdom there was no 'droit administratif', has been considered either an oversimplification justified by its immediate audience—the students of

[82] See Wade (78) 30 ('our law has been curiously lazy about it'); Craig (n 77) 437.
[83] Bachof (n 67) 373.
[84] See G Miele, 'Italian Administrative Law' (1954) 3 ICLQ 421, 444.
[85] Law No 79-587 of 11 July 1979. For further analysis, see G Vedel and P Delvolvé, *Le système français de protection des administrés contre l'administration* (Sirey 1991) 142.

his courses—or as a species of political thought,[86] more precisely of nineteenth-century Whiggism. We need not take sides in this debate: suffice it to observe that Dicey not only used the rhetorical device of antithesis in order to highlight the divide between French administrative despotism and the English rule of law, but he also took the contrastive approach to comparative law to extremes: the approach that mainly (or only) highlights the differences between the legal systems under examination as opposed to the 'integrative' approach, which emphasises similarity.[87] As observed right from the first volume in this series,[88] both approaches are questionable in descriptive and prescriptive terms. Descriptively, they fail to take some elements into account. Prescriptively, they are biased, even though the bias favours commonality or diversity. For both these reasons, they are of limited scientific value. Our first comparative study showed shown that even at the end of the nineteenth century there was an area of commonality. This largely depended on borrowings. The importance of the French construction of administrative law was recognised, for example, by Otto Mayer, the founder of modern German administrative law.[89] And this new comparative enquiry confirms it. There was a clear commonality in the legislative regulation of administrative procedure adopted in *Mitteleuropa*.

The second remark concerns the relationship between public law and its social and institutional environment. Dicey was not at all isolated in his belief that there was a biunivocal and not dissociable relationship between a social group and its law. His belief was based on the broader assumption that all law is inextricably linked with the spirit of the people, of each people; that is, in the terminology of the German historic school, a *Volksgeist*.[90] The weaknesses of this assumption are too well known to require more than a passing mention here. Suffice it to refer to the reception of Roman law in Germany to understand that exchanges and borrowings often characterise the history of our legal institutions. Our previous diachronic comparison confirmed this with regard to the creation of special administrative courts in Europe after 1861, when the French model was imitated, with various adjustments, by Austria, Germany, and Italy. This comparative enquiry confirms it still further, calling for greater attention to a process that has gone relatively unnoticed over the last five decades or so. After Austria adopted its administrative procedure legislation, some of its neighbours had no codification of the standards

[86] See M Loughlin, *Public Law and Political Theory* (Clarendon 1992) 141 (for whom Dicey's view was a variant of conservative normativism).

[87] For this distinction, see RB Schlesinger, 'The Past and Future of Comparative Law' (1995) 43 AJCL 477.

[88] della Cananea and Bussani (n 2) 219.

[89] Mayer (n 79) French translation by the author II (for whom 'c'est le droit français qui a servi de guide et de modèle', that is to say, French administrative law has been regarded as a model). See also AH Feller, 'Tendencies in Recent German Administrative Law Writing' (1932) 18 Iowa L Rev 144 (for whom 'the German theory started as an offspring of the ... French system').

[90] FK Savigny, *Vom Beruf unserer Zeit für Gesetzgebung und Rechtswissenschaft* (1815).

set by national courts nor even a shared concern for ensuring a proper and fair administration. There was, instead, the diffusion of a new way to regulate the discharge of administrative functions and powers.[91]

This connection between diffusion and innovation is interesting and important for examining how much European administrative law's 'common core' has evolved. In our previous diachronic comparison, we observed the emergence of a common core in several corners of Europe, concerning the general principles of administrative action.[92] These principles, including legality, due process of law, and publicity, were mainly defined by the courts in order to prevent abuse of power by public authorities. The conceptual and institutional justification of judicial intervention lay, with some variants, in the necessity to ensure that administration functioned according to the law. If certain powers were attributed to a public authority, such as a ministry or a local body, to achieve specific goals under certain conditions, then the court's function was to check that only those goals were pursued (otherwise, there would be an abuse of power or *détournment de pouvoir*) only when those conditions were present (otherwise, there would be either an error of fact or an error of law) and in respect of specific procedural requirements. However, an excess of emphasis on judicial review tends to overrate how the courts work and underrate how administrative institutions work.[93] With the growth of government, while the traditional court-centred model remained more or less unchallenged in the 'major' legal systems of Europe, in others, a 'movement for administrative procedure legislation' emerged.[94] It did so within a particular spatial and temporal cluster, at the heart of which lay the Austrian legislation.

Interestingly, some ideas and institutions continued to be shared within this cluster, notwithstanding regime changes after 1945.[95] This was also the case for Spain in some respects. Even more interestingly, during the last part of the time frame in question, administrative procedure legislation was also adopted by the Scandinavian countries and later by Germany, followed by Italy, the Netherlands, and several other nations,[96] including France, which had long been opposed to it.[97] Thus, with justification, it can be said that a 'patrimoine juridique européen' has emerged;[98] that is, a common legal heritage.

[91] For this observation, see Langrod (n 7) 534; G Langrod, 'La nouvelle loi Yugoslave sur la procédure administrative non contentieuse' (1957) 10 R Adm 631; Isaac (n 7) 109.

[92] della Cananea and Mannoni (n 27).

[93] See Weil (n 68) 243 (observing that the French legal literature is 'uninterested in how the administrative decisions are taken ... when one speaks of "administrative procedure" ... what is meant ... is the procedure in the courts').

[94] B Schwartz, 'The Model State Administrative Procedure Act' (1958) 33 Wash L Rev & St B J 1, 2.

[95] L Potesil and others, 'Simplification of Administrative Procedure on the Example of the Czech Republic, Poland, Slovakia, and Hungary' (2021) 11 Adm Sci 9.

[96] G della Cananea, 'The Regulation of Administrative Procedure in Europe: A Historical and Comparative Perspective' (2020) 32 ERPL 223.

[97] See Weil (n 68) 243.

[98] Langrod (n 7) 533. In a slightly different vein, Ebherard Schmidt-Aßmann has argued that the 'idea of procedure constitutes basic expression of a common European administrative law': 'Structures

IV. The Overlooked Importance of Austrian Administrative Law

A final reflection on the neglected influence of Austrian administrative procedure legislation in public law scholarship may not be out of place. The adoption of administrative procedural legislation was a functional response to the emergence of the administrative State and, theoretically, 'the finest practical product of Kelsen's School of Law'.[99] As functional necessities were largely similar, and Kelsen's theory had a profound influence in many parts of Europe, including France and Italy,[100] it might be interesting to reflect on the attention devoted to Austrian administrative procedure legislation.

Let us imagine an administrative lawyer faced with issues concerning administrative procedure between 1925 and 1970. He or she would have readily concluded that there was no general domestic legislation in the field. It would have been possible, however, to make the following schematic argument for change: although the national tradition lacked a general legislative framework but had a powerful administrative court, Austria had taken a different path. Alternatively, at the most basic level, a comparative viewpoint might have been helpful for a theoretical approach to the study of administrative procedure. However, what emerges from our reports is that it was only at this most fundamental level that Austrian law and legal culture were given any consideration by a handful of scholars in Italy[101] and by (virtually) none in France. One possible explanation is that there was a language barrier to communication, a difficulty in communication between peoples using different languages.

This explanation, however, is not satisfactory because there were public lawyers, such as Roger Bonnard in France, with a good knowledge of German and Austrian legal experience, particularly with regard to administrative judicial review.[102] The same applies to Italy, where most public lawyers worked in the cultural framework of the general theory of the State elaborated by the great Austrian jurist Georg Jellinek (*allgemeine Staatslehre*),[103] but especially after 1915, the importance

and Functions of Administrative Procedures in German, European and International Law' in J Barnes (ed), *Transforming Administrative Procedure* (Global Law Press 2008) 66.

[99] See R Parker, 'Book Review of L. Adamovich, Handbuch des österreichischen Verwaltungsrechts. Vol. 1. Allgemeiner und materiellrechtlicher Teil' (1953) 3 AJCL 287, 288; Schambeck (n 8).

[100] See, among others, N Bobbio, 'Law and Force' (1965) 49 Monist 321 (for whom Kelsen's theory of legal rules had 'become the common heritage of modern philosophy of law'); O Jouanjan (ed), *Hans Kelsen. Forme du droit et politique de l'autonomie* (PUF 2010).

[101] Including, among others, AM Sandulli, *Il procedimento amministrativo* (Giuffrè 1940) 5; Pastori (n 7) 95; Miele (n 84) 444.

[102] R Bonnard, *Le contrôle juridictionnel de l'administration. Etude de droit administratif comparé* (1934 Dalloz 2006) 251. In the foreword to the new edition, Bernard Pacteau has emphasised Bonnard's comparative approach, as well as his 'curiosity' regarding public law in Germany in the 1930s.

[103] For further remarks, see MR Di Simone, 'Le Code civil autrichien en Italie' (2011) 89 Rev hist droit fr étrang 115.

of Austrian ideas and institutions, such as the Civil Code, was neglected.[104] This suggests that a cultural divide emerged as a consequence of the Great War. This conjecture seems to be confirmed by Schefold's careful analysis of the belated translation of Santi Romano's masterpiece ('The Legal Order').[105] At the beginning of the twentieth century, Schefold observed, Romano had been asked to write a book on Italian public law for German readers. However, although the book was ready by 1915 when the Great War began, the project was abandoned. With its nationalist propaganda, the war had destroyed the 'world of yesterday' to borrow the title of Stefan Zweig's superb description of those events.[106]

Whether or not this explanation is sound for France and Italy, it is hardly applicable to Germany as it shared the same language, had been part of the Holy Roman Empire with Austria, had been its ally during the Great War, and, as observed by Augsberg in this volume, Austrian administrative law was the 'most closely related' to that of Germany.[107] Other hypotheses must, therefore, be further developed and verified. We should ask ourselves whether a comparative approach of the type envisaged here would have been regarded as outside the acceptable bounds of study for a public lawyer. In other words, a mainstream lawyer would have thought that little was to be gained from this kind of enquiry. Factually, Augsberg finds that there were few and cursory references to Austrian legislation. Perhaps this was so because the German tradition left 'public authorities ... free in their choice of procedure' and did not criticise 'the relatively great informality of administrative procedure'.[108] Georges Langrod gave a slightly different explanation, observing that German legal culture was more reluctant to acknowledge the importance of administrative procedure[109] because of the weight traditionally accorded to the administrative act (*Verwaltungsakt*).[110]

The underlying assumption is that the salient traits of a legal system can only be adequately understood against its underlying legal theory (and to some extent the political theory) a given society espouses. An approach of this type can usually

[104] G Jellinek, *Allgemeine Staatslehre* (O Häring 1900), translated into both French and Italian. His influence is highlighted, among others, by S Cassese, 'Lo stato presente del diritto amministrativo italiano' (2010) 60 Riv trim dir pub 389, 395.

[105] S Romano, *L'ordinamento giuridico* (Sansoni 1917), translated into German by Roman Schnur in 1975. Schefold's work is 'La recezione dell'Ordinamento giuridico in Germania' in M Mazzamuto (ed), *Santi Romano e l'ordinamento giuridico (1917–2017)* (Editoriale scientifica 2020) 319. See also Cassese (n 104) 395 (for the thesis that Italian public lawyers paid less attention to both Austrian and German legal cultures after 1945).

[106] S Zweig, *Die Welt von Gestern: Erinnerungen eines Europäer* (1942), English translation by A Bell, *The World of Yesterday. Memoires of a European* (U Nebraska Press 2013).

[107] Augsberg (n 66).

[108] Bachof (n 67) 373.

[109] G Langrod, 'L'autocritique de l'administration fédérale allemande' (1960) 13 R Adm 646, 651.

[110] O Mayer, *Deutsches Verwaltungsrecht* (1894), French translation by the author, *Le droit administratif allemand* (Giard & Brière 1905) 122 (where the administrative act is defined as 'acte d'autorité emanant de l'administration, act qui determine, vis-à-vis du sujet, ce qui, pour lui, doit être droit dans le cas individuel', that is to say it is adopted by a public authority and defines the law for the individual in a particular case).

focus on a central concept of public law: the rule of law. With its traditional emphasis on sound administration, Austrian legal culture was the first to acknowledge the increasing importance of the administrative State and define, at the legislative level, some essential standards of conduct for all public authorities. Other legal cultures were reluctant to agree on the importance that Austrian legal culture had given to the 'administrative' side of *Rechtsstaat*. An alternative account might draw on the differing role ascribed by constitutional theorists to parliamentary democracy. For Kelsen, after parliamentary rule had replaced constitutional monarchy:

> all conceivable political progress, the creation of a just social order, and the dawn of a new and better age were expected from a constitution that would allow popular representation to play a decisive role in forming the State's will.[111]

In conclusion, while administrative law owes much to France for its regulation of administrative powers based on specialist courts, during the nineteenth century[112] the development of administrative law owed much to Austria, with its innovative legislative reform of 1925, a model for policymakers and scholars in Europe.[113]

[111] H Kelsen, *Vom Wesen und Wert der Demokratie* (1929), English translation in AJ Jacobson and B Schkink (eds), *Weimar. A Jurisprudence of Crisis* (U California Press 2002) 95. See also A Jakab, 'Two Opposing Paradigms of Continental European Constitutional Thinking: Austria and Germany' (2009) 58 ICLQ 933 (arguing that the distinctive traits of the Austrian and German legal theories depended on the fact that the former reflected Kelsen's heritage, while the latter were influenced by Schmitt and Smend).

[112] For a different opinion, according to which France 'invented administrative law', see S Cassese, 'Le droit tout puissant et unique de la société: Paradoxes of Administrative Law' (2010) 22 ERPL 171, 175.

[113] Differently and exaggeratedly, Parker (n 99) 288 asserted that the French administrative system was 'much overrated'.

Questionnaire

Introduction

This is the questionnaire for use at the second historic workshop organised within the framework of the Common Core of European Administrative Laws (CoCEAL) project. The CoCEAL project is a new comparative research initiative in the field of administrative law, approved and funded by the European Research Council by way of an 'Advanced Grant—Excellent Science' for the period 2016–21. The project is presented on its website www.coceal.eu and is described in detail by the PI, Giacinto della Cananea in his article in the *Maastricht Journal of European and Comparative Law* (2019) 26(2) 217–50.

The workshop aims to highlight the influence of the 1925 *Austrian Allgemeine Verwaltungsverfahrensgesetz* (AVG) on the administrative procedure legislation of other countries.

In answering this questionnaire, you should only consider the **period from 1920 to 1970**. Please consider every question only in reference to the years 1920–1970.

We are aware that different countries have experienced different developments in administrative procedure codifications (some countries adopted an AVG during the years 1920–1970: some countries adopted an AVG later on, and some still do not have an AVG). However, we decided to create just one questionnaire that would be the same for everyone. As specified below, if your country did not have an AVG between 1920 and 1970, you can answer the questions considering the discipline of administrative procedure as stemming from other sources (sector-specific laws, case law, general principles, etc.).

Section A General questions

1. Did your country enact a law on administrative procedure between 1920 and 1970?
   If the answer to question number 1 is YES, then please also answer questions 2–6.
   If the answer to question number 1 is NO, then please answer only questions 5–6.
   Please specify:

2. in what kind of institutional and political context the AVG was enacted;
3. if there are federal and State AVGs in your country;
4. if there are some sector-specific AVGs in addition to the general AVG, and how the possible conflicts or overlaps were solved;
5. Did your Constitution contain any principles on administrative procedure?
6. What were the sources of law (case law, laws, general principles, natural law, academia, others) for administrative procedure? How were the principles of administrative procedure defined?

Section B Explicit references

B.1. Explicit legislative references (if your answer to question number 1 is NO, then do NOT answer Section B.1. Go directly to Section B.2)

7. Is there any evidence (preliminary drafts, parliamentary discussions reports, scholarship) that your country's legislator took the Austrian General Law on Administrative Procedure of 1925 into account when preparing and approving the national legislation on administrative procedure? If your country is a federal State, please consider both federal and State legislation, if applicable.

B.2. Explicit jurisprudential and academic references

8. Are there any citations referring to the Austrian AVG in case law? Did courts use general principles (also deriving from Austrian law) *secundum legem*, *extra legem* and/or *contra legem*?
9. Are there citations from the Austrian AVG in academic works such as treaties, monographs, and articles in law journals?

Section C Substantive influence

10. For the purposes of our research, we make the preliminary assumption that the most interesting elements of the Austrian General Law on Administrative Procedure of 1925 are the following:
    i. completeness of the preliminary investigation and fact-finding process
    ii. the right to a hearing
    iii. the requirement to give reasons
    iv. the organisation of remedies (broadly speaking: administrative and jurisdictional)

Are these elements in your national legislation on administrative procedure? (If your answer to question number 1 is NO, please answer this question considering the regulation of administrative procedure as defined in question number 6)

Section D Factual methodology

Hypothetical cases

CASE 1 (Authorisation) Mr Schultz wants to obtain authorisation to open a pharmacy. What kind of procedure will take place? What kind of procedural rights are granted to Mr Schultz? If the administration denies the authorisation, what kind of remedies can Mr Schultz exercise?

CASE 2 (Disciplinary procedure against a civil servant) The administration intends to dismiss Caius, a civil servant, for inappropriate behaviour (several people witnessed him drinking in his office during working hours). What kind of procedure will be followed? Must Caius be informed? Does he have the right to respond? What procedural right does Caius have? If the measure against him is adopted, can he challenge it? And what kind of remedies can he exercise?

CASE 3 (Expropriation procedure) The authority intends to expropriate the house of Mrs Sempronia to make way for a railway line. What kind of procedure must be followed? Who must be informed? Who may intervene? What procedural rights does Mrs Sempronia have (the right to a hearing, the right to full knowledge of the findings, the right to present documents, the duty of the administration to take the documents presented by the parties into serious consideration, the right to challenge the decision about the location of the railway)? If the expropriation act is adopted, who can challenge it? Moreover, what kind of remedies can be exercised?

CASE 4 (Planning) An authority decides to build a new school in a particular location. What kind of procedure must be followed? Who must be informed? Who may intervene? If the decision is adopted, who can challenge it? Moreover, what kind of remedies can be exercised?

Section E The Personal Factor

Many scholars and judges of the former Austro-Hungarian Empire moved to other countries (or became citizens of other countries, albeit remaining in the same place) during or after the First World War, becoming scholars and judges in other countries and contributing to the spread of Austrian legal influence. Is there any example of this in your country? Are you aware of any personal interaction between your country and some Austrian institution or person that contributed in some way to spreading the influence of the Austrian AVG?

Selected Bibliography

Antoniolli, W, *Allgemeines Verwaltungsrecht* (Manzsche Verlag 1954)

Auby, JB, 'General Report' in JB Auby (ed), *Codification of Administrative Procedure* (Bruylant 2014) 27

Auby, J-M, *La procédure administrative non contentieuse* (Dalloz 1956–27)

Bähr, O, *Der Rechtsstaat. Eine publizistische Skizze* (Wiegand 1864)

Baumgart, M and H Habel, *Law on the Supreme Administrative Tribunal and Law on Administrative Proceedings* (Bibljoteka Prawnicza 1933)

Becker, F, *Das allgemeine Verwaltungsverfahren in Theorie und Gesetzgebung. Eine rechtsvergleichende Untersuchun* (W Kohlhammer Verlag 1960)

Becker, F, 'The Development of German Administrative Law' (2017) 24 George Mason LR 453

Becker, HJ, 'Fritz Werner—Präsident des Bundesverwaltungsgerichts von 1958 bis 1969. Erinnerungen an eine große Richterpersönlichkeit' in P Häberle, *Jahrbuch des öffentlichen Rechts der Gegenwart* (Mohr Siebeck 1987) 105

Bernatzik, E, *Rechtsprechung und materielle Rechtskraft* (Manz 1886)

Bettermann, KA, 'Verwaltungsakt und Richterspruch' in *Gedächtnisschrift für Walter Jellinek* (Isar Verlag 1955) 361

Bettermann, KA and E Melicharin (eds), *Veröffentlichungen der Vereinigung der deutschen Staatsrechtslehrer*, vol 17 (de Gruyter 1959)

Bonnard, R, *Le contrôle juridictionnel de l'administration. Etude de droit administrative comparé* (Librairie Delagrave 1934)

Bonnard, R, *Précis de droit administratif* (Librairie Générale de Droit et de Jurisprudence 1943)

Brunstein, JL, *Das Administrativ-Verfahren und seine Reform* (Manz 1900)

Capitant, D, 'Geschichte der Verwaltungsgerichtsbarkeit in Frankreich' in K-P Sommermann and B Schaffarzik (eds), *Handbuch der Geschichte der Verwaltungsgerichtsbarkeit*, vol II (Springer 2019) 1335

Chapus, R, *Droit administratif général* (15th edn, Montchrestien 2001)

Ciesielski, Z, 'Sawicki Stanisław (1907-1944)' in Polish Biographical Dictionary, vol XXXV (Publishing House of the Polish Academy of Science 1994)

Clavin, P, *Securing the World Economy: The Reinvention of the League of Nations, 1920–1946* (OUP 2013)

Concha, G, *Politika II. Közigazgatástan* (*Policy II. Public Administration*) (Grill 1905)

Craig, P, *Administrative Law* (8th edn, Sweet & Maxwell 2016)

Czapliński, W, 'Socially of Administration and the Duty to Justify Decisions' (1936) 8 GAiPP 231

de Laubadère, A, *Traité élémentaire de droit administratif* (Librairie Générale de Droit et de Jurisprudence 1953)

della Cananea, G, 'The Italian Administrative Procedure Act: Progresses and Problems' [2011] Ius Publicum Network <www.ius-publicum.com/repository/uploads/12_01_2012_9_44_DellaCananea_EN.pdf> accessed 2 February 2022

della Cananea, G and M Bussani, 'The Common Core of European Administrative Laws: A Framework for Analysis' (2019) 26 Maastricht J Eur & Comp L 217

Delvolvé, P, *L'acte administratif* (Sirey 1983)

Eberle, EJ, 'The West German Administrative Procedure Act: A Study in Administrative Decision Making,' [1984] 3 Penn State Intl LR 67

Ermacora, F (ed), *Österreichische Bundesverfassungsgesetze* (Böhlau Verlag 1989)

Erwin, H, 'Machtspruch' in A Cordes and others (eds), *Handwörterbuch zur Deutschen Rechtsgeschichte*, vol 3 (2nd edn, Erich Schmidt 2016) 1119

Ferrari Zumbini, A, 'Judicial Review of Administrative Action in the Austro-Hungarian Empire: The Formative Years (1890–1910) (2018) 1 It J Pub L 9

Ferrari Zumbini, A, *Alle origini delle leggi sul procedimento amministrativo: il modello austriaco* (Napoli Scientifica 2020)

Ferrari Zumbini, A, 'Standards of Judicial Review of Administrative Action in the Austro-Hungarian Empire' in G della Cananea and S Mannoni (eds), *Administrative Justice* Fin de siècle: *Early Judicial Standards of Administrative Conduct in Europe (1890–1910)* (OUP 2020) 45

Fleiner, F, *Institutionen des deutschen Verwaltungsrechts* (6th–7th edn, JCB Mohr–Paul Siebeck 1922)

Giannini, MS, *Il potere discrezionale della pubblica amministrazione* (Giuffrè 1939)

Gneist, R, *Der Rechtsstaat und die Verwaltungsgerichte in Deutschland* (Springer 1872, 2nd edn 1879, reprint 1958)

Goršić, F, *Komentar Zakon o opštem upravnom postupku od 9. novembra 1930. godine (Commentary of the Law on General Administrative Procedure of November 9, 1930)* (Geca Kon 1931)

Hauriou, M, *Précis élémentaire de droit administratif* (Recueil Sirey 1938)

Hausner, R, 'Origin of the Presidential Decree on Administrative Procedure' (1933) 15 GAiPP

Hausner, R, 'Three Laws on Administrative Proceedings' (1929) 8 GAiPP

Hellbling, EC, *Kommentar zu den Verwaltungsverfahrensgesetzen*, 2 vols (Manz 1953-54)

Hellbling, EC, 'Die Landesverwaltung in Cisleithanien' in A Wandruszka and P Urbanitsch (eds), *Die Habsburgermonarchie 1848–1918*, vol II (Austria Academy of Sciences Press 1975) 190

Herrnritt R, *Das Verwaltungsverfahren: Systematische Darstellung auf Grund der Neuen Österreichischen und Ausländischen Gesetzgebung* (Springer 1932)

Hoetzel, J, *Nové správní řízení* (1928) 6 Právník 266

Hoetzel, J, *Československé správní právo, část všeobecná* (Melantrich 1934)

Horáková, M and V Tomoszková, *Správní řízení v zemích EU. Rakousko, Polsko, Slovensko a Maďarsko* (Linde Praha 2011)

Hostiou, R, *Procédure et formes de l'acte administratif unilatéral en droit français* (Librairie Générale de Droit et de Jurisprudence 1975)

Isaac, G, *La procédure administrative non contentieuse* (Librairie Générale de Droit et de Jurisprudence 1968)

Iserzon, E, *Administrative Proceedings. Criminal-administrative proceedings. Compulsory proceedings in administration. The Act on Court Administrative Tribunal. The Union Regulations—Jurisprudence* (Księgarnia Powszechna 1938)

Jandy-Jendrośka, K, 'System of Jurisdictional Administrative Proceedings' in T Rabska and J Łętowski (eds), *System of Administrative Law*, vol III (Publishing House of the Polish Academy of Science 1978)

Janowicz, Z, *Code of Administrative Proceedings: Commentary* (Wydawnictwo Naukowe PWN 1992)

Jochum, H, *Verwaltungsverfahrensrecht und Verwaltungsprozeßrecht. Die normative Konnexität von Verwaltungsverfahrens- und Verwaltungsprozeßrecht und die Steuerungsleistung des materiellen Verwaltungsrechts* (Mohr Siebeck 2004)

Judson, PM, *The Habsburg Empire: A New History* (Belknap 2016)
Kałuski, W, *Administrative Proceedings: A Systematic Handbook with the Text of the Current Regulation and Specimens of Applications and Settlements* (Związek Pracowników Administracji Gminnej RP 1929)
Klappstein, W and G-C von Unruh, *Rechtsstaatliche Verwaltung durch Gesetzgebung. Entstehung und Bedeutung des Schleswig-Holsteinischen Landesverwaltungsgesetzes für das rechtsstaatliche Verwaltungsrecht* (R v Decker's Verlag, G Schenk 1987)
Kley, A, *Grundriss des liechtensteinischen Verwaltungsrechts* (LPS 23, VLAG 1998)
Klonowiecki, W, *Party in Administrative Proceedings* (Towarzystwo Naukowe KUL 1938)
Kmieciak, Z (ed), *Administrative Procedure in the Habsburg Succession Countries* (University of Lodz and Wolters Kluwer Polska 2020)
Kohl, G, 'Von der Doppelgleisigkeit der Verwaltung zur mittelbaren Bundesverwaltung—ein Überblick' (2021) 11 Beiträge zur Rechtsgeschichte Österreichs 315
Kopp, F, *Verfassungsrecht und Verwaltungsverfahrensrecht. Eine Untersuchung über die verfassungsrechtlichen Voraussetzungen des Verwaltungsverfahrens in der Bundesrepublik und die Bedeutung der Grundentscheidungen der Verfassung für die Feststellung, Auslegung und Anwendung des geltenden Verwaltungsverfahrensrechts* (Beck 1971)
Koropatnicki, D, *Kommentar zum Allgemeinen Verwaltungsverfahrensgesetz* (Buchhandlung Altes Rathaus 1927)
Kostić, L, *Komentar Ustava Kraljevine Jugoslavije iz 1931. godine (Commentary of the 1931 Constitution of the Kingdom of Yugoslavia)* (G Kon, a.d., 1934)
Kostić, L, *Administrativno parvo—reprint* (2000)
Koubi, G, L Cluzel-Metayer and W Tamzini (eds), *Lectures critiques du code des relations entre le public et l'adminiostration* (Librairie Générale de Droit et de Jurisprudence 2018)
Krbek, I, *Zakon o opštem upravnom postupku (Law on General Administrative Procedure)* (Naklada 'Obnova' 1931)
Lehne, F, 'Zur Geschichte der Verwaltungsstreitsache in Österreich' in Verwaltungsgerichtshof (ed), *90 Jahre Verwaltungsgerichtsbarkeit in Österreich* ([self-published] 1966) 26–39, 33
Lilić, S, *ZUP & ZUS—Komentar Zakon o opštem upravnom postupku i Zakona o upravnim sporovima sa komparativnim zakonodavstvom (LGAP & LAD—Commentary of the Law on General Administrative Procedure and the Law on Administrative Disputes with Comparative Legislation)* (Savremena administracija 1997)
Lilić, S, *Posebno upravno pravo (Special Administrative Law)* (Pravni fakultet 1998)
Longchamps, F, 'The Problem of the Durability of an Administrative Decision' (1961) 12 Państwo i Prawo 910
Majstorović, B, *Komentar Zakona o opštem upravom postupku (Commentary of the Law on General Administrative Procedure)* Beograd, 1957.
Majstorović, B, *Komentar Zakona o opštem upravnom postupku—drugo izdanje (Commentary of the Law on General Administrative Procedure—Second Edition)* (Savremena Administracija 1959)
Majstorović, B, *Komentar Zakona o opštem upravnom postupku—treće izdanje (Commentary of the Law on General Administrative Procedure—Third Edition)* (Zavod za javnu upravu 1961)
Majstorović, B, *Komentar Zakona o opštem upravnom postupku—četvrto izdanje (Commentary of the Law on General Administrative Procedure—Fourth Edition)* (Službeni list 1965)
Mannlicher, E, *Die österreichische Verwaltungsreform des Jahres 1925* (Springer 1926)
Mannlicher, E and E Coreth, *Das Verwaltungsverfahren. Mit einer Einleitung, erläuternden Bemerkungen, Materialien, einschlägigen anderen Gesetzen und Verordnungen* (2nd edn, Verlag der österreichischen Staatsdruckerei 1927)

Mannori, L and B Sordi, 'Science of Administration and Administrative Law' in H Hofmann, P Grossi and D Canale (eds), *A Treatise of Legal Philosophy and General Jurisprudence*, vol 9, *A History of the Philosophy of Law in the Civil Law World, 1600–1900* (Springer 2009) 225

Mayer, O, *Deutsches Verwaltungsrecht*, vol I (3rd edn, Duncker & Humbolt 1923, reprint 1969)

Merkl, AJ, *Allgemeines Verwaltungsrecht* (Springer 1927)

Michael, L and F Wollenschläger, 'Verfassung im Allgemeinen Verwaltungsrecht—Bedeutungsverlust durch Europäisierung und Emanzipation?' (2015) 75 Veröffentlichungen der Vereinigung der Deutschen Staatsrechtslehrer 131

Miele, G, 'Italian Administrative Law' (1954) 3 ICLQ 421

Morelon, C, 'Introduction' in P Miller and C Morelon (eds), *Embers of Empire. Continuity and Rupture in the Habsburg Successor States after 1918* (Berghan 2019) 3

Ogris, W, 'Die Rechtsentwicklung in Cisleithanien 1848–1918' in A Wandruszka (ed), *Die Habsburgermonarchie 1848–1918*, vol II (Austrian Academy of Sciences 1975) 538

Olechowski, T, *Die Einführung der Verwaltungsgerichtsbarkeit in Österreich* (Manz 1999)

Olechowski, T, 'Die Entwicklung allgemeiner Grundsätze des Verwaltungsverfahrens' in M Holoubek and M Lang (eds), *Allgemeine Grundsätze des Verwaltungs- und Abgabenverfahrens* (Linde 2006) 13

Olechowski, T, 'Geschichte der Verwaltungsgerichtsbarkeit in Österreich' in K-P Sommermann and B Schaffarzik (eds), *Handbuch der Geschichte der Verwaltungsgerichtsbarkeit in Deutschland und Europa*, vol II (Springer 2019) 1099

Pahlow, L, 'Administrativjustiz' in F Jaeger (ed), *Enzyklopädie der Neuzeit*, vol I (Metzler 2005) 79

Panejko, J, 'Public Health' in KW Kumaniecki, B Wasiutyński and J Panejko (eds) *Polish Administrative Law in Outline* (Księgarnia Powszechna 1930)

Pastori, G (ed), *La procedura amministrativa* (Neri Pozza, 1964)

Pastori, G, 'The Origins of Law n. 241/1990 and Foreign Models' (2010) 2 It J Public L 259

Patyi, A, 'A közigazgatás "rendezése" és a kodifikáció iránti igény' ("Arrangment" of public administration and the need for legislation) in A Patyi and A Zs Varga, *A közigazgatási eljárásjog alapjai és alapelvei* (*Fundamenents and Basic Principles of Administrative Procedures*) (Dialóg-Campus 2019) 77

Patyi, A, A Rixer and G Koi (eds), *Hungarian Public Administration and Administrative Law* (Schenk Verlag GmbH 2014)

Piątek, W, 'Problems of Reconstruction of General Principles of Administrative Proceedings' in JP Tarno and W Piątek (eds), *General Principles of Administrative Proceedings. Volume II. Part 2* (Wolters Kluwer 2018)

Pratobevera, CJ, 'Ueber die Gränzlinien zwischen Justiz- und politischen Gegenständen und das Verhältniß der Gerichtshöfe zur landesherrlichen Macht' in *Materialien für Gesetzkunde und Rechtspflege in den Oesterreichischen Erbstaaten* 1 (Geistinger 1815) 1

Pünder, H, 'Administrative Procedure—Mere Facilitator of Material Law versus Cooperative Realization of Common Welfare' in C Waldhoff and H Pünder (eds), *Debates in German Public Law* (Hart 2014) 239

Quaderer-Vogt, R, *Bewegte Zeiten in Liechtenstein, 1914 bis 1926*, 3 vols (Chronos and VHVFL 2014)

Rajchl, J (ed) *Správní řád 10 let v akci* (Univrzita Karlova 2016)

Rozmaryn, S, 'On the General Principles of the Code of Administrative Proceedings' (1961) 12 Państwo i Prawo 887

Rozmaryn, S, 'About the Draft Code of Administrative Proceedings' (1961) 4 Państwo i Prawo 631
Sandulli, AM, *Il procedimento amministrativo* (Giuffrè 1940)
Saunier, S, *Recherche sur la notion de formalisme en droit administratif français* (Presses universitaires d'Aix-Marseille 2007)
Schädler, E, *Für ein historisch-kritisches Verständnis des Verfahrensrechts, Versuch einer Apologie anhand von Beispielen aus dem Landesverwaltungspflegegesetz* (Arbeitspapiere LI 54, LI 2016)
Schädler, E, 'Zur Herkunft des Landesverwaltungspflegegesetzes: eine überprüfende Rekonstruktion' in Liechtenstein-Institut and Historischer Verein für das Fürstentum Liechtenstein (eds), *Geschichte erforschen—Geschichte vermitteln, Festschrift zum 75. Geburtstag von Peter Geiger und Rupert Quaderer* (LPS 59, VLAG 2017)
Schäffer, H, 'Administrative Procedure in Austria: 80 Years of Codified Procedure Law' (2005) 17 ERPL 871
Schambeck, H, 'The Development of Austrian Administrative Law' (1962) 28 Int Rev Admin Sc 215
Schefold, D, 'Riforme amministrative, riforme del procedimento amministrativo e il ruolo della dirigenza pubblica: il modello tedesco' in S Gambino (ed), *Dirigenza pubblica e innovazione amministrativa* (Maggioli Editore 1992) 95
Schefold, D, 'Selbstverwaltungstheorien: Rudolf Gneist und Hugo Preuß' in D Lehnert and C Müller, *Vom Untertanenverband zur Bürgergenossenschaft* (Nomos 2003) 97
Schneider, JP, 'Chapter 10. Germany' in JB Auby (ed), *Codification of Administrative Procedure. Proceedings of the International Academy of Comparative Law Congress on 'Codification' May 2012* (Bruylant 2014) 203
Slapnicka, H, *Österreichs Recht außerhalb Österreichs. Der Untergang des österreichischen Rechtsraums* (Verlag für Geschichte und Politik 1973)
Sorace, D, 'Administrative Law' in JS Lena and U Mattei (eds), *Introduction to Italian Law* (Kluwer 2002) 125
Starczewski, E, 'Draft Law on Administrative Proceedings' (1926) 23 GaiPP
Starczewski, E, 'On the Administrative Proceedings Act' (1926) 12 GAiPP 185
Staša, J, *K pozapomenutým padesátinám jednoho zákona*, (2018) 1–2 Správní právo 89
Stefanović, J, *Komentar Zakon o opštem upravnom postupku od 9. novembra 1930. godine (Commentary of the Law on General Administrative Procedure of November 9, 1930)* (Geca Kon 1933)
Stjepanović, N, *Administrativno pravo FNRJ—opšti deo* (Administrative Law of FPRY—General Part) (Naučna knjiga 1954)
Stjepanović, N, *Položaj gradjana i organizacija u uravnom postupku (Position of Citizens and Organizations in Administrative Procedure)* (Savremena Administracija 1957)
Stjepanović, N, *Upravno pravo SFRJ - Opšti deo - knjiga II (Administrative Law of SFRY - General Part Vol. II)* (Zavod za izdavanje udžbenika 1964)
Stolleis, M, *Geschichte des öffentlichen Rechts in Deutschland*, vol 2 (Beck 1992)
Stolleis, M, *A History of Public Law in Germany: 1914–1945* (OUP 2004)
Stolleis, M, 'Entwicklungsstufen der Verwaltungsrechtswissenschaft' in W Hoffmann-Riem, E Schmidt-Aßmann and A Voßkuhle (eds), *Grundlagen des Verwaltungsrechts, vol. I: Methoden—Maßstäbe—Aufgaben—Organisation* (2nd edn, Beck 2012) § 2, 63
Stolleis, M, *Geschichte des öffentlichen Rechts in Deutschland. Vierter Band: 1945–1990* (Beck 2012)
Stolleis, M, *Public Law in Germany: A Historical Introduction from the 16th to the 21st Century* (OUP 2017)

Supiński, W, *Administrative Proceedings: Outline of Theory with Commentary* (Polska Drukarnia Narodowa 1933)

Tarno, JP, `Functions of the General Principles of Administrative Proceedings` in JP Tarno and W Piątek (eds), *General Principles of Administrative Proceedings. Volume II. Part 2* (Wolters Kluwer 2018)

Taylor, AJP, *The Habsburg Monarchy: 1809–1918* (first published 1948, Penguin 1990)

Tezner, F, *Das Handbuch des österreichischen Administrativverfahrens* (Manz 1896)

Tezner, F, *Die landesfürstliche Verwaltungsrechtspflege in Österreich vom Ausgang des 15. bis zum Ausgang des 18. Jahrhunderts*, vol II (Hölder 1902)

Tezner, F, *Das österreichische Administrativverfahren, dargestellt auf Grund der verwaltungsrechtlichen Praxis. Mit einer Einleitung über seine Beziehung zum Rechtsproblem* (Österreichische Staatsdruckerei 1922)

Tezner, F, *Die rechtsbildende Funktion der österreichischen verwaltungsgerichtlichen Rechtsprechung, IV. Das österreichische Administrativverfahren. Systhematisch dargestellt auf Grund der verwaltungsrechtlichen Praxis* (2nd edn, Österreichische Staatsdruckerei 1925)

Thoma, R, 'Über die Grundrechte des Grundgesetzes für die Bundesrepublik Deutschland (1951)' in R Thoma, *Rechtsstaat—Demokratie—Grundrechte. Ausgewählte Abhandlungen aus fünf Jahrzehnten*, edited by H Dreier, (Mohr Siebeck 2008) 468

Ule, CH, 'Verwaltungsreform als Verfassungsvollzug' in CH Ule and others (eds), *Recht im Wandel. Festschrift 150 Jahre Carl Heymanns Verlag KG* (Heymanns 1965) 53

Ule, CH and F Becker, *Verwaltungsverfahren im Rechtsstaat. Bemerkungen zum Musterentwurf eines Verwaltungsverfahrensgesetzes* (Grote 1964)

Urbanowicz, S, 'New Law on Administrative Proceedings' (1928) 24 Gazeta Sądowa Warszawska 371

Varga, A Zs, *Die Entwicklung des Rechts der öffentlichen Verwaltung* (*The development of public administration law*) in G Máthé (ed), *Die Entwicklung der Verfassung und des Rechts in Ungarn* (*The development of the constitution and law in Hungary*) (Dialóg Campus 2017)

Vasváry, F, *A magyar közigazgatás központi alapszervei* (*Central Institutions of Hungarian Public Administration*) (Politzer 1902)

Wade, HWR and CF Forsyth, *Administrative Law* (11th edn, OUP 2014)

Waline, M, *Droit administratif* (Sirey 1963)

Wawro, G, *A Mad Catastrophe: The Outbreak of World War I and the Collapse of the Habsburg Empire* (Basic Books 2014)

Werner, F, 'Verwaltungsrecht als konkretisiertes Verfassungsrecht' [1959] DVBl 527

Wess, MA, *The Grand Strategy of the Habsburg Empire* (Princeton UP 2018)

Wiener, C, *Vers une codification de la procédure administrative* (PUF 1975)

Wille, H, *Liechtensteinisches Verwaltungsrecht, Ausgewählte Gebiete* (LPS 38, VLAG 2004)

Zakrzewski, A, 'Jakub Sawicki 1899–1979' in *Profiles of Scholars. Professors Warsaw University after 1945 S–Ż, Monumenta Universitatis Varsoviensis 1816–2016* (Warsaw University Publishing House 2016)

Zametica, J, *Folly and Malice: The Habsburg Empire, the Balkans and the Start of World War One* (Shepheard Walwyn 2017)

Index

For the benefit of digital users, indexed terms that span two pages (e.g., 52–53) may, on occasion, appear on only one of those pages.